It seems with every book I've read
The pages get inside my head.
The latest book that I checked out
Came with pirates strewn about.

Pages in My Head

I turned the page to chapter four
Where I was handed down an oar
And rowed until my hands were raw.
Then the rocky coast I saw.

It loomed against the darkening sky;
A castle bold was standing high.
See how with the books I've read
The pages get inside my head?

–Nancy Bopp

Reading 5 for Christian Schools®
Second Edition

Bob Jones University Press, Greenville, South Carolina 29614

This textbook was written by members of the faculty and staff of Bob Jones University. Standing for the "old-time religion" and the absolute authority of the Bible since 1927, Bob Jones University is the world's leading Fundamentalist Christian university. The staff of the University is devoted to educating Christian men and women to be servants of Jesus Christ in all walks of life.

Providing unparalleled academic excellence, Bob Jones University prepares its students through its offering of over one hundred majors, while its fervent spiritual emphasis prepares their minds and hearts for service and devotion to the Lord Jesus Christ.

If you would like more information about the spiritual and academic opportunities available at Bob Jones University, please call

1-800-BJ-AND-ME (1-800-252-6363).

NOTE:

The fact that materials produced by other publishers may be referred to in this volume does not constitute an endorsement by Bob Jones University Press of the content or theological position of materials produced by such publishers. The position of the Bob Jones University Press, and the University itself, is well known. Any references and ancillary materials are listed as an aid to the student or the teacher and in an attempt to maintain the accepted academic standards of the publishing industry.

READING 5 for Christian Schools® Second Edition
Pages in My Head

Produced in cooperation with the Bob Jones University School of Education and Bob Jones Elementary School.

for Christian Schools is a registered
trademark of Bob Jones University Press.

© 2002 Bob Jones University Press
Greenville, South Carolina 29614

First edition © 1982 Bob Jones University Press

ISBN 1-57924-371-1

15   14   13   12   11   10   9   8   7   6   5   4   3   2

Contents
Lessons

Viewpoints

Regions

Creatures Great and Small

Endeavors

Reflections

Acknowledgments

A careful effort has been made to trace the ownership of selections included in this textbook in order to secure permission to reprint copyrighted materials and to make full acknowledgment of their use. If any error or omission has occurred, it is purely inadvertent and will be corrected in subsequent editions, provided written notification is made to the publisher.

Robert Francis "The Base Stealer" from *The Orb Weaver* ©1960 by Robert Francis, Wesleyan University Press by permission of University Press of New England

"Coronation Day" by Lois Hoadley Dick from *False Coin, True Coin*. Copyright © 1993 by Bob Jones University Press.

"Floradora Doe" Copyright © 1984 by Jack Prelutsky. Used by permission of HarperCollins Publishers.

"His First Bronc," by Will James. From *Young Cowboy,* Copyright 1935 by Charles Scribner's Sons; copyright renewed © 1963 by Auguste Dufault. Reprinted by permission of the Will James Art Company.

"A Just Judge", "The King and the Shirt", "Three Rolls and a Pretzel", from *FABLES AND FAIRY TALES* by Leo Tolstoy, translated by Ann Dunnigan, copyright © 1962 by Ann Dunnigan. Used by permission of Dutton Signet, a division of Penguin Putnam Inc.

"Mijbil—Iraq to London" by Gavin Maxwell. Adapted from *The Otter's Tale,* Copyright © 1962 by Gavin Maxwell Enterprises Ltd.

"The Monkey, the Mirror and the Red Paint" from *Jungle Doctor's Monkey Tales* by Paul White. Copyright 1957. Used by permission from Ruth White from Paul White Productions, Lindfield NSW, Australia.

"Pinocchio", by C. Collodi (translated by Walter S. Cramp). First published in *Pinocchio, the Adventures of a Marionette* by Ginn and Company in 1904.

"The Quarrel" by Eleanor Farjeon. Reprinted by permission of Harold Ober Associates Incorporated. Copyright © 1933, 1961 by Eleanor Farjeon.

"Rufus and the Fatal Four" from *RUFUS M.* by Eleanor Estes, copyright 1943 by Harcourt, Inc. and renewed 1970 by Eleanor Estes, reprinted by permission of the publisher.

"Snowflakes" from *All Day Long* by David McCord. Copyright © 1965, 1966 by David McCord. By permission of Little, Brown and Company (Inc.).

"A Spear for Omar" by Heddy Rado from *All Kinds of Courage.*

"Venture to Mierow Lake" by Gloria Repp from *Mik-Shrok*. Copyright © 1998 by Bob Jones University Press

"We, the People" illustrated by Nora Unwin. Copyright © 1974. Artwork used by permission of the University of Oregon Library.

"A Wonderful Man" from *In One Door and Out the Other* by Aileen Fisher. Copyright © 1969, 1997 Aileen Fisher. Used by permission of Marian Reiner for the author.

Project Coordinators	Project Editor	Cover
Vicky L. Burr	Sarah White	John Bjerk
Janice A. Joss		
Susan J. Lehman	**Designers**	**Composition**
Jeri Massi	Holly Gilbert	Carol Larson
Karen T. Wooster	Elly Kalagayan	
		Photo Acquisition
		Cindy Mauk

Photo Credits

The following agencies and individuals have furnished materials to meet the photographic needs of this textbook. We wish to express our gratitude to them for their important contribution.

"Almost Real"
Pictures taken by Dawn Watkins with permission from the National Marionette Theater, Brattleboro, Vermont.

Basketball Hall of Fame: 370 (bottom)

BJU Press Files: 207-9 (border)

Corel Corporation: 249, 267 (both), 293-94, 296, 347, 518 (brass), 520 (chandelier), 526 (fuselage), 528 (harvesting), 529 (hyaena), 536 (procession, quartz), 538 (rigging), 539 (scaffolding), 545 (wharf)

Digital Stock: cover (girl reading book), 1, 83, 120-21 (all), 179, 352 (bottom), 370-73 (basketball border), 373 (bottom both), 428-29, 456, 534 (orangutan)

Sam Laterza: 469-70

Library of Congress: 118

PhotoDisc, Inc.: cover (paper), title page (paper), 123 (both), 191, 261, 265-66, 269, 295, 323, 342, 345, 427, 442, 490-514 (border), 516 (ancient), 517 (awning), 519 (canyon, caribou), 526 (ferry, galabia), 528 (hedgehog), 531 (laser), 536 (python), 538 (rodent, salute), 542 (talon), 545 (vermin)

Unusual Films: 13, 71, 75, 78 (both), 209, 348-51 (all), 352 (cutover, disengage)

Dawn Watkins: 79, 80, 81 (all), 82 (both), 207 (girl), 324-27, 329-32, 334-35

www.arttoday.com: 122, 522 (crayfish), 525 (ermine), 530 (jade), 535 (pheasant, porcelain), 546 (zinc)

1

LESSONS

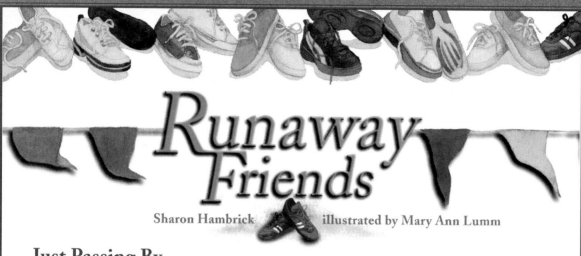

Runaway Friends

Sharon Hambrick   illustrated by Mary Ann Lumm

Just Passing By

The only good thing about going to a new school was that my new classmates didn't know how fast I could run. So, when we lined up for the year's first race, I could run like turbocharged lightning right through the finish line. Then I would listen to the amazed comments of the kids as I pretended not to be breathing hard.

"Rachel's fast!" they'd say. Or, "You run like the wind, Rachel."

After that happened, I'd have friends. People liked to be friends with me once they knew I was the fastest kid my age on two feet. It happened the same way every year.

That's right. Every year I was in a different school.

I lived with my grandparents in their RV. During the summers, Grandpa would drive all over a section of the United States or Canada. Then, when it got close to time for

school to start, he would start looking around for a nice RV park to stop in for the school year.

It wasn't always like this. When I was younger, before I needed to go to school, we drove around all the time. Grandma called it a permanent vacation, and Grandpa called it the "freedom of the road." By the time I was seven, I'd had

my picture taken in front of forty-nine of the fifty state capitol buildings. Yes, we had driven all the way up to Juneau, Alaska. You can't drive to Honolulu, Hawaii, but my Grandpa threatened to once.

"Zollie," he said to my Grandma, "let's get some pontoons and take this thing Pacific!"

Grandma Zollie just laughed, but I didn't. I was half-afraid he would try it someday, and there I would be, flailing my arms in the middle of the ocean, gasping for breath, waiting for the Coast Guard. You can't run your way out of trouble when the trouble is the Pacific Ocean, and running was the only way I knew how to succeed.

There was good and bad to the way we lived, but the best part of being the new girl every year was that I got to astonish everyone with how extraordinarily speedy I was. Frankly, I had never been beaten in a race, ever. Not even the fastest boy could beat me when I put myself in gear and turned on my speed.

This year, after driving through the Plains States and the Southwestern States for our summer tour, Grandpa sighed a deep sigh and pulled in to the Flyin' High RV Park in Albuquerque, New Mexico. I was not amused.

Albuquerque isn't even the capital city of New Mexico. There aren't any trees there, there's hardly any water, and in the summer (when we arrived) it's as hot as the Sahara Desert.

"Please don't pay the space rent, Grandpa Sam," I said. "Let's keep driving. We could get to San Diego in a few days. There are good schools there. Think of the beaches I could run on. Think of the cool water. Think of Sea World."

Grandpa wasn't interested in sea life or salt water this year, so we put up the awning, set out the lawn chairs, said "howdy" to the neighbors, and then trudged down the road to this year's school to sign me up.

That's how I got to be standing in the relay line at Bible Community School, looking to my right and grinning my head off. Here I was, ninety-one pounds of lean, mean running machine. And there, standing next to me, was a short boy with blond hair who barely came up to my shoulder. I figured he couldn't weigh more than about fifty pounds, and I was sure there wasn't one

ounce of muscle on his skinny frame.

"Run to the fence," Mr. Herman said. "Touch the fence. Then turn around and run back. And may the best team win!"

Then the shot went off. It wasn't a real shot, of course. It was Mr. Herman's whistle, but I liked to imagine I was running at the Olympic Games and the audience was screaming my name:

"Rachel Barnwell! Rachel Barnwell! USA!! USA!!!!"

I took off like a bullet from a gun, so fast I amazed even myself. Imagine my surprise when I saw Kyle out of the corner of my eye! I had never seen anyone out of the corner of my eye be-fore, because

usually my closest competitors were seven or eight strides behind me. Well, I sped up faster than ever. I kept my eyes on my goal—the fence up ahead—and kicked off those paces so fast they didn't know what hit them.

About four paces from the fence, I slowed down the tiniest bit so I wouldn't slam right into it. I made a neat, flawless turn, my fingers just grazing the chain-link. I was so pumped up inside to win this race, I did the turn perfectly! I wanted to erase Kyle from the list of people I had seen out of the corner of my eye.

Pretty soon, I heard the screaming.

I was used to it. It happened every year when people realized what a champion runner I was, so I knew what was going on: they were cheering for me! Only somehow they got it wrong. Instead of "Rachel! Rachel!" what I heard was "Kyle! Kyle! Go, Kyle!"

That ignited my fuse, I'll tell you! I ran faster than I had ever run before, and quick as anything I was over the line, slapping hands with the person behind me. I turned around in time to see Kyle race over the line after me, tag the next runner, and then flash a big grin at our teacher, Mr. Herman. A whole group of kids surrounded him and pounded his back like he'd won the Kentucky Derby.

I was breathing hard and staring harder, trust me, because this was a thing that had never happened to me before. I had won the race, but Kyle was being congratulated. Weird school, I thought. Can't wait to hit the road to my new school next year. Maybe I can get Grandpa to park in San Diego.

"You're fast," Kyle said to me as we walked back to class.

"Yeah," I said, "faster than you."

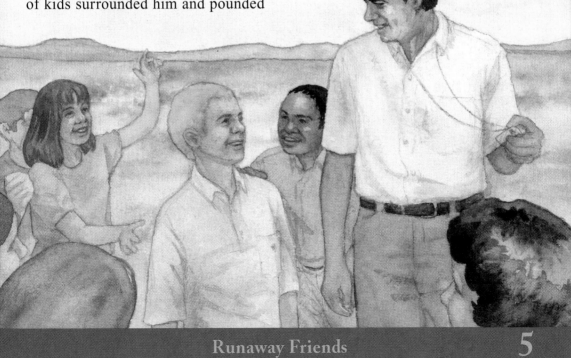

I sat in my seat in class, wrapped up in a big lump of sadness. Winning races was how I had always begun making friends at school. It wasn't going to work at this school, and I didn't know how else to get people to like me. That Kyle kid had badly messed things up for me. For some reason, they cheered for the losers at this school! I'd show them how fast I was again. Next time they'd cheer for me for sure!

So I challenged Kyle to races at recess. I won every time. Some of the girls cheered for me, but mostly all the loud shouting was for the little guy with skinny legs. Finally, after beating Kyle and everyone else four races in a row to the fence and back, I gave up. I walked over to the group of kids who were crowded around Kyle, and I stuck my head right in there.

"How come you guys all cheer for Kyle?" I said. "I'm way faster than he is."

All the kids got quiet, and I felt a big presence behind me. It was Mr. Herman, my teacher.

"Rachel," he said, "Kyle was in a terrible accident last year. The doctors thought he would never walk again. The whole school rooted for Kyle all year. We prayed for him every day many times. Seeing Kyle run is like seeing God answer prayer right out there in plain view where we can see it."

Boy, did I feel small and slimy. There I'd gone and run a boy into the ground who couldn't even walk a year ago.

"Sorry, Kyle," I said. "Nobody told me. How was I supposed to know, anyway?"

"It's okay, Rachel," Kyle said. "I like running against you."

"You do?"

"Yep," he said. "And guess what? Someday I'm going to beat you."

I laughed. "You'll never beat me."

Chrissy apologized to me for not explaining things earlier.

"We assumed you knew about Kyle," she said, "so we thought you were being mean to keep beating him."

It was hard for me to make new friends, even after Chrissy's talk, because I didn't know how. Running had been my ticket to friendship and party invitations before. Grandma gave me some pointers, though, when I asked her.

"Ask them about their families and hobbies," Grandma said. "And whatever you do, don't brag."

I followed her advice. I didn't talk about the forty-nine capital cities or my six-and-a-half minute mile. I didn't mention how Grandpa had "made a killing" on the stock market when he was

younger and that's why he could be on vacation all the time.

Grandma was right. By asking about other people's lives, I found out a lot about my new friends. Chrissy had a coin collection and three brothers. Her father worked downtown, and her mother stayed home. Marcie's parents were both dentists and they had four German shepherds! Lori's sister was the city tennis champion. The two of them lived with their aunt and uncle who ran a little grocery store.

Here to Stay

Everything started to go along really nicely. Then one day when I was minding my own business, enjoying my life, my school, and my friends, Mr. Herman announced Fall Field Day.

"There will be races and prizes, everyone!" he said. "And of course the Mothers' Club will serve hot dogs, potato chips, and soda pop all afternoon."

We all cheered. My pulse sky-rocketed with excitement. Then I realized something. All those recesses, when I had been making friends with the girls, little old Kyle had been running. In fact, now that I looked at him, he didn't seem quite as skinny as he had been. When the next recess came around, I wanted to run to prove that I could run him into the ground, but Chrissy called, "Hey, Rachel, come talk!" I looked at the fence. I looked at Chrissy. That's when I decided I wanted to have friends more than I wanted to beat Kyle.

Besides, he couldn't beat me, could he?

On Fall Field Day, I jumped out of bed and started running around inside the RV. There wasn't a lot of room to run, of course, so I ran out-side. I was so excited. I was going to run, and Grandma and Grandpa would be there to watch me win!

After morning classes, we went outside for our hot dog lunch and the races. Chrissy won a blue ribbon for winning the carry-a-cotton-ball-on-a-spoon race. I got a red ribbon for being in a relay race where we had to stop at the halfway point and pop a balloon by stomping on it. Some of the kids had trouble popping their balloons, and I screamed myself hoarse yelling, "Jump on it! Jump on it!"

Finally, it was time for the real race—the one between Kyle and me. It wasn't just between the two of us, of course. It was a relay race: run to the fence, touch the fence, run back. There were five kids on each team, but Kyle and I were both the final runners for our teams.

I figured there was no way for my team to lose. If the fourth runner tagged me before his team's fourth runner tagged Kyle, I would be ahead of him, and I would win. If we were tagged at the same time, I would win because I had always been able to beat him. And, in the worst possible case, if he got a head start on me, I could always turn on those built-in rockets Grandpa said I was born with and run so fast past Kyle he wouldn't be able to catch up with me for a week.

The whistle blew. Both number-one runners ran like their lives depended on it. I tried not to scream too much, but my stomach was tight and nervous. "Come on, run!" I said fiercely under my breath. I looked over at the seats where Grandma and Grandpa were sitting, watching.

My team's first runner came in a little bit ahead of Kyle's runner, but the second runners came in about the same time. Our third runner was a little bit slow making the turn, but by the time the fourth runners were heading back toward Kyle and me, it looked like a dead-even race. I wiped my sweaty hands on my clothes and looked over at Kyle. He was staring straight ahead, and determination was written all over his face. I bit my lip. When the runner slapped my hand, I took off faster than I ever had before.

Nothing mattered now but running and winning. I didn't look to the right or the left. I kept my eyes straight ahead of me. Up ahead was the fence.

I made the turn perfectly. Kyle was two or three steps behind me, but I wasn't taking any chances on losing to him. Not when Grandma and Grandpa were on the sidelines. I could hear Grandpa shouting, "Go, Rachel! Come on, Rachel!" My team was ahead of me, screaming, jumping up and down. Just a few more yards and—

I didn't see the rock. It was just a small rock, but when my foot landed on it, I knew I was going down hard. I heard myself scream. I felt my ankle twist sharply under me as I crashed onto the ground, landing hard. I closed my eyes. All Kyle would have to do now would be to trot slowly across the finish line, and his team would win. I had lost. In front of my grandparents and new friends, I had crashed. I couldn't wait for summer so we could drive far away from Albuquerque and never come back.

"Rachel, you okay?"

I opened my eyes. There was Kyle standing over me! He was sweaty and breathing hard.

"Are you all right?" he said again.

"Go ahead, Kyle," I said. "Win the race. It's okay."

He smiled. "Are you crazy? I know what it's like to be hurt." He grinned at me as I began to hear the approach of other people coming to see how I was. "Besides," he said, "when I beat you it's not going to be because you got hurt. It's going to be because I'm faster than you."

Grandma Zollie nudged Kyle out of the way. She patted my hand, called for a "doctor in the house," and started to pray aloud for my full recovery.

They called the race a tie, but I knew better. Kyle could have beaten me, but he chose not to. They told me later that he stayed away from the finish line the rest of the afternoon. He didn't want anyone to say he had won.

The way I figured it, I was the winner that day: I'd found a place and a school and a bunch of friends that I really liked and wanted to keep.

"Grandpa," I said that night, as he was tucking me into bed, "have you ever thought about selling the RV and buying a house without wheels?"

"You about ready to settle down and not have your friends roll away at the end of the year?"

"Yes, Grandpa."

"Well, we knew the day was coming, didn't we, Zollie?"

Grandma nodded. Grandpa patted my head as I settled down into my pillow to sleep.

A Wonderful Man

Aileen Fisher

My father carries a pearl-handled knife
with three steel blades that are as big as life:
one is longest, and one is littler,
but the shortest one is the sharpest whittler.

My father whittles me whistles from sticks,
and uses his knife when there're things to fix,
and he whittles me darts and arrows with wings
and sailboats and rabbits and other such things.

And sometimes he asks me, "Would *you* like to try
to whittle a little something with me standing by?"
So I whittle something as well as I can . . .
Say, but my father's a wonderful man!

His First Bronc

Will James • illustrated by Preston Gravely

Billy was a born cowboy; the only kind that ever makes the real cowboy. One day Lem told him he could have a certain black horse if he could break him. It was a little black horse, pretty as a picture. Billy went wild at the sight of him, and ran into the corral to get as close a view of the horse as he could.

"I've always wanted to break in a horse. That'll be lots of fun."

The next morning Lem found Billy in the corral with the new horse.

"Well, I see you're busy right early, Billy."

"He's some horse, ain't he?" he said.

"He sure is," agreed Lem. "And your first bronc, too."

An hour or so later Billy had his saddle on the black horse, and cinched to stay. By this time quite a crowd had gathered around. The foreman, the cowboys, all the ranch hands were watching. All was set but taking the hobbles off the horse's front feet and climbing on. Some of the men offered to do that for Billy but that young cowboy refused. He wanted to do it all himself; it was his bronc.

Billy gathered his hackamore rope and a hunk of mane to go with it, grabbed the saddle horn with his right hand and, sticking his foot in the stirrup, eased himself into the saddle. He squirmed around until he was well set, like an old bronc fighter, saw that the length of reins between his hands and the pony's head was just right, then he reached over and pulled off the blindfold.

Billy's lips were closed tight; he was ready for whatever happened. The pony blinked at seeing daylight again, looked back at the boy sitting on him, snorted, and trotted off.

A laugh went up from all around. Billy turned a blank face toward his father and hollered.

"Hey, Dad, he won't buck!"

Another laugh was heard and when it quieted down Lem spoke up.

"Never mind, son," he said trying to keep a straight face, "he might buck yet."

The words were no more than out of his mouth, when the little black lit into bucking. Billy was loosened the first jump for he'd been paying more attention to what his dad was saying than to what he was sitting on. The little pony crowhopped around the corral and bucked just enough to keep the kid from getting back in the saddle. Billy was hanging on to all he could find, but pretty soon the little old pony happened to make the right kind of a jump for the kid and he straightened up again.

Billy rode pretty fair the next few jumps and managed to keep his seat pretty well under him, but he wasn't satisfied with just sitting there; he grabbed his hat and began fanning. All went fine for a few more jumps and then trouble broke loose. Billy dropped his hat and made a wild grab for the saddle horn.

But the hold on the saddle horn didn't help him any; he kept going, up and up he went, a little higher every jump, and pretty soon he started coming down. When he did that he was by his lonesome. The horse had gone in another direction.

"Where is he?" said Billy, trying to get some of the earth out of his eyes.

"Right here, Son," said his father, who'd caught the horse and brought him up.

He handed the kid the hackamore reins and touched him on the hand.

"And listen here, young feller, if I catch you grabbing the horn with that paw of yours again, I'll tie it and the other right back where you can't use 'em."

Those few words hit the kid pretty hard. There was a frown on his face and his lips were quivering at the same time. He was both ashamed and peeved.

His father held the horse while Billy climbed on again.

"Are you ready, cowboy?" Lem looked up at his son and smiled.

After some efforts the kid smiled back and answered.

"Yes, Dad, let him go."

The pony lit into bucking the minute he was loose this time and seemed to mean business from the start. Time and again Billy's hand reached down as if to grab the saddle horn, but he kept away from it.

The little horse was bucking pretty good, and for a kid Billy was doing mighty fine, but the horse still proved too much for him. Billy kept getting further and further away from the saddle till finally he slid along the pony's shoulder and to the ground once again.

The kid was up before his dad could get to him and began looking for his horse right away.

"I don't think you'd better ride him any more today, Sonny," Lem said as he brushed some of the dust off the kid's clothes. "Maybe tomorrow you can ride him easy."

But Billy turned and saw the horse challenging him, it seemed, and he crossed the corral, caught the black, blindfolded him and climbed on again.

Then Lem walked up to Billy and said so nobody else could hear, "You go after him this time, Billy, and just make this pony think you're the wolf of the world. Paw him the same as you did that last calf you rode."

"Y-e-e-ep!" Billy hollered as he jerked the blind off the pony's eyes. "I'm a wolf!"

Billy was a wolf; he'd turned challenger and was pawing the black from ears to rump. Daylight showed plenty between him and the saddle but somehow he managed to stick on and stay right side up. The horse, surprised at the change of events, finally let up on his bucking; he was getting scared and had found a sudden hankering to start running.

After that it was easy for Billy; he rode him around the corral a couple of times and then, all smiles and proud as a peacock, he climbed off.

Billy had ridden his first bronc.

Card Catalog

"So they don't have libraries in your country?" Chris asked. He and Raul walked through the county library doors.

Raul shook his head. "Not in my small town."

"Over here is what we call the *card catalog*," Chris said. He pointed to a large, rectangular wooden structure with many small drawers.

"What is that for?" Raul said.

"You can know where to find any book you want."

Raul wrinkled his brow.

"Here—I'll show you." Chris opened a drawer in the card catalog.

The card catalog is an important resource tool in your search for a book. The name of every book in the library is recorded on at least three cards in the card catalog. The drawers are organized and labeled alphabetically so that you can search for any book by its *title*, by its *author*, or by at least one *subject* heading.

Subject Cards

The *subject* heading is usually in all capital letters to display the difference between the title and the subject. If you were to look in the drawer marked with the letter *H* for *horses*, you might find a subject card that looks like this:

Subject Card

Subject

HORSES
636.1
RIC Richardson, Julie   *Author*   *Title*
          Horses and Ponies / Julie Richardson; illustrated by Libby
          King. Rourke Corp., 1982.
          Describes the types of horses and ponies that are found
     in various countries and discusses how they are used for
     work and for sport and how they are fed and cared for.
     Includes index.
          ISBN 0-86592-755-3
               [1. Horses 2. Ponies] I. King, Libby, illus. II. Title.
     III. Series
     SF 302.R5   1982   636.1   82-9018

Author Cards

A favorite author of horse stories is Marguerite Henry, who wrote *Misty of Chincoteague.* Perhaps you would like to read some more books by Marguerite Henry. You could also look up the name *Henry* in the card catalog drawer marked with the letter *H* for books that she wrote. All the books by Marguerite Henry that the library carries are listed on separate cards one after the other. One of the cards listed for the author Marguerite Henry might look like this:

Author Card

Author

F
HEN Henry, Marguerite, 1902–   *Title*
        Stormy, Misty's Foal / Marguerite Henry; illustrated by Wesley Dennis.
            —Chicago: Rand McNally, ©1963.
        Summary: A huge storm bursts upon Chincoteague Island just as Misty
    is about to give birth to her foal.
        ISBN 0-528-82083-4
            [1. Ponies—Fiction. 2. Chincoteague Island—Fiction]
    I. Dennis, Wesley, ill.   II. Title

    PZ10.3H43   1963   86-29892
    [Fic]

Title Cards

The same information is also recorded on a card by the book title as shown below.

Title Card

            Stormy, Misty's Foal
F
HEN Henry, Marguerite, 1902–
        Stormy, Misty's Foal / Marguerite Henry; illustrated by Wesley Dennis.
            —Chicago: Rand McNally, ©1963
        Summary: A huge storm bursts upon Chincoteague Island just as Misty
    is about to give birth to her foal.
        ISBN 0-528-82083-4
            [1. Ponies—Fiction. 2. Chincoteague Island—Fiction]
    I. Dennis, Wesley, ill.   II. Title

    PZ10.3H43   1963   86-29892
    [Fic]

Call Numbers

Let's look again at the subject card on page 19. The numbers and letters in the upper left-hand corner are the *call number.* The call number tells the location of the book in the library. If a library is organized with the Dewey decimal system, the books are on the shelves in numerical order. Often certain sections, such as fiction, are organized and labeled alphabetically by the last name of the person who wrote them. The examples of the author and title cards on page 20 indicate that the book is located in the fiction section under the author's last name, *Henry.*

Computer Search

Computers are another valuable resource for learning. Following the same organization pattern as the card catalog, the computer in the library can locate information about any book available. You can search for a book, a recording, or other information by title, author, subject, or keyword. Look at the author search for Marguerite Henry below.

A search to find books by the author gives all the titles that the library carries.

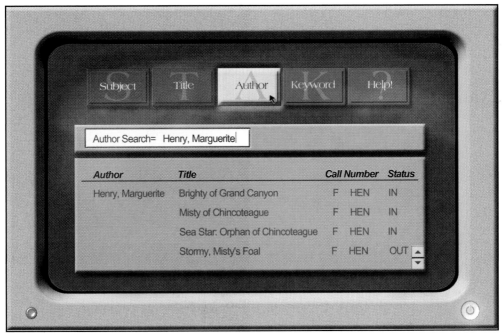

Author	Title	Call Number	Status
Henry, Marguerite	Brighty of Grand Canyon	F HEN	IN
	Misty of Chincoteague	F HEN	IN
	Sea Star: Orphan of Chincoteague	F HEN	IN
	Stormy, Misty's Foal	F HEN	OUT

Author Search= Henry, Marguerite

Now look at a search by subject. Would you like to read a book or look up specific information in the encyclopedia about horses? Once you find the general subject, the computer displays more selections.

Finding a book by subject may mean a search through several levels before getting to the selection.

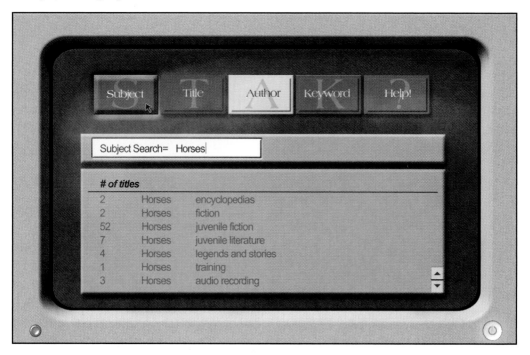

Here are more books to choose from the *juvenile fiction* category shown on the third line above.

Notice that two of the books have already been checked out of the library.

If you know the title of the specific book you want to read, try the title search as shown below.

Advancing technology offers the ability to expand the search for information beyond your library. This makes it possible to borrow a book from another library or access computer connections to find current information.

So whether it's finding facts for a report, researching a historical record, pursuing up-to-date information, or reading for pleasure, the library contains a wealth of knowledge. Now you know how to begin your search as you explore the library and beyond.

A search by title quickly gives the location and status of the book.

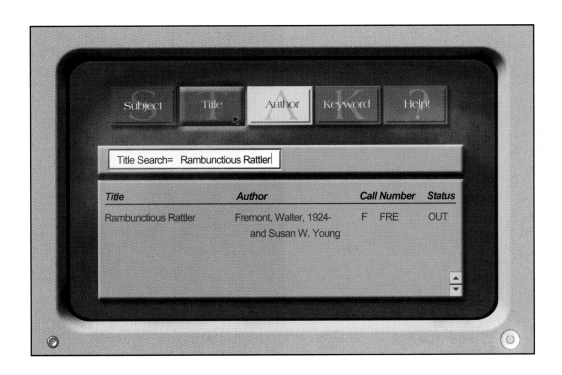

Lessons from Mr. Lee

Jeri Massi

illustrated by Johanna Berg

The royal bodyguard of the Korean emperor developed the martial art tae kwon do over a thousand years ago. At the time, the people called it hwarang-do, which means "the way of the flower of manhood." People in nearby China and Japan had also developed their own martial arts and sometimes used them to help in the study of pagan religions like Zen and Taoism. These religions demand stern physical training and discipline, and for this reason pagan priests sometimes use the martial arts to assist them in their training. Many good karate and tae kwon do teachers conduct schools without any association with pagan beliefs, and as Bill learns in this story, sometimes a karate teacher can teach a boy one of the most important lessons he will ever learn.

Willing to Learn

The sun was setting. I hurried on my way up Clover Road, past the quiet houses and neat lawns. I walked as fast as I could.

A front door slammed. Two boys came out of one of the houses. They saw me and looked away. But after I was past them, I heard them laughing. I looked back and saw one of them imitating me, holding his left hand clenched against his chest.

I looked down at my feet and kept going. Soon I couldn't hear them anymore.

Clover Road led to the highway. I walked past a bakery and a dry cleaner's, then came to a one-story building that was marked by a single sign. The sign said

Lee's Tae Kwon Do School
Mr. Lee, Head Instructor
Fifth-Degree Black Belt

An Asian man stood in the doorway, looking up at the pink and orange sky. Then he looked down at me.

"Can I help you?" he asked. His eyes were black and sparkling like dark oil.

"I want to learn karate," I told him.

"Lot of people want to learn that," he said. "Why come here to learn?"

I pointed down the highway with my good arm. "I live a few blocks away. I can walk here," I said. "At least until the days start getting shorter."

"Huh. Sensible," he agreed, putting his long, slim hands on his hips. His skin was a smooth tan color and contrasted sharply against the snowy whiteness of his karate uniform. "You come here and sit down," he said. "Watch a while." He pointed to a row of folding chairs that were lined up against the wall inside. "You are how old?"

"Ten."

"Okay."

I did as he told me. He walked away. I rubbed my bare toe into the rough carpet and watched the students as they strolled across the room in their billowy white uniforms.

Mr. Lee stepped into his tiny private office. He came out with a

26

long cloth strip in his hands. It was his black belt, but years of use had worn it to gray. He wrapped it twice around his hips, knotted it, and waited while the students lined up to face him.

An American and a Korean flag were hanging on the wall behind Mr. Lee. He and his students said the Pledge of Allegiance to the American flag. Then the students bowed to him. He bowed to them, clapped his hands, and class began.

The students groaned and toiled through calisthenics, sit-ups, and stretching exercises. Many of the people had white belts, and many had green belts. Some had brown belts. Only two wore black belts. Mr. Lee told one of the men with a black belt to take over.

"You come with me," he said to me. We went into his office.

"So," he said to me. "You take karate from me because you live close. Any other reason?"

I shrugged.

"You like sports? Play football?"

"No."

"Baseball?"

"No, . . . sir."

"You don't play baseball?" he asked, his shining dark eyes getting wide. "What kind of American boy are you?" He smiled a strong, white smile at me.

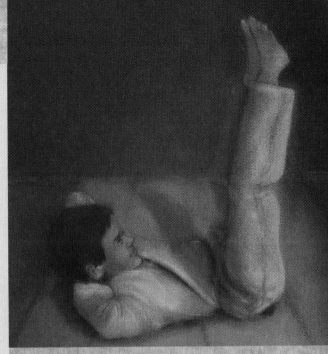

For an answer, I offered him my left arm. I knew that look, always of surprise and fear, that came into people's eyes when they saw my arm. They usually tried not to stare at it.

His smile faded, and he took hold of my babyishly tiny left hand in his big brown one. "Hurt you?" he asked.

"No. It's just too small." I felt my eyes stinging with tears. I swallowed a couple times and said, "My other one is normal. Can I still learn karate here?"

"Yes." He leaned across his desk and pulled a sheaf of papers from a basket. "You promise to work hard?"

"Yes, sir."

"You good boy? Obey law? Go to school every day?"

"Yes, sir."

"Take papers to your parents. If they sign, I let you come to my school."

"Okay."

"I see you tomorrow night. Your name is?"

"Bill."

He shook hands with me. "I am Mr. Hyong Lee. Maybe you knew that."

"Yes, sir. Good-bye."

I learned how to wear a *gi* and tie my white belt the right way. I was the newest student, so I always stood at the end of the line when we pledged allegiance and bowed to Mr. Lee.

The exercises stretched my legs and my back and pulled at my stomach until I felt like a rubber band. Mr. Lee made us do sit-ups very slowly, with our feet in the air and our toes pointed straight up.

One of the men with a black belt taught me how to punch. It was hard, because in tae kwon do students don't throw their shoulders forward like boxers would. They use their hips instead. At first I felt awkward about punching with my left arm, but Mr. Lee told me to do it.

"Other people think that arm no good," he said. "But God not make mistakes."

Working Hard

One evening when I was walking up to the karate school—tae kwon do school as we called it—some of the older kids were out playing stickball on the street.

"Hey, let's see you chop down that tree!" one of them called out to me. I pulled my folded-up *gi* closer and tried to ignore them as I passed. Some of them imitated me doing karate, clenching their arms to their chests and yelling, "Hiyah! Hiyah!"

I was almost running by the time I got to Mr. Lee's.

"Hello, Billy," Mr. Lee called as I ducked past him into the training hall, or *dojo*.

"You okay, Billy?" he asked.

I threw my *gi* onto a folding chair and asked, "When am I going to learn how to fight?"

He bent down. "Only been three weeks. Still early."

"But when? How long does it take?"

He shrugged. "I study karate all my life. I still not a fighter. Never wanted to be one."

"You can fight," I said. "I've seen you."

"Spar, maybe. Fighting means hurting. I not hurt other people."

I looked down and didn't say anything.

He straightened up and put his hands on his hips. "Somebody picking on you, Billy?"

I nodded.

"Older boys?" he asked.

"Junior high boys."

"What they say?"

"They laughed at me for my arm and for taking karate."

"Huh," he said, then added, "Many people fear what they not understand. They think martial art is fight, fight, fight; yell and scream and break board. Maybe you thought that too at first."

I nodded.

"Some people," he continued, "maybe do that. But we not do that in my *dojo*. We practice hard, learn discipline. But some people make fun. That is same with your arm. People fear it a little bit. It look strange to them."

"I'm tired of people laughing at me," I told him. "I want God to give me a normal arm!"

He squatted down so that he could see me face to face. His glittering dark eyes were serious. "God may not give new arm; He give skill instead. Mr. Lee cannot make older boys leave you alone; he make you see how foolish they are. Someday you see, it not the arm or leg that make you who you are. It is how you live. If Lord Jesus is pleased with you, not matter what others say. Fighting not help you."

Then he stood up and walked away.

I learned how to do the basic kicks. At first when I practiced them, I nearly fell over each time I tried. My legs got tired. My feet got tired. My ankles and knees felt like they'd been twisted and turned every which way. After class I could barely get into my street clothes, and my short walk home seemed like a long hike.

One night it started to rain during the lesson. By the time I had struggled back into my clothes, it was pouring outside.

Mr. Ryan, the man who had taught me to punch, called me over. "Hey, Billy, I can give you a ride home. I live over by Clover Road," he said. "Call your folks and ask if it's all right."

There was a phone in Mr. Lee's office. I called quickly and got permission.

I folded my damp *gi* together and followed him out to his little Volkswagen. Mr. Lee smiled and waved to us.

We climbed in and pulled out with a jerk as the little car jumped forward.

"Tired out?" Mr. Ryan asked, squinting at the windshield as he guided the car onto the highway.

"Uh-huh."

"Where's your house?"

"All the way down to the end of the street."

"You always walk to class?"

"My dad works at night and he takes our car. I don't mind so long as it's light outside."

He turned the car onto Clover Road. A few of the older kids were still out. They moved aside for us as we rumbled through. A few

of them saw me and pointed. Mr. Ryan ignored them.

"I can start picking you up for class," he told me.

"Thank you."

"You're a hard worker, a good student. This your house?"

"Yes. Thanks."

My mother was hurrying down the driveway with an umbrella. "Thank you so much for bringing Billy home," she called to him as I scrambled out. I winced at the name Billy. When Mr. Lee used it, it wasn't so bad, but when Mom said it, I felt like a kid.

"Are you Mr. Ryan?" she asked.

"Yes, I am. If it's all right, I can pick him up for class," he called over the rumbling of the car.

"Oh, that would be fine. Billy talks so much about you and Mr. Lee." I felt my face burning.

"Very nice meeting you, ma'am. I better let you get in out of the rain. Bill, I'll see you tomorrow night."

"Good-bye."

I felt a lot better going to class with Mr. Ryan. The kids up the street stared at us when we drove past. They pointed at me a couple times at first, but Mr. Ryan always ignored them. After a while they stopped. Mr. Ryan was tall and looked like a mountain climber. He had thick, curly hair and dark eyes. Although he was not old, his face was craggy and he rarely smiled. He wasn't the sort of man that people laugh at.

I learned how to do jump kicks and spinning kicks. At first all the turning and spinning made me dizzy, but I worked on keeping my balance. Mr. Lee could leap through the air, twirl around in a blur, and touch his foot against my ear as lightly as though I were made of porcelain and he were afraid of breaking me. But I also saw him leap through the air and drive his foot through three pine boards. Sometimes he would toss a board into the air and then break it with a punch or kick before it hit the ground.

Taking the Test

The school year started; I continued my lessons from Mr. Lee. The air outside was crisp and clear, but it was still hot inside the *dojo* when we trained.

"You ready for green-belt test?" he asked me one night.

My mouth went dry. I nodded, waiting for him to name a day.

"I think I test you next week. You very good student. Older boys still pick on you?"

I shrugged. "I come with Mr. Ryan now, so they don't have a chance to."

"You could walk to class," he observed. "Then drive home with Mr. Ryan."

"I like driving with him both ways."

He nodded and looked down at me. "When you first come here," he said gently, "you carried left arm way up here, like this." He pressed his left arm to his chest. "Seemed like you were afraid people should see it. Now you do not care anymore. You swing arms a lot now."

"Nobody here makes fun of it," I said.

"You not ashamed of it in here anymore. We respect how God chose to make you. You are used to it; we are used to it."

"But other people outside the *dojo* will make fun of it."

He cocked his head. "Those boys still so important?"

I didn't know what to say. Finally he said, "Okay, okay, enough of that. Let me see you punch."

I punched for him a couple times. "More?" I asked.

"No. Let me see you kick. Try a side kick." I snapped out a side kick for him. He nodded and asked to see more. It was the first time he had ever tutored me. I supposed it was to get me ready for my green-belt test. Mr. Ryan and a couple of older students strolled across the *dojo* and watched us. Mr. Lee went through all the kicks with me. We practiced self-defense together, and I showed him the first *kata*, a routine of karate techniques that's sort of like a drill. He did not say much. When we were finished, he nodded.

"You coming along pretty well," he said. "You very good student. Wish all my students work as hard as you."

He walked away. Mr. Ryan looked down at me. "Mr. Lee doesn't say that to many people," he told me.

After class when Mr. Ryan was driving me home, I said, "Some of the older kids on the street laugh at me for my arm."

"I noticed that," he replied. "It's hard to ignore, isn't it?"

"Yes." I could hardly hear my own voice.

Mr. Ryan said no more until we were at my house. Then he looked at me straight on. "I can tell you what Mr. Lee would say: 'How God made you is His choice. How you live with that is your choice.'"

I sat with my hand on the door handle a long time.

"Would you mind," I asked, "if I walked to class next time?"

"Nope. I'll drive you home afterwards."

"Thanks."

On Monday night after dinner I folded up my *gi* and set off for the *dojo* while it was still light outside. I tucked my *gi* under my arm.

The boys up the street were sitting on the curb, talking. My heart beat harder, but I thought about

Mr. Lee. Everything he had to say was a million times more important than jeers and catcalls from these boys.

They stopped talking and watched me. Some of them started laughing. I kept walking with my head up. I could sense that they were imitating me, but I didn't look back at them this time. It was time to stop thinking more of older kids who picked on me than of what God thought of me. I just wanted to get to the karate school,

test for my green belt, and tell Mr. Lee I had walked to class.

I passed the boys and walked on to Mr. Lee's. He was standing in the doorway. His hands were clasped behind his back.

"You early, Billy," he called.

"I started early," I said. "I walked."

"Boys pick on you?"

"I just kept walking, Mr. Lee. I never looked back." I swung my *gi* into my hand and looked up at his sparkling black eyes. "You were right. It wasn't important anymore."

"You make a big step," he said. "I have something for you." He pulled a green belt from behind his back and put it into my hand.

"But I haven't tested!" I exclaimed.

"You tested last week with me," he replied. "And now tonight you ready for green belt from Mr. Lee."

The belt was new and stiff, folded up and held together with rubber bands. I knew that tonight I would be standing with all the green-belted students. But I also knew I had passed another test, and that reward was even better than a black belt. I was sure of it.

Fables and Folktales

illustrated by John Bjerk

Storytelling has always been a good way to explain an idea. Many stories that are part of our literary heritage have been told and retold to help pass on to new generations the values and ideas that are important to a country. Fables and folktales are two kinds of stories that teach.

Fables

No doubt you have been reading fables in one form or another since kindergarten or first grade. Aesop, a Greek slave, was probably the greatest fable writer of all time. Aesop's fables, like most others, are very short stories and come to the point quickly. There are few details about the setting, and characters (most often animals) have names but little other description. The story always draws a moral or a lesson, which is sometimes stated at the end of the fable.

Some of the morals of Aesop's fables have become famous, like the one in "The Maid and Her Milk Pail."

That moral has become the well-known saying "Don't count your chickens before they hatch." The fable "The Wind and the Sun" teaches that gentleness can accomplish what force cannot. "The Boy Who Cried Wolf" teaches that liars are not believed even when they tell the truth, and the famous story about the hare and the tortoise demonstrates that "slow and steady wins the race."

Think of other fables you have read. Very likely they can be traced to the Greek slave who wrote them down hundreds and hundreds of years ago.

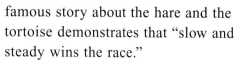

Folktales

Uncle Remus stories, like "Mr. Wolf Makes a Failure," are examples of folktales. Most experts believe that the slaves of the southern colonies brought the Brer Rabbit tales with them from Africa and over the years made them fit the language and customs of the American South. These stories were told and retold by the slaves. Joel Chandler Harris finally wrote them down. Mr. Harris worked hard to keep the dialect of the storytellers as he wrote.

"Hans Clodhopper" is another example of a folktale. It was passed on orally from person to person until someone finally wrote it down. Some other folktales that you probably know are "Cinderella" and "Little Red Riding Hood," which came from France. "Hansel and Gretel," "The Bremen Town Musicians," and "Snow White" are German tales. The Grimm brothers, who collected the German tales, are two of the major collectors of folktales. You can find books of their folktales in most libraries. You probably read some of the English tales to your little brothers and sisters. "The Story of the Three Little Pigs" and "Jack and the Beanstalk" are two in a long list of favorite tales Joseph Jacobs wrote down for English children.

Folktales are often similar to each other; for example, in many of them there are either three sisters or three brothers (as in "Hans Clodhopper"), and the youngest one is almost always the winner in the end.

You can always tell which characters are good and which are bad in a folktale, and you can be sure the bad characters will be punished in the end. Although the lesson isn't written out as it is in a fable, you can usually figure out what the moral of a folktale is.

Mr. Wolf makes a Failure

The collection of folktales known as Uncle Remus stories comes to us from Joel Chandler Harris, who heard such tales while he lived in the American South. He used dialect to preserve the tales as the storyteller, Uncle Remus, tells how Brer Rabbit out-wits his enemies.

adapted from the story by Joel Chandler Harris • illustrated by Tim Davis

"I see your ma's got company," said Uncle Remus, as the little boy entered the old man's door with a huge piece of mince-pie in his hand.

"Well, I saw the pie lying there, Uncle Remus, and I just thought I'd fetch it out to you."

"My, my, honey," replied the old man, looking over the child with admiration. "My, my, honey. It ain't Thanksgiving time, and they ain't got no business layin' a mince meat pie 'round loose. This here pie," Uncle Remus continued, holding it up and measuring it with an experienced eye, "will give me

strength to pursue on after Brer Fox and Brer Rabbit and the other beastesses."

Here the old man paused, and proceeded to demolish the pie—a feat accomplished in a very short time.

Then he wiped the crumbs from his beard and began:

Brer Fox feel so bad, and he get so mad 'bout Brer Rabbit, that he don't know what to do, and he look mighty downhearted. By and by, one day while he was goin' along the road, old Brer Wolf come up with him. When they got done howdyin' and askin' after one another's family, Brer Wolf, he allowed that there was somethin' wrong with Brer Fox, and Brer Fox, he allowed there wasn't, so he went on and laugh and make great to-do. But Brer Wolf, he got mighty long head, and he sorter broach about Brer Rabbit's carryin's on, 'cause the way that Brer Rabbit deceive Brer Fox done got to be the talk of the neighborhood. Then Brer Fox and Brer Wolf they sorter talked on, they did, 'til by and by Brer Wolf he up and say that he done got a plan fixed to trap Brer Rabbit. Then Brer Fox asked how. Then Brer Wolf up and tell him that the way to get Brer Rabbit was to get him in Brer Fox's house.

"How you goin' get him there?" says Brer Fox.

"Fool him," says Brer Wolf.

"Who goin' to do the foolin'," says Brer Fox.

"I'll do the foolin'," says Brer Wolf, "if you'll do the gamin'."

"How you goin' do it?" says Brer Fox.

"You run along home, and get on the bed, and make like you're dead, and don't you say nothin' 'til Brer Rabbit comes in and puts his hands on to you," says Brer Wolf, "and if we don't get him for supper, Joe's dead and Sal's a widow."

"This look like a mighty nice game," Brer Fox agreed. So then he ambled off home, and Brer Wolf, he marched off to Brer Rabbit's house. When he got there, it looked like nobody was at home, but Brer Wolf he knocked on the door—blam! Blam! Nobody came. Then he knocked again—blim! Blim!

"Who there?" says Brer Rabbit.

"Friend," says Brer Wolf.

"Too many friends spoils the dinner," says Brer Rabbit; "which one's this?"

"I fetch bad news, Brer Rabbit," says Brer Wolf.

"Bad news is soon told," says Brer Rabbit.

By this time Brer Rabbit done come to the door.

"Brer Fox died this mornin'," says Wolf.

"Where are your mournin' clothes, Brer Wolf?" says Brer Rabbit.

"Goin' after them now," says Brer Wolf. "I just call by for to bring the news. I went down to Brer Fox house little bit ago, and there I found him stiff."

Then Brer Wolf lope off. Brer Rabbit sat down and scratch his head, he did, and by and by he say to himself that he believe he sorter drop round by Brer Fox's house. No sooner said than done. Up he jump, and out he went. When Brer Rabbit got close to Brer Fox's house, all look lonesome. Then he went up nearer. Nobody stirrin'.

Then he look in, and there lay Brer Fox stretch out on the bed just as big as life. Then Brer Rabbit make like he's talkin' to himself.

"Nobody around for to look after Brer Fox—not even Brer Turkey Buzzard ain't come to the funeral.

"I hope Brer Fox ain't dead, but I expect he is," says Brer Rabbit.

"Even down to Brer Wolf done left him. It's the busy season with me, but I'll set up with him. He seem like he dead, yet he might not be," says Brer Rabbit.

"When a man go to see dead folks, dead folks always raises up a leg and hollers, *wahoo!*"

Brer Fox he stayed still. Then Brer Rabbit he talked a little louder: "Mighty funny. Brer Fox looks like he's dead, yet he don't do like he's dead. Dead folks raise a leg and hollers *wahoo!* when a man comes to see him," says Brer Rabbit.

Sure enough, Brer Fox lift up his foot and holler *wahoo!* and Brer Rabbit he tear out the house like the dogs was after him.

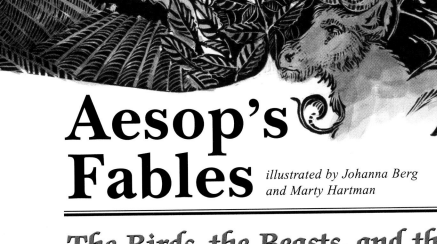

Aesop's Fables

illustrated by Johanna Berg and Marty Hartman

The Birds, the Beasts, and the Bat

he birds and beasts once went to war. The bat— which could not be said to be bird or beast—at first kept out of the way of both, but when he thought the beasts would win the day, he was found in their ranks, and to prove his right to be there, he said, "Can you find a bird that has two rows of teeth in his head, as I have?" At last the birds had the best of the fight, so then the bat was seen to join their ranks. "Look," said he, "I have wings, so what else can I be but a bird?"

"To fly with all winds" was thought base in the bat by both sides of the fight, and he could not get bird or beast to own him, and to this day he hides and skulks in caves and stems of trees, and does not come out until dark when all the birds of the air have gone to roost, and the beasts of the field are wrapt in sleep.

One must not blow hot and cold.

The Field of Corn

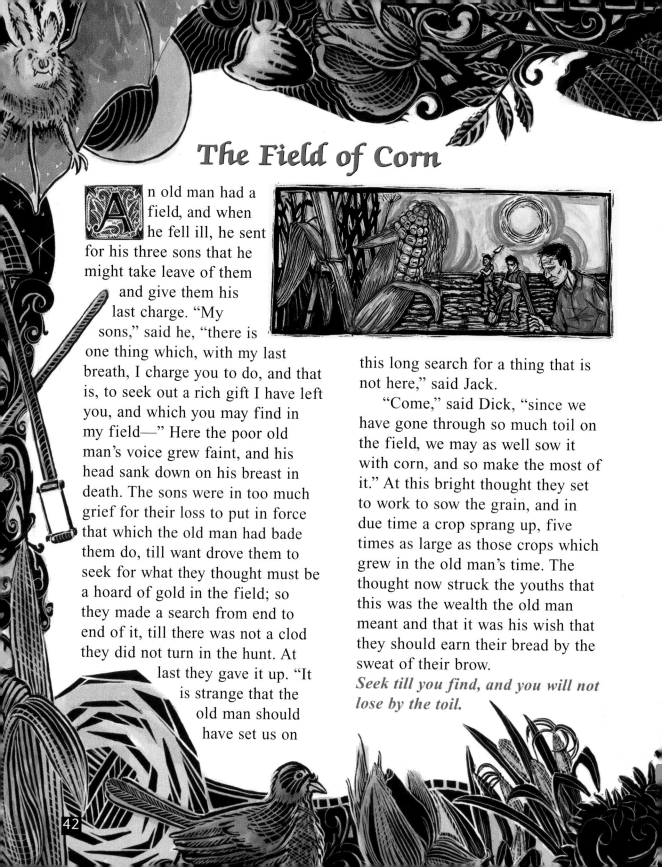

An old man had a field, and when he fell ill, he sent for his three sons that he might take leave of them and give them his last charge. "My sons," said he, "there is one thing which, with my last breath, I charge you to do, and that is, to seek out a rich gift I have left you, and which you may find in my field—" Here the poor old man's voice grew faint, and his head sank down on his breast in death. The sons were in too much grief for their loss to put in force that which the old man had bade them do, till want drove them to seek for what they thought must be a hoard of gold in the field; so they made a search from end to end of it, till there was not a clod they did not turn in the hunt. At last they gave it up. "It is strange that the old man should have set us on this long search for a thing that is not here," said Jack.

"Come," said Dick, "since we have gone through so much toil on the field, we may as well sow it with corn, and so make the most of it." At this bright thought they set to work to sow the grain, and in due time a crop sprang up, five times as large as those crops which grew in the old man's time. The thought now struck the youths that this was the wealth the old man meant and that it was his wish that they should earn their bread by the sweat of their brow.

Seek till you find, and you will not lose by the toil.

42

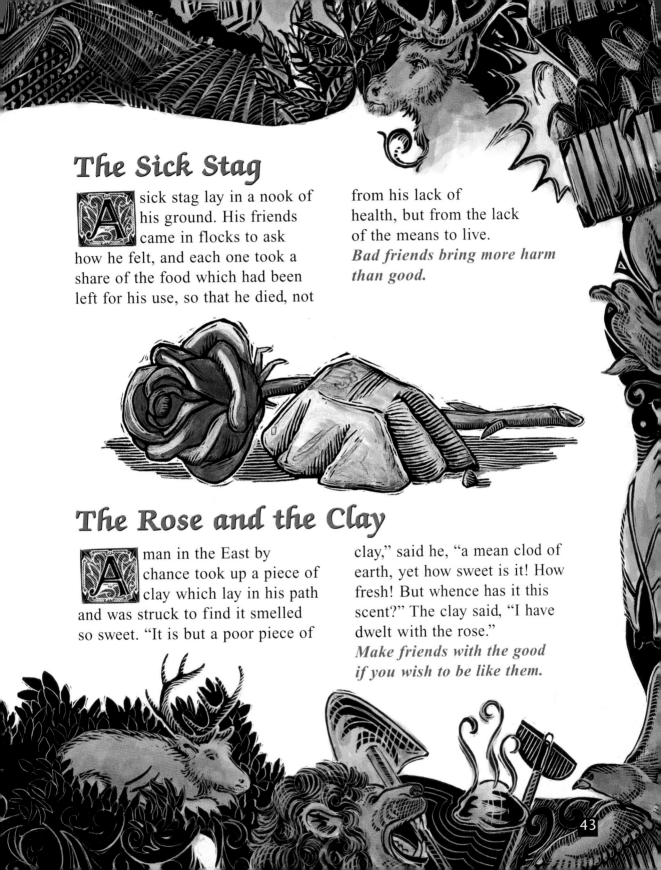

The Sick Stag

A sick stag lay in a nook of his ground. His friends came in flocks to ask how he felt, and each one took a share of the food which had been left for his use, so that he died, not from his lack of health, but from the lack of the means to live.

Bad friends bring more harm than good.

The Rose and the Clay

A man in the East by chance took up a piece of clay which lay in his path and was struck to find it smelled so sweet. "It is but a poor piece of clay," said he, "a mean clod of earth, yet how sweet is it! How fresh! But whence has it this scent?" The clay said, "I have dwelt with the rose."

Make friends with the good if you wish to be like them.

The Maid and Her Milk Pail

One day, as a young maid went down the road with her pail of milk on her head, she was heard to say, "This pail of milk will fetch me so much, which sum I will lay out in eggs; these eggs will bring a score of chicks, and they will be fit to sell just at the time when fowls bear a good price: so that on May-day I shall have a new gown. Let me see . . . yes, green will suit me best, and green it shall be. In this dress I will go to the fair, and all who are there will pay their court to me; but with a proud look I shall turn from them."

Wrapt in this dream of joy, she gave a toss of the head to suit the words, when down came the pail of milk and with it the eggs, the chicks, the green gown, and all the bright thoughts of what she should do at the fair.

Count not your chicks till they are out of the shell. Each "may be" hath a "may not be."

A Just Judge

Leo Tolstoy

*illustrated by
Kathy Pflug
and Tim Davis*

An Algerian king named Bauakas wanted to find out whether or not it was true, as he had been told, that in one of his cities there lived a just judge who could instantly discern the truth and from whom no rogue was ever able to conceal himself. Bauakas exchanged clothes with a merchant and went on horseback to the city where the judge lived.

At the entrance to the city a cripple approached the king and begged alms of him. Bauakas gave him money and was about to continue on his way, but the cripple clung to his clothing.

"What do you wish?" asked the king. "Haven't I given you money?"

"You gave me alms," said the cripple; "now grant me one favor.

Let me ride with you as far as the city square; otherwise the horses and camels may trample me."

Bauakas set the cripple behind him on the horse and took him as far as the city square. There he halted his horse, but the cripple refused to dismount.

"We have arrived at the square; why don't you get off?" asked Bauakas.

"Why should I?" the beggar replied. "This horse belongs to me. If you are unwilling to return it, we shall have to go to court."

Hearing their quarrel, people gathered around them shouting, "Go to the judge! He will decide between you!"

Bauakas and the cripple went to the judge.

There were others in court, and the judge called upon each one in turn. Before he came to Bauakas and the cripple, he heard a scholar and a peasant. They had come to court over a woman: the peasant said she was his wife, and the scholar said she was his. The judge heard them both, remained silent for a moment, and then said,

"Leave the woman here with me, and come back tomorrow."

When they had gone, a butcher and an oil merchant came before the judge. The butcher was covered with blood and the oil merchant with oil. In his hand the butcher held some money, and the oil merchant held onto the butcher's hand.

"I was buying oil from this man," the butcher said, "and when I took out my purse to pay him, he seized me by the hand and tried to take all my money away from me. That is why we have come to you—I holding onto my purse, and he holding onto my hand. But the money is mine, and he is a thief."

Then the oil merchant spoke. "That is not true," he said. "The butcher came to me to buy oil, and after I had poured him a full jug, he asked me to change a gold piece for him. When I took out my money and placed it upon a bench, he seized it and tried to run off. I caught him by the hand, as you see, and brought him here to you."

The judge remained silent for a moment, then said, "Leave the money here

with me, and come back to-morrow."

When his turn came, Bauakas told what had happened. The judge listened to him and then asked the beggar to speak.

"All that he said is untrue," said the beggar. "He was sitting on the ground, and as I rode through the city, he asked me to let him ride with me. I set him behind me on my horse and took him where he wanted to go. But when we got there, he refused to get off and said that the horse was his, which is not true."

The judge thought for a moment, then said, "Leave the horse here with me, and come back to-morrow."

The following day many people gathered in court to hear the judge's decisions.

First came the scholar and the peasant.

"Take your wife," the judge said to the scholar, "and the peasant shall be given fifty strokes of the lash."

The scholar took his wife, and the peasant was punished. Then the judge called the butcher.

"The money is yours," he said to him. And pointing to the oil merchant he said, "Give him fifty strokes of the lash."

He next called Bauakas and the cripple.

"Would you recognize your horse among twenty others?" he asked Bauakas.

"I would," he replied.

"And you?" he asked the cripple.

"I would," said the cripple.

"Come with me," the judge said to Bauakas.

They went to the stable. Bauakas instantly pointed out this horse among the twenty others. Then the judge called the cripple to the stable and told him to point out the horse. The cripple recognized the horse and pointed to it. The judge then returned to his seat.

"Take the horse; it is yours," he said to Bauakas. "Give the beggar fifty strokes of the lash."

When the judge left the court and went home, Bauakas followed him.

"What do you want?" asked the judge. "Are you not satisfied with my decision?"

"I am satisfied," said Bauakas. "But I should like to learn how you knew that the woman was the wife of the scholar, that the money belonged to the butcher, and that the horse was mine and not the beggar's."

"This is how I knew about the woman: in the morning I sent for her and said, 'Please fill my inkwell.' She took the inkwell, washed it quickly and deftly, and filled it with ink; therefore it was work she was accustomed to. If she had been the wife of the peasant, she would not have known how to do it. This showed me that the scholar was telling the truth.

"And this is how I knew about the money: I put it into a cup full of water, and in the morning I looked to see if any oil had risen to the surface. If the money had belonged to the oil merchant, it would have been soiled by his oily hands. There was no oil on the water; therefore the butcher was telling the truth.

"It was more difficult to find out about the horse. The cripple recognized it among twenty others,

even as you did. However, I did not take you both to the stable to see which of you knew the horse, but to see which of you the horse knew. When you approached it, it turned its head and stretched its neck toward you; but when the cripple touched it, it laid back its ears and lifted one hoof. Therefore I knew that you were the horse's real master."

Then Bauakas said to the judge, "I am not a merchant, but King Bauakas. I came here in order to see if what is said of you is true. I see now that you are a wise judge. Ask whatever you wish of me, and you shall have it as a reward."

"I need no reward," replied the judge. "I am content that my king has praised me."

Three Rolls and a Pretzel

Leo Tolstoy • illustrated by Tim Davis

Feeling hungry one day, a peasant bought himself a large roll and ate it. But he was still hungry, so he bought another roll and ate it. Still hungry, he bought a third roll and ate it. When the three rolls failed to satisfy his hunger, he bought some pretzels. After eating one pretzel he no longer felt hungry.

Suddenly he clapped his hand to his head and cried, "What a fool I am! Why did I waste all those rolls? I ought to have eaten a pretzel in the first place!"

THE KING AND THE SHIRT

Leo Tolstoy
illustrated by Tim Davis

A king once fell ill. "I will give half my kingdom to the man who can cure me," he said.

All of his wise men gathered to decide how the king could be wife; or if he had children, they were bad—everyone had something to complain of.

Finally, late one night, the king's son was passing by a poor

cured. But no one knew. Only one of the wise men said what he thought would cure the king.

"If you can find a happy man, take his shirt, put it on the king—and the king will be cured."

The king sent his emissaries to search for a happy man. They traveled far and wide throughout his whole kingdom, but they could not find a happy man. There was no one who was completely satisfied: if a man was rich, he was ailing; if he was healthy, he was poor; if he was rich and healthy, he had a bad

little hut and he heard someone say,

"Now, God be praised, I have finished my work, I have eaten my fill, and I can lie down and sleep! What more could I want?"

The king's son rejoiced and gave orders that the man's shirt be taken and carried to the king and that the man be given as much money as he wanted.

The emissaries went in to take off the man's shirt, but the happy man was so poor that he had no shirt.

Hans Clodhopper

Hans Christian Andersen
dramatized by Doris Fisher Harris

illustrated by Tim Davis

CAST

FATHER: Ambitious and pushy man

FRANZ: Conceited son

LUDWIG: Vain son

HANS: Quiet, sincere, and clumsy son

SUITOR I: Proud hunter

SUITOR II: Arrogant wrestler

SUITOR III: Conceited sword fighter

PRINCESS: Witty daughter of the king

GIRLS: Three giggling girls

SCENE I

The three boys are seated in a circle: Ludwig is polishing his shoes, Franz is polishing his sword, and Hans is staring vacantly into space. The door opens, and their father bursts into the room.

Father: *(excitedly)* My sons, your fortune is made!

Franz: We could use a fortune.

Ludwig: We could use a penny.

Hans: Have you noticed it is a beautiful day?

Father: Oh, be quiet! Who cares about the weather?

Franz: He does. The simpleton of the family.

Ludwig: He is always gazing at the sky.

Father: Come here, my clever boys. *(Franz and Ludwig move to him.)* The messenger said the king's daughter is to be married.

Franz: So!

Ludwig: What?

Father: I have heard that she is so beautiful that every man who meets her loses his voice. She has grown tired of this and has vowed to marry the man who has the most to say for himself.

Franz: I shall win her.

Ludwig: I shall win her and her money.

Franz: I can say the Latin dictionary by heart.

Ludwig: I can say all the laws of the country by heart.

Franz: I can say all the newspapers front and back for the last three years.

Hans: I can decorate beautiful horse harnesses.

Ludwig: Be still, Hans!

Father: *(to Franz and Ludwig)* Very well, very well. You shall go today.

Franz: I shall take our coal black horse.

Ludwig: I shall take the white.

Father: Hans, go saddle the horses for your brothers.

Hans: Yes, Father. *(Exit, shuffling, staring at the sky)*

Father: Now my clever sons, go upstairs and pack. But first put this oil on your mouth so that you can talk better. *(takes small bottle from pocket and boys oil their mouths)*

(Exit Father, Ludwig, and Franz; Father with an arm around each boy)

SCENE II

Enter Father, Hans following

Hans: Father?

Father: Now, I must be sure they have what they need.

Hans: Father?

Father: What is it, Hans?

Hans: Father, I want to go to the court and talk to the princess, too.

Father: Don't be silly. You do not have the brains to win the princess.

Hans: May I have a horse?

Father: Your brothers have taken our horses.

Hans: May I have fine clothes like my brothers?

Father: We have no more money.

Hans: If I mayn't have a horse, I'll take the billy goat. He is my own, and I will ride him to the castle. May I?

Father: Very well, but I fear you will make a fool of yourself.

(Exit Hans, Father following)

SCENE III

The three boys are seated, resting on a hillside
just outside the castle; each has a bag.

Ludwig: See what I have found for the princess. *(opens his bag)* Here is a wild rose. I will tell her it looks like her. Girls like that.

Franz: That is nothing. See what I found. *(opens his bag)* Girls like diamonds better than flowers.

Hans: See what I found on the way. *(opens his bag)*

Ludwig: Ugh. It's a dead bird.

Hans: I found it. It was beautiful. Perhaps I will have time to cook it.

Ludwig: You are silly!

Franz: What else is in your bag?

(Hans pulls an old wooden shoe out of his bag.)

Franz: Clodhopper! It is only an old broken wooden shoe. Are these your gifts to the princess?

Hans: *(simply)* She may have whatever I have.

Ludwig: What are you doing?

Hans: *(gets on his knees and scoops up sand)* Did you ever see such fine sand? It is soft and beautiful. I will put some in my pocket.

Franz: What kind of gifts are these to bring to a princess?

(Exit Franz and Ludwig)

Hans: *(calling after them)* I will bring her all I can. This is all I have!

(Exit Hans, trudging after them)

SCENE IV

The boys enter the castle and find three suitors ahead of them. The princess is seated with three maids-in-waiting behind her. As the brothers and the other suitors come before the princess, the girls giggle.

Suitor I: *(gets up and nervously goes to stand in front of the princess)* O beautiful Princess, I am the most famous hunter of the land, *(voice begins to leave him)* and I come to claim your hand— *(realizes that he cannot speak)*

Princess: This will never do, will it, girls?

Girl I: No indeed.

Girl II: How silly he looks.

Girl III: His face is red.

Princess: Away with you. *(Exit Suitor I, angrily)*

Suitor II: *(rushes in)* Your Highness, I am the best wrestler— *(voice leaves him)*

Suitor III: *(rushes in, almost colliding with Suitor II)* I am the greatest swordsman! I—I— *(voice leaves him)*

(Princess laughs as men wildly gesture and try to express themselves.)

Princess: Away with all of you.

(Exit the three suitors, trying to talk)

Girl I: Did you see his face?

Girl II: Did you see his feet?

Girl III: Did you see his ears?

(Franz and Ludwig come stumbling before the princess, each eager to be first.)

Franz: Your Majesty, I can say the Latin dictionary by heart— *(voice leaves him)*

Ludwig: I can say the law books— *(voice leaves him)*

Princess: *(wearily)* Get out!

(Exit Franz and Ludwig, Princess watching)

Princess: Did any of those stuck-up fools think I would marry him? *(notices Hans)* Here's one more. Very well. But I am hungry and I want my lunch, so please be quick.

Hans: It is lunch time. I'm hungry too.

Princess: Do you expect me to feed you?

Hans: No. I have a bird to be roasted. *(pulls bird from bag)*

Princess: Do you have something to roast it in?

Hans: Yes, here is my roasting pot. *(pulls out shoe)*

Princess: You are a man of good sense. Where shall we get something to catch the dripping oil?

Hans: Here, I have sand in my pocket. *(puts sand in bottom of shoe)* Will you lunch with me?

Princess: *(comes and takes Hans's arm)* I like you. You have an answer for every problem. And you don't boast. I will have you for a husband.

(Princess takes Hans by the hand and leads him up to the throne. He smiles and sits down. She places a crown upon his head and a robe around him and goes to doorway and calls.)

Princess: Come and see the rare and wise man who will be king of the realm.

(Others come on where they have exited. The suitors are angry, and the brothers are amazed.)

Princess: *(standing beside Hans and taking his hand)* And now, king of my heart, let's have lunch.

Pinocch
and the Gold Coins

C. Collodi • illustrated by Tim Banks

For over a hundred years the novel Pinocchio *has been a favorite with children. The original story was written in Italian and then translated into other languages as its popularity increased. The puppet Pinocchio has many adventures and suffers many misfortunes when he tries to live without working or studying. Convinced that it is easy to become rich and enjoy life, he joins a marionette circus and is almost used as firewood by the circus's fire-eater. The man spares Pinocchio, then gives him five gold pieces and sends him on his way home. But once again Pinocchio strays from what he knows is the path of duty.*

The Promise of Gold

Pinocchio had not gone half a mile when he met a Fox lame in one paw, and a Cat blind in both eyes. The Fox, who limped, leaned heavily on the Cat; and the Cat, who was blind, was guided by the Fox.

"Good morning, Pinocchio," said the Fox, saluting him politely.

"How do you know my name?" asked the marionette.

"I know your papa very well."

"When did you see him?"

"I saw him yesterday at the door of his house."

"What was he doing?"

"He was in his shirt sleeves and he trembled with the cold."

"Poor Papa! But he will tremble no more after today."

"Why?"

"Because I have become a great, rich man."

"You a great, rich man!" said the Fox, and he laughed aloud. The Cat also laughed, but in order not to be seen laughing he stroked his mustache with his two front paws.

"What are you laughing about?" said Pinocchio, taken aback. "I hate to make your mouths water, but I have here, as you shall see, five beautiful pieces of gold."

And he pulled out of his pocket the money that Fire Eater had given him. At the sound of the money the Fox involuntarily stretched his leg that was paralyzed and the Cat opened wide his eyes that looked like two green lamps; but it was all done so quickly that Pinocchio did not see anything.

"And now," said the Fox, "what do you intend to do with all that money?"

"First of all," replied the marionette, "I shall buy a coat for my papa, all covered with gold and silver and with buttons of brilliants. Then I shall buy a new A B C card for myself."

"For yourself?"

"Yes, indeed, because I wish to go to school and begin to study."

"Look at me!" said the Fox; "because of my passion for studying I have lost a leg."

"Look at me!" cried the Cat; "because of my love for studying I have lost both eyes."

In the meantime a Blackbird flew near them and said, "Pinocchio, do not listen to the counsel of bad companions. If you do, you will be sorry."

Just as soon as the Blackbird had said that, the Cat sprang and caught him by the back. Before the Blackbird had time to say "Oh!" the Cat ate him up, feathers and all. Then the Cat cleaned his mouth and closed his eyes and became as blind as he was at first.

"Poor Blackbird!" said Pinocchio. "Why did you treat him so badly?"

"I did it to teach him a lesson. Another time he will know that he ought not to meddle with other people's business."

They walked along a short distance when the Fox, stopping suddenly, said to the marionette, "Should you like to double your money?"

"What do you mean?"

"Should you like to make of those miserable five pieces, ten? a hundred? a thousand?"

"Why, of course! And how can you do it?"

"It is very easy. Instead of going home, come with us."

"And where do you want to take me?"

"To the Country of the Owl."

Pinocchio thought a little and then said resolutely: "No, I will not go. My father expects me. Who knows but that the poor old man, when I did not return yesterday, was worried and wept for me? I have been a bad boy, and the Talking Cricket was right when he said, 'Disobedient boys never get along well in this world.'"

"Then," said the Fox, "you want to go home? All right! Go home, but it will be the worse for you."

"Yes, it will be the worse for you," said the Cat.

"Think well, Pinocchio, for you have thrown away a fortune."

"A fortune," said the Cat.

"Your five pieces might be two thousand by tomorrow."

"Two thousand," repeated the Cat.

"But how is it possible that they can become so many?" asked Pinocchio, whose mouth was wide open with astonishment.

"I will explain to you," said the Fox. "You must know that in the Country of the Owl there is a magic field called 'The Field of Wonders.' You make a little hole in the ground and you put inside, for example, one piece of gold. Then you cover over the hole with a little earth, water it with a few drops of water from a fountain, put on a little salt, and go to bed and sleep quietly. In the meantime, during the night, the gold piece begins to grow and blossom; and the next morning, returning to the field, guess what you find? Why, you

find a tree loaded with gold pieces!"

"If I bury five pieces," said Pinocchio, all excited, "how many shall I find next morning?"

"It is easy to count," replied the Fox. "You can do it on your fingers. Every gold piece will make five hundred; and therefore, multiplying each by five, you will have two thousand five hundred."

"Oh, how beautiful!" cried Pinocchio, dancing with joy. "When I have all those gold pieces I will give you five hundred of them and I will take the other two thousand to my papa."

"A present to us!" cried the Fox disdainfully as if he were offended. "No, indeed!"

"No, indeed!" said the Cat.

"We," said the Fox, "work only to enrich others."

"Only others," said the Cat.

"What good people!" thought Pinocchio; and forgetting all about his papa, the new coat, and the A B C card, he said to the Fox and the Cat, "Come on, then; I will go with you."

The Path of Danger

They walked and walked and walked until they arrived at the Red Lobster Inn, tired to death.

"Let us stop here a little," said the Fox, "just long enough to get something to eat and rest ourselves. At midnight we can start again and tomorrow morning we shall arrive at the Field of Wonders."

They entered the inn and seated themselves at the table, but none of them was hungry. The poor Cat felt very much indisposed and could eat only thirty-five mullets with tomato sauce and four portions of tripe; and because the tripe did not taste just right he called three times for butter and cheese to put on it.

The Fox would willingly have ordered something, but as the doctor had told him to diet, he had to be contented with a nice fresh rabbit dressed with the giblets of chicken. After the rabbit, he ordered, as a finish to his meal, some partridges, some pheasants, some frogs, some lizards, and some bird of paradise eggs; and then he did not wish any more. He had such a distaste for food, he said, that he could not eat another mouthful.

Pinocchio ate the least of all. He asked for a piece of meat and some bread, but he left everything

on his plate. He could think of nothing but the Field of Wonders.

When they had supped, the Fox said to the host, "Give me two good rooms, one for Mr. Pinocchio and another for me and my companion. Before we go we will ring the bell. Remember, however, to wake us at midnight so that we can go on with our journey."

"All right, sir," replied the host; and he winked his eye at the Fox and the Cat, as if to say, "We understand each other."

Pinocchio had scarcely jumped into bed when he fell asleep and began to dream. He seemed to be in a field full of arbors, and each arbor was overgrown with vines covered with large bunches of grapes. Instead of grapes, however, they were all gold pieces, that made a noise when the wind blew—*zin-zin-zin-zin*. It was just as if they said, "Here we are! Let who will come and take us." When Pinocchio was on the point of reaching for them, he heard a loud knocking at the door of his room. It was the landlord who came to tell him that the clock had struck midnight.

"And are my companions ready?" asked the marionette.

"Better than that! They left two hours ago."

"Why were they in such a hurry?"

"Because the Cat received word that his father was very sick with frosted feet and that he was in danger of losing his life."

"And they paid for the supper?"

"What do you think those people are? They are too highly educated to insult a gentleman as good as you are."

"Oh, yes! That affront would have displeased me very much," said Pinocchio, hastily. Then he asked the landlord, "Did they say where I should meet them?"

"At the Field of Wonders, this morning at daybreak."

Pinocchio paid a gold piece for his supper and that of his companions and then departed. He groped his way along, because outside the inn it was so dark that he could not see anything. It was very quiet and not even a leaf stirred. Some birds flying along the road struck Pinocchio on the nose with their wings. He jumped back and cried out with fear, "Who goes there?" The echo of the surrounding hills took up his words and repeated, "Who goes there?" "Who goes there?" "Who goes there?"

As he walked on, he saw on the trunk of a tree a little creature that shone with a pale opaque light, just like a candle behind a globe of transparent porcelain.

"Who are you?" asked Pinocchio.

"I am the Talking Cricket," it replied, with a little voice that seemed to come from another world.

"What do you want with me?"

"I wish to warn you. Go back, with your four gold pieces that you have left, to your papa, who cries and thinks he shall never see you again."

"Tomorrow my papa will be a very rich man because these four pieces will become two thousand."

"Do not trust those who promise to make you rich in one night, my boy. Usually they are mad or deceitful. Listen to me and go back."

"I want to go on."

"The hour is late."

"I want to go on."

"The night is dark."

"I want to go on."

"The road is dangerous."

"I want to go on."

"Remember that boys who always do what they want to will sooner or later repent."

"The same old story! Good night, Cricket."

"Good night, and may you escape from the assassins!"

The Talking Cricket had hardly said these words when he suddenly disappeared, just as if some one had blown the light out, and the road was darker than ever.

"Truly," said the marionette to himself, starting again on his way, "how unfortunate we poor boys are! Everybody scolds us, everybody warns us, and everybody gives us advice."

But Pinocchio was not able to finish his reasoning, because at that moment he thought he heard a rustling in the leaves behind him. He turned to look and saw in the dark two coal sacks covering two figures which ran toward him on the tips of their toes.

"Here they are, truly!" said Pinocchio to himself. Not knowing what to do with the four gold pieces, he put them into his mouth and under his tongue. Then he tried to run away. But he had hardly started when his arms were seized and he heard two hollow voices say to him, "Your money or your life!"

Not being able to reply on account of the money in his mouth, Pinocchio made many bows and gestures in order to make his captors understand that he was a poor marionette and that he did not have a cent in his pockets. "Come on and stop fooling! Out with it!" the brigands cried.

And the marionette made signs with his hands and head, which meant, "I have none!" . . .

"Ah! do you make-believe you are deaf? Wait a little and we will show you how we shall make you give up the gold."

Then they began to handle the marionette very roughly, but Pinocchio managed to liberate himself from their hands. Jumping a hedge that bordered the road, he began to run across the fields with the assassins after him, like two dogs after a rabbit.

After a run of fifteen miles Pinocchio could go no farther. Fearing that he was lost, he climbed to the top of a large pine tree and sat on one of the branches. The assassins also tried to climb; but when they got halfway up they slipped and fell to the ground, rubbing the skin off their legs and hands as they dropped.

However, they did not consider themselves conquered. On the contrary, they collected a bundle of sticks, and, placing them around the tree, set fire to them. In less time than it takes to tell it, the pine tree took fire and blazed like a candle blown by the wind. Pinocchio, seeing that the flames mounted higher and higher, and not wishing to be roasted, jumped down from the top of the tree. Away he ran, just as before, with the assassins always behind and never getting tired. . . .

When he arrived at a certain point, he thought he heard some one. Indeed, he saw on the road whom do you suppose?—the Fox and the Cat, that is, the two companions with whom he had supped at the inn called the Red Lobster.

"Here is our dear friend Pinocchio!" cried the Fox, hugging and kissing him. "How did you ever get here?"

"It is a long story," said the marionette, "and I will tell you when I have time. I met some assassins on the road."

"Assassins? Oh, my poor friend! and what did they want?"

"They wished to rob me of my money."

"Infamous!" cried the Fox.

"Most infamous!" said the Cat.

"But I started to run," continued the marionette, "and they ran after me." . . .

"And your money, where is that?"

"I have it all, less the piece I spent at the inn called the Red Lobster."

"And to think that instead of four pieces they might become two thousand by tomorrow! Why did you not follow my advice? Why do you not sow them in the Field of Wonders?"

"Today it is impossible. I will go another time."

"Another time will be too late," said the Fox.

"Why?"

"Because that field has been bought by a rich man, and after tomorrow no one will be permitted to sow there any more."

"How far is the Field of Wonders from here?"

"Hardly two miles. Will you come with us? In half an hour we shall be there. You can sow the money quickly, and after a few moments you can return home with your pockets full. Will you come with us?"

Pinocchio hesitated a little because he thought of the advice of the Talking Cricket; but, after the fashion of foolish, heartless boys, he finally yielded. With a shake of his head he said to the Fox and the Cat, "Come on, I will go with you." And they started.

The Payment for Fools

After having walked half a day they arrived at a city called Stupid-catchers. As soon as they entered the city Pinocchio saw that all the streets were full of sick dogs that gaped for food; clipped sheep that shook from the cold; featherless chickens that begged for alms; big butterflies that could not fly any more because they had sold their beautiful wings for a few pennies and were ashamed to be seen; and pheasants that limped, bewailing their brilliant gold and silver feathers now lost to them forever.

In the midst of the crowd of beggars and unfortunates they

passed from time to time several fine carriages filled with people, each of whom turned out to be a Fox or a thieving Magpie or a Bird of Prey.

"Where is the Field of Wonders?" asked Pinocchio.

"Only a few steps farther."

And so it proved. They walked through the city, and outside the walls they stopped in a field which looked much like other fields. No one was in sight.

"Here we are at last," said the Fox. "Now you must stoop down and dig a hole and put the money inside."

Pinocchio obeyed, dug a hole, put in the money, and then covered it over with earth.

"Now then," said the Fox, "go to that well and take a little water and sprinkle the ground where you have sown."

Pinocchio went to the well. Because he had nothing in which to carry water, he took his hat and,

filling it, came back and sprinkled the spot where he had sown the money. Then he asked, "Is there anything else?"

"Nothing else," replied the Fox. "Now we shall go away. You may return here in about twenty minutes and you will find a large vine with its branches covered with money."

The poor marionette, nearly crazy with joy, thanked the Fox and the Cat a thousand times and promised them a beautiful present.

"We wish nothing," they replied. "To us it is enough to have taught others the way to get rich without doing anything; and we are as contented as we can be."

Thus saying, they bowed to Pinocchio and, wishing him a good harvest, went away.

The marionette, returning to the city, began to count the minutes one by one. When he thought it was time to go back he took the road that led to the Field of Wonders. And while he walked along his heart beat like a big hall clock—*tic-toc-tic-toc*. Meanwhile he was thinking to himself, "And if, instead of two thousand, I should find five thousand? Oh, what a rich man I should be! I would have a palace and a thousand wooden horses and carriages

to amuse me; I would have a cellar filled with good things, a library filled with candy, Dutch cake, almond cake, and cinnamon stick."

Thus imagining, he arrived at the field. He stopped to look for the large vine with many branches, but he saw nothing. He took a few steps more. Nothing. He entered the field and went right to the hole where he had planted his money. There was nothing there. Then he became thoughtful and began to wonder what he should do next.

Just then he heard a whistling in his ears as if some one were laughing. Looking up, he saw on a tree a big Parrot who was preening his feathers.

"Why do you laugh?" asked Pinocchio in an angry voice.

"I laugh because in cleaning my feathers I tickled myself under my wings."

The marionette did not reply. He went to the well and sprinkled again the place where he had buried his money. When he had done this he heard a laugh more impertinent than the first one. It sounded very loud in the solitude of the field.

"Well," said Pinocchio, wrathfully, "tell me, if you can, ignorant Parrot, why you laugh now."

"I laugh at those silly heads who believe everything that is told them."

"Do you refer to me?"

"Yes, I speak of you, poor Pinocchio. You are foolish enough to think that money, if sowed properly, will grow like grain and plants. I thought so once, and in consequence I have today very few feathers. Now that it is too late to mend matters, I have made up my mind that in order to get together a few pennies it is necessary to work with your hands or invent something with your head."

"I do not understand," said the marionette, who already began to tremble with fear.

"I will explain better," said the Parrot. "Know, then, that while you were in the city the Fox and the Cat returned here. They took the money and then fled like the wind. And now they cannot be caught."

Pinocchio remained with his mouth wide open. Unwilling to believe the words of the Parrot, he began with his hands and nails to dig out the dirt where he had planted his money. And he dug and dug and dug until he had made a hole large enough for a haystack; but the money was not there.

After this sad adventure, a cruel judge throws Pinocchio into jail for acting unwisely. Months later, the marionette tries to return home when he is released. He becomes more and more careful about his choices, showing he is growing up. But he still makes mistakes. In his many adventures he is forced to act as a watchdog, is almost put into jail again, is turned into a donkey, and is swallowed by a great dogfish. At long last Pinocchio gets home to his father, Gepetto, and is turned into a real boy.

How To Make a Puppet

Darrell Koons

Although we think of puppets as mostly for children today, they have entertained adults as well as children over the years. In Japan, puppetry has become a fine art. The Japanese have serious and suspenseful puppet shows that last for hours. Their puppets may be simple, but they have been used expertly to bring an audience of men and women to tears.

Puppets can be made of anything from simple paper bags or socks to fine porcelain. One way to make a puppet is to use papier-mâché, a paste mixed with paper. The papier-mâché is spread over the framework or skeleton to form the puppet's head. This process takes a long time because it requires several days of drying time between steps.

Step 1: Getting Started

First, consider what the puppet should look like. Puppets have their own characteristics and personalities, just like people. Try sketching the puppet on paper. How would a grandma look? A princess? A fox? Or a clown? Remember that the puppet may change even while it is under construction.

Step 2: Gathering Materials

Gather the following materials.

wheat paste

newspaper

acrylic or tempera paints

5½ × 3½" piece of poster board or light cardboard

masking tape

yarn or corn silk

Duco cement or white glue

leather or felt

cloth for the costume

variety of accessories for the puppets

Wheat paste is available at wallpaper or interior decorating

shops. Mix only enough paste for one session at a time. Discard any paste not used to avoid leftover paste's spoiling.

Next, decide whether or not to use waterproof paint. Acrylic paint is waterproof and won't rub off when dry. However, it won't wash out of fabric either, so be sure to wear an old shirt when painting. Tempera paint will wash out of most clothing, but it isn't waterproof. Therefore, a puppet painted with tempera paint should never get wet.

Duco cement works best for gluing on the hair but must be used in a well-ventilated area. White glue can be used instead.

Step 3: Making the Head

Ready? First, begin with the form for the puppet's head. Wad up one full sheet of newspaper and crumple it into the size of an orange. Next, shape the poster board into a tube around two of your fingers and tape it together. Push the tube into the newspaper wad, leaving enough of the tube showing to form a neck for the puppet.

Now the frame is ready for the papier-mâché. Spread newspaper on the work area to protect the sur-face. Then unfold one sheet of newspaper, laying it out flat. Spread paste over the sheet of newspaper. Tear large strips of pasted newspaper and shape them over the head form. Use smaller and smaller pieces until the head is shaped. Continue adding strips of pasted newspaper to the poster-board tube, making the neck and shoulders of the puppet.

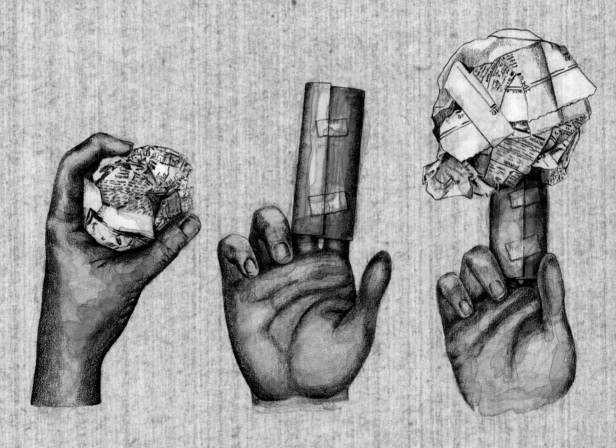

It is also possible to shape the detail of the puppet's face while the papier-mâché is wet. Push in the wet papier-mâché to make indentations for the eyes. Build up and shape the cheeks, nose, eyelids, and lips with more pasted paper. Then put the puppet in a safe place to dry.

Step 4: Painting

Wait until the puppet's head is completely dry before painting. Mix the base color and paint the entire head and neck. (A clown might have a white face, and other puppets might have varying skin color.) While the base color is still wet, blend a little red over the cheeks.

Once the puppet has dried again, use a pencil to lightly sketch the puppet's eyes, nose, and mouth. Look at a classmate's eyes. Notice that the eyelid covers part of the eye. Sketch the puppet's eyes with eyelids too.

Now paint the background color of the eye white. Make sure the colored part is neither too bright nor too dark. Paint the pupil black; then put a dash of white in both pupils to make the eyes seem to sparkle.

Most puppets look better with a slightly open mouth because then

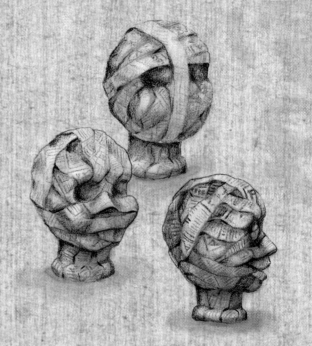

they look more like they are talking. Use a dark brown or black in the middle of the mouth. Teeth may also be painted to look as if the puppet's mouth is slightly open.

Then paint the lips, using red if the puppet is a woman or a darker tone if the puppet is a man.

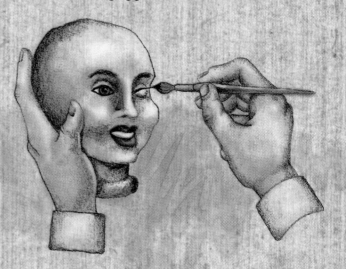

Step 5: Attaching the Hair

What should the puppet's hair look like? Will it be long and braided or short and curly? What color would be best? Let the paint dry, and then glue on the hair. If corn silk is used, it needs to be glued only across the head. To use yarn, put a line of stitching across the center of several strands of yarn and then attach the wig with glue. To make short or curly hair, glue individual bits of yarn all over the puppet's head.

Step 6: Adding the Costume

To make the puppet's hands, draw a pattern of the thumb and a mitten shape for the other four fingers. Cut out two mitten-hands from leather or a double thickness of felt that has been glued together. Paint the leather or felt the same base color as the puppet's head.

Cut two pieces of cloth six to eight inches wide for the puppet. Put the two pieces of cloth together, right sides facing each other. Stick the mittens inside the sleeves, pointing toward the center with their thumbs up. Sew the costume together, turn it inside out, and pull it over the puppet's neck like a shirt.

Accessories like eyeglasses, a belt, a bandanna, or a hat can also be added.

Get together with your classmates to write the script for your puppet show.

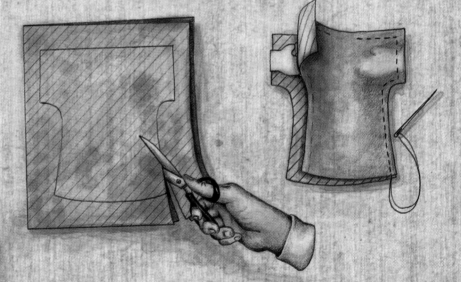

ALMOST REAL

Susan W. Young

String Puppets

What is about two feet tall, can walk but never speaks, can run but cannot see, can move but cannot feel? A marionette, of course.

The word *marionette* is French for "little Mary." The earliest string puppets portrayed stories from Scripture, stories that often included Mary, the mother of Jesus. Perhaps the word *marionette* was originally used to refer to the small puppet representing Mary. Today the word *puppet* and the word *marionette* are used interchangeably.

Although a marionette is always a puppet, a puppet is not always a marionette.

A marionette is a jointed puppet controlled by strings or wires attached to various parts of its body. The strings make it possible for the puppet to move and gesture like a real person. The number of strings varies from puppet to puppet. The more strings, the more elaborate the movement can be. Each marionette has its own control to which all of the strings are attached.

Practice and Imagination

Operating a marionette takes practice, patience, and imagination. A good puppeteer must coordinate his hand movements with what the puppet needs to do. Each movement of the control causes an instant response from the puppet most of the time, so it is important to move gently, without jerking.

Many great puppeteers work first as apprentices, practicing hundreds of hours with one puppet to perfect their skill. Being a puppeteer is more than just being able to move the puppet properly; it means being able to focus on making the puppet seem to come alive.

Part of making a marionette come alive is knowing how to show what the puppet character is supposed to be thinking or feeling. A good puppeteer observes himself and the people around him, carefully noting how the head and body move when a person is thinking, listening, crying, or laughing.

Because a marionette's face cannot move, the puppeteer must show the puppet's emotion

through other movements of his body. Allowing the head to fall forward lets the audience know that the puppet is shedding tears or is embarrassed. Moving both

arms up at the same time can
show surprise. Laughter can be
shown by moving the control to

cause the puppet to shake all
over.

A marionette can stand, sit,
bow, run, or kneel. It can fight

with its fist, draw a sword, or hammer a nail. It can act nervous, surprised, scared, or angry.

Some of these actions may require a curved hand or something sewn or glued to the hand. In *Pinocchio*, Pinocchio must grow ears and a tail when he has stayed too long on the island. Cloth ears and a tail are inserted into the puppet's head and back. When the time comes for these to appear, special strings pull out each ear and the tail. In *David Copperfield,* Mrs. Gummidge often cries into her apron. The corner of her apron is glued to her hand so that by simply raising her hand she can lift the corner of her apron to her eyes

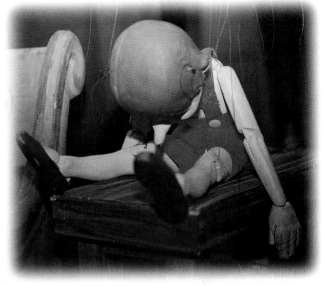

to dry a tear. In other plays, an organ grinder can turn the handle of his organ, two puppets can toss a ball, or another can play a flute. And all can look real and believable in this world of puppets.

On-Stage Performances

Once the puppeteer has mastered his own puppet or puppets, he is ready to join the other puppeteers on the bridge above the puppet stage. This area may seem too small for even one puppeteer, but often four or five work together here.

As the puppets move through the play, not only must each individual puppet look and act natural, but he must also respond to his fellow puppets in a natural way. Each puppet must appear to listen and respond to the other puppets just as real people respond to each other. Actions must speak to other characters as well as to the audience.

Finally, the voices of the puppeteers must speak for the puppets to the audience. Their voices must be understandable and must fit the character of the puppets. A high, piping voice would be more natural for Pinocchio than for Geppetto, for example.

The life put into a marionette comes down the strings from the puppeteer. As the puppet moves to the master's hand, the marionette can become happy or sad, funny or angry, energetic or tired. And once it moves, a puppet can seem, for a moment, like a "real live boy."

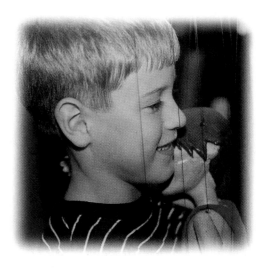

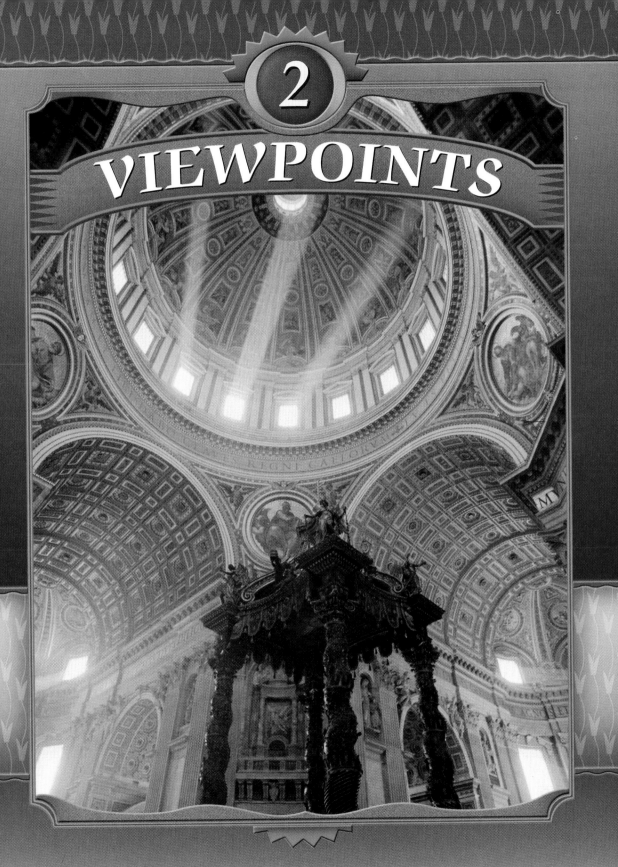

2

VIEWPOINTS

BIG Brother

Henry Becker • illustrated by Paula Cheadle

A Warrior

Well, to start with, my name is Timothy, and I'm in fifth grade at Trinity Christian. I have an older brother just like a lot of boys around here. Well, not just like a lot of other boys. My older brother is mentally disabled.

My brother's name is Brad. He's fourteen, but he doesn't go to school anywhere. Mom and Dad work with him at home a lot, and a tutor comes in once a week. He's getting to where he can almost tie his shoes by himself and dress himself with some help. But he moves funny and doesn't talk very well. He can't read at all right now, but Mom and Dad hope he'll be able to someday.

At first when I was growing up, I didn't really understand what was wrong with Brad. Mom would take him out for a walk every afternoon and I played games with him some, and for a long time I didn't even care that he was slow. Mom and Dad acted like everybody had a

mentally disabled brother in their family—I mean, it was like nothing was different from normal. And they said, "Brad is the Lord's special blessing to us." I never really understood that, but it didn't make much difference.

But then I started to notice other boys my age. They had big brothers who would play with them and teach them neat stuff. And all I had was Brad. Brad just smiles and says really simple things and looks at magazines a lot, especially the *National Geographic,* because he likes the colorful pictures. I play little-kid games with him like Candy Land and bounce the ball. He can't teach me how to hold a bat or how to shoot a basket. I started wanting a big brother like everybody else.

Then this year came. This year two things happened. We moved to this new place, and Mom had another baby, which means that I have a new little sister. Mom

84

couldn't take Brad for his walks in the afternoon. So since I am in the fifth grade now, my parents decided I was old enough to do it.

That was fine with me. I mean, I like Brad.

The first day everything was okay. I helped Brad with his jacket and everything, and we went for our walk. I had to go slowly so he could hold on to my arm and get his balance. (Mom and Dad figure this walking will help his coordination. You know, help him to be able to move better.) We went a different way from the way Mom would go so we could stop at the pet store. Brad looked in the window at a puppy for what seemed like an hour. But I didn't mind too much. I always like looking in the pet store. Brad kept saying, "Look at the little puppy, Timothy." The puppy really was great. It kept jumping up at the window and licking the glass in front of Brad's face. It made Brad laugh.

Well, the first walk went pretty well. In fact, I kind of enjoyed it. Brad was a little tired out by the time we got home, but he was happy. He kept talking about the puppy. I told Mom all about it, and she was glad we had a good time. I told Dad about it at supper too.

The second day—that's the day that was really bad. I got home from school and had my snack and did some homework. Then I got Brad ready to go for our walk again. He was excited because we'd had so much fun the day before. I was excited too, because it was fun to see him happy.

But when we got down to the end of the street, a bunch of boys were there, maybe five or six. Most of them were a year or two older, but some of them were my age. I knew some of them. The biggest one, the one leaning against the mailbox, was Mike Richardson. And I knew Gino Borelli too. He's in my class at Trinity.

Mike said, "Hey, Mitchell!" But it wasn't a friendly kind of hey. It was the kind where you know somebody's about to do something rotten. That's why they use your last name, too. They just want to sound tough.

Then Mike said, "Hey, Mitchell, what have you got there? Kinda big for a two-year-old, isn't he?" And he laughed, and all the other boys laughed, and I got so mad I could feel my ears turning hot. I looked at Brad, and he looked a little confused, and I was afraid he was about to cry. I guess he figured out they were talking about him, but I knew that if he cried it would make things even worse.

Then Mike stuck his tongue out of the corner of his mouth and crossed his eyes and walked funny, a little bit like my brother walks, and he made all kinds of horrible slobbery noises. And all the other boys just laughed and laughed. Gino Borelli was laughing too.

Brad's eyes were getting bigger and bigger, but he still wasn't saying anything. By then I was so mad that I didn't care if Mike was bigger than I was. I jumped on him and started beating him up as hard as I could. I was saying "Nobody's-going-to-talk-about-my-brother-like-that" between punches. And I was crying a little bit, but I don't think they could tell. I'd given Mike a good punch before all the other boys jumped on me and pulled me off him and gave me a few good punches of their own. They said, "Get out of here, kid." And Gino Borelli, who's the same age as I am, was saying it too.

Well, I finally took Brad's hand and started back for home. He was crying by then and could hardly walk. I didn't say much. I guess I kind of jerked him to try to make him walk faster. I was afraid he'd cry about not getting to see the puppy, but he didn't say anything about that. I guess the fighting really scared him. He kept saying, "Bad boys. They were bad boys, Timothy."

I didn't mean to say anything, but I was mad. So I said, "Why couldn't you be like a regular big brother? You're supposed to take care of me. And I have to take care of you instead."

I was kind of mad at myself then for saying that. But Brad didn't answer me, and I figured he probably didn't even understand.

Well, there was no way I could keep everything a secret from Mom. I mean, Brad went to her as soon as we got home and just cried and cried, but she couldn't understand anything he was saying except "bad boys," so she had to ask

Big Brother 87

me. She would have found out anyway, because my clothes were ripped a little and dirty all over. I had a few bruises, too.

Well, I told Mom everything, and she didn't say an awful lot. Mostly she just said, "Well, we'll wait and talk about it with Dad." That usually scares me, because it means I've done something bad. But this time I didn't even care much. I just went into my room and closed the door and lay on my bed. Brad was still crying and that was making the baby cry, so Mom had her hands full; but I just didn't feel like going out there to help her. And she never asked me to come. I guess she probably talked to Brad about how those bad boys didn't understand how special he was and stuff like that.

Well, when Dad got home I had to tell him the story all over again.

Then he and Mom talked to me alone. I don't remember a lot of what they said. They quoted some Bible verses about loving your enemies and turning the other cheek. But the main thing I was thinking about was what Dad said at first—that was what kept me from remembering everything else they said. He said, "You know, Timothy, you're going to have to go back out there and apologize to those boys."

I got kind of mad, I guess. I said, "Dad, they were making fun of Brad! Why do I have to apologize for beating Mike up when he was making fun of Brad?"

That was when Dad quoted all the verses. But all I could think of was Mike Richardson's mocking Brad.

But finally I said I would go. Dad talked to me about all the things I should say, and then he prayed with me. That made me feel a little better, but I still didn't eat much supper that night. I didn't sleep an awful lot either.

A Witness

The next day I didn't even ask Brad if he wanted to go for a walk. He just stayed in his room and looked at magazines. Every once in a while he would come and say something to Mom about the bad boys and how they didn't love Jesus. Mom was really patient with him and explained about Jesus' love for others.

It was time to go. Mom prayed with me and then I walked down the two blocks to where I knew the guys would be. There they were, and Mike Richardson was leaning against the mailbox. They watched me coming and laughed. I just went over and over in my mind the things Dad had told me to say. And I prayed. I prayed a lot.

"Hey, Mitchell," Mike yelled at me. "Where's your big brother today?"

I ignored what he said, just like Dad had told me to do. As soon as I got close enough I said, "Mike, I'm sorry I lost my temper yesterday, and I'm sorry I hit you."

Well, Dad had said that would startle them so much that I could keep on talking. He was right. I said, "I love Brad, even if he is different. We learn patience from him . . . and love . . . and the Lord gave

him to us for a reason. I should have explained things to you yesterday, because fighting doesn't solve anything. I disobeyed the Lord yesterday when I hit you." I stopped then and took a deep breath. I was shaking all over, and I prayed that they wouldn't be able to tell. Now this was the place where Dad had said, "Even if they keep on making fun of you, they'll still respect you." So I stuck my hands in my pockets and waited for them to make fun of me.

But it wasn't as much as I expected. Mike just said, "Well, will you look at the preacher man. Why don't you shake your Bible at us a little, huh?" And the other boys laughed, but it was a weak laugh, and I could tell they all felt uncomfortable. In fact, they all started to walk away, like the mailbox corner wasn't interesting anymore. Mike

Richardson left too, but he said, "So long, Preacher." And he stuck his hands inside his jacket and went away whistling, like what I had said hadn't made any difference to him.

I had watched Gino Borelli the whole time I was talking. He was the one my dad had been most concerned about. So even though I was still shaking a little, I prayed that Gino would stick around so I could say something to him.

But he didn't. He was about the last one to leave, and he looked at me sort of with surprise, I guess, but he walked away when the other boys did.

When they had all left, I went back home. I had to go to my room for a while until I stopped shaking, but by the time Dad was home I was able to come out and tell him and Mom all about it. They were glad. And Dad said, "Son, it's like I said–they may still pick on you occasionally, but it will be just to test you. I think all of those boys respect you more now. And maybe you'll still have a chance to witness to some of them, especially Gino Borelli."

I prayed for chances to witness to Gino the next few days, but a chance didn't come. He seemed to be avoiding me. In the afternoons I just walked with Brad around the

back yard. But by Monday he was feeling better, and when I mentioned the puppy, he jumped up and down and clapped his hands. So we walked down the two blocks and I held my breath, but there was no one at the mailbox. Brad didn't seem to remember—he just kept talking about all the things around him, but especially about the puppy. When we got to the pet store, there was a different puppy in the window—a brown one instead of a black one—but he was just as cute. I don't think Brad even noticed the difference. He just jumped up and down and tapped on the glass. Finally we went inside, and the store manager was really nice. He pulled the puppy out and let Brad hold it for a few minutes. I wouldn't have thought Brad could be so gentle. He even said soft little things to the puppy.

Tuesday when we went for our walk again, we turned the corner and saw three boys at the mailbox—Mike Richardson and one of his friends and Gino Borelli. I could hardly believe it, and my stomach tied up in knots. I hadn't prayed before I left.

They all three started making fun of Brad, like they had rehearsed it or something. But Brad was the one that surprised me this time. He spoke out so clearly, clear enough for everybody to understand. He said, "You're bad boys. You don't love Jesus. That makes you bad boys. Boys that don't love Jesus won't go to heaven."

That was probably the most I had ever heard Brad say at once. And it stopped the boys cold. They laughed a little, but they left. That sort of surprised me, because they could have made fun of the way Brad talked. But they didn't even turn around.

Then the Lord gave me the courage to call Gino's name. "Hey, Gino," I said. "Wait up." And he waited. Almost like he had been hoping I would call. The other boys didn't look back. I prayed a quick prayer as he came closer.

"Gino," I said, "why don't you come to the pet store with us?"

He didn't say anything. He just smiled and shook his head and went on home. But Dad and Mom had both said it would take time.

The last week or so, Gino has started being nicer to me at school. In fact, today I invited him over to my house for next weekend to play games with Brad and do some other stuff. He kind of laughed when I talked about Candy Land, but he said he would play the game if I promised not to tell anybody else about it.

Brad and I walked down to the pet store almost every day last week. I decided to start saving up to buy him a puppy for his next birthday. After all, he did help me out that last day that the bullies showed up. I don't know if I would have known what to say if he hadn't taken over.

Oh, yeah. After Brad helped me that time, I said, "Hey, Brad, thanks for what you did. I was really glad to have your help."

And Brad put his arm around me and smiled. And he said, "That's okay, Timothy. That's what a big brother does."

The Quarrel

Eleanor Farjeon • illustrated by Mary Ann Lumm

I quarreled with my brother,
I don't know what about,
One thing led to another
And somehow we fell out.
The start of it was slight,
The end of it was strong,
He said he was right,
I knew he was wrong!

We hated one another.
The afternoon turned black.
Then suddenly my brother
Thumped me on the back,
And said, "Oh, *come* along!
We can't go on all night—
I was in the wrong."
So he was in the right.

Adventure on Gull Island

Milly Howard

illustrated by Johanna Berg

Mangrove Cove

Jennifer stretched out face down on the dry boards of the dock and peered through one of the cracks. Below her, the shadowed water swirled around the posts, and slashes of sunlight rode the tiny ripples of seawater. A huge splash of water over her brought her to her feet.

"Jeremy!" She ran after her twin as he headed down the beach with his empty pail. "If you don't quit sneaking up on me, I'll . . . !"

"You'll what?"

She caught up with him. In a flash, she grabbed his pail, filled it in the surf, and drenched his sun-bleached hair.

Jeremy laughed. "Okay! We're even."

They sat down on the edge of the dock, watching the mild surf until Jennifer began to feel lulled by its steady cadence.

"They're not here yet." Jeremy's words pricked their frail bubble of peace.

Jennifer tossed a shell into the water and sighed. "How come Aunt Helen married a widower with an eleven-year-old son? And why does he have to spend the summer with Gramps just because we do?"

Jeremy didn't answer.

Jennifer remembered what Gramps had said just before he left to meet the plane. "You two make Anthony feel welcome, you hear?" He had rested one hand on Jennifer's shoulder and roughed up Jeremy's hair with the other. "He may not be your real cousin, but he has the same heavenly Father you do; and that makes him more than a cousin. He's your Christian brother." Gramps's blue eyes had twinkled as he smiled. "He's a bit of a land-lubber, though. City-bred. You two'll have to show him the ropes."

A gleam of sun on a white sail caught Jennifer's eye. "Here they come," she said.

As the day sailer bumped against the dock, the twins scrambled up to help secure the boat and stow the sails. Gramps held out an arm to the boy with him and helped him onto the dock. "Twins, this is Anthony," he said. "Anthony, the one with short hair is Jeremy; the one with long hair is Jennifer."

Jeremy thrust out a hand. "Nice to meet you, Anthony."

Sunlight glinted off Anthony's glasses, hiding his eyes. "I'd rather be called Tony." He shook Jeremy's hand rather stiffly, and he nodded at Jennifer.

"Hi," she said, a little too brightly.

"Jennifer, why don't you and Tony chat a bit while Jeremy and I take the suitcases up to his room?" Gramps and Jeremy headed for the summer house with Tony's things.

Tony shifted uneasily. His eyes followed the white curve of sand and water that formed the cove.

"It's called Mangrove Cove," Jennifer said, watching him. "We're protected from the ocean here, but we're still on it."

Tony took off his glasses, and his face lost its owlish look. He rubbed them on his shirt to clean

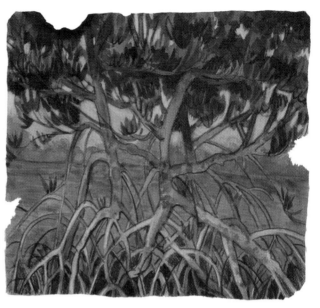

away specks of ocean spray. "Why's it called Mangrove Cove?"

"Look down there." She pointed to the left curve of the cove. "Those are mangroves. Gramps says they may have started the island. Their roots catch sand and mud and finally form a landmass."

"How old is this island then?"

"Gramps says some of the mangroves are hundreds of years old." She turned as Jeremy ran down the porch steps. "Jeremy, hasn't Gull Island been on the charts since the seventeenth century?"

Jeremy nodded. "You should see some of the old maps Gramps has!" he said.

Tony's features relaxed as he grinned. "Wow! Like pirate maps? I'd like that!"

The three children turned up the grassy slope to the house. Jeremy elbowed Jennifer and whispered, "He's not so bad." Jennifer shrugged.

While Jeremy took Tony on a tour of the house and yard, Jennifer set the table on the screened porch. The wind blew softly over the row of old bottles that lined the railing, producing a hollow tune. Dinner music, Gramps called it.

Jeremy and Tony raced each other up the steps and slid into their seats.

"You'll have to get the twins to show you the island, Tony," Gramps said. "They've explored around on their own the last two summers, and Jen girl here can even handle a boat." He winked at her.

"Thank you, sir." Tony grinned.

"And by the way, call me Gramps."

Jennifer sat down stiffly in her chair. "Soup's getting cold, Gramps." She felt Jeremy's and Gramps's eyes on her face but ignored them. Gramps took his seat at the head of the table and said the blessing.

The breeze off the cove cooled as they ate. Finally Gramps pushed back his chair and reached for the big Bible that lay on a side table. He lit the hurricane lamp and turned the pages. Jennifer listened to the rise and fall of his voice as he read aloud. Around them the song of the bottles crescendoed with the wind.

Later, as the sunset faded, Gramps told stories of pirates and treasure. He finally stopped and smiled at Tony. "Long day, wasn't it, Tony? I suspect tomorrow will be as full as you and these twins can pack it. How about early to bed?"

In the tower bedroom, Jennifer climbed into her alcove bed, yawned, and swung the casement window open. The beam from the lighthouse on the northern tip of the island silvered the trees. Just offshore a tiny light moved steadily along the curve of the cove. She stared at it for a moment. "Probably just a night trawler." Before leaning back in bed, she peeked out again, but the light was gone. Jennifer pulled up her sheet and closed her eyes.

Odd One Out

Most mornings Jennifer was the first one up, roused by the rhythmic crash of the surf. But restless dreams of pirates, maps, and unlighted boats had filled the night. The sun was streaming through the window when she awoke, and she rolled over to face it. Two figures were heading up the beach toward the house. The taller one carried a basket, and every so often he bent and picked up something from the sand. He turned his head, and Jennifer saw the sparkle of sunlight on his glasses. Tony! And—Jeremy!

Outraged, she bounced off the bed, yanked open a drawer, and dressed quickly. She glanced back out the window. The boys had just entered the cove. They were chattering to each other like old friends. Jennifer thrust a foot into one sneaker, snatched the other, and tramped angrily down the stairs.

Gramps glanced up from the stove. "Is that the latest style?"

Jennifer blinked. "What?"

"The hair." Gramps raised a bushy eyebrow and grinned. "Looks like you tangled with an electric eel."

Jennifer ran a hand through the tangles. "I forgot to brush it."

"In a hurry to catch the boys, eh?"

"Jeremy left without me!" Jennifer exploded. "Just wait until I get my hands on him!"

"Hold on, Jenny." Gramps took the pan off the stove. "You were sleeping late, so I asked Jeremy to take Tony shell hunting. High tide last night probably gave them good pickings. Now, you've got about fifteen minutes before we eat—just enough time to spend a few minutes with your Bible. How about it?"

Jennifer stared, speechless. Then she whirled and stamped back upstairs, fighting back tears. "Gramps seems to think it's just fine that I'm the odd one out," she thought.

After breakfast, the twins cleared the table and did the dishes while Gramps took Tony into the study to show him the maps.

"Tony sure knows a lot about shells," Jeremy said. "Probably about as much as Gramps does."

Jennifer frowned at him.

"Well, almost," Jeremy mumbled. "He is good, Jen."

Lips tight, Jennifer reached for another plate.

"Gramps said he'd come exploring with us today," Jeremy said.

"Let's surprise him and make a picnic lunch."

By the time the sun was high, the boat was loaded with their gear and the picnic basket. Gramps took his place in the stern beside the tiller, and Jeremy and Tony operated the sails. Jennifer cast off the mooring lines and leaped in. One quick glance revealed that her usual job was taken. Slumped against the side of the boat, she stared at her sneakers.

"Come and sit by me, Jen girl," Gramps said. "When we get past the breakers, you can take over."

Jennifer smiled at Gramps. Taking the tiller when he was in the boat was a special treat.

The boat cut cleanly through the breakers and headed out to sea. "It's like flying!" Tony shouted.

Gramps moved over, and Jennifer squeezed between him and the tiller. Gramps's big hand completely covered hers as he helped her guide the boat along the island coastline. Jennifer glanced down at his brown hand, gnarled and wrinkled with age. "His heart must be big too," she thought. "He loves me and Jeremy, yet he still has room left over to love a new grandson."

Gramps pointed toward the shore. "I thought we'd anchor in

Sebastian Cove and explore Catfish Inlet." He took the tiller again and guided the boat past some outcroppings of coral reef. When the bottom touched sand, Jeremy and Tony leaped overboard and hauled the boat ashore. Gramps climbed out with the anchor, wrapped the line around a tree, and jerked. "She'll hold, Jen girl!" He reached to help Jennifer out of the boat.

Gramps unrolled his map and led the way around the sandy shoreline.

"Come on, Jen!" Jeremy called.

Jennifer passed Gramps and splashed after Jeremy and Tony. Around the bend, the inlet expanded and formed a small, protected cove with a high white mound, half covered with rough bushes, rising at one end. The boys charged across the cove and scaled the mound, but Jennifer turned and waited for Gramps to catch up.

"Come on up!" Tony called. "You've got to see this!"

Treasure Hunters

Jennifer and Gramps struggled to the top and stood wordlessly beside the boys. Beyond the mound the inlet curved into an open stretch of water.

"A land-locked harbor!" Gramps exclaimed. "This isn't on the map."

"We're not the first to find it, though," Jeremy said. "Look over there."

On the other side of the stretch of water, a boat rode at anchor. Long and lean, it looked as powerful as a Coast Guard cutter.

"How'd it get in here?" Tony asked.

Gramps rubbed his chin. The boat lay motionless, not a sign of life on board. "Probably came up the inlet during high tide when the water was deep enough. The question is, why? What would people who own a boat like that want unless they're treasure hunters?"

As Jennifer looked at the boat, something tugged at her memory—something about lights and darkness. Shrugging, she gave up and turned away. "I'm going down—" she began. Suddenly, footsteps crunched below them.

Startled, they turned to see a burly man approaching, thrusting his way up the mound. Scowling, he waved a rifle at them.

"What're you doing here?" he shouted.

Gramps's eyes narrowed, and his face tensed. "Exploring. What about you?" he said quietly.

The man's face flushed with anger. "None of your business. You're on private property. Off!" He pointed down the mound.

"Just hold your peace, stranger," Gramps said firmly. "We'll leave."

Gramps put an arm around Jennifer and led her down with Jeremy and Tony scrambling right behind them. Jennifer turned once and saw the man standing, legs apart, watching them head back across the cove. Gramps motioned for them to keep silent until they were out of hearing.

"Whose property is it?" Jeremy asked when they reached the boat. "What right does he have to this end of the island?"

Gramps opened his map and frowned. "Well, I know one thing for sure," he said. "It's never wise to argue with an angry man holding a loaded gun." He held the map so they could see. "No sign of deep water. The inlet ends in the cove. This map was made in 1806, but it's been accurate so far. Sorry, kids—looks like I got us into trouble. It probably wasn't on our property."

"What's this?" Tony indicated a sun drawn on the map.

Jeremy looked over his shoulder. "It's the lighthouse."

"Built in 1798 by Old Cap'n Trevor," Gramps said. "You'll have to look for the light tonight—it's about a mile from our house."

"Can we go see it?" Tony asked.

"I'll check on that when we get home," Gramps said. "I'll have to arrange to get it unlocked so we can go inside, since the Coast Guard owns and operates it now." He looked at his watch. "For right now, what do you say we find a beach where we can eat our lunch?"

Just before bedtime that night, Gramps folded a little piece of paper into Jennifer's hand. "Read it before you go to sleep tonight," he whispered, patting her shoulder.

In her room, Jennifer sat on the windowsill and read the Scripture reference written on the paper. "I John 1:7a." She leafed through the pages of her Bible till she found it. "But if we walk in the light, as he is in the light, we have fellowship one with another."

Jennifer sighed and stared out at the brilliant beam of the lighthouse. "Gramps wants me to see Tony as my Christian brother," she said out loud. "Okay. I'll try."

Jeremy forked a pancake onto his plate the next morning. "Where are we going today, Gramps?" he asked.

Gramps passed him the butter. "Haven't heard back from the Coast Guard yet. My friend there said he'd check on that hidden harbor and that boat, but we'd better stick close to home until we know more."

By late afternoon, Jennifer had grown restless. She wandered into the study where the boys were playing checkers and perched on the arm of Gramps's chair to watch.

"Gotcha," Tony said. He jumped three of Jeremy's men.

Jennifer grinned, waiting for the usual explosion that erupted when she beat Jeremy, but he just laughed and began setting up a new game. "Just wait, Tony," he said. "This time I'll win."

Jennifer watched, anger rising inside. "They could have asked if I wanted a turn," she thought.

The boys were silent, intent on their new game. Jennifer sighed loudly, but neither of them looked up. She gave the stool beside the boys a vicious kick, sending it rolling across the game and scattering the pieces.

Jeremy scrambled around on the floor to retrieve the pieces. "Jennifer, go away!" he yelled.

Jennifer spun around and ran through the kitchen, slamming the screen door behind her. Tears stung her eyes as she plunged through the underbrush. She pounded up the path to the shadows of the live oaks. Although the grasses stung her legs, she kept going. Out of the trees, she found herself on the path to the lighthouse at the northern tip of the island. She clambered up the rocks.

The lighthouse stood like a sentinel on the cliff. Jennifer circled slowly around the tall tower and the deserted house that leaned against it. She tipped her head back to see the room where the lamp was housed at the very top. "If we walk in the light, as he is in the light . . ." The words from the Bible verse whispered in her mind.

She kicked a shell and walked toward the lighthouse keeper's house. Halfway there she stopped. The padlock on the door hung from the broken hasp, and the door wasn't completely closed. When she looked back, she saw Jeremy and Tony scrambling up the rocks after her, so she hurried to the door, swung it open, and stepped inside.

As her eyes became used to the darkness, she picked her way between stacks of wooden crates. Through the gloom she could see the broad door, barred on the outside, that led into the lighthouse tower.

"Jennifer! Jennifer-r! Wait for us!" The boys shoved the door open. "Jennifer?" Jeremy whispered. "Is that you?"

For a moment, Jennifer considered not answering. Finally she said, "Who else?"

"Hey, Jennifer, I'm sorry," Jeremy said. "I shouldn't have yelled. Come on, you know we aren't supposed to be in here without permission."

"Yeah, let's play pirates," said Tony. "The Coast Guard just called and said the boat was gone, so it's safe to play in the live oaks. You can be the captain, Jennifer."

"Okay." Jennifer moved forward and banged her shin against a crate. "What *is* this stuff?"

Tony leaned over to inspect the crate closest to the door. "The lid's broken on this one. It has some metal rods in it."

"Better not touch it," said Jeremy. "Hey, let's get out of here."

Jennifer peered out the door down the path that led to the sea. She caught her breath. "Jeremy. Here comes that man we saw at the mound—and someone's with him!"

"Get back inside," Tony whispered. "Follow me!"

They rushed across the room to the barred door. Jeremy unbarred it, revealing a small room with steps leading upward. "These steps must go up to the tower," he whispered. "Quick! Get inside and pull the door closed partway." Crouched behind the wooden staircase, the three hardly dared to breathe.

The Lighthouse Keeper

The front door was shoved open, and two men entered. "I thought I told you to shut that door!" the first man said angrily. "Any fool could see the lock's broken!"

"I did close it, Lee," his companion said. "The wind must have blown it open."

"Always some excuse. I'll be glad when this shipment is delivered. That old graybeard will have the Coast Guard on us before we know it."

"Aw, he won't do anything. He didn't give you any trouble, did he? I don't see why we even had to move the stuff."

"You know what the sentence is for selling guns?" Lee's voice rose. "I sure do, and I don't aim to spend my life behind bars!"

"Relax, would you? The deal's over tonight, and then we'll be on our way to Bermuda."

Lee lit a hurricane lamp. The children shrank farther back. After Lee had checked the broken crate, he held the lamp high to check the other boxes. With a cry of annoyance, he crossed the room to study the crate beside the tower door. "Another cracked one! Can't you do anything right?"

He leaned down to run his hand across the far end of the crate, and the lamp slipped forward. As he tried to keep the oil from spilling out of the lamp, he lurched forward, hitting the tower door. It slammed and the bar fell solidly into place.

The children stared at each other in the dim light. "What'll we do?" Jennifer whispered.

Tony put his finger to his lips and leaned against the door. After a while he straightened up. "They're gone," he said, "and we're locked in."

"Gramps will never find us," Jeremy said. He pushed desperately against the barred door. "We're not supposed to be in here."

"He thinks we're playing in the live oaks," said Tony. "That's where we told him we'd be."

Jennifer groaned. "I got us into this."

"It wasn't your fault," Tony said. "And don't worry; we'll find a way out. Jeremy, why don't you go up and see how big those slits in the tower are?"

"Okay. Come on, Jen."

Jennifer clumped up the stairs behind Jeremy and surveyed the lamp room while he examined the slits. He turned back, his face discouraged. "These slits are hardly wide enough for a cat to get through," he called down.

"I thought so," said Tony as the twins descended. "But we have to do something!" When they reached him, he was bent over, rummaging through the materials under the stairs.

"Did you find anything?" Jeremy asked.

"Two empty paint cans, a brush, an old tarp, and two ladders," answered Tony.

Jennifer shivered, but not from cold. "What good are they?" she asked.

Tony didn't answer. "Let's all go upstairs. Maybe there'll be something we can use in the lamp room."

At the top of the winding stairs, they pulled the heavy door open. A search around the circular room yielded nothing useful.

"We'll have to wait, then," Jeremy said. "The smugglers might get away, but Gramps will find us. He'll come looking when we don't show up for supper."

"There ought to be some way we could warn the Coast Guard about those gun smugglers. They shouldn't get away. Who knows who they're selling those guns to!" Jeremy's usually cheerful face was grim and tense.

After a long moment, Tony spoke slowly. "At home," he said, "we pray for God's help."

Jennifer looked at Jeremy. She smiled at Tony. "So do we. You want to start, Tony?"

When they all lifted their heads again, Tony looked thoughtful. "I know a way to warn the Coast Guard, but we'll have to wait until dark."

"What? What?" Jennifer leaned forward eagerly.

"That tarp downstairs is big enough to block one side of the lamp room," Tony said.

"And?" Jennifer asked.

"And the light wouldn't show through on that side!" Jeremy said. "We could block the one toward the mainland where the Coast Guard station is located. That wouldn't get any ships into trouble, but the dispatcher would send someone to check on the lamp!"

"You've got it, Tony!" Jennifer said. "You're all right!"

By late afternoon they were ready. It had taken some time to carry the ladders up the stairs to the lamp room, and the tarp had not been easy to carry either. They pushed, shoved, and dragged it between the three of them, stair after stair. When they finally had it in place, it covered an entire block of windows. "It's actually going to work!" Jennifer said.

For a while they sat without speaking, watching the dim light from the slits gradually dissolve into darkness. "Jeremy?" Jennifer said quietly. "Why don't you tell some of Gramps's stories? Tony hasn't heard—"

A sudden scrape and a bump sounded below. The children jumped to their feet and leaned against the door. The crates were being moved!

"The smugglers came by sea, or they would have seen the blocked light," Tony whispered. "The big boat is probably anchored offshore."

"They'll be taking the crates out in a rowboat," Jeremy added. In the darkness, Jennifer could tell he was grinning. "It'll take them a long time."

Minutes dragged into an hour as the scraping and thudding continued. Then suddenly—a crash!

"Someone else is here!" Tony whispered.

They heard shouts and scuffling. A gunshot echoed into the night. Then all was quiet.

The children listened tensely. Footsteps reverberated outside the door where they hid. The bar lifted and the door slowly creaked open. A figure holding a flashlight appeared in the doorway.

"Jeremy? Jen girl? Tony?" a familiar voice called.

"Gramps!" Jennifer jumped up and launched herself into his arms.

"So this is where you three were," Gramps said. "If you only knew how worried I was—but it never crossed my mind that you were trapped by smugglers!"

The bulky figure of a Coast Guard lieutenant entered the room. "What are these kids doing here?"

"We got locked in," Jeremy began.

"And we heard the smugglers talking about guns," Jennifer interrupted.

"So we tried to warn the Coast Guard," Tony finished.

The lieutenant stared at them. "One at a time," he said. "Don't tell me—*you* blocked the light!"

"Only toward the mainland," Tony said hastily. "We knew you would come and check on it, sir."

"Yes, we made a fine haul tonight," the lieutenant said. "We've heard about this group, but we didn't know they were operating this far up. Congratulations, kids—good work."

Jennifer looked up at Gramps. "Gramps, it's all my fault—I ran away mad."

Gramps gave her a hug. "I just thank the Lord you're all okay. How about supper?" He grinned at their enthusiastic replies. "How about you, Lieutenant?"

"Right after I fix this light," the lieutenant said.

"Oh, we just put that old tarp over the windows," Tony said. "It'll come right down."

The lieutenant stopped on his way up the stairs. "Kids!" he said and burst into laughter.

Jennifer beamed. "It was Tony's idea."

Gramps ushered them out the door. "You three'll have an adventure tale to beat all. After supper you can tell me the whole story."

Jennifer grabbed Gramps's big hand. "Thank you for the verse, Gramps. Being together there in the lighthouse . . . I guess we learned what fellowship is with friends and the Lord."

"But if we walk in the light, as he is in the light, we have fellowship one with another." (I John 1:7)

Beacons and Bells

Becky Davis • illustrated by Preston Gravely

In "Adventure on Gull Island," Jennifer, Jeremy, and Tony explored a lighthouse that was over two hundred years old. The children saw the keeper's house too, but nobody lived there anymore.

Ever since men first started traveling by water, rocky coasts and dangerous shoals have taken the lives of sailors who were driven into them by storms or who didn't see them soon enough. Long ago someone thought of constructing a tall building with a light to warn sea travelers of the dangers ahead.

One of the first—and definitely the most famous—lighthouses was built over two thousand years ago in Egypt. Thousands of the pharaoh's slaves worked over twenty years to build it. The lighthouse, called the Pharos, stood over four hundred feet high, with a huge fire burning on top. Mirrors made the fire seem even brighter. Stories say that the light could be seen for over thirty miles! The Pharos was one of the Seven Wonders of the ancient world.

After the Pharos was destroyed, no other lighthouse quite as splendid was ever built. For one thing, lighthouses were hard to construct because of where they had to be built. One of the most fearsome places was the Eddystone rocks, which jutted out of the English Channel. These rocks were not quite high enough to be seen from a distance, but they were high enough to wreck many a passing ship. Since many seamen lost their lives on these rocks, the English government finally hired Mr. Henry Witstanley to build a lighthouse in 1698.

The Eddystone rocks curved and jutted so much that no one thought a lighthouse could be built there. Besides, Henry Witstanley had a reputation—as a "kook"! He had an inventor's mind, but he used it in strange ways. In his own house he had so many weird contraptions and trick devices that he charged admission for people to walk through! The lighthouse he built had extra balconies, flag-poles, odd fixtures, and other gadgets, just right for a man like Henry Witstanley. But it did stand—for almost four years. No ships crashed into the rocks during that whole time. Then a storm hit, one of the worst that the Eddystone rocks had ever known. Henry Witstanley was killed in the light-house when the storm destroyed it.

A new lighthouse was erected on the Eddystone rocks, and then another, and then another. The last one, finished in 1882, still stands,

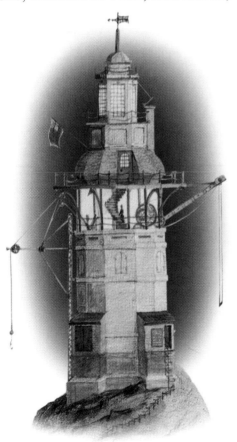

partly because of the many im-provements that have been made in lighthouse construction.

One improvement that has been made over the centuries is in the light itself. In the Pharos a huge bonfire burned at the top. In later lighthouses the lighthouse keeper tended hundreds of candles. Then oil lamps with reflectors were used. But it wasn't until Thomas Edison invented the light bulb that light-houses became really effective and required less maintenance, or care, by the lighthouse keeper.

The lighthouse keeper is the faithful man who makes sure that the lighthouse is operating constantly to warn passing seamen of possible dangers. If a lighthouse is built on land, like the one in "Adventure on Gull Island," the keeper's house may be built along-side the lighthouse tower. A door leads right from the keeper's house to the tower. But some lighthouses have been constructed on a solitary rock surrounded by water. As the lighthouse keeper climbs up the many steps to the light, he passes each room of his home. At the very top is the thousand-watt bulb—about the size of a volleyball—and the huge rotating lenses that send the strong beacons of light over the water.

But during a thick fog, passing fishermen can't see even the powerful beacon from the lighthouse. Hundreds of years ago, seamen realized that some sort of warning sound was needed for foggy days and nights. They tried cannons for a while, but the short blasts couldn't tell them much about how far they were from the rocks. Then huge fog bells were used. But the fog bells were hard for the lighthouse keepers to work; so they became unpopular. Finally someone realized that if steam was channeled just the right way, it made a very loud noise. And thus the foghorn was invented—a huge machine powered by steam that sends out a long, low sound over the water.

New electronic devices and other inventions allow many lighthouses to work almost by themselves. In many cases, as in "Adventure on Gull Island," it is no longer necessary for one man to live next to or inside the tower and carefully maintain it every day. The Coast Guard, which is always stationed near the lighthouse tower, can watch the lighthouse and visit it if the bulb needs to be changed, if the foghorn needs to be activated, or if something seems to be wrong.

A lighthouse keeper's life has always been thought of as a lonely one, and it's true that it used to be solitary. But since electricity has brought the radio, telephone, and other conveniences, a lighthouse keeper's life doesn't have to be as lonely. Motorboats can take him to the mainland much faster than boats of the old days, too. Most lighthouse keepers now live with their families on their little rocky islands year round. They seem to love the beautiful ocean and quiet privacy.

As lighthouses are improved, there will be even less need for full-time attendants. But for centuries seamen have owed their safety near the shores to the faithfulness of the lighthouse keepers.

THE GOSPEL LIGHT

Becky Davis

More than a hundred years ago, men used oil-lamp lighthouses to warn ship pilots of dangerous coastlines. In the dark and for a great distance, the lighthouse would send out its warning. But if a sea captain had to navigate his ship close to that ragged shore, the lighthouse keeper placed smaller oil lamps along the coast to lead the pilot to the harbor.

Lorraine Harbor along the great Lake Erie had this kind of coastline. But one night in the late 1800s the lighthouse keeper of Lorraine Harbor was tired. He decided that since no ship had ever navigated that treacherous coastline at night, no one would need the lower lights along the coast that night. Instead of trimming the lamps along the shore and filling up their oil reservoirs, the lighthouse keeper went to bed.

But while he slept, a terrible storm blew up. And indeed a ship did come along, tossing and plunging, trying to enter the harbor, watching the lighthouse, and searching desperately for the lower lights. Because they had not been lit, the ship crashed into the jagged rocks and sank. Only a few men survived.

When Mr. Philip P. Bliss heard this story, he was angry that such a terrible thing had happened simply through careless neglect. But the more he thought about it, the more he realized that he and many other Christians were just like the lighthouse keeper. Lost souls in the

night are often dashed along the coastline even while the light of Christ's love is shining. This tragedy occurs because Christians, who are the lower lights to lead people to Christ, do not have their lamps trimmed and bright. Mr. Bliss promptly wrote a song. His metaphors compared our heavenly Father to the great lighthouse and Christians to the lower lights along the shore. He hoped that his song would remind Christians all over the world of their responsibility to lead souls to Christ.

Let the Lower Lights Be Burning

Philip P. Bliss

Philip P. Bliss

1. Bright-ly beams our Fa-ther's mer-cy From His light-house ev-er-more,
2. Dark the night of sin has set-tled, Loud the an-gry bil-lows roar;
3. Trim your fee-ble lamp, my broth-er: Some poor sail-or tem-pest tossed,

But to us He gives the keep-ing Of the lights a-long the shore.
Ea-ger eyes are watch-ing, long-ing, For the lights a-long the shore.
Try-ing now to make the har-bor, In the dark-ness may be lost.

Let the low-er lights be burn-ing! Send a gleam a-cross the wave!

Some poor faint-ing, strug-gling sea-man You may res-cue, you may save.

REFERENCE TOOLS

Libraries provide information about many subjects, from aardvarks to zyzzyvas. They contain facts from places as different from each other as Arizona and New Zealand. The amount and content of information varies with each reference tool. To understand a topic it is best to consult several reference materials.

Each reference tool has a specific purpose. After reading "Adventure on Gull Island," let's see what we could find out about mangrove coves. Although a dictionary describes a mangrove, an encyclopedia gives more detail to help us imagine what a mangrove looks like. Then you might use an atlas to see the actual location of a place such as Mangrove Cove if it were a real place. A geographical dictionary is another reference tool that might give information about a specific place, such as Mangrove Cove.

Dictionary

A dictionary lists words in alphabetical order and gives their definitions. A good dictionary will also give the pronunciation of the word and its function as a part of speech. The *etymology* of the word (how the word came into existence) is interesting and helpful as well.

The dictionary states that a mangrove is a type of tropical tree. The word *mangrove* may have come from a Portuguese word. The dictionary gives several meanings for the word *cove*. A cove could be a body of water, a cave, or a valley area tucked between mountains. From reading the story "Adventure on Gull Island," you have a mental picture of tropical trees in a small area near a body of water. Although a dictionary might have an illustration of a mangrove, an encyclopedia is a better choice to refer to for a picture of a mangrove.

Encyclopedia

A dictionary usually has more entries than an encyclopedia, but an encyclopedia gives more information. Like the dictionary, the encyclopedia lists its entries in alphabetical order. Certain words or subjects

The Atlas

If Mangrove Cove were a real place in Florida, an atlas could show the exact location. As you did more research about Florida, you would discover that Florida has more coastline than any other state except Alaska. To plan a trip to Florida, you would need to know more about the surrounding area.

Some atlases provide detailed maps; a traveler could trace turnpikes and major highways to find the larger airports and cities. The atlas also gives information about the transportation systems of any state, such as roads, railroads, and waterways. Physical features such as the Everglades, uplands, lake lands, swamps, and the coastal plains are shown. The atlas also tells the rainfall and climate in any particular state throughout the year.

A person doing research for any reason, whether for travel plans or for a homework assignment, can start with these three sources. You can use the dictionary for brief, accurate definitions, the encyclopedia for informative articles, and the atlas for geography and description.

might also be illustrated. The encyclopedia tells us that there are different types of mangroves and that they grow in certain areas. Further details include explaining the parts of the tree and their uses. An encyclopedia provides a complete explanation and gives more illustrations. Now you have a greater understanding of mangroves than the dictionary definition gave you.

Mangrove Forest at the Mangrove Aquarium.

Expand your search to find a place to stay near the Mangrove Aquarium, find directions to its location, learn about the climate, or discover special places of interest nearby. Computer access to current information is not a substitute for other reference tools, but it can add to the scope of knowledge.

The availability of this varied and instant information requires guidance and good judgment. Ask an adult for advice if you come across questionable materials online. Learn to use the tools available, but beware of letting the tools use you.

Beyond Books

Computer reference tools are also valuable for research. With a computer you can access information from a variety of sources on any topic. Pictures, videos, or audio clips help you see and hear the information. Searching *mangrove trees* and *Florida* might lead you to find out about the Florida

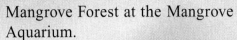

THE TAL-OMEGA

Jeri Massi
illustrated by Del Thompson and John Bjerk

*When Bruce learned of the contest to
send the first child through space to
the research center on
Jupiter 2, he jumped
at the chance. As an
orphan, he longed to
be a part of something
special, to belong. Now, after
being declared the winner, he is in
the second week of his voyage into
space. For a week he has eaten and
talked with the Tal-Omega crew, and he has seen
space through the portholes of the ship. For a boy
with no family, this week of hard work, horseplay,
and high adventure has been like a dream come
true. Little does he know that his newfound contentment will soon be threatened.*

Mutiny

"Tal-Omega—Tal-Omega.
Seven days out from orbit. 0600
hours. Crew roster is as follows:
Captain John Denton, helm.
Lieutenant Laurence Richards,
navigation. Lieutenant Dwight
Finelli, communication and survey.
All levels acknowledge." Bruce
was already accustomed to the
computer's daily request.

Dr. Hanson looked up. "Sickbay
acknowledges." He turned to
Bruce. "I'm going to anesthetize
you, Bruce."

"Yes sir."

"That injury's going to require a
little surgery, nothing serious. If we
were on Earth, you wouldn't even
need to spend the night in the hospital. I'm going to call in Simmons

and Mitchell to prep you while I decontaminate." He reached up to a small hatch in the low metal roof.

"Had to get my arm caught in that hatch door," Bruce thought.

At the moment he felt no pain, but the thought of immediate surgery frightened him. He wished he could be somewhere else. But not really. He had never felt as comfortable with a group of people as he did with the men of the *Tal-Omega* spaceship. For the briefest moment his mind turned to the second moon of Jupiter that would be his home. He would indeed be a newcomer at the school there, for all the students on Jupiter 2 had been born there and had never met a boy from Earth.

For the first time, memories of green grass and blue sky filled him with homesickness. "Even the greenhouses on Jupiter 2 won't be like Earth," he thought, "like home."

"Now just breathe easily, Son. Simmons and Mitchell will come in to prep you for surgery. I'll be back in a minute to give you an injection." Dr. Hanson placed a mask on Bruce's face and ruffled the boy's hair. The doctor was a gray-haired man, ramrod straight with keen gray eyes that seemed to see everything. Instinctively, Bruce had liked and trusted him from the beginning of the voyage.

Bruce tried not to inhale deeply. In a moment he noticed that he wasn't as nervous as he had been the moment before. Then the walls,

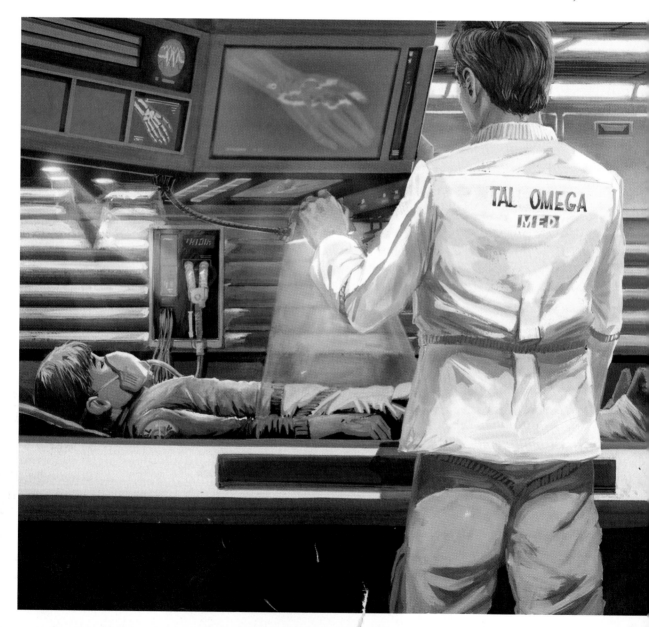

normally so close and cramped, looked far away. They blurred, and he relaxed. "And so pretty," Bruce thought happily, as the bank of controls surrounding the cubicle glowed like many Christmas lights. The screen just above his bed showed a computer image of his hand with highlights in red for the areas where there was damage. In another moment it, too, blurred.

Bruce closed his eyes and yawned. He heard, rather than saw, the doctor leave. The swish of the sickbay door caused him to lift his eyelids sleepily. Two shadowy figures came in. Simmons and Mitchell, Bruce thought vaguely, then closed his eyes again. Of the fifteen crew members, Simmons and Mitchell were his least favorite. They were simple ship-mechs. They could function in any department of the ship, doing semi-skilled work.

"He's out. Cut that gas," Mitchell said.

Simmons slid back the shield. Then he leaned over Bruce. "Poor kid. He really tore up that arm."

"Quit stalling and set that dial," Mitchell said. His voice sounded far away. As Bruce came in and out of a daze, their voices seemed to get louder and softer, then garbled, then clearer. He had no sense of time, but at some point while they were setting up, Mitchell was saying, "His life won't be worth a plugged nickel soon enough."

"I'm not hurting any kid—"

"Don't you turn on us now, Simmons!"

"You threatening me?"

"You can lay to it, man. Lay to it. I'll see to it that nobody turns traitor on us."

"I just never thought it would come to roughing up a kid."

"It won't. He'll join us as soon as he sees the flash of a laser. I'll have him eating out of my hand within an hour of the takeover. Won't I, Brucey-boy? Haha."

Bruce struggled to speak but could only manage an inaudible sigh. The voices faded as he drifted deeper into sleep.

Sometime later a voice again intruded into his dreamlike state.

"Bruce, I'm going to put you to sleep now."

"Don't kill me." He struggled "I won't tell. Don't put me to sleep."

"It's just an injection, Son. It's time to operate."

"No, Mitchell, I won't tell."

Then darkness descended and Bruce knew nothing else.

When he opened his eyes, Bruce's first thought was for his arm. He turned and looked at it, waggling his fingers. Everything seemed to be working. The delicate laser surgery had fastened his torn skin back together. He moved the arm and felt a little pain, but it wasn't too bad.

He lay back and tried to relax, wondering why he felt so strange. Something nagged at the back of his memory. "You'd think I was scared to death," he thought wearily. He closed his eyes. Memories of the events just before the operation teased him. He could almost hear the voices fading in and out. Patiently, he forced himself to relax and concentrate. Bits and pieces of the conversation began to fall into place. His uneasiness grew.

The swish of the door interrupted Bruce's thoughts. Dr. Hanson entered the tiny sickbay. "How are you doing, Bruce? The computer tells me you're feeling a little stressed."

Bruce just regarded the doctor silently.

Hanson smiled at him and spoke to the computer. "Dr. Hanson requesting personal readout, vital signs, and recovery analysis for current subject, please. Visual display only." The information appeared on the main screen. Hanson frowned at it and then glanced at Bruce.

Carefully, he checked the read-outs from the computer. He checked Bruce closely.

"I think I'll keep you here for the off-watch, Son," he said. "I sleep close by. The computer can tell me if you wake up or need anything."

"Please, sir, I don't want to sleep."

"If you need company, I can stay and go a few rounds of voice-activated checkers with you," Dr. Hanson said gently.

"No, I—" To his horror Bruce felt tears coming into his eyes.

"No, I—" he tried again. And then he burst out crying. He was ashamed of it, but he couldn't stop.

"Steady, boy. You're all right." Dr. Hanson put his hands on Bruce's shoulder.

"Something's wrong," Bruce sobbed. "I can't remember what it is."

"You had a bad dream going under the anesthetic, Son," the doctor said. "That's all. We call it angst. It's common out in space. You'll be all right."

"No, it wasn't a dream. It was more like . . ." The bits of overheard conversation finally clicked in Bruce's mind. "Mutiny!" he exclaimed.

Suddenly Dr. Hanson leaned close, his hand closed over Bruce's mouth. "Be quiet!"

Bruce tensed. "Not Dr. Hanson, too," he said inwardly.

"Don't use that word unless you mean it," Dr. Hanson said. "And if you mean it, don't say it so loudly." He slowly took his hand away. "Now, tell me what you know."

Bruce thought he should keep silent and bravely demand to see the captain first. But instead he heard himself saying, "Mitchell and Simmons thought I was asleep. They were talking about a takeover. They expected to have me join them as soon as I got scared enough."

Dr. Hanson drew back a little. "Well? Will you?"

Bruce could feel his hands trembling from fear, but he said, "I'm with the captain."

"Are you, boy?"

"If I get out of here alive, I will go straight to him and tell him." His words made him feel a little braver. A week ago he would not have believed it of himself.

"You're a good kid," Dr. Hanson said, relaxing a little. "But don't go to the captain. Mitchell would be on to you in a second. I'll get the captain down here. The crew would expect him to come and see you, your being so young. I'll tell him you're awake and a little pale. When he comes we'll tip him off. Wouldn't it be good to know who's in on it, though?"

"You're not with them, then?" Bruce asked, shakily.

Dr. Hanson suddenly laughed. "No, Bruce. But mutiny—" He lowered his voice. "That word's poison out here. No place for hysterics if a crew's in the middle of that dirty business."

Dr. Hanson spoke toward the computer screen.

"Captain to sickbay, please," he said.

A Matter of Time

In a couple of minutes Captain Denton walked in, bowing his head a little to avoid bumping it on the low bulkhead. The computer arranged for more air conditioning. The two grown men and the boy on the bed filled up the room. Dr. Hanson murmured the story to Captain Denton.

"Mitchell and Simmons are both on duty," the captain said. "They traded shifts with two of the other men."

"Who else is up there?" Dr. Hanson asked.

"Joe Hands—"

"I wouldn't trust him with my granny's glasses!"

"You don't think—" Captain Denton cut himself off as the emergency lock hummed on the sickbay door. He and Dr. Hanson tugged at it, then punched the emergency number code on the computer panel.

"It won't let us out!" Dr. Hanson said.

"This is Captain Denton," the captain said to the computer. "Open the sickbay door."

"Access to sickbay denied," the computer said.

"This is Captain Denton, serial number 321836. Open the door. That's a direct order," Captain Denton said.

"Denied," the computer replied. "No access to sickbay without proper clearance. Your code number is obsolete."

"Anderson!" Captain Denton smacked his fist into the palm of his other hand. "Yesterday he told me that fuel was leaking into the protective covering that houses part of the computer's memory. I gave him five minutes to clean it and sent Mitchell in with him."

"That's it, then," Dr. Hanson said. "Simmons, Mitchell, Hands, and Anderson."

"And they're all on duty on the bridge," the captain said. "They've planned carefully, all right."

"Well, we can do a little maneuvering on our own. I'm still the ship's doctor and I have a secure medical computer." Dr. Hanson punched up a sequence on the computer and said, "This is Dr. Hanson. Run an emergency check for food poisoning among the crew. Alert to all subjects sleeping or unconscious."

"Why are you worried about food poisoning?" Bruce asked.

"I'm not, Son. But the computer will give me a chart of the

layout of the ship's personnel— where everybody is. I have a hunch that the mutineers probably locked all the loyal men into the crew's cabin during the shift change a half-hour ago. Anybody not on shift was probably in his bunk."

A schematic map appeared on the computer's viewing screen. It showed red flashes in one of the cabins.

"Right you are," the captain said. "Six men are in their cabin—locked in, no doubt. And Simmons and Mitchell are going to make sure there's no communication between us and the other prisoners."

Dr. Hanson sat down next to Bruce. "So here we are," the doctor said.

"What will they do to us?" Bruce asked.

"Maroon us, I reckon," Captain Denton replied. He leaned against the bulkhead and frowned in thought. "We're heading out to the research station on Jupiter 2, and I know there's nothing out there they could want. My guess is that the mutineers are gold hunters."

Dr. Hanson nodded. "And we're only an hour and a half away from Mars."

"Mars?" Bruce asked. "Is there gold on Mars?"

"Some people think so," Captain Denton replied. "Private scout ships have gone out and picked up traces of it. But there's been nothing official—scientific reports are against it."

"They would maroon us on Mars?" Bruce asked. "We can't live on Mars."

"Not on the surface, anyway," Dr. Hanson agreed. "But they'll let us suit up for it."

"Even so, that would give us only an extra day," Captain Denton said.

Dr. Hanson looked at Bruce a little worriedly and nodded.

"Bruce, why did you compete for the Jupiter trip?" the captain asked.

Bruce shrugged. "I don't have any family on Earth," he replied. He hesitated, then said, "So I thought if I grew up on Jupiter 2 and learned how to work in a space research center, I could get a good rank in the Space Force and then really be a part of something."

Captain Denton said, "Now you're a part of something, Bruce. You didn't turn coward and run after Mitchell to beg him for anything. You did what was right. And now you're sitting here with the two of us."

"I'd rather be here than with them," Bruce answered.

"Even if it means getting marooned on Mars?" said the doctor.

"It won't mean that. We can think of something," said Captain Denton.

"Doctor—what surgical lasers do you have to cut into that panel?" asked Captain Denton.

"Let's see if we can short-circuit the wiring that's keeping the door closed." He turned to Bruce. "What's your take?"

Bruce's heart jumped a little bit at being included in the planning. "Won't the computer alert somebody?"

"Perhaps. But we might be able to get out before they do anything especially nasty—like cut off the air in here."

"We could try to cut our way through the door itself," Dr. Hanson said.

"Could we have a back-up plan, just in case?" Bruce asked.

Captain Denton looked at him. "Like what?"

Bruce nodded at the trash chute. "If we open that for a couple of minutes and let some air get into it, I'm small enough to climb through it. I can crawl up the trash chute and get anything you need."

For a minute both men were silent. Then the doctor whistled through his teeth. Captain Denton looked thoughtful. "If we could get to the loyal men—but we don't have any weapons."

"I've got two laser pistols up in a hatch in the bulkhead," Dr. Hanson offered. "Not much for eight men." He glanced around.

"On the other hand—" Denton began.

"What?" Dr. Hanson asked.

Bruce's heart was beating hard. "You know—" Captain Denton glanced at the sealed bags of drugs overhead. "Chemicals in the right combinations—"

"Explosives!" Hanson exclaimed. "I should've thought of that right away."

Dr. Hanson dropped to the floor and crawled under the foldup bed. He slid back a cupboard door in the wall. "Most of my chemicals are stored down here in rubber compartments," he said with a grunt.

"You got sleeping gas, Doc?" the captain asked.

"Good old nitrous oxide," Dr. Hanson replied. "Otherwise known as laughing gas. Enough of it should put them to sleep eventually, before they get too excited about orbiting around Mars. But we ought to blast them with it soon, before we come closer to Mars, because nothing fights sleep in a man like greed."

"How do we channel the gas to the bridge?" the captain asked.

"Put it in the humidifier," the doctor answered. "A room the size

of the bridge has its own humidifying tank. That way we can knock them all out."

Captain Denton nodded. "Here, Son," he said, buckling a holster around Bruce. "You know how to use a laser pistol?"

"Yes, sir."

"Don't hesitate to use it if you have to."

"Okay."

The doctor held up six gauze bundles, three in each hand. "These packets explode on impact—so don't trip." He gently pushed them into the pockets of Bruce's jumpsuit. Finally he handed the pressurized canister of sleeping gas to the boy.

"Climb over to the air-conditioning units and put the sleeping gas in the humidifier," Captain Denton said. "First, empty the water. You might flood some of the crawlspace, but it shouldn't damage anything. Then go to the crew's cabin and try to get in. Cut your way out from there with the laser. We'll do the same here and meet you at the bridge half an hour from now. By then all those boys should be sleeping."

"Wait," Dr. Hanson said. "What if somebody jettisons the trash?"

Bruce stopped. He hadn't thought of that.

Captain Denton looked away. "You're right. They might suspect our plan. They know we've got Bruce." He glanced at Bruce. "We'll try something else. If Simmons and Mitchell are planning to maroon us, they wouldn't have any qualms about jettisoning you into space."

"But Captain Denton," Bruce exclaimed. "We'll all die anyway if I don't try it!" He stooped down and opened the trash chute door, letting some fresh air into the stagnant, dirty trash tunnel. He was glad there were no rats or bugs in space. The first puff of air from the chute sent out a filthy smell. Bruce's eyes watered. "Whew!"

Captain Denton put a restraining hand on his shoulder. "Son, this is no game. You could be killed."

Bruce stood up. "I know. But when we were all planning it, I—" How could he explain to Captain Denton how much he wanted to try

it, even if it failed, even if he got thrust out into space? "You see, I never did anything like—I mean, I never really had friends before and I—" Then he hit on the answer. "You'd do it yourself if you could fit!"

Captain Denton nodded. "But I'm the captain."

"We'll all get killed if I don't. It would just be a matter of time."

"The boy's right about that," Dr. Hanson observed.

Captain Denton relented. "All right. Go ahead then." He thrust out his hand. "Remember, you have thirty minutes. Doc and I will cut a way out of here."

Bruce shook hands with him, then with Hanson. "Wait a second," Hanson said. He opened a cabinet and pulled out an aerosol can. "The pain killer injected into your hand should keep it from hurting, but this might help, too." He sprayed a silky, gummy substance onto Bruce's hand. In an instant the substance hardened into a tough, rubberlike glove. "That'll keep out infection," Hanson said.

Space Force

Bruce checked his equipment again, then crawled into the tunnel.

The tunnel was narrow, like a thin tube, just wide enough for a small boy to shinny through, squelching his way through a swamp of discarded printouts, sour milk, water, coffee, sodden bits of unused soap, leftover food, and plain old dirt that clung to the walls.

Clutching the canister in one hand, the boy bellied his way through the waves of trash. It billowed around him so that in places he had to keep his hands pressed under him instead of up by his shoulders. Even then his head and back would scrape the roof. There was no turning around in here—no going back. He wondered what would happen if he couldn't force his way out a trash chute.

He pushed himself through a mountain of paper and saw light gleaming ahead. It was the mess trash chute. He got up to it and forced it open with his good hand. Nobody was in the mess hall.

The tunnel was too narrow for him to bring his knees up to climb out. He pulled himself through with his hand and elbow. Don't trip, Dr. Hanson had warned him. If he fell it would be the end of him.

Slowly he eased through the opening until his hands could reach the floor. Then he crawled out on both hands and scrambled with his feet until he was out of the tunnel.

Bruce let out the water in the humidifier, deposited the gas canister inside, and activated it.

Noiselessly, he returned to the trash chute and pulled on the door. Nothing happened. He yanked again, then braced both feet against the wall, grabbed the stubborn handles with both hands, and pulled for all he was worth. He thought his heart would crack from the strain.

The computer's voice interrupted him. "Please wait until trash disposal is completed. Trash chute depressurized during disposal."

He almost fell to the floor, stunned, barely catching himself on his feet. If he had entered the tube a moment earlier, he would be floating out in space now.

"Who jettisoned it?" he wondered. "Was it somebody who knew I was in there?"

Maybe Dr. Hanson really was a mutineer! He still had a

laser pistol of his own. Had he used it on the captain and then jettisoned the trash?

Bruce swallowed. Suddenly the computer said, "Trash disposal complete. Tube sealed."

"Maybe," he thought, "Mitchell was listening through the intercoms." If so, he'd be on his way to the humidifiers to get the gas out. On the other hand, if Dr. Hanson was a mutineer, he might keep jettisoning the trash to make sure Bruce was out of the way, because he knew that Bruce had a laser pistol.

What could he do? Bruce looked around the room, knowing that escape any other way was impossible.

"Besides," he told himself. "I don't know if Dr. Hanson's in or out, and I gave my word to get to the other men and free them. There's no other way." He pulled open the trash chute door.

"At least it's clean this time," he told himself. He gripped the rim of the chute and climbed in.

Soon he was squirming his way to the crew's cabin.

He reached it in no time and banged on the door, panting with relief and fear.

There was a scrabbling noise and then the hatch opened. All he could see was legs, and then one of the men, Finelli, bent down.

"Hey, it's Bruce. Heave to, somebody. Give me a hand." The six men hauled him out and grouped around him, talking all at once.

"Well, wasn't that smart?"

Lieutenant Finelli's face went white. "We jettisoned that trash not three minutes ago so one of us could try to squeeze out through the tube! You could have been killed!"

The shock of relief made Bruce's knees sag. Jettisoning the trash had been an accident! "The captain's in sickbay," Bruce said. "He gave me thirty minutes to put sleeping gas in the humidifier, find you, and get to the bridge."

"That probably leaves us fifteen minutes," Finelli said. "Hand out the explosives. Who's an engineer here? Let's figure out how to blow out the door with that laser pistol."

It took fourteen and a half minutes to cut a way through the door. Just as they emerged, the captain and the doctor were coming up the narrow, tubelike hallway.

"The computer ran a scan for me," Dr. Hanson said. "Everybody's gone nighty-night on the bridge."

Denton said, "Let's go tuck them in, shall we?"

The sleeping mutineers were confined to the brig, and Bruce returned to his cabin. But after the next watch he was called to Captain Denton's quarters.

"Come in, Bruce."

Bruce stepped into the captain's cabin. It was fairly roomy, considering the size of the ship itself. There were a bed, a desk, and some wall hangings. Captain Denton was at the desk. "Come here, Son."

Captain Denton looked up from his work. His gaze was business-like yet friendly.

Suddenly Bruce swallowed hard. Now he knew that he didn't want to go to Jupiter 2, with its scientists and technicians who would poke him and ask him questions and examine him and feed him carefully and record everything about him. He didn't want to be a new kid again. He wanted to stay with Captain Denton and Dr. Hanson and live aboard the *Tal-Omega.*

"You've got your uniform back into good shape, I see."

"Yes, sir."

Captain Denton's keen eyes held Bruce's attention. "Anybody tell you that we've aborted the mission to Jupiter 2?"

Bruce jumped a little. "No, sir."

"Can't make it, now that we're short-handed this way. We've turned around—heading back to Earth for a new crew before going out again. The Space Force will detour a freighter to get supplies to Jupiter 2."

Bruce nodded a little. He felt relieved, but he could sense that Captain Denton had more to tell him.

"I know of a school," the captain continued, "that trains people for space flight. Would you like to join the Space Force? I'll show you the school when we get back to Earth."

"Will they accept me?" Bruce asked, his eyes shining.

"Well, I've sent my report about the mutiny on to Earth. You're big news now—a hero. Sure, the Space Force would take you. And I'll help you all I can."

"What about Jupiter 2?" Bruce asked.

"There are other kids who want to go, Bruce. A replacement will be sent out on the next flight."

"Okay. I—I mean, thank you." Bruce stumbled over the words. Suddenly he thrust out his hand to the captain. "Thank you very much."

Captain Denton smiled and shook his hand with a firm, hard shake. "Thank *you,* Bruce."

Fees of Indenture

Andy Thomson
illustrated by Preston Gravely

A Price to Pay

"Here, man, throw that bundle down there," Captain Taylor said, turning from the ship's clerk. He thrust his hands into his breeches pockets and spread his elbows out wide.

"Aye, sir," the sailor said, dropping a bundle of straw and rags onto the dock. The rags stirred feebly and then were still again.

The captain eyed the bundle distrustfully. "The little wench is alive?"

The sailor looked down. The rags and straw nearly hid the girl, but he saw that she was breathing. "For a while, Captain."

"We've sold all the hardy folk," the clerk put in. "You'll take a loss on her and those four others aboard with the fever."

"Ah, that's a triple loss on her, then—both parents died aboard. I wish I had never laid eyes on such a miserable wench. Four times I had her whipped. Four times! And now she gets revenge by dying on my hands—No!" he exclaimed suddenly as his eyes caught sight of one of the townsmen. "See that goodman over there? Call him over here." The captain thoughtfully stroked the edge of his frock coat between his thumb and forefinger.

He had snatched profit from the grip of loss before. The clerk brought the goodman with him across the wooden slats of the dock.

"Nay sir, nay. I have enough," the man said. "Not for any price will I take another, nor a sick one at that. I have enough servants.'"

"See here what a bargain that one yonder might be. She has the price of both parents' indentures on her bill, yet I would release her to you for only half her own rate," the captain insisted. "That's a tenth of what I could ask."

"And I could pay the burial and church fees? Many thanks, but no," the man replied.

"Oh come, friend, she may yet recover, now that she's on blessed land."

"No, *friend,*" the man said, accenting the last word. "You've taken loss on the wench I see, but I know you. You will still try to stuff a few more coins in your pocket while leaving burial fees to another. Besides," and he nodded back to the bundle, "there might be a buyer for you. The Widow Bradbury."

The captain saw that a gray-haired woman was kneeling by the pallet of straw, examining the feverish girl. The town physician, fresh off the ship from examining the other indentured servants, was standing by her.

"Why, the little girl would make a pleasant companion," the captain began, wheedling. The physician looked up sternly.

"You still mean to sell her?"

"Of course."

"Think of the mercy of God, sir, and release her. The girl's more dead than alive. Let the Widow take her. She at least will bear the burial costs if it comes to that."

"Doctor, you would beggar me. Volunteer your own goods to the service of the Lord, not mine," the captain replied smoothly. "I have my own tender little ones at home, dependent upon my business ventures abroad, and—"

"Enough of those lies, man."

The woman looked up. "I will buy her," she said, preventing the doctor from arguing any further. "How much do you ask?"

"He wants more than you have, good lady," the doctor interrupted.

"There are my savings, doctor," she said softly.

"What? Make yourself and the girl destitute?"

"Half her rate, madam," the captain said quickly. "It's a fair deal, for I'm in a hurry to leave port, and I am not completely heartless."

"Only mostly," the doctor added under his breath.

"I haven't got that much," the Widow said. "Not readily available."

"Ah well, more's the pity. She would have made a fine—"

"She'll only die if you keep her," the woman said. By now she had one arm under the girl's head. "What profit would that be?"

"No despair," he answered quickly, winking to the clerk. "I can take some money from you now in earnest. If the girl lives, then you may pay me when I return in two months. If you haven't the money then, I will take her off your hands and resell her."

She nodded, and the clerk wrote down the transaction.

"I doubt him, madam," the doctor whispered, picking the child up off the straw and rags. "Bear in mind that he lives off broken hearts."

The captain pretended that he hadn't heard it, but he smiled. Soft, sentimental people like the Widow Bradbury were just the people to buy up these little ones. No doubt within two months she would have restored the girl to her full worth, and he would manage to regain his losses.

"Her name is Elizabeth," he said.

It was night when Elizabeth awoke. She had been washed and her hair had been cut close because of the fever and the vermin from the straw. But she didn't feel these comforts, only the heavy warmth of a quilt over her, and she saw that the walls were straight, not bowed. The lamplight flickered, but it did not bob up and down. She was on land. Land.

"The ship—" she began. "My mother—"

"Poor girl. Rest. The ship is gone from port by now," a voice said. It was a woman's voice. "Your parents are in God's hands now and He has brought you into mine."

Her eyes closed and she fell asleep again until the next morning. When broth was put to her lips, she drank it.

"Mother?" she asked, confused.

"You are with me now," the voice said, and instantly Elizabeth remembered having been awake the previous night.

The girl closed her eyes. She was in Philadelphia at last, alone. Scarcely out from Dover, Mother had died in the stinking hold of the ship. Father had followed soon after, leaving her with nothing but their indentures to pay. And now, she realized, she had been sold, but she had no memory of the scene on the docks.

Only a few days ago the fever had laid hold on her, yet it had been severe. Even now she was weak, but the last nine weeks had taught her that weakness would not be tolerated. The frail and sickly would die.

"My name is Elizabeth," she began bravely, trying to get up, "and I can spin—"

"Enough of that," the woman said, and gently forced her back to the bed. "I don't hold with slavery. We can save enough to pay the rest of your price, and then you may live with me until you can make your own way in the world." The girl lay back, surprised at being ordered to rest. For the first time she felt the comfort of where she was: the clean bed and orderly room. Under the soft quilt her body relaxed, but her eyes, though tired, keenly watched the Widow Bradbury, who, under the law, was Elizabeth's absolute authority and who could sell her or keep her at will, no matter what she said about letting her go. But the Widow did nothing more dramatic than smooth the covers and the feather pillow.

After a moment Elizabeth moved closer and rested her head on the woman's arm. Unfaltering, she looked into the Widow's eyes. "Thank you," she whispered. And then the girl fell asleep.

But already the Widow had heard the comments from the clerk and other crewmen about Elizabeth. She foresaw that much time would go by before the girl would thank her again.

The voyage had hardened Elizabeth. Perhaps, the Widow Bradbury thought, she had been hardened even before that by the debtor's prison and the cold, hard streets of London.

She did not cry for her parents. And after that one moment of gratitude in the Widow's arms she did not again speak kindly or softly to the older woman. She seldom spoke at all.

She spun when there was spinning to do, and she wove when the spinning was done, and she accompanied Mistress Bradbury to town to sell the yarn and cloth they had made.

Unwillingly, she attended Sunday meetings, morning and evening, with her mistress. She did not fidget. No, she sat still and her hard brown eyes glared at every word. She held her head high, kept her jaw tight, and spoke nothing to anybody there.

"Nay, the ship's hold—cruel place that it is—did not break her," the physician said softly one Sunday morning when he and his wife met the Widow in the street where new planking was being laid for a sidewalk. Elizabeth was walking ahead, absorbed in looking at the straight, raw planks of wood. "It bent her sore," he continued. "She may never be straightened, Widow."

Mistress Bradbury looked sober. "She has seen grief, doctor. Though now Satan has bent her to hate God, yet she may be made straight." Her eyes looked vague for a moment. "Once she felt gratitude. She may feel it again."

Elizabeth looked back, sensing that she was being discussed. Now that the morning service was over she was eager to get back home. There was only catechism at home to be learned, but often the Widow

would read to her from the *Book of Martyrs*. That was something, at least. Hearing that other people had suffered made Elizabeth feel better for some reason. And it proved to her that God would make anybody suffer: His own Son, His own people—and her.

"Come, Elizabeth, walk with me," the Widow called. Elizabeth joined her, and they bade good day to the doctor and his wife. But as they started home, the minister joined them. He was a young, serious man with a quick step under his long black frock. She knew that he was studying her with his large, serious eyes.

"And how is our Elizabeth this Sabbath?" he asked gently.

"Well," she said shortly.

"Mind your manners, my girl," the Widow said.

"And you, sir?" Elizabeth dutifully asked.

"Well, thank you," he replied, smiling at her. He suddenly stooped down so that he could see her eye to eye. She had never seen a minister do such a thing. "Elizabeth, is it really well with you?" he asked. "Is your soul safe with God?"

"I have nothing safe with God," she replied angrily. She turned away and kept walking. The minister stood up, looked for a moment at the Widow, and then turned in at his own door.

"I will not go back to that church any more," she said when they returned to the three-room house where the Widow lived.

"You must come to meeting, Elizabeth," the Widow replied gently.

"I will not, I say. And no one can make me."

"I will, if you force me."

Elizabeth hesitated on that, then insisted, "No, I will not. You are not my mother."

"But you are my ward, and you will obey me, child."

"No, I say. No!"

"I mean that you should obey me," the Widow said. "Give in now, and I won't be angry. It is a normal expectation that you attend the meetings with me, nothing cruel. If your pride rebels again and makes you say no, I will switch you." She glanced meaningfully at a dry switch lying in the kindling box alongside the fireplace.

"No! There, I say it again. I will not go."

"Elizabeth."

Elizabeth knew the switching would come. By now she knew that the Widow would always keep her word, even on whippings. Nevertheless, the girl held her head up.

"Bring me the switch," the Widow said.

The girl took a breath and obeyed. "Aye, that I'll do." Elizabeth brought it to her and held it out.

After it was over, tears of resentment sparkled in the girl's eyes as the Widow handed it back to her. But the girl only said, "You'll need something harder than that. For I was whipped aboard ship with a leather thong." Lip trembling, she thrust the switch back into the woodbox.

"I thought a lighter punishment given by one who loves you would succeed where cruelty failed," the Widow replied. Elizabeth only stood still with her head down and didn't answer.

"Child, I have been good to you; I have nursed you, prayed for you, and now I've whipped you. Does nothing touch your heart?" she asked.

Elizabeth looked up. "I don't know," she said wearily. "Maybe you should stop trying. You say God loves me, yet He has given me harder punishments than you could ever give me. What hope do I have with Him? If I love Him, He will kill me, and if I hate Him, He will also kill me."

"The company of unrepentant sinners taught you that, child."

"I was born to unrepentant sinners."

"You can be born again."

In that moment she almost gave in, at least to the arms of the Widow, to be comforted. But in the end she resisted and walked away.

"Very well," Elizabeth said. "I will obey my mistress and go to the meetings with her."

A Prayer for Mercy

A few more weeks went by. The Widow began to instruct her in reading and ciphering, using a hornbook and a slate. Elizabeth could soon spell out her own name. She began to pick her way through parts of the Widow's great musty-smelling Bible. It was not a book she would have chosen, but parts of it were easier than the *Martyrs,* and the Widow owned only those two books to choose from.

Often the Widow would bid Elizabeth read aloud while she spun at the wheel, listening. "I have no quarrel against your handiwork, child, but my eyes grow too dim for reading," she would say. "So I will let your eyes read while my hands see the spindle and yarn." It was true. The Widow needed no eyes for her work.

Elizabeth began to realize that she was having an easy time of it. Though by law the Widow owned her, she was as free as though they were mother and daughter instead. Elizabeth began to feel anxious about the remainder of her bill. Would they have enough to pay it?

"Oh, rest yourself about that, dear girl," the Widow assured her. "We have done well with the loom, and I will take some from my savings if all else fails. It is all I have, but surely I can spare enough to complete payment on half of a child's passage."

Yet the physician, who often looked in on the Widow to see how she did, was worried. "Mark me," he said. "Slave traders that hark from Africa and England are not to be trusted. He will think he's given you a bargain, and it will needle him."

"God's hand is on her," the Widow replied. "On her life, at least, if not her soul yet. Let every captain rise against me, so long as God assists me."

Elizabeth was at the spinning wheel when the Widow said this. The girl looked up and cocked an eyebrow but added nothing.

"Child, would you run to the market for me for dye?" the Widow asked, smoothing some of Elizabeth's hair back into the girl's stiff bonnet. "Master Kettlewell is holding some for me to make his vest."

"Aye, Mistress," Elizabeth said, standing up.

"My trap is outside, girl. I will take you. Kettlewell's shop is on my way," the doctor said. "God give you a good day, Widow."

"And you, Doctor. Hurry home, Elizabeth."

The market was close, for the Widow's house each year seemed to be more and more drawn into the city of Philadelphia as it grew around her. In minutes the horse was trotting over cobblestones, and Elizabeth could see the tall masts and riggings from the wharf leaning this way and that over the rooftops like crazily tilting trees. "There you are, Elizabeth." The doctor said, pulling the horses to a stop. "Can you manage your way home alone?"

"Yes."

She gathered up her bulky skirts and leaped out. He laughed at her and watched while she crossed the cobblestones to get to Kettlewell's. Then he stopped. There was Captain Taylor coming down the sidewalk, a month early! The doctor reined in and tied the reins to the brake. Hurriedly, he climbed out.

Elizabeth trotted out of the shop.

"Hi! Go back!" the doctor called, suddenly afraid, but Taylor saw her.

"You there!" He seized her arm. "I know you."

The doctor crossed in three quick strides. "Leave her alone, Captain."

"Well said. Of course." He obeyed. "I was just admiring the Widow's work, Doctor."

The doctor released Taylor's grip on Elizabeth. "Aye. The Widow's work. Bear that in mind."

"Oh that, of course," Taylor laughed. "I'm as willing as you for the Widow to keep her, though I admit, I am calling a bit early for my payment."

"What brings you back this soon?" the doctor demanded.

"Sickness aboard ship. Fever spread to the crew. We could not have managed Barbados. I thought I would take advantage of my return to collect the balance due me. If you remember, we did not agree to a term of payment."

"Enough. The Widow has it," the doctor said, waving his words away.

"Money for the parents' passage and the girl's."

"You thief! It was half the girl's passage!" the doctor exclaimed.

"No, friend, that isn't what the Widow signed. She must pay all indentures to keep the child."

"I'll see you hanged for your sleight of hand with widows and the fatherless!"

"On the contrary, I have my contract. A judge will award the girl to me." He lifted Elizabeth's chin, and she pulled away.

"Pretty thing. I can sell her for the full price now."

"Come along, Elizabeth," the doctor said, pulling her away.

"And speaking of hanging, Doctor," Taylor called, "have a care the Widow does not try to flee with her, else it will be the Widow who is hanged, not me—for kidnapping!"

The doctor lifted Elizabeth into the trap and then jumped in. "Oh, the villainy of the man! He would have spirited you away instantly, had I not been watching. No, no," he added hurriedly, seeing how white she was. "Think nothing of my words. A dozen men there were nearby who know you. He'd not have tried it, I daresay."

"What would it have mattered?" she asked, tears springing to her eyes. "I'm trapped, aren't I? The Widow cannot pay my parents' passage as well as all of mine. My own full fare was only half of theirs. The Widow meant to pay only half of mine!"

"Can you really believe the Widow will let you be sold, Elizabeth?" he asked.

"What choice will she have?"

"One can always choose to do right—to do kindly. She and I will think of something. Don't worry. God has His hand in this. While He keeps us, no hand can hurt us."

"And what if He gives me up to Taylor?"

The doctor shook his head. "When you're a woman of prayer someday, Elizabeth, you'll know God's love better. I tell you, the Widow is sure she will keep you, and as she knows God's face better than most do, I would trust her opinion."

He pulled the horse to a stop. She leaped out. "I will look at the garden," she said suddenly, keeping her head down.

"The garden?" he asked. "Now?"

"Yes."

He didn't argue. "All right, but stay nearby."

She went out to the garden, then past it to the hillside, still bare of houses, and threw herself down to the ground. "Oh God, have mercy on me and don't let me be sold back into slavery," she begged. "I have no hope but You, now. I've hated You every day of my life, but have mercy on me if You can make Yourself do it, and keep me with the Widow." Then she cried. She cried for a long time, remembering the hold of the ship, the death of her parents, the moaning and the dying and the griefs she had felt. Her sudden memories left her trembling. "Oh please," she added. "If You really love me, and if You've really

wanted my soul all this time, have mercy on me and change my heart. Forgive my sin and save me!"

She looked up. The doctor was coming up the hillside. "Be of good cheer, girl." He pulled her to her feet. "The Widow's given her savings for you. You'll be all right, now. I will go pay Taylor."

He wiped a tear from her cheek. "She's calling for you."

"Thank you!" Elizabeth exclaimed and ran down the hillside, her soft muslin dress flapping and billowing.

She ran into the house. The Widow was by the hearth.

"You've used up your savings for me!" Elizabeth exclaimed, running and clutching her by her skirt. "Now it will be the poorhouse for you, as sure as we live!"

"Why, you've been crying, child."

"You've bought my life, but you've used your own!"

The Widow sat down in her rocking chair. "I have a pair of hands, Elizabeth. I can save again. Besides, it was God's will to buy you back."

"That way?"

"Yes."

"I've been wicked to you!" she blurted out. "Forgive me, Widow."

"I do, daughter. Come here." She opened her arms, and Elizabeth came into them, closed her eyes, and leaned her head on the woman's shoulder. "I knew that sooner or later God would touch your poor broken heart and begin to heal you," the Widow said.

"Will you keep me, please?"

"I will adopt you," she whispered. "Then it will be settled once and for all."

Elizabeth pulled back a little. "Is that God's will, too?"

"It is." She smoothed the girl's hair. "He may let the heart break in order to bring it to repentance, but then He gathers it back with greater mercies. Wait and see, Elizabeth."

The girl closed her eyes again and hid her face once more on the shoulder, crying tears of remorse and gratitude. "I will. I promise I will."

Floradora Doe

Jack Prelutsky
illustrated by John Bjerk

Consider the calamity
of Floradora Doe,
who talked to all her plants, because
she thought it helped them grow,
she recited to her ivy,
to her fennel, ferns, and phlox,
she chatted with her cacti
in their little window box.

She murmured to her mosses,
and she yammered to her yew,
she babbled to her basil,
to her borage and bamboo,
she lectured to her laurels,
to her lilac and her lime,
she whispered to her willows,
and she tittered to her thyme.

She gossiped with a poppy,
and she prattled to a rose,
she regaled her rhododendrons
with a constant stream of prose,
then suddenly, one morning,
every plant keeled over, dead.
"Alas!" moaned Floradora.
"Was it something that I said?"

THE BEGINNING OF THE ARMADILLOS

Rudyard Kipling • illustrated by Tim Davis

The following story, written in the form of a fable, is really poking fun at the theory of evolution. It shows an impossible but humorous theory of how armadillos might have evolved.

Rudyard Kipling was a British writer who grew up in India when it was governed by England. As a boy he heard many of India's folktales and animal fables, and later in life he wrote his own versions of them in two of his books, Just So Stories *and* The Jungle Book. *Although he pretends to be telling his story seriously, he makes his characters—especially the confused Jaguar—so silly that the reader can see Kipling's sense of humor.*

Which Is Which?

This, O Best Beloved, is another story of the High and Far-Off Times. In the very middle of those times was a Stickly-Prickly Hedgehog, and he lived on the banks of the turbid Amazon, eating shelly snails and things. And he had a friend, a Slow-Solid Tortoise, who lived on the banks of the turbid Amazon, eating green lettuces and things. And so *that* was all right, Best Beloved. Do you see?

But also, and at the same time, in those High and Far-Off Times, there was a Painted Jaguar, and he lived on the banks of the turbid Amazon too; and he ate everything that he could catch. When he could not catch deer or monkeys he would eat frogs and beetles; and when he could not catch frogs and beetles he went to his Mother Jaguar, and she told him how to eat hedgehogs and tortoises.

She said to him ever so many times, graciously waving her tail, "My son, when you find a Hedgehog you must drop him into the water and then he will uncoil, and when you catch a Tortoise you must scoop him out of his shell with your paw." And so that was all right, Best Beloved.

One beautiful night on the banks of the turbid Amazon, Painted Jaguar found Stickly-Prickly Hedgehog and Slow-Solid Tortoise sitting under the trunk of a fallen tree. They could not run away, and so Stickly-Prickly curled himself up into a ball, because he was a Hedgehog, and Slow-Solid Tortoise drew in his head and feet into his shell as far as they would go, because he was a Tortoise; and so *that* was all right, Best Beloved. Do you see?

"Now attend to me," said Painted Jaguar, "because this is very important. My mother said that when I meet a Hedgehog I am to drop him into the water and then he will uncoil, and when I meet a Tortoise I am to scoop him out of his shell with my paw. Now which of you is Hedgehog and which is Tortoise? Because, to save my spots, I can't tell."

"Are you sure of what your Mummy told you?" said Stickly-Prickly Hedgehog. "Are you quite sure? Perhaps she said that when you uncoil a Tortoise you must shell him out of the water with a scoop, and when you paw a Hedgehog you must drop him on the shell."

"Are you sure of what your Mummy told you?" said Slow-and-Solid Tortoise. "Are you quite sure? Perhaps she said that when you water a Hedgehog you must drop him into your paw, and when you meet a Tortoise you must shell him till he uncoils."

"I don't think it was at all like that," said Painted Jaguar, but he felt a little puzzled; "but, please say it again more distinctly."

"When you scoop water with your paw you uncoil it with a Hedgehog," said Stickly-Prickly.

"Remember that, because it's important."

"But," said the Tortoise, "when you paw your meat you drop it into a Tortoise with a scoop. Why can't you understand?'

"You are making my spots ache," said Painted Jaguar; "and besides, I didn't want your advice at all. I only wanted to know which of you is Hedgehog and which is Tortoise."

"I shan't tell you," said Stickly-Prickly, "but you can scoop me out of my shell if you like."

"Aha!" said Painted Jaguar. "Now I know you're Tortoise. You thought I wouldn't! Now I will." Painted Jaguar darted out his paddy-paw just as Stickly-Prickly curled himself up, and of course Jaguar's paddy-paw was just filled with prickles. Worse than that, he knocked Stickly-Prickly away and away into the woods and the bushes, where it was too dark to find him. Then he put his paddy-paw into his mouth, and of course the prickles hurt him worse than ever. As soon as he could speak he said, "Now I know he isn't Tortoise

at all. But,"—and then he scratched his head with his unprickly paw—"how do I know that this other is Tortoise?"

"But I *am* Tortoise," said Slow-and-Solid. "Your mother was quite right. She said that you were to scoop me out of my shell with your paw. Begin."

"You didn't say she said that a minute ago," said Painted Jaguar, sucking the prickles out of his paddy-paw. "You said she said something quite different."

"Well, suppose you say that I said that she said something quite different, I don't see that it makes any difference; because if she said what you said I said she said, it's just the same as if I said what she said she said. On the other hand, if you think she said that you were to uncoil me with a scoop, instead of pawing me into drops with a shell, I can't help that, can I?"

"But you said you wanted to be scooped out of your shell with my paw," said Painted Jaguar.

"If you'll think again you'll find that I didn't say anything of the kind. I said that your mother said that you were to scoop me out of my shell," said Slow-and-Solid.

"What will happen if I do?" said the Jaguar most sniffily and most cautious.

"I don't know, because I've never been scooped out of my shell before; but I tell you truly, if you want to see me swim away you've only got to drop me into the water."

"I don't believe it," said Painted Jaguar. "You've mixed up all the things my mother told me to do with the things that you asked me whether I was sure that she didn't say, till I don't know whether I'm on my head or my painted tail; and now you come and tell me something I *can* understand, and it makes me more mixy than before. My mother told me that I was to drop one of you two into the water, and as you seem so anxious to be dropped I think you don't want to be dropped. So jump into the turbid Amazon and be quick about it."

"I warn you that your Mummy won't be pleased. Don't tell her I didn't tell you," said Slow-Solid.

"If you say another word about what my mother said—" the Jaguar answered, but he had not finished the sentence before Slow-and-Solid quietly dived into the turbid Amazon, swam under water for a long way, and came out on the bank where Stickly-Prickly was waiting for him.

A Little Bit of Both

"That was a very narrow escape," said Stickly-Prickly. "I don't like Painted Jaguar. What did you tell him that you were?"

"I told him truthfully that I was a truthful Tortoise, but he wouldn't believe it, and he made me jump into the river to see if I was, and I was, and he is surprised. Now he's gone to tell his Mummy. Listen to him!"

They could hear Painted Jaguar roaring up and down among the trees and the bushes by the side of the turbid Amazon, till his Mummy came.

"Son, son!" said his mother ever so many times, graciously waving her tail, "what have you been doing that you shouldn't have done?"

"I tried to scoop something that said it wanted to be scooped out of its shell with my paw, and my paw is full of per-ickles," said Painted Jaguar.

"Son, son!" said his mother ever so many times, graciously waving her tail, "by the prickles in your paddy-paw I see that that must have been a Hedgehog. You should have dropped him into the water."

"I did that to the other thing; and he said he was a Tortoise, and I didn't believe him, and it was quite true, and he has dived under the turbid Amazon, and he won't come up again, and I haven't anything at all to eat, and I think we had better find lodgings somewhere else. They are too clever on the turbid Amazon for poor me!"

"Son, son!" said his mother ever so many times, graciously waving her tail, "now attend to me and remember what I say. A Hedgehog curls himself up into a ball and his prickles stick out every which way at once. By this you may know the Hedgehog."

"I don't like this old lady one little bit," said Stickly-Prickly, under the shadow of a large leaf. "I wonder what else she knows?"

"A Tortoise can't curl himself up," Mother Jaguar went on, ever so many times, graciously waving her tail. "He only draws his head and legs into his shell. By this you may know the Tortoise."

"I don't like this old lady at all—at all," said Slow-and-Solid Tortoise. "Even Painted Jaguar can't forget those directions. It's a great pity that you can't swim, Stickly-Prickly."

"Don't talk to me," said Stickly-Prickly. "Just think how much better it would be if you could curl up. This *is* a mess! Listen to Painted Jaguar."

Painted Jaguar was sitting on the banks of the turbid Amazon sucking prickles out of his paws and saying to himself—

"Can't curl, but can swim—
  Slow-Solid, that's him!
Curls up, but can't swim—
  Stickly-Prickly, that's him."

"He'll never forget that," said Stickly-Prickly. "Hold up my chin,

Slow-and-Solid. I'm going to try to learn to swim. It may be useful."

"Excellent!" said Slow-and-Solid; and he held up Stickly-Prickly's chin, while Stickly-Prickly kicked in the waters of the turbid Amazon.

"You'll make a fine swimmer yet," said Slow-and-Solid. "Now, if you can unlace my back-plates a little, I'll see what I can do towards curling up. It may be useful."

Stickly-Prickly helped to unlace Tortoise's back-plates, so that by twisting and straining Slow-and-Solid actually managed to curl up a tiddy wee bit.

"Excellent!" said Stickly-Prickly; "but I shouldn't do any more just now. It's making you black in the face. Kindly lead me into the water once again and I'll

practice that side-stroke which you say is so easy." And so Stickly-Prickly practiced, and Slow-Solid swam alongside.

"Excellent!" said Slow-and-Solid. "A little more practice will make you a regular whale. Now, if I may trouble you to unlace my back and front plates two holes more, I'll try that fascinating bend that you say is so easy. Won't Painted Jaguar be surprised!"

"Excellent!" said Stickly-Prickly, all wet from the turbid Amazon. "I declare, I shouldn't know you from one of my own family. Two holes, I think, you said? A little more expression, please, and don't grunt quite so much, or Painted Jaguar may hear

us. When you've finished, I want to try that long dive which you say is so easy. Won't Painted Jaguar be surprised!"

And so Stickly-Prickly dived, and Slow-and-Solid dived alongside.

"Excellent!" said Slow-and-Solid. "A little more attention to holding your breath and you will be able to keep house at the bottom of the turbid Amazon. Now I'll try that exercise of wrapping my hind legs round my ears which you say is so peculiarly comfortable. Won't Painted Jaguar be surprised!"

"Excellent!" said Stickly-Prickly. "But it's straining your back-plates a little. They are all overlapping now, instead of lying side by side."

"Oh, that's the result of exercise," said Slow-and-Solid. "I've noticed that your prickles seem to be melting into one another, and that you're growing to look rather more like a pine-cone, and less like a chestnut-burr, than you used to."

"Am I?" said Stickly-Prickly. "That comes from my soaking in the water. Oh, won't Painted Jaguar be surprised!"

They went on with their exercises, each helping the other, till morning came; and when the sun was high they rested and dried themselves. Then they saw that they were both of them quite different from what they had been.

The Beginning of the Armadillos 165

"Stickly-Prickly," said Tortoise after breakfast, "I am not what I was yesterday; but I think that I may yet amuse Painted Jaguar."

"That was the very thing I was thinking just now," said Stickly-Prickly. "I think scales are a tremendous improvement on prickles—to say nothing of being able to swim. Oh, *won't* Painted Jaguar be surprised! Let's go and find him."

By and by they found Painted Jaguar, still nursing his paddy-paw that had been hurt the night before. He was so astonished that he fell three times backward over his own painted tail without stopping.

"Good morning!" said Stickly-Prickly. "And how is your dear gracious Mummy this morning?"

"She is quite well, thank you," said Painted Jaguar; "but you must forgive me if I do not at this precise moment recall your name."

"That's unkind of you," said Stickly-Prickly, "seeing that yesterday you tried to scoop me out of my shell with your paw."

"But you hadn't any shell. It was all prickles," said Painted Jaguar. "I know it was. Just look at my paw!"

"You told me to drop into the turbid Amazon and be drowned," said Slow-Solid. "Why are you so rude and forgetful to-day?"

"Don't you remember what your mother told you?" said Stickly-Prickly:

"Can't curl, but can swim—
    Stickly-Prickly, that's him!
Curls up, but can't swim—
    Slow-Solid, that's him!"

Then they both curled themselves up and rolled round and round Painted Jaguar till his eyes turned truly cart-wheels in his head.

Then he went to fetch his mother.

"Mother," he said, "there are two new animals in the woods today, and the one that you said couldn't swim, swims, and the one that you said couldn't curl up, curls; and they've gone shares in their prickles, I think, because both of them are scaly all over, instead of one being smooth and the other very prickly; and, besides that, they are rolling round and round in circles, and I don't feel comfy."

"Son, son!" said Mother Jaguar ever so many times, graciously waving her tail, "a Hedgehog is a Hedgehog, and can't be anything but a Hedgehog; and a Tortoise is a Tortoise, and can never be anything else."

"But it isn't a Hedgehog, and it isn't a Tortoise. It's a little bit of both, and I don't know its proper name."

"Nonsense!" said Mother Jaguar. "Everything has its proper name. I should call it 'Armadillo' till I found out the real one. And I should leave it alone."

So Painted Jaguar did as he was told, especially about leaving them alone; but the curious thing is that from that day to this, O Best Beloved, no one on the banks of the turbid Amazon has ever called Stickly-Prickly and Slow-Solid anything except Armadillo. There are Hedgehogs and Tortoises in other places, of course (there are some in my garden); but the real old and clever kind, with their scales lying lippety-lappety one over the other, like pine-cone scales, that lived on the banks of the turbid Amazon in the High and Far-Off Days, are always called Armadillos, because they were so clever.

So *that's* all right, Best Beloved. Do you see?

No Longer a Slave

Eileen M. Berry

illustrated by Kathy Pflug

Onesimus turned over on his straw mat. Through the window in the slaves' quarters he could see the stars. Nighttime in Colosse was always so still. How he wished for some of that stillness to seep into him. But there was no room for it.

"I will go to Rome." The thought came like the toll of a gong, and Onesimus sat up. He could leave for Rome tomorrow. Philemon would never find him there.

His heart began to pound at the thought of freedom. No more long hours of labor. No more menial tasks. No more mocking words from the high-ranking servants about the low-class Phrygian slaves.

"But if I am to go away, I must have money," he thought. He smiled to himself in the darkness. "Philemon has plenty of that. My only problem is how to get it."

"But Philemon has been kind to you." Onesimus heard the words in his mind, almost as though they had been spoken. A twinge of guilt made him pause. But a moment later he argued with that inner voice. "Philemon, yes—and his wife, Apphia. But no one else. Philemon may be what they call a Christian, but his servants are not. I am not welcome here. I have no home anywhere. What reason do I have to stay?"

While the stars slowly faded before the dawn, Onesimus lay wakeful, planning his escape.

Onesimus watched all the next day for his opportunity. And when it came, it was perfect.

Philemon's manservant came from the master's chamber to the cooking quarters, where Onesimus was stoking the fire. The manservant sat down, lounging with his feet toward the blaze. He and the cook exchanged stories of the day, and Onesimus listened.

The manservant drew his feet up suddenly. "I have left the master's water jar in the chamber. He wanted it filled." He caught sight of Onesimus and settled back, stretching his legs out once more. "You, slave, fetch it for me."

As Onesimus hurried to obey, he could hear the manservant laughing with the cook.

"I will have the last laugh this time," he said to himself. "They will never see me again."

Onesimus entered the chamber. Immediately he noticed a gilded box on a table. Precious stones gleamed inside. He chose a few, hoping they would not soon be missed, and hid them inside his tunic. Onesimus hesitated only a moment at the chamber door. Then he turned and fled out to the street and away.

Two weeks later, Onesimus awoke to feel hard stone beneath him. Ah, yes. He had spent the night here on the steps of an empty arena. He was cold and stiff—but he was finally in Rome. That was all that mattered. He felt inside his tunic for the bag of coins he had received in exchange for the jewels. The familiar lump was still there.

The sun slanted into his eyes. Onesimus squinted. He sat up quickly. The sun was already high in the sky. "It must be close to midday!" He groaned and rubbed his sore limbs. "I must buy myself some bread."

The streets of Rome were teeming with people and animals. Onesimus elbowed his way through the throng, keeping his eyes on the ground.

"Hail, my friend!" a voice boomed just to his right.

Caught off guard by the friendly tone, Onesimus glanced up. His eyes met those of Marcus.

"Your face is very familiar. I have seen you in the house of Philemon—have I not?" Marcus watched him, and his eyes, though keen, were kind.

Onesimus remembered now. This man was one of those Christians; he visited often at Philemon's home, bringing news from Rome. Onesimus could not afford to have him suspect what had happened. He forced a smile in return. "You are right, my lord. My master has sent me to Rome on an urgent mission. I return to Colosse today."

Marcus raised his eyebrows. "The Philemon I know would send none but his most trusted servant on an errand of such urgency."

Onesimus glanced down at the dusty road and shuffled his feet. "And that is just what I am." He raised his head, trying to appear confident. "I'm no longer a lowly slave. I've been promoted since I became a Christian."

Marcus did not answer for a moment, and Onesimus felt his face flush under the older man's sharp gaze. "I am glad to hear that, my brother," he said at last. "You have chosen well. When last I visited the house of Philemon, you were a source of great strife in his household."

"I suppose I was." Onesimus looked at the wall just beyond Marcus.

Marcus was silent for what seemed an eternity. Then he stepped forward and placed a hand on Onesimus's shoulder. "Since you are a Christian now," he said, "there is someone you must meet. He is my friend, and he lives very near here."

Onesimus took a step backward. "But I must be on my way—"

Marcus lifted a hand. "You can spare an hour, can you not? I rather think your master would approve the idea."

Onesimus trudged along behind Marcus. How smoothly Marcus threaded his way through the crowds! He spoke to a man or a woman here and there, and always his voice sounded the same—friendly and gracious. Onesimus quickened his pace, eager yet reluctant to follow.

Marcus led Onesimus down another busy street, then suddenly stopped. On some steps sat a man with a gray beard, talking to a group of people gathered about him.

"What is his name?"

"Paul," Marcus whispered.

no longer. We who were dead in our sins may be alive to God through Jesus Christ. This is God's gift, given freely, not earned by our good works."

Onesimus touched the lump beneath his tunic. The money pouch was still there. It seemed to weigh more now than it had before; in fact, he felt he might sink with the weight of it. When Paul locked eyes with him for a moment, Onesimus almost believed Paul knew about his sin.

But Paul was speaking. "You who are slaves to sin and aliens from God in your minds can be brought near to Him by the blood of Jesus Christ. I beseech you, beloved people—be reconciled to God and be free!"

The apostle lifted his eyes toward heaven and prayed. Then he quietly dismissed the people.

Onesimus wanted to leave, but he could not. For the first time in years, he felt something stronger than the hatred in his heart. Greater than all his bitterness was a longing to know this Jesus. But he was as Paul had said—a slave to sin and an alien from God. He rested his hand on the money pouch again.

A firm hand touched his shoulder. Marcus was beside him again.

Marcus motioned him to move forward, but Onesimus did not move. Already the words Paul was speaking held his complete attention.

"Do you not know that you who are without Christ are the slaves of sin?" he said. "Sin is your master. But thanks be to God, Jesus Christ died, was buried, and rose again that we might be the slaves of sin

"Onesimus, I have not been fooled by your claims."

Onesimus's hands went cold. He forced himself to meet the eyes of Marcus, expecting to see mockery there. But he saw only concern and kindness.

"Why don't you become a Christian—truly?" Marcus asked quietly.

"I would like to," Onesimus said. "But you do not understand—I am not fit to be a Christian. You do not know what I have done."

Marcus nodded. "Already you have come closer to Christ than those who believe themselves to be fit," he said. "It does not matter what you have done. The blood of Jesus Christ alone can cleanse you. Come—I would like you to meet Paul and talk with him."

When Onesimus left with Marcus an hour later, the weight he had carried was gone. He still had the money from the stolen jewels, but now he knew that he must restore it to Philemon—and he wanted to. The hatred and guilt had lifted from his heart. He was, as Paul had said, a new creature in Jesus Christ. All things had become new.

"Will you stay in Rome for a while?" Marcus asked.

"Yes," said Onesimus. "Paul wants to teach me more about Christ. He will write Philemon a letter to explain."

"You will accept my offer to stay in my home then? My wife and I would count it a privilege to give shelter to a new brother in Christ."

"You are very kind. I will stay."

The streets were quiet now; many had gone to their homes for the noon meal. Onesimus marveled at the difference between this quietness and the noise of the bustling crowd only hours before.

"Do you think Philemon will receive me when I return to him?" Onesimus asked. "I have greatly wronged him."

"Philemon is a follower of Christ," Marcus said. "He knows what it is to be fully forgiven. You have no need to fear."

Onesimus walked on with a light step. Even if he remained Philemon's slave, how different it would be. Inside, he was a slave no longer.

Types of Fiction

Some stories, such as "Fees of Indenture" and "No Longer a Slave," take place more than a hundred years ago. Some stories take place in the future, such as "The *Tal-Omega*." But many stories that you read could happen today.

Modern Realistic Fiction

Many stories take place in the present. They use everyday settings such as a city block, a pet store, or a corner mailbox. These stories include realistic objects and events—a flashlight, an old lighthouse, a picnic, the beginning of summer vacation. A story that takes place in the present and uses familiar objects and events is called *modern realistic fiction.* "Big Brother" and

"Adventure on Gull Island" are examples of modern realistic fiction.

In "Big Brother," Timothy has to learn to accept his mentally disabled older brother, Brad. The author of "Big Brother" uses this story to tell us the sad truth that some people, even Christians, can be cruel to people who act or look different. Writers often use this type of literature to show us problems that people have to overcome. But not all modern realistic fiction has been written by Christian authors. Some authors try to teach falsehood in their stories by giving the wrong answers to modern-day problems. A wise reader will remember that fiction is "made up" by the author, no matter how real the fiction seems.

Historical Fiction and Biblical Fiction

"Fees of Indenture" takes us to the past. Indentured servants, wooden sailing ships, and hand-woven cloth are all parts of history. Stories that show what life was like in the past are *historical fiction.* Historical fiction gives the reader an idea of the differences in the past and present. For instance, the law no longer permits Americans to buy and sell children, nor do children have to pay the debts of their parents. Yet these conditions were a part of life in early America.

Good historical fiction also shows the *sameness* of the past and present. People as cruel as the captain of the slave ship still try to "live off broken hearts" today, though they may not be selling slaves. And, like the widow, Christians today must still choose to do right, to love the Lord, and to seek lost sinners. Historical fiction should help us to see that the battle between right and wrong never changes in time.

Similar to historical fiction, good biblical fiction presents facts with historical research. Good biblical fiction is always true to Scripture but approaches the story in a personal way. We know that Onesimus was a runaway slave who turned to Christ. In the book of Philemon, Paul admonishes Philemon to receive Onesimus when he returns. But we are not told why Onesimus left.

The author weaves historical research into the biblical fiction account. This information supports the plot and setting. Knowing about the cities of Rome and Colosse helps the author and the reader realize what it would have been like to live at that time in history.

Science Fiction and Fanciful Fiction

The term *science fiction* usually makes us think of space ships and laser guns. Science fiction almost always takes the reader to the future, like the story "The *Tal-Omega*" does. Often the setting used in science fiction is a futuristic world, a distant planet, or a spaceship. But the key to literary

science fiction is that it emphasizes science and intelligence in its setting and characters. In "The *Tal-Omega,*" Bruce, Dr. Hanson, and Captain Denton save the ship by using strategy. They rely on their knowledge of the ship and the doctor's knowledge of chemistry to outwit their captors.

Fanciful fiction, on the other hand, may take place in the future or in another world, but it does not emphasize science. The author of fanciful fiction creates his own world of make-believe characters and events. "The Beginning of the Armadillos" is fanciful fiction. The reader knows that animals don't talk, and certainly he understands that no turtles or porcupines ever taught themselves to change so that they became armadillos. To enjoy fanciful fiction, the reader must allow himself to believe the impossible while reading the story.

Sometimes authors blend science fiction with fanciful fiction to give us stories that contain space ships and new inventions as well as fanciful characters. It is common for writers to combine these two types of literature.

No matter what the type, good literature always looks at conflict from God's point of view. Good literature will always show love and purity as good, and it will always show sin as wrong and destructive.

Whether the story takes place in the past, present, or future, the author presents the setting to show the character in a more personal way. Understanding the character and setting makes the reading of fiction a pleasure.

3

REGIONS

Ma and Muffin

Jamie Turner   *illustrated by Paula Cheadle*

Little Golden Fireball

The three little children circled their grandfather's big armchair in front of the fireplace and tugged at his sleeve.

"Oh, Grandpa," begged Meg, the oldest, "please tell us a story."

"A story?" said Grandpa. "And what makes you young'uns think I have another story to tell?"

"You always have another story, Gramps," said Nora.

Grandpa scratched his head. "I reckon I've told you every story I've ever heard at least a dozen times."

"Then tell us one you didn't hear," suggested Mark. "Make one up."

Grandpa tugged at his beard. "Mmm . . . now there is one I hadn't thought about." He opened his eyes and smiled. "How would you like to hear a story about a boy named Micah and his dog?"

"Yes! Yes! Oh, please! Do tell us!" the children all said at once as they sat down around Grandpa's feet.

Grandpa leaned forward to adjust the pillow behind his back, and then he started.

If you had known Micah's ma the way he knew her, you'd understand why he was so fearful of bringing the pup home when he found it.

Micah Ward and his ma lived in Mississippi at the time—right in the heart of the delta, where the land was as gummy black as licorice and as flat as a giant johnnycake. Micah's pa had been a cotton farmer before he died, sharing part of Mr. Deal's land and working for him. After Pa's death Mr. Deal had let Micah and his ma keep living in their little two-room house. To pay their rent, Ma helped Cass Deal in the garden and around the big house.

One day Micah was walking home after school. He had stopped to examine a dead blackbird whose legs stuck straight up in the air in a wonderful way. As Micah was crouched down beside the bird, he heard a shrill, squeaky noise. It was the same kind of sound the Deals' baby girl, Dovey, made when she patted her hands and squealed. Micah thought at first it was coming from the dead bird, and he all but fell backward in surprise. Then he caught sight of an old ripped cardboard box over in some tall grass and saw it wiggle just a little. He left the blackbird and crawled over to the box.

When he lifted the flap on one corner, he saw a pair of the shiniest molasses brown eyes, a little brush of yellow tail whipping back and forth, and a rosy, grainy tongue hanging out underneath a little wet raisin of a nose. All this was attached to the cutest little flop-eared pup Micah had ever seen.

The pup's whole body was wagging in time with his tail. Micah took him out of his box and lifted him up. He was exactly the color of Ma's sweet muffins—the ones she made only at Christmas time because they called for a whole cup of sugar.

"Howdy there, Muffin," Micah said and then let out an Indian whoop. He had him a pup that someone had likely dumped along the highway.

"Let's you and me go home, Muffin," Micah said, tucking him under one arm and his arithmetic book under the other. Muffin was twisting and yipping with excitement as Micah set off at a trot.

Suddenly Micah stopped in his tracks. What would Ma say when he came in toting a pup? He knew she'd think of Muffin as nothing but a pack of foolishness.

You see, Ma was different from other grown-up women that Micah knew. For one thing, she didn't wear lacy collars and smell sweet like honeysuckle the way Miss

Cates did. Miss Cates was Micah's schoolteacher. She had soft brown hair and stepped daintily like a little wren. But Ma moved like a loaded river barge in her heavy shoes, and she smelled mostly like cornmeal and ammonia.

And Ma didn't generally act cheery the way Cass Deal did. Cass was always laughing and humming while she worked, and sometimes she quoted poetry, like "The world is so full of a number of things, I'm sure we should all be as happy as kings." But Ma mostly grunted and sighed. The only thing she ever quoted was Bible verses when she thought they fit a certain situation. Sometimes she quoted, "The heart is deceitful above all things, and desperately wicked," like when she caught Micah popping blackberries into his mouth instead of putting them in the pail.

Ma didn't tolerate a lick of nonsense, and Micah knew sure and certain what she'd say about the pup. But when he looked down at Muffin, he knew he had to try to convince Ma somehow to let him keep the pup.

He cut across the field at an angle and put Muffin inside the old fenced chicken yard. Then he went inside to face Ma.

As soon as he opened the door, his heart felt as low as the wet floor Ma was scrubbing. Micah had learned from experience that Ma's mood on scrubbing day was not a thing to be trifled with. She didn't even look up or stop when he walked in but grunted and said, "Now stay out till I'm done, won't you? I left you an apple right by the door. That'll tide you over to supper time."

But Micah, figuring it would be hard for Ma to get up from her hands and knees and chase him with a hickory switch, decided not to put it off. He took a good bite of apple to wet his whistle, swallowed, took a deep breath, and spoke to her across the wet floor.

"Ma, I found me a dog—the cutest little pup, Ma—and his name's Muffin 'cause he's all gold and yellow-brown, and I saw him by the dead bird in the grass, and I think he must be terribly hungry and lonesome, and I can keep him in the old chicken pen out back, and . . . oh *please,* Ma!" The words came tumbling out all helter-skelter, but Ma understood perfectly.

Her scrub brush stopped swishing, and her broad frame rocked back heavily on her heels. The furrows between her eyes got deeper, and her stormy gray eyes were threatening some mighty bad weather.

"Micah Abner Ward, I can't believe what I'm hearing." She rolled her eyes upward. "Here I am barely able to feed our own two mouths, and you bring home an old mutt to stand around with his jaw hanging open. He can't stay, Micah, so just put the notion out of your mind right this instant."

"But Ma, he can eat table scraps, and you won't have to tend to him at all. I'll do it all, I promise!" Micah said.

"Table scraps!" she snorted. "And since when do we have any of those left with the way you eat? No, Micah, he'll have to go."

Ma was a solid woman, as stout as an oak stump, and she had a will to match. Micah stood there with his eyes swimming in tears. Ma's mouth gave a twitch. Hurriedly, she started scrubbing again with fresh vigor. "He can stay out back tonight, but we'll get rid of him first thing tomorrow." She glanced up, adding quickly, "Now that's the end of the matter. Go on out and leave me in peace."

Supper that night was a solemn business, and after Micah had sopped his last chunk of cornbread in his glass of buttermilk, he asked to be excused.

"Go on outdoors," Ma said gruffly, "and since this is the hound's only night here, you might as well take him this last hunk of cornbread to add to the piece you stuffed inside your britches pocket when you thought I wasn't looking. I'm not a mean woman, Micah, but I am sensible. Cute little pups grow into horsesized hound dogs that could eat more than you and me put together. Now say your good-byes to the dog tonight and get it over with."

Wiggles and Giggles

Grandpa stopped here and reached over to stir the logs on the fire. Then he got his nail clippers out of his pocket and slowly examined his hands. He snipped off a fingernail or two, frowning and whistling all the while.

The children shifted anxiously.

"Go on, Gramps!" one of them said. "Did Micah have to take the dog back where he found him? What happened, Grandpa?"

Grandpa looked up, pretending to be startled. "Oh! I wasn't sure you were listening to me."

"Please finish it!" they clamored.

"I guess I'll go on." Grandpa chuckled a little and plumped the pillow up a bit more. Then he settled back and continued.

Well, after Micah excused himself from the supper table that night, he went out back and gave the pup some water along with the cornbread and then brought him around to the front porch to play with him. A little bit later Ma came out and sat down in her rocker to do a lapful of mending. She grunted extra hard and began to sew furiously.

"Look, Ma," Micah said after a little while. "Ain't he a dandy?" He was grabbing Muffin with both hands and roughing around with him, rolling him over and pushing him in play. Muffin was barking a shrill little yap and coming right back for more.

Ma just grunted and kept her eyes on her sewing.

The next time Micah rolled the puppy over extra hard, he went tumbling over and over and ended up right close to Ma's rocker. Muffin stood up, but this time instead of coming back to Micah for more playing, he set his eye on Ma and started yipping around her rocker and wagging his whole body, trying to get her to notice him. Her stitches got downright violent, and she kept her eyes glued to her lap. Then Muffin jumped up on the side of her rocker, but he was so short he couldn't get his paws to catch hold and stay. So he flipped backward and landed in a little squirmy heap and then got up and tried it all over again.

Micah stared with his mouth hanging open, disbelieving the pup's boldness. Ma just kept on sewing.

Then Muffin started nosing around her feet and just plain showing off with little leaps and dog hollers. He even got down on his back and whirled his little legs in the air like he was riding a bicycle upside down. Then when that didn't work, he grabbed the hem of her skirt and gave a little tug. Ma got mad then and kicked her foot at him and swatted the air like she was after a pesky housefly. "Git!" she said.

But Muffin thought she was playing with him, and he just went crazy, jumping back and forth and nipping at her shoe.

Well, Ma was plumb confused about how to act with all of Muffin's goings-on, and she finally let out one giant puff of air, picked up her mending, and stomped on into the house, slamming the door harder than Micah ever did when she fussed at him for doing it.

Muffin ran to the door and stood there yelping and pawing at the screen, with his head over on one side like he thought maybe Ma was teasing him and playing hide-and-seek.

Early the next morning Ma left the house, and when she came back she said to Micah, "Take the pup over to the Deals' house on your way to school. Cass said they'll take him."

When Micah didn't answer, she said, "Be grateful, boy, that you can at least see the critter once in a while. You know we can't afford to keep him, and I done the best I could for ye." She dropped her heavy hands onto his shoulders. Her voice softened as much as Ma's voice could. "It ain't easy t' be poor, Son, but at least you can see the pup now and then."

"But seeing a dog," thought Micah, "isn't the same as having him for your very own."

He did as he was told, however, and made sure he rubbed the tears off his face before he got to school.

Micah had never had a worse day than that one turned out to be. He got his lessons all mixed up and even labeled his map of Canada upside down. He walked straight home after school without even going by the Deals' to see Muffin. If Muffin couldn't be his, he decided, it would hurt too much to see him.

But that night during supper, they heard a scratching and whining at the screen door. Looking up, they saw Muffin peeking in, and his tail was wagging so fast it was just a yellow blur.

"Muffin!" Micah cried.

"Stay put," Ma said, but she was too late. Micah had already jumped up and run to the door. When he opened it to go out, Muffin skittered inside faster than a water bug. He headed straight for Ma and started up again. He fell at her feet in a jiggly heap and squirmed and yelped for her to pat him. She tried to pretend he wasn't there, but it was awful hard to do

when the pup was going haywire right at her feet.

Just then Cass Deal came panting up the front steps.

"That little feller is quick!" she laughed. Her eyes were sparkling with fun as she picked Muffin up. "Sorry, Mattie," she said to Ma. "He shot out the gate before I could stop him." Muffin whined as she carried him away.

The next night Ma and Micah were sitting on the porch after supper. Micah was struggling over a long-division problem, and Ma was darning holes in his socks. Without warning, a little golden fireball streaked up the steps. By the time Cass Deal arrived, Muffin had yarn tangled around his front paws and Ma was flapping her old faded red-checked apron at him and saying, "Scat!"

Things kept going on like this. Muffin was absolutely smitten with Ma, and every chance he got he'd dig or sneak his way out of the Deals' yard and hightail it over to the Wards'. Then he'd bark and dance around Ma while she tried to shoo him away. Cass finally quit trying to chase him and just waited for Micah to bring him back home.

One day in late October Miss Cates dismissed school a half hour early. Micah hurried home. He was aiming to ask Ma if he could go over and help Cass Deal gather pecans or rake leaves to earn some cash money.

Micah was heading up the front steps when he stopped in surprise. The door was propped open a little way, and inside he could see Ma sitting with her back to him. She

was bent over a little and appeared to be talking to the floor.

"You're a little rascal if there ever was one," Micah heard her say. "Yes sir, you're just stuffed full of mischief. Now stop it, you little scamp. I'm gonna whip you good and proper if you don't be-have yourself."

And she laughed, really laughed, and then picked up a furry little ball of wiggles and shook it in play. The little fur ball barked in response and tried to lick her face, and she laughed again right out loud. There could be no mistaking that bark. It was Muffin as sure as the Mississippi River is wet.

"All right, you little scalawag," she went on, "it's time to take you back outdoors." And with that, she turned around with the laugh still on her face and her eyes all crinkled at the corners. When she saw Micah, she stopped dead.

At first, she looked embarrassed and then sort of mad, but then finally the corners of her mouth pinched in and she gave a little halfway smile. Then she came on outside and got hold of herself.

"Well, quit your gawking. For pity's sake, what's a body to do when a pup won't leave her alone, but torments her until all she can do is give up and love him? I talked to Cass Deal this morning and told her we'd take the pup back. I aimed to surprise you with him—well, I can see you're surprised, all right. Pick your jaw up, Son."

She looked down at Muffin, who was twisting and yipping as if he'd got hold of a firecracker on the Fourth of July. Micah couldn't think of a word to say, but his grin could have lit up the whole cotton field on a moonless night.

Grandpa looked into the fire a minute, and the children sat quietly. Meg sighed contentedly.

"So Micah got to keep Muffin for his very own dog, Grandpa?" asked Mark.

Grandfather nodded. "Yes, sir, he did. And Muffin was the best little dog a boy ever had. He lived almost thirteen years with Micah and Ma, and no one cried harder than Ma when the little fellow died. I can still see her stroking his tired little head tenderly and crying without shame the day he died. I keep remembering too how Muffin won Ma's heart when he was a pup by just being nice and steady as the sun shines. She finally *had* to give in and be nice right back." Grandpa chuckled softly.

"Grandpa," said Nora, "Micah had the same last name as ours, didn't he? I think you must have known that boy and his little dog. Did you, Grandpa?"

"Yes," said Grandpa, smiling at his grandchildren. "I knew that little boy very well—about as well as I know my own self."

MAP SCALES

Comparison of Map Scales

"Right in the heart of the delta, where the land was as gummy black as licorice and as flat as a giant johnnycake"— Mississippi was home to Ma and Micah. Many exciting stories like "Ma and Muffin" and "Venture to Mierow Lake" take place in states where day-to-day life depends on a body of water for food, income, and transportation. About half of the states in the United States border the coastline. Two of these coastal states are Mississippi and Alaska. Not only is Alaska the largest state in the United States, it also has more coastline than any other state.

Look at the maps above. Compare the map of Mississippi, a southern state, to that of Alaska. At first glance, you might think that these two states are about the same size. Actually, Alaska is nearly ten

Mississippi

Mississippi R.

Jackson
Meridian

Hattiesburg

Biloxi

Scale
0   100   200
1 inch = 200 miles

Alaska

Yucon R.
Fairbanks

Anchorage
Juneau

Scale
0   500   1000
1 inch = 1,000 miles

times larger than Mississippi. The reason that the states look as though they are about the same size on these maps is that they are drawn on different scales.

What is a scale? A scale shows the relationship of how many miles are represented by the map. Map scales allow travelers and students to compare distances.

The scale of miles on the map of Mississippi shows us that one inch on the map represents 200 actual miles in Mississippi. We can quickly find that the width of the state of Mississippi is about 200 miles. Now notice that the scale of miles on the map of Alaska tells us that one inch on the map represents about 1,000 actual miles in Alaska. By measuring the width of Alaska on the map (2.3 inches), we can multiply to find that the width of the entire state of Alaska is about 2,300 miles.

Skill Lesson: Map Scales   189

Reasons for Map Scales

The maps below, drawn on the same scale, show how the sizes of Mississippi and Alaska really compare. This scale, however, is too small for the map of Mississippi to contain any details about the state.

Mississippi's map drawn on a larger scale could show cities and geographical features such as lakes. There are times when a map drawn on a larger scale may be needed for locating expressways, rivers, airports, battlefields, national forests, and other points of interest.

Maps of the world or of large countries are usually drawn on a small scale so that they can show a large area. A map with a very large scale could show many more details such as cities, street names, and even restaurants.

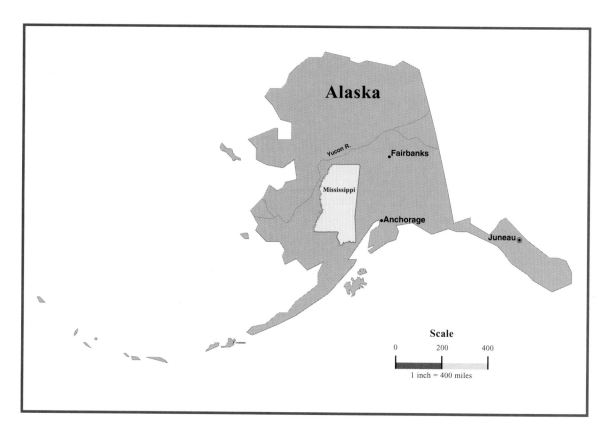

Alaska

Yucon R.

Fairbanks

Mississippi

Anchorage

Juneau

Scale

0   200   400

1 inch = 400 miles

Mt. McKinley in Alaska

Look again at the first maps of Alaska and Mississippi. Use the map scales to find out whether it is a greater distance from Anchorage to Fairbanks in Alaska or from Jackson to Biloxi in Mississippi.

Although the distance from Jackson to Biloxi appears to be greater, remember that the Mississippi map is drawn on a larger scale with fewer miles shown for each inch on the map. Now you know how a specific map can guide you on your travel adventures.

The Six Travelers

dramatized by Becky Davis
illustrated by Justin Gerard

CAST

Narrator	Runner
Soldier	Friend
Strong man	Merchant
Huntsman	Daughter
Blower	Guard
Townspeople	Stagehands

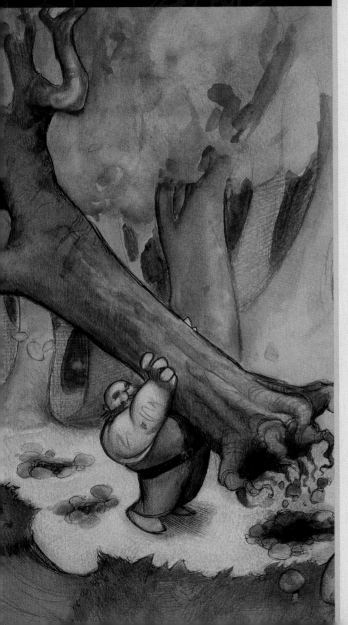

SCENE I

Soldier enters at stage left and makes his way to center stage. He clutches a small pouch with a drawstring, pulling out three coins.

Narrator: Once there was a soldier who had served in a wealthy merchant's personal guard for many years. But when he was finally discharged, he received only three farthings to help him make his way in the world, even though he had served faithfully.

Soldier: Three farthings! The merchant has storehouses full of gold to the ceiling. But to me, who risked life and limb for him, he grants only three farthings. I shall have to see what I can do to make my way in the world with so little.

(At stage right, Strong man is surrounded by several "uprooted" trees.)

Narrator: As the soldier went on his way through the forest, he saw a man uprooting trees as if they were blades of grass. When the strong man had uprooted two dozen trees, he stopped and noticed the soldier.

Strong man: Well, how now, my fine soldier?

Soldier: A long life of service, with but three farthings to show for it!

Strong man: Ah, a certain merchant's doing, I'll warrant. I know of how he takes advantage of poor people. He overcharges us till we haven't a cent, just so he can fill his own coffers to the brim with gold.

Soldier: Then come with me to seek an audience from him. A man of your strength could be a great asset in our plea.

Strong man: You have convinced me! Let me first take this firewood to my mother, and I will join you.

Narrator: So saying, the strong man took up one of the trees and wrapped it around twenty-three others. He disappeared through the forest but soon returned to the waiting soldier.

(Exit Strong man stage right, carrying a bundle of trees, then re-enter to join Soldier. The two walk toward stage left.)

Strong man: Now we are off to make our way in the world and seek an audience from an unjust merchant! Perhaps together we will be able to make our way in the world.

Narrator: The strong man and the soldier traveled on for several miles when they saw a man . . .

(The two walk toward stage left, pantomiming conversation, until they notice Huntsman at center stage. He is aiming a musket offstage.)

Soldier: How now, what is this, my good man? You aim with your gun, but I cannot see a target.

Huntsman: My dear fellow, two miles from here is a fly sitting on a flower petal, and I wish to shoot out its right eye.

Strong man: Ah! An aim like that could serve some purpose in our travels.

Soldier: Surely! Do come with us. We are off to seek an audience from an unjust merchant.

Huntsman: Ah, yes. I know of how that merchant takes advantage of poor people. He cheats us of our livestock only so that his barns can be full. I will gladly come with you. Together we will be able to make our way in the world.

Narrator: So the three companions set off. They had traveled several more miles when . . .

(The three stop, fan themselves with their hands, mop their brows, and notice three "windmills" [students] in the corner of stage left, "windmilling" with their arms. Blower stands across from them.)

Huntsman: *(puzzled)* What is this? Not a breath of wind, but three windmills all turning!

Strong man: A remarkable sight, surely.

Soldier: Perhaps we will find the answer farther down the road. Let us continue.

Huntsman: There is a man. Perhaps he will know something about the mystery of the windmills.

Strong man: My, what a nose he has! Almost big enough for a man to rest upon. And see how he holds one nostril and blows through the other!

Soldier: How now, my good man? What are you doing with your nose?

Blower: Did you not pass three windmills turning, a mile down the road? There is no wind today, so I came out to blow

196

and make them turn. If I had gotten any closer, there is a chance I would have blown them over completely. Sometimes my nose gets out of control.

Soldier: Ah, but what a man to accompany us on our travels! Surely a nose like that would be of some use. Do accompany us. We are on our way to seek an audience from an unjust merchant.

Blower: Ah, yes, I know the one. He takes advantage of poor people. I will gladly come with you. I had best put a clothespin over my nose, though, so as not to blow one of you away by accident. Then together we can make our way in the world.

(Blower clips the end of the cardboard nose with a clothespin. Exit the four travelers at stage left, then re-enter. They pantomime walking and conversing toward center stage. Enter Runner and Friend from stage right and walk to center stage.)

Narrator: So the unusual group set out once again on their journey. By and by they came upon two men walking together. One of them, though, was hopping down the road on one foot.

(Runner hops while steadying himself on the arm of Friend, who carries a hat.)

Blower: I must say, that fine fellow can move faster on one leg than any of the rest of us can on two!

Soldier: How now, my good fellow? Why do you have one leg buckled up under you like that?

Runner: And good day to you, sir! If I were to unbuckle my other leg, I would move so fast that my friend here would soon be left in the dust and would probably never see me again. Now that would be a shame, wouldn't it?

Soldier: Ah, a fine man you would be to accompany us on our quest! You never know when a talent like that may have some purpose. We are on our way to seek an audience from an unjust merchant. Come with us, and by all means bring your friend along too.

Runner: Ah, yes, my friend and I will gladly come and join the cause of justice. Together we will be able to make our way in the world.

(Together, the six approach the merchant's castle. Several townspeople wait at the castle, whispering and sharing news.)

Friend: *(waving the hat in his hand)* And so as not to disappoint you by any means, I will reveal that I have a talent too. I must always carry my hat in my hand, for when I place it upright on my head, such a terrible frost comes that trees will fall right over from the ice that forms on them.

Soldier: Splendid! Splendid! Six travelers like us will surely make our way in the world!

SCENE II

Narrator: And so the little group traveled on until they saw before them their destination: the merchant's stately castle. There they heard talk in the streets.

Blower: Ah! The word is that the merchant is looking for a husband for his daughter.

Runner: I have heard that she is beautiful, but just as cruel as her father.

Strong man: People are saying that the man who can win a race with her will win her hand in marriage.

Friend: The racers are supposed to run from the castle to a mountain spring and back again with a cup of water from the spring.

Huntsman: Oh, but if the man loses the race, he will also lose his head. That is part of the bargain. And I have heard that the merchant's daughter is as swift as a deer.

Soldier: Ah, there's always a catch to it. But perhaps we can show the merchant a thing or two about what six "ordinary" men can do.

Runner: *(excitedly)* Oh, I will gladly race for you, if you do indeed want to win the hand of such a girl. I will unbuckle my leg to be sure to win.

Narrator: So the soldier walked up to the castle to see the merchant.

Soldier: Sir, I am ready to try for the hand of your beautiful daughter.

(Merchant appears behind the desk/castle.)

Merchant: *(mocking)* Ha! You are merely a soldier! Better men than you have tried and have not lived to tell the tale. You must bargain to be beheaded if you lose the race.

Soldier: Very well; I would still like to try. However, I would like to request that my servant run for me.

Merchant: Your servant may run for you, but when he loses the race, both he and you will lose your heads! Agreed?

Soldier: So be it.

Narrator: The race was set. The runner and the beautiful daughter took off. Although the girl was indeed swift, the runner passed her easily. He ran to the mountain spring, filled his cup, and headed back. But he was worn out from all his travels, so he stopped to rest and fell asleep. Soon the merchant's daughter caught up with him.

(The merchant's daughter and Runner leave at stage left to fill their cups. Runner re-enters before the girl, and lies down with his head on a large "rock" at stage left. He sets his full cup beside him.)

Daughter: *(startled and panting)* How now? What is this? My challenger—asleep! Well, let us see if he can win the race with no water in his cup! *(She empties his cup.)*

Narrator: And so saying, she poured out every last drop and raced on, laughing to herself. But fortunately the huntsman was on the castle roof.

(Travelers stand together near the castle. Huntsman squints into the distance.)

Huntsman: *(pointing toward Runner)* Look, my good soldier! I can see the runner from here. He has fallen asleep and the girl has poured out his cup of water.

Soldier: I cannot see him, my good huntsman, but if we do not help him, the six travelers will soon be four travelers!

Huntsman: I will gladly shoot the rock out from under his head.

(*As Huntsman aims, Runner dislodges the "rock" with a quick motion of one hand, which is tucked behind or beside it.*)

Narrator: Saying that, the huntsman took quick aim and fired, sending the rock rolling down the hill. The moment the rock disappeared from under his head, the runner awoke.

Runner: Ah, I see that the merchant's daughter has been up to some mischief, but it will not serve her, even so.

(*Runner leaps up, grabs his cup, and runs out to refill it. He then runs to the castle, passes the girl, who is pantomiming running, and waits, panting, until she arrives.*)

Narrator: The runner ran back to the spring, filled his cup again, and passed the girl to win the race with a good ten minutes to spare.

Daughter: (*to her father*) No matter what the rules of the race were, I refuse to marry a common soldier!

Merchant: Do not fear, my dear. You shall not have to. (*to the men*) Come, my good men. You have won the race, and you shall be honored.

SCENE III

Stagehands set table at center stage.
Behind the table, an iron-barred window is visible.

Narrator: So saying, the merchant took the six travelers into a great iron room with walls of iron, doors of iron, and windows with iron bars across them.

Soldier: *(surprised and delighted)* Ah, a fine treat! You have set before us many wonderful things to eat.

Merchant: Yes, and I hope you will enjoy them immensely.

Narrator: So saying, the merchant disappeared from the room. He hurried downstairs and ordered the cook to stir up a great fire under the room, great enough to heat up the iron and roast the six travelers alive.

(All six travelers "eat" and mop their brows.)

Blower: My, but it is getting rather hot in here.

Huntsman: Especially under my feet. I cannot help wondering if the merchant is up to some mischief.

Soldier: *(very excitedly)* I do believe there is a fire under us! And the iron will heat up so hot that we will surely be roasted alive!

Friend: Ah, not necessarily so, my good soldier. Perhaps you have forgotten about my hat.

Narrator: So saying, the runner's friend put his hat upon his head. Immediately the six friends felt the heat no more.

Instead they began to shiver. A long time later, the merchant opened the door.

Merchant: Well, two hours have gone by. Certainly they should be roasted by now.

Soldier: Most gracious host, could you please let us out? We are s-suffering a mild case of frost-bite in this cold room.

Narrator: The merchant was in a speechless rage, but he let the men leave the room.

Daughter: *(proudly)* Father, I still refuse to marry that common soldier!

Merchant: Perhaps we can devise another plan, my dear. *(to the soldier)* Good sir, if you were to take all the gold you could carry, would you be willing to relinquish your right to marry my daughter?

Soldier: I think that would be agreeable. But allow me two weeks first.

SCENE IV

Narrator: During that two weeks, the soldier hired tailors to make the largest sack in the world. They used all the material they could find to sew it together.

Soldier: I am ready. My servant will carry the gold for me.

(Strong man enters from stage left, dragging a large bag to meet the merchant at center stage. Two students bring in a child's wagon piled with "gold.")

Strong man: Here is my sack!

Narrator: When the merchant saw the size of the sack and the strength of the strong man, he turned a little pale, but he ordered a wagonload of gold to be brought.

Strong man: Why, what is this? It barely covers the bottom of the bag! That will hardly do!

Narrator: The merchant turned a little paler at that, but he ordered more gold to be brought.

Strong man: Truly, sir, your men will have to do far better than this.

Narrator: Before long the merchant had emptied every room in his stately castle of the gold that was there. And still the sack was not full.

204

Strong man: See here, sir. I am not choosy. I will take anything you have to offer in order to fill my sack.

(Two students return from stage right with a wagon. The wagon is loaded with faux fur coats and several household items.)

Narrator: So the merchant called for jewels, furs, and fine silk. He called for cups and plates and fine silver. And still the strong man's sack was not full.

Strong man: Ah, well, we must put an end to this sooner or later. And besides, if a man's sack is not quite full, why, he can close it that much more easily.

Narrator: So saying, the strong man hoisted the sack onto his back and walked away with it to join his five friends.

(Strong man walks to join travelers at stage right.)

Merchant: What? That man is walking away with all the riches I own! This cannot be! What am I to do?

Daughter: Father! Order your personal guards to be sent out to capture that soldier! Tell them that he stole your riches.

Merchant: *(firmly)* That I shall. Guards!

Narrator: And so an entire regiment of guards came to find the six friends rejoicing over all the riches that the strong man had brought back to them.

(Guard appears at center stage, as if the remainder of the regiment were behind him.)

Guard: You are under arrest for stealing all these riches!

Soldier: Oh, no, good sir. We came by these riches honestly.

Guard: Nevertheless, you are all under arrest.

Blower: Ah! This is where I come in. I was afraid I would not be able to help in this whole great adventure.

Narrator: So saying, the blower removed the clothespin from his nose and gave a little puff with one nostril. Every man in the regiment flew up into the air and floated there under the power of that blast.

(Guard jumps up on a chair when Blower blows.)

Guard: Mercy! Mercy! Let us down!

Blower: Only if you promise to take this message to the merchant: Any man you send to arrest us will also be given a ride in the air.

Guard: We will! We will!

Narrator: So the blower let the guards down gently and fastened the clothespin back on his nose. The guards ran back to the palace, never to be seen again.

(Guard runs off-stage.)

Soldier: Well, my good friends, shall we be off? I believe we have succeeded in making our way in the world.

Narrator: And so the six friends lived together happily ever after, using their riches wisely to help not only themselves, but other poor people around them.

Soldier: After all, we knew what it was like to be poor.

Narrator: And what of the merchant and his daughter? Well, they discovered that they did indeed have three farthings left, so we can assume that they also were able to make their way in the world.

common 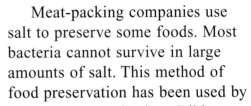 Salt

Candy Jamison

Salt Makes a Difference

Does a bite of pickle appeal to you? What about a soft pretzel, fresh from the oven, or a big plate of French fries from your favorite restaurant? One thing that makes pickles, pretzels, and French fries taste so good is the salt in these foods.

In parts of the world where people eat mostly cereals (grains), vegetables, or boiled meats, they usually add common salt to their food. This common salt is sodium chloride. It is important to health.

For example, a strong, steady heartbeat depends partly on the sodium from common salt. In the United States we "iodize" our common salt before eating it. Iodized salt contains a small amount of the compound potassium iodide. This compound helps keep the thyroid gland healthy and prevents an illness that causes *goiter*.

Meat-packing companies use salt to preserve some foods. Most bacteria cannot survive in large amounts of salt. This method of food preservation has been used by people since Bible times. Christians are called "the salt of the earth" in Matthew 5:13 because their presence in the world holds back corruption.

People who live in northern climates use salt to melt the ice and snow on roads in the winter. When salt is added to water or ice, a saltwater mixture forms. This mixture freezes at a much lower temperature than pure water does. Because this mixture freezes at a lower temperature, early car owners added salt to the water in radiators. This did help prevent the water in the radiator from freezing in the winter. But it also made the radiator rust faster. Today, car owners use antifreeze to protect their radiators.

Salt Is Everywhere

Seawater

Common salt is the most abundant kind of salt in seawater. Common salt and other salts enter the seas through the water cycle. In this cycle, water follows a series of steps over and over again. First, water evaporates. Then it precipitates as snow, rain, or sleet. Next, water flows through or on the ground to the lowest place it can. It will drain into rivers and streams first. These rivers and streams dissolve minerals and salts from the land over which they flow. Eventually they will empty into the sea, depositing their dissolved cargo there. Finally, water evaporates again. When water evaporates from the seas to enter the water cycle again, the salts are left behind.

The seas are growing a little saltier every day as streams and rivers bring salts to them. Evolutionists once thought that they could judge the earth's age by figuring out how fast this salt accumulated. But did the seas start out without salt? And have they always gotten saltier at the same rate? Evolutionists assume the answer to both of these unanswerable questions is yes. Even with these assumptions, though, their calcula-

tions led them to believe that the earth was only a few million years old. Their evolutionary theories required the earth to be billions of years old. They gave up attempting to judge the earth's age from the accumulation of salt in the seas.

Natural Brines

Water that contains large amounts of salt is called *brine water*. Seawater can be called brine water. But the term usually refers to waters containing more salt than is in seawater. The Dead Sea (really a lake) and the Great Salt Lake are both examples of natural brines. They both receive salt from rivers. But in each example the water enters the lake and evaporates, leaving the salt behind, because the lake has no outlet. This fact makes both "lakes" much saltier than the seas. If you were to swim in either the Dead Sea or the Great Salt Lake, you would notice the high salt content right away. You would find it easy to float in the salty water, and any cuts that you might have would sting as soon as they touched the water.

Rock Salt

When common salt crystallizes, it is called rock salt. Rock salt is found either in great flat beds or in salt domes. Although salt beds are found in Pakistan and Iran, not much salt is removed from them. Salt is removed, however, from the salt beds in the United States and Canada. Salt is also removed from salt domes, humped salt deposits that are from one thousand feet to two miles across and several thousand feet deep. Some salt domes in North America extend more than three thousand feet deep, and some in Europe are believed to extend downward fifteen or even twenty thousand feet.

Evolutionists have a theory of how salt beds and salt domes came to be: saltwater seas or lakes evaporated very slowly to form salt beds, sometimes very deep in the ground; then great pressure or high temperatures made some of these deep salt beds come to the surface and form salt domes. But the evolutionists face a problem that they don't want to admit: there is no evidence to back up this theory.

Creationists believe that God made the salt beds when He made the land and that the salt domes formed as a result of the Flood. Evolutionists say that we hold this belief by faith. However, no one was present to observe the formation of the salt beds, so evolutionists must accept their ideas by faith too.

The difference between the evolutionist and the Creationist is what he puts his faith in: man's ideas or God's truth. The Bible tells us that God made the earth by speaking it into being. Just like everything else in nature, salt formations remind us that He is the Creator.

View of the Dead Sea

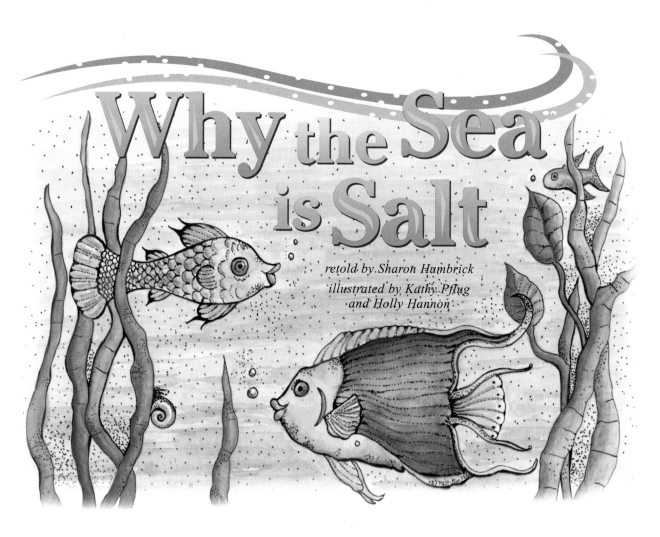

Why the Sea is Salt

retold by Sharon Hambrick

illustrated by Kathy Pflug
and Holly Hannon

"Grandpa," Charity asked, "why is the sea salty?"

Grandpa Rumpole looked across the sandy dunes, out to the edges of the horizon where the sun sat sinking. He remembered that once he had sat upon this very hill overlooking the sea and had asked his grandfather the same question.

"Your great-great-grandfather explained it to me," Grandpa Rumpole said. He patted Charity's head and smiled at her. "The story goes like this."

Charity looked out across the sea and listened.

So long ago that no one really remembers it, there lived two brothers. Pierre was so rich he owned a mountain of gold, but Hector was a poor lad who had only one mule. Pierre's wife was well-fed and fat, but Hector's wife

210

was sickly and skinny. One day Hector and his wife were so hungry they thought they would have to eat their mule.

"Before we eat Ferdy," Hector said, "I will ask Pierre to help us."

So Hector rode Ferdy five miles to Pierre's grand estate to ask for food.

"Minnie is sick and has no food," he said. "Will you give me some food and medicine for her, Pierre?"

"Give you food?" Pierre said. He waved his arm toward his huge mansion. "Does this look like a poorhouse for those who cannot earn their own bread?" Pierre laughed. Then he said, "All right, Hector. You're my brother, so I'll help you. If you give me that mule, I will give you a pound of bacon."

Hector dismounted and patted Ferdy on the nose. "Good mule," he said. He bound up the pound of raw bacon in his kerchief and started on the long walk home. He knew Minnie was waiting by the fire, shivering and coughing in hunger and cold.

As he walked, Hector grew more and more sad. Minnie needed more than bacon. She needed milk, berries, and fruits. She needed a doctor and medicine.

"Why did I visit Pierre today?" he thought. "There is only a little bacon, and I no longer have Ferdy to help me in my work. We are ruined!"

He sat down, cradled his head in his hands, and cried. Just then a little old woodchopper appeared.

"What is the matter?" the woodchopper asked.

"My wife is sick and starving. I traded my mule for this pound of bacon, and when we have eaten it, my wife and I must starve."

"Take that pound of bacon to the Land of Nowhere," said the woodchopper, "and you will find help."

"Where is the Land of Nowhere?" Hector asked.

The woodchopper beckoned Hector to follow him into the woods. Beyond a cluster of trees stood a shining house made all of glass. "That is the Land of Nowhere," the woodchopper said. "Everyone in the Land of Nowhere loves bacon more than any other food. When they see you have a whole pound of bacon, they will offer you more riches than you can imagine, but do not sell the bacon for money."

"Why should I not sell the bacon?" Hector asked. "Minnie is dying. The money would help her."

"There is something better than money in the Land of Nowhere," the woodchopper said. "Tell the people of Nowhere that you will accept no payment other than the little hand grain grinder that stands behind the door. Do not take any payment other than the grinder."

Hector shook his head. "What good will a grain mill do for me? I have no grain."

"Do what I ask," the woodchopper said. "When you come back out with the grinder, I will show you how to make it work."

Hector thanked the woodchopper for the good advice. Then he approached the shining glass house and knocked. A cheerful woman answered the door, but when she saw that Hector carried a pound of fresh bacon, she began to plead with him.

"Give me that bacon," she said. "I will give you one hundred francs for it."

"Bacon?" said a large man in the room, "for bacon I will give you a thousand francs!"

Hector thought of Minnie at home and what the money could do to help her. "No," he said, "I will sell the bacon only for the grain grinder that stands behind the door."

The people of the Land of Nowhere shouted. They pled. They flattered. But Hector's resolve would not budge.

"Only the grain grinder," he said.

At last, the people of Nowhere gave him the grain grinder. "Give us the bacon now," they said. Hector clutched the hand mill tightly and rushed out of the shining glass house.

"Good," said the woodchopper, clapping his hands. "Take this home to your sick wife. Say, *Grind, little mill. Grind milk and fruit for Minnie.*"

Hector did as he was told and soon Minnie was sitting up in bed. After a few days, she was as good as new. The village people were astonished at her recovery.

"It was the hand mill Hector purchased for me," she said. "The hand mill gave us milk."

Word of the hand mill spread over the whole kingdom. Everyone came to see it. Hector and Minnie would order the mill to grind out candy for children and flowers for young ladies. All the people of the village were happy.

Then one day Pierre, Hector's rich brother, heard tidings of the mill.

He rode up to Hector's small house. "I must have this mill," he said.

"I bought the mill," Hector said. "You will have to be content with your mountain of gold."

Pierre turned away angrily. "I will have that mill." He grabbed the mill and rode off into the night. "I have my mill!" he shouted.

Minnie cried quietly, but Hector took her hand and smiled. "Don't worry, Minnie," he said. "Last night, I asked the grain grinder to grind out gold coins for us. We are rich beyond our wildest dreams."

Pierre's head was full of dreams. He pictured rivers of gold and mountains of diamonds. "I will rule all the world," he thought.

Just then, robbers appeared from among the trees. They stole the horse and the grinder.

The robbers were sailors, and, as quickly as they could, they returned to their ship that was docked in the harbor.

"Captain," they said, "you will never have to go in search of salt again. We have captured the grain grinder that can grind out anything in all the world."

"Let us put out to sea," said the Captain, "and see what this grinder will do." He smiled. "I will be very happy if I can grind salt and not have to sail around the earth to find it."

"Little grinder, grind me salt," the Captain shouted. The sailors cheered as the grain grinder began to grind salt. Salt poured from the grinder into all the buckets and tubs of the ship. When the cargo hold was full, the captain shouted, "Enough, little mill, stop grinding salt."

But the mill did not stop. What the captain did not know was that although anyone could get the mill to start working, only its rightful owner could tell it to stop. The captain shouted. He pled. He got down on his knees and shook the little mill, but still it ground salt and more salt. All that night and through the next day salt poured from the mill.

At last a sailor shouted, "We are lost!" And so it was, for now the ship was so heavy with salt that it began to sink into the ocean.

"Stop, stop, little mill," the Captain and sailors cried, but the mill did not stop. The ship sank to the bottom of the ocean.

"And the mill never stopped grinding salt, Charity," Grandpa Rumpole said. "It's there at the bottom of the ocean to this day, grinding away. And that's why the sea is salt."

"Is that true, Grandpa?" Charity asked, leaning on Grandpa Rumpole's shoulder and looking out at the sea.

"Only in the Land of Nowhere," said Grandpa.

Damon and Pythias

adapted by Becky Davis   *illustrated by Preston Gravely*

Long ago two friends named Damon and Pythias lived in Syracuse, a city in Sicily ruled by a strong and cruel tyrant named Dionysius. Because they were good young men who loved truth, Damon and Pythias both chafed under the rule of Dionysius. In fact, one day Pythias spoke against King Dionysius in public.

When he heard of it, the king was furious. Immediately he ordered that Pythias be thrown into prison and sentenced to die in one month. And so it was.

When Pythias heard that he was to be executed in one month's time, he was brave enough to request an audience with the cruel king to make a request.

"O Dionysius," he said, "I realize that I am sentenced to death in one month. I beg, though, O King, that I may be granted leave to sail home to my parents to say good-bye to them one last time."

Dionysius threw back his head and laughed loud and long. "Young man, you are braver than any man I have ever seen." His face grew hard. "You are also more foolish. Only a very stupid ruler would allow a prisoner to leave at all. And you want to travel far away for an entire month! Back to the dungeon with you. There you will sit until the day of your death."

When Damon heard that Pythias had been denied his request, he too begged audience with the king.

"O Dionysius," he said, "I beg that you hear my petition. Let Pythias go to his home to say good-bye to his parents. I will stand in his place until then. If he has not returned by the day appointed for his execution, I will be executed for him."

For a moment Dionysius was speechless. "Now I have seen a man even more foolish than Pythias," he said. "Yes, I will grant your request. But I am sure that you will never see your friend again. In one month you will die."

"Pythias will return," Damon answered confidently. "He is a friend whom I trust in everything."

So Damon was cast into the dungeon and Pythias was allowed to go free. He boarded the ship and sailed far away to bid his parents good-bye. And day after weary day Damon sat in the dungeon, trusting his dear friend Pythias to return.

Finally, the day appointed for the execution arrived. Pythias had not returned, and Damon was summoned before the king. "Your friend has not returned!" Dionysius sneered. "What will you do now?"

"I am sure that he has been detained against his will," Damon replied stoutly. "He will come if he possibly can."

In the meantime, though," Dionysius shouted, "you will go to the executioner!"

But just as Damon was being led to the executioner, he heard a clatter of hoofs and a familiar voice.

"Stop! Stop!" It was Pythias! "My ship was detained in a storm," he panted.

"I have done all I can to arrive in time. Do not allow Damon to die in my stead. I have returned." And he ran to Damon to take his place.

King Dionysius watched in amazement. "Halt!" he demanded of the executioner. "These men must go free. They have been nobler than I." He covered his face with his hands and said, "I only wish that I could be worthy of such a friendship as the one that I see between Damon and Pythias."

LEGENDS

illustrated by Preston Gravely and Lynda Slattery

Damon and Pythias would have lived over two thousand years ago. Do you think their story is true? History does tell us that there was a tyrant named Dionysius who was harsh to his people. Dionysius, we know, exacted heavy taxes and believed in his own absolute power. But what about Damon and Pythias? Were they real?

Cicero, the famous Roman statesman, was one person who made the story of Damon and Pythias famous. It's likely that the two friends really existed, but different details of what really happened have been told and re-told so that you might hear several versions of their story with no two versions being exactly alike.

In another version of this story, Pythias arrived in Syracuse as a prisoner from a conquered land and was condemned to death by a whim of Dionysius.

Other people tell the story so that Pythias was a nobleman who took part in a plot to kill Dionysius and was caught. Stories that contain some truth and are passed down from generation to generation are called *legends*.

A legend can be almost completely accurate or almost all fiction. "Damon and Pythias" is close to being accurate, unlike the stories of Robin Hood, for instance. Although a real Robin Hood probably existed, storytellers and songwriters created most of his adventures for him in stories and in songs.

King Arthur is another example of a man who has become a part of legend. Historians think that Arthur was a successful general who lived in the sixth century. Yet we know him as a king and as the head of the Knights of the Round Table. If the legends are true, Arthur filled his days with jousts and tournaments, slew dragons all over England, and rescued fair maidens. What is more likely is that he spent his life fighting off invaders who wanted to conquer his land.

People enjoy legends because legends provide them with heroes.

Damon and Pythias symbolize friendship. Robin Hood was the symbol of what English farmers admired: generosity, courage, and wit. And King Arthur stands for true, unselfish kingliness as well as dignity and fearlessness.

Legends usually grow up around famous people. Think of the stories you have heard about George Washington and Abraham Lincoln. The story of Washington chopping down his father's cherry tree is a modern example of a legend. Even today people are passing down to their children the stories of great men and women.

SOME SPECIAL DAY

Marie C. Poley

illustrated by Preston Gravely

Searching

Jesse poked his digging stick a little farther into the dirt, wriggling it in circles as it went deeper. Again, nothing! He'd been searching most of the morning, getting his sneakers wet and his pants muddy to the knees, and still no arrowheads, not even a piece of flint. He rubbed a grimy fist across his hot face and wished for a drink. "Best be getting back," he said to himself.

He whistled for Rusty, the crossbreed farm dog that served as watchdog, hunting dog, and companion. His dad called him the "Heinz dog" after Heinz's 57 varieties. Jesse smiled and squinted toward the last place he had seen Rusty. Sure enough, down through the plowed field came his buddy with his pink tongue sliding out one side of his mouth. Rusty was covered with burrs and mud from his nose to his tail, even muddier than Jesse himself.

"You didn't find anything either, huh, Rusty?" asked Jesse. He knew the dog had been digging into groundhog holes all along the field near the fence. That was the best place to look for arrowheads!

Hunting arrowheads, flints, and other Indian relics was something Jesse had learned to enjoy while riding on the tractor as Dad did the farm work. A Pennsylvania farmer all his life, Jesse's dad had found many relics in the fields. He could spot them easily from the tractor while plowing, harrowing, or harvesting. Jesse's mom had arranged Dad's Indian relic collection on a piece of hunter green velvet. On snowy evenings one winter, Dad had built a glass-topped table for the collection, and it now sat in a place of honor near the fireplace where, when the fire was roaring, the pieces of quartz caught the light and shone like gems.

Jesse loved to scan the table, spying out his favorite pieces. He hoped he could someday collect enough of his own to display, but it was very hard to find an arrowhead that wasn't chipped or damaged. So far, he had seven arrowheads, five of pure white quartz and two black flint pieces. Only two of the quartz stones were whole, and one was worn so smooth that it was hard to tell whether it was a true arrowhead.

"Mom, I'm home!" Jesse called into the kitchen.

Mom was setting the table. She smiled at her son. "Any success with the great exploration?" she asked. "You were gone quite awhile today, and by the looks of you and Rusty, not too much dirt was left unturned."

Jesse grinned and put his arm around her while he helped himself to a piece of sliced carrot from the table. "I didn't find anything and neither did Rusty, but we're both hungry. What's for supper?"

"I made potato salad, and we'll cook pork chops on the grill," she replied. "We'll eat as soon as Dad comes in with the plow." No sooner had she spoken than they could hear the rumbling growl of the huge tractor and the clanking of the plow.

Jesse pushed open the screen door, leaped off the porch, and ran to his dad, who stopped the tractor long enough for Jesse to scramble onto the seat beside him. They rode the last few hundred feet together, with Rusty jumping and barking and biting at the big tires.

"Won't he ever learn?" Dad called good-naturedly above the roar of the tractor. He pulled to a stop and shut off the engine.

"He just wants to come too, Dad!" Jesse hollered, then realized that the great engine had been turned off. He laughed and lowered his voice. "Rusty gets jealous because I get to ride and he has to stay on the ground. Someday I'm going to give him a ride!"

"Well, that will be some special day when I let that Heinz dog ride on my tractor," Dad teased. "And it'll be some special day before I let you drive this tractor alone, Son." Jesse knew Dad was serious about that part.

He sighed. Other kids got to drive tractors for their dads. Jesse's father had done it himself as a boy—and had wrecked the family tractor by driving it over a riverbank. That was why he wouldn't let Jesse do it.

"Sorry, Son," he would say. "But it takes responsibility to drive a big, tough machine. You'll have to wait."

The Petermans enjoyed dinner and the cool evening together. Jesse recounted his adventures with Rusty and assured his dad that his chores were done. Then Dad read the Scripture, and each of them prayed in turn. By 9:30 they were all in bed; morning on the farm came early.

Jesse groaned and rolled over in bed. He had heard Mom calling his name and, as usual, stayed where he was until she sounded insistent. Knowing he had only a few minutes to get washed and dressed, he

finally hopped up, pushing Rusty off the bed.

"Are you ready for us to find our treasure today, boy?" he whispered to Rusty as he scratched the dog behind his ears. Rusty scurried toward the steps. Boy and dog bounded down the stairs in a mad race. As always, Rusty's feet hit the hall floor first and Jesse's hit a split second later.

"You win again, you 'woofy' dog." Jesse laughed. Rusty had won this game every morning since he was a puppy.

"Jesse, this morning you need to get the calves fed and watered and gather the eggs," Dad reminded him during their breakfast. "Mom said you missed a few of the eggs last time." He pushed back his plate and looked at Jesse. "Your hobby is great, Son, but remember that chores and time with the Lord come first. Concentrate on the important things as much as you do on your fun."

"Sure, Dad, but—" Jesse thought of how inviting the farm was. He wished Dad could see how wonderful it was to call his time his own, forget everything, and go roaming over the farm, looking for arrowheads.

"No excuses, Jesse. If you want to do things like run the tractor and help with the important work, you have to show me you're dependable. And that also means coming the first time your mother calls you in the morning."

Jesse looked down and nodded. He knew Dad was right. "Yes, sir."

Dad stood up, put his arms around Jesse's shoulders, and gave him a big bear hug. "Wanna' wrestle?"

"Yeah!" Jesse wriggled to get a grip on his dad's great forearms, and moments later the wrestling match was on in the living room.

About two hours later, Jesse had finished his chores and was following a small trail through the woods—one that he had read about in a book on historical Indian trails in Pennsylvania. All at once, Rusty began barking and crashing in the underbrush a few yards away.

That bark meant Rusty was on the trail of wildlife. Jesse scrambled toward the sounds.

"Get him, Rusty, get him!" he said even before he could see what Rusty had cornered. Then, as he crashed through the trees on the bank of the stream, his eyes opened wide. There on a stump just above the stream was the biggest raccoon he had ever seen. The angry animal was spitting and growling at Rusty, who kept bounding at the stump. The water swirled and foamed around some of the roots that were thrust out from the bank. The stream fell into a small pool before gradually winding through the woods.

Jesse knew that coons could be vicious when cornered, so he tried to pull Rusty away by his collar. "Not this time, boy," he murmured. But the dog, determined to finish off his prey, bounded back toward the coon. As Rusty landed on the stump, it gave way a little from the bank. Just then Jesse saw a glint of quartz at its base. A couple of arrowheads lay right in the hole that was laid bare. Jesse fell to his knees to grasp at the treasures, but just then the whole stump crashed into the water, taking the dog and most of the bank with it. Jesse's heart sank as the arrowheads fell into the water too. But a terrible yelp from Rusty made him leap to his feet. In the water, the big coon had clenched its teeth into the side of the dog's neck.

Both animals went underwater, thrashing wildly about. Jesse leaped into the stream. He started screaming and hitting the coon with his digging stick, trying to pull Rusty up at the same time. Dad had once said that a coon could drown a dog, even one as big as Rusty. The water was one of a coon's best defenses.

Jesse clenched his teeth and pounded the coon again. This time it let go, growling and showing its teeth, but just as the dog was gaining its footing, the coon flew at him. The dog yelped again and tried to turn to face the attack. But once more the coon's sharp teeth found their mark, this time on the dog's ear. The coon dragged Rusty underwater.

Trembling, Jesse scrambled into the current and lifted the largest rock he could find. Then he stumbled over to the struggling animals as they rolled near the surface. It was all Jesse could do to stand up straight and land the rock squarely on the coon's back. But the big coon just shook itself and went down on Rusty's head again. Jesse hefted another rock.

The dog wasn't fighting now; he was crying. Jesse hit the coon again, this time on the head. The stunned coon rolled downstream with the current. Jesse summoned all his strength to pull Rusty from the stream.

As he stumbled up the bank, Jesse desperately prayed that Rusty would be all right. He wasn't sure the dog was even alive. Blood and water oozed off Rusty's head and neck, and when Jesse set him down, he didn't move at all.

Jesse crumpled to the ground and cradled Rusty's head in his lap, murmuring and stroking him gently. Rusty stirred then but had no more strength to move.

Jesse knew he had to get help quickly. He took off his shirt, spread it on the ground, and gently laid Rusty on it. Then he grabbed both sleeves and, trying not to hurt the dog, pulled him up the trail toward the open field.

A Place of Honor

In the cleared field, Jesse spotted his dad on the moving tractor in a cloud of dust. He left Rusty where he lay and ran as fast as he could over the uneven ground. Once he fell and, gritting his teeth against the pain in his knees, scrambled to his feet and ran on.

Dad saw Jesse coming and slowed the tractor to a halt. He switched it off.

"Dad," Jesse called, "Rusty's hurt real bad—he tangled with a coon. I'm not sure if he's going to live. Help me, Dad, please!" He clambered up onto the seat with his father. Dad switched on the engine again, and the big tractor rumbled down to the woods.

Dad's face was strained as he looked at the injured dog. "Son,

you'll have to drive the tractor while I hold Rusty. He's too heavy for you to keep hold of while you try to keep yourself on," Dad said. "Think you can do it?"

Jesse swallowed hard. "I'll drive slow enough so it won't hurt Rusty," he said, hoping his dad would advise him.

"Right. Nice and easy, Son, over the smooth ground, but take the bumps slow."

Together they positioned Rusty on the tractor and Dad held him securely. Jesse climbed up onto the high, hard seat. He cautiously pulled the throttle down a notch.

Jesse pressed the clutch, and the big giant lumbered across the field. He wanted to glance back and see how Rusty was, but he decided not to risk taking his eyes off the route in front of him. He drove up the wide path, trying to keep the tractor from bumping too much.

Mom ran out to meet them. Using all his strength, Jesse pushed down slowly on the brake to avoid a jerking stop. Quickly he hit the clutch to disengage the engine and switched the tractor off. All three worked together to lower the dog to the ground. "Kate," Dad said, "call the vet and tell him we're bringing in a badly injured dog. I'll get the truck."

In twenty minutes that seemed like forever to Jesse, the three of them were pulling into the veterinarian's drive. An assistant came out to take Rusty. Dr. Bradley, the vet, told them to stay in the waiting room as he examined the dog. In a few minutes he came out.

"Well?" Jesse asked anxiously.

"Coons shouldn't be out in the day. It's a good thing Rusty's current in his vaccination," the vet said. "Plenty of stitches, and it's still hard to tell how all that water's going to affect his lungs. But he's strong and healthy; he's got a good chance to recover. I can give you a better answer tonight."

In the pickup on the way home, Jesse gave his dad an account of the episode at the stream. When he came to the part about the stump's breaking off into the stream, he remembered the arrowheads that were lost.

"They were beauties, Dad. But I don't even care about them now. I won't care if I never find another arrowhead as long as Rusty will be all right." Jesse glanced at his dad with sadness in his eyes. "Do you think he'll be all right, Dad?"

"I don't know, Son. We'll have to leave it in the Lord's hands."

After they got home, Dad pointed to the tractor. "You want to take it to the barn, Jesse?" He held out the keys.

Jesse shook his head. "No." He looked away, and Dad slowly put the keys in his pocket. Jesse felt his father's eyes on him.

"Why not, Jesse?"

"It scared me up there. I knew I had to be careful for you and Rusty and keep going, but you were right. I'm not old enough."

Dad smiled. "You felt responsible," he said. "And that means you are." He pulled the keys out again and held them in front of Jesse in his big hard palm. "You're right—it's no joke to drive a tractor. But just tell the Lord you're scared, and ask Him to guide you. Pretty soon you'll see how much you've depended on Him all along, and you won't be scared anymore. That's what it is to do the Lord's will, Son—depending on Him for everything and trusting Him." He hesitated, then asked again, "Won't you take the keys, Son?"

Jesse looked up. This time he nodded. "I guess I will." And he took them.

Dad put a hand on Jesse's shoulder. "Jesse," he said, "part of growing up is learning new things—and part is losing old things, hard as that is." He was looking at Rusty's food dish over on the porch steps. Jesse swallowed and nodded.

Dad patted him soundly. "Go on now. You park that thing and come inside."

The veterinarian called that night while Jesse was helping Mom with the dishes. Dad talked to him. Jesse stood by, forgetting the dish in his hand.

Dad hung up and smiled. "Rusty's come through the worst of it, and the vet expects him to make

it. We can probably bring him home at the end of the week."

Mom gave Jesse a hug. "Thank the Lord. Rusty's been a good dog. Pretty soon everything will be just the same again," she said.

"I wonder," Dad said. He winked at Jesse, who smiled for the first time since that morning.

For the next few days, Jesse stayed around the farm, played some ball with the neighbor boys, and waited for Rusty's return. Several times he went down to the field with his Dad to watch the planting, or he scouted out new places where the chickens were hiding their eggs. He was even on time for breakfast.

When Dad came in for dinner one night, he pulled out a soiled handkerchief and laid it near Jesse's plate. "I finished up in the

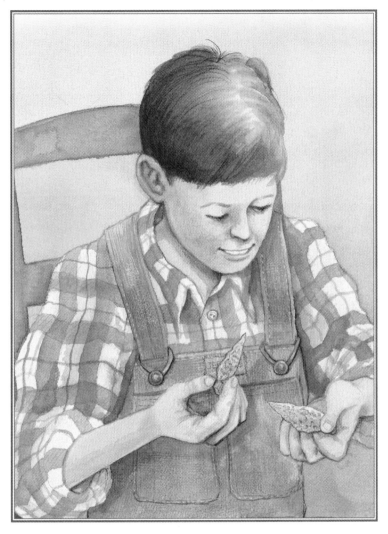

finger around the smooth edges. "It's one of the arrowheads from under the stump, isn't it? Thanks, Dad," he managed to get out. "It's the best one I've ever seen."

Dad put his arm around his son's shoulder and hugged Mom with the other arm.

Jesse set the arrowhead aside. "You know, nothing's been just the same since Rusty got hurt. I guess I've learned a little more about what's most important."

Mom smiled. "Dad always said it would be some special day when you drove the tractor—and he was right."

Dad set the arrowhead on the kitchen counter. "I'll put that in the case tomorrow after I bring Rusty home."

"I'll help," Jesse offered. He grinned at his dad. "Can I go park the tractor?"

river field today. Here's something I found. It was just downstream from where that raccoon fought with Rusty. It's for you, Jesse."

He smiled at Mom as Jesse opened the cloth. Inside the dusty white folds lay a beautiful—and yes, perfect—arrowhead. Jesse gasped. He picked it up and ran his

Snowflakes

David McCord

illustrated by Debbie King

Sometime this winter if you go
To walk in soft new-falling snow
When flakes are big and come down slow

To settle on your sleeve as bright
As stars that couldn't wait for night,
You wouldn't know what you have in sight—

Another world—unless you bring
A magnifying glass. This thing
We call a snowflake is the king

Of crystals. Do you like surprise?
Examine him three times his size:
At first you won't believe your eyes.

Stars look alike, but flakes do not:
No two the same in all the lot
That you will get in any spot

You chance to be, for every one
Come spinning through the sky has none
But his own window-wings of sun:

Joints, points, and crosses. What could make
Such lacework with no crack or break?
In billion billions, no mistake?

Venture to Mierow Lake

From Mik-Shrok *by Gloria Repp*

illustrated by Jim Brooks

Steve and Liz Bailey are missionaries who have just started working in Koyalik, a small Eskimo village on the coast of Alaska. The time is 1950: these Eskimos cannot read or write, they must hunt for meat in order to stay alive, and they do not own snowmobiles. They welcome white people and are curious about their ways.

Steve has found a helper and friend in Victor, a young Eskimo who speaks a little English. Victor interprets whenever Steve wants to talk to the Eskimos, and he allows Steve and Liz to have church services in his home.

As the story opens, Steve has learned that another village, located far inland at Mierow Lake, is open to hearing about the gospel, and he has been praying for an opportunity to visit. But it is midwinter, and he knows that taking such a long and dangerous trip without an experienced companion would surely end in disaster.

So Far, So Good

On Sunday, three families came to the meeting at Victor's house. There were several babies and young children who made the usual noises, but their mothers tended to them, and no one seemed distracted.

The Eskimos listened carefully, first to Steve as he told a Bible story in English, and then to Victor, who translated the story into Eskimo.

Victor must be doing a good job, Steve thought. People nodded or smiled or looked serious in all the right places.

Victor's wife, Nida, invited Steve and Liz to come back that

Venture to Mierow Lake 233

evening. Liz baked a cake, and Steve brought along their note-books, hoping to pick up some useful Eskimo expressions. He still found it hard to unscramble the long Eskimo words.

That evening, Victor told one hunting tale after another in his broken English. As he listened, Steve couldn't help thinking again that Victor would be the perfect person to guide him to Mierow Lake. He'd already asked him to go, but the young Eskimo always had something more important to do.

Suddenly, to Steve's delight, Victor began talking about the trip to Mierow Lake as if it would be a great adventure. "First thing, we ask Gus. That old trader, he know where to go."

Victor's eyes twinkled. "Your dogs good and strong now?" he asked. "Need to be strong this trip."

"Getting stronger every time I take them out. Now they last longer than I do."

"How about your new dog? That *mik-shrok?*"

"Oh, Mikki? He's grown a lot. Of course, he gets special food." Steve smiled at Liz. "But he's worth it." Then Steve told Victor how he'd been trying out different leaders and how Mikki had won the fight with Bandit.

"That dog, he pull with heart," said Victor. "And he . . . what you call him? Smart cake?"

Liz giggled, then she put a hand over her mouth. Steve nodded. "Smart cookie. Yes, he sure is. I think I'll keep him as leader. The Lord sent us a good dog."

"Nida," Liz said, "we don't want to leave you here alone. Could you come too?"

Nida smiled and shook her head. Victor answered for her. "Nida take boys and go visit sister in Nome. She stay for a week or little bit longer. May be I bring her nice fox skin. May be we get a caribou." His eyes gleamed. "Gus say caribou run by Mierow Lake. We go soon; how about Wednesday?"

On Monday, Steve made sure he talked to each person who had ever come to a Sunday service or to Liz's story time. He tried to explain where they would be going and why they'd be away for a week or more.

That night he and Liz talked about the visits they had made. "I don't want them to think I'm just off on a hunting trip with Victor," he said. "But I'm not sure they understood me. I don't think any of them are true Christians, either."

"They're so friendly," said Liz. "They want to be nice, and they smile and agree with everything you say. The children are well behaved and amazingly polite. I wish we could figure out what they're really thinking."

"That's one reason we've got to learn Eskimo," said Steve. "Be sure to pack our notebooks. And by the way, do you know how to make bannock?"

"No," said Liz. "What's that?"

"A kind of crisp biscuit that's good to take on trips. You mix flour, lard, salt, baking powder, and water to make a stiff dough, then you fry it."

Steve consulted with Gus, the owner of the trading post, to make sure they'd be prepared for the worst weather.

"You and Victor will need to shoot some game along the way," said Gus. "But if you have to wait out a blizzard, you'll want something to keep you alive." He scratched the bald spot on top of his head. "Remember that the dogs will need plenty to eat. Most of the time they'll hunt on their own, but take along some dried salmon too."

Steve listened carefully, then he bought a small sturdy tent, a camping stove, some bales of dried salmon, and plenty of dried food such as beans and oatmeal.

When he packed the sled, he first spread out a heavy canvas tarp to line it. On the tarp he piled the bales of dried salmon and all their supplies. Then he pulled the tarp up and around and tied it snugly in place. On top, tucked under the ropes, went the ax, the guns, their snowshoes, and the big iron skillet.

He handed Liz a canvas bag. "We'll hang this below the handlebars."

"What's it for?"

"My hunting knife, the dog chains, maybe some extra rawhide. Better put in that extra waterproof match safe too."

"How about some chocolate and a few pieces of bannock?"

"Good idea!"

They left long before daybreak and drove for hours under bright moonlight. Steve felt as if they were traveling in another world—a frozen world of white and silver and shadowed black.

Liz rode on the sled for a long time, then she jumped off, saying she was cold. "I'll run with the dogs for a while," she said. "I'll tell Mikki to do me proud."

Victor must have heard her remark, for he called to Steve, "What's that—*do me proud?*"

"She wants Mikki to do such a good job that she'll be proud of him." He glanced at the dog. Mikki seemed to be pulling for the sheer joy of it, his floppy ear standing straight up in the wind. "So far, so good."

Victor grunted in agreement, and as they drove on, Steve heard him muttering, "So far, so good."

The first stretch of the river was familiar because of Steve's short trips inland. Late that morning, the sun rose slowly in a glow of pink, and in just a few hours, it began to set again. But they pushed on in the dusky light and finally reached the landmark known as Tall Rocks.

Huge icy boulders marked the fork of the river Gus had said to

watch for. Behind the boulders rose the towering cliffs that had given the place its name.

Victor nodded toward the cliffs. "Rabbits in there."

They unloaded the sleds quickly and set up the tents. Then Steve and Victor grabbed their rifles. "I'll start a fire and get things ready," Liz said. "Good hunting!"

Back behind a clump of alders, Steve shot a snowshoe rabbit, and then Victor got one too. They crept through a snow-covered willow thicket and shot four more. "Dogs can hunt here too," said Victor.

After they returned to camp, Steve and Victor unharnessed the dogs and sent them to forage for their supper. One by one, the dogs came back to the fire, and Steve chained them close by. They curled up and watched the preparations for supper, looking contented.

The fragrance of wood smoke and sizzling meat reminded Steve of other winter camp-outs when he'd been a boy. But those trips had been just for fun—what a difference tonight!

He and Victor cut spruce boughs to use as cushions under the sleeping bags, and they all slept soundly.

Will They Listen?

On the second day, the river wound through a long rocky canyon, then opened out into a broad valley edged by mountains. When they stopped for the night, there were no sheltering rocks, but Victor knew what to do.

After the tents were up, he cut snow blocks and piled them around the base of each tent to keep out the wind. They didn't see any game, so they fried the rabbits they'd shot the night before and threw the bones to the dogs.

That night, Steve had hardly enough energy to feed the dogs and climb into his sleeping bag. If he was so tired, what must Liz be feeling? She hadn't said a word of complaint. But she'd been quick to accept the seal oil Victor offered for her windburned face. And she had fallen asleep before he blew out the candle.

For a long while he listened to an owl hooting deep in the forest. What would the people at Mierow Lake be like, he wondered. Lord, help me to tell them about You, somehow. And Victor needs You too . . .

After several hours of travel the next morning, they left the river at the pile of red-streaked rocks Gus had described and turned onto a dogsled trail. Gus had said the shortcut would save a whole day's travel. The trail climbed up into the mountains through a forest of tall spruce trees. The grade was so steep that it was hard to keep the sleds upright, but the dogs pulled steadily onward.

Canada jays flitted through the trees, and chickadees called from every side. Liz pointed out the birds she knew and asked Victor about the others, but he wasn't sure of their English names.

Once Steve's team lurched forward in a sudden burst of speed, and the sled rocked dangerously on the narrow trail. Steve shouted to Mikki, and the dog slowed obediently to his usual trot.

Victor chuckled and pointed to tracks in the snow. "We cross rabbit trail. Dogs think it supper time."

By late afternoon they had climbed to the top of an especially high ridge, so they stopped for a rest. The sinking sun had turned the sky, clouds, and mountain peaks to gold. Below them spread a long valley, also touched with gold.

"Look!" exclaimed Liz. She waved at a flat, snow-covered expanse edged by rows of cabins.

"Victor, do you think that's Mierow Lake?"

"Looks like." He grinned. "So far, so good."

The dogs must have sensed the end of the trip, for they raced down the mountainside, and Steve had to jump on both runners to keep the sled on the trail. As they drew closer to the village, he counted the cabins. More than Koyalik. Looked deserted, though. Where had everybody gone?

Halfway through the village, they saw an old woman carrying a bucket. Victor spoke to her briefly. "Caribou hunt," he told Steve. "Men come back tomorrow, may be."

"Ask her if there's any place we could stay," said Steve.

Victor discussed Steve's question with the woman for a long time. Steve caught a word here and there that he recognized, but he couldn't make sense of anything they said. An icy wind rose and seemed to blow right through him. The dogs drooped in their harnesses, waiting.

Finally, Victor turned back to them. "There is house at end of village. Nobody live there. Very old."

"I don't mind," said Steve, "as long as it has a roof and walls."

Victor spoke to his dogs, and they plodded slowly through the village. Steve's team followed to where a cabin stood close to the frozen lake.

More like a hut, Steve thought. It's plenty small. But it does have a roof.

The door hung off its hinges, and he pulled it open cautiously. Someone had once used the cabin for storage, judging by the dusty shelves and rows of nails in the log

walls. The window had no glass in it. The dirt floor was littered with rubbish. And dogs had been kept in here.

Liz took a step backward. She looked up at Steve, and he put an arm around her. "It's just for a few days. We can clean it up."

Victor helped them shovel out the rubbish, and at bedtime that night, Steve whispered to Liz, "Even without a stove, it's better than sleeping in a tent."

She nodded, yawned, and a minute later fell asleep. He lay awake for a while longer.

Cold air crept past the paper he had tacked over the window, and he pulled the sleeping bag more snugly around his shoulders.

God had brought them safely to Mierow Lake; he was thankful for that. But he didn't know these people, and it probably had been a long time since they had seen a white man. Would they even listen to his message?

I guess I'll just have to wait, he thought. Until tomorrow.

The hunters returned the next day in high spirits. They had shot several caribou, and everyone in the village would get a share. Perhaps no one would starve this winter.

After the feast that evening, Steve tried speaking to a group of the men. Most of them understood English, and they listened carefully.

He started by introducing himself and Liz and Victor, and he told them a little about the work in Koyalik. When they nodded and smiled, Steve breathed a little more easily.

Then he showed them one of Liz's Bible storybooks and told the story of David as a young boy.

The pictures must have looked strange to them, Steve thought—all those people with white faces wearing brightly colored long clothes. And which of the Eskimos had ever seen a lion? But they leaned forward eagerly to see, and they exclaimed at the picture of David killing a bear.

Afterwards, Steve said to Liz, "This is so different from Koyalik. I can answer their questions by myself! I've been trying out a little Eskimo on them too, and they're helping me learn."

Steve preached twice on the second day, and he and Liz spent all their spare time visiting with the people. Steve had hoped that Victor would come with them, even though he wasn't needed to translate, but after a few visits,

Victor grew restless. Finally, he went off in the afternoon and shot a caribou and a wolf, and he came back smiling.

The third day, the day they had to leave, came much too quickly.

One of the young men said, "The book with pictures. Can you let us have it a little while? Then you come back and get it?"

Steve felt like shouting for joy. Several of the young couples could read English, so even though he and Liz couldn't stay, God might use the book to teach them about Himself.

He smiled at the friendly, fur-ruffed faces that surrounded him and spoke his confidence aloud. "Yes! God will bring us back."

Vasko's Christmas Rescue

Dawn L. Watkins
illustrated by Paula Cheadle

Something Warm

If it had not been December, Vasko might have given up hope. He huddled in a corner where two old buildings met and tried to think of something warm. He had not eaten since the morning before—a piece of dark bread no bigger than his hand—but today he was sure that something would happen. It was nearly Christmas, and Christmas was hope.

A shiver ran over him. *That's good,* he thought. *If I am shivering, I'm still warm inside.* His grandmother had told him stories about his father, a sailor, and his father's father, a ship's captain. They braved many winter storms at sea, where icy waves ripped over the decks, drenching every sailor. His grandmother had made her voice deep and repeated his grandfather's words: "We were all of us chilled to the marrow, but if we could shiver, we knew we were still alive."

"I'm alive," Vasko said to the wind. And he shivered again. *Think of something warm,* he reminded himself.

"Boy!" said a voice beside him.

Vasko looked up. A man glowered down at him.

"This is my property," the man said. "Get out of here."

"Couldn't I just stay here the night?" Vasko asked. "I won't hurt anything, yes?"

"Cur boy! Get out, I say!" The man lunged at him, and Vasko sprang away like a rabbit into the deeper snow. "And don't be slinkin' back here neither!"

Vasko floundered through the drift at the far end of the building and into the street in front. A carriage thundered past, snow spraying up from the wheels and the horses' hooves. The harness jingled and a girl's laughter skittered over him from inside the black depths of the carriage.

Vasko tried to imagine what it was like inside the cab. The girl was probably his own age and dressed in a velvet coat with white

242

fur at the neck. She surely carried a white muff. Her father would be throwing the lap robe over her legs and telling her that soon they would be home.

He even imagined a stack of boxes beside her, each one filled with some fine food he had seen in shop windows and occasionally found in bins behind the grand inn at the town center. He thought her cheeks would be rosy, and her nose might be cold, but not her toes or her fingers.

He thought her father would be tall, maybe an officer. Vasko could barely remember his grandmother and grandfather now, but he knew that once he had been cared for.

The carriage made the end of the street and turned the corner. Vasko wished for the briefest of seconds that he could be in such a carriage and have someone to care if he were cold or tired. *If only my captain grandfather were here—he would see to me.*

"Vasko," he said to himself, "think of something *warm,* not about cabs that are not for you." He made himself walk with a purpose. Too many times in too many towns he had been shouted at for standing in front of a store, for scaring off his betters from coming in to make purchases.

At the next alley, Vasko spied an empty barrel on its side. Quicker than a blink, he was in it, out of the wind. Fish. The barrel had contained pickled herring or maybe menhaden. His stomach growled, and this time he could not ignore the hunger eating at his insides.

He began to feel the cold in his marrow too. The bells of the church rang out the hour—one, two, three, four. Four o'clock in the afternoon. Dusk was the worst part of the day, the hardest part to keep heart in.

Suddenly the barrel went right-side up. Vasko tumbled around, knees over nose. He scrambled to stand up and defend his new home. He got his hand on the lip of the barrel and struggled to his feet.

A man in a wool cap jumped back. "What's this?"

Vasko looked the man right in the eye. "Is this your barrel?"

"Yes, boy, it is. What might you be doing in it?"

"Taking up housekeeping, I am."

The man laughed a great burst of a laugh and bent forward with his hands on his knees. "Well, I never!" And then in a swift movement, he grabbed Vasko by the shoulders and popped him out of

"What you got there, Cappy?" said one.

"A pickled herring," said the man. "Or rather—a *frozen* herring." He pushed slow down than he could disappear. He tipped the bowl all the way up, drained it, and licked the rim.

The heat of the fire seeped in from the outside and the warmth of the broth filled him from the inside. And when the two met, he felt suddenly overwhelmingly sleepy.

He lowered himself to the hearthstones—knees, hands, a shoulder—and he was asleep.

Vasko's Christmas Rescue 245

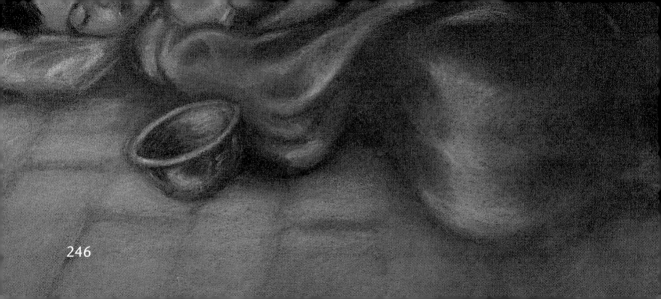

The Best of All Mornings

He woke up in a bundle of blankets. The fire was still going. He looked around.

"Well, there he is," said the man who had hauled him in out of the snow. Somehow he did not look as big to Vasko as he had outside in the alley.

"Is it morning?"

"Indeed. And night. And morning again." The man smiled. "The best of all mornings! It's Christmas!"

Vasko sat up. "Christmas!"

The man handed him a piece of soft bread and a handleless cup with milk. "Merry Christmas to you."

Vasko at last remembered his manners. "Thank you. And thank you for supper—whenever that was."

The man nodded. "What's your name?"

"Vasko." He noticed for the first time the brass buttons on the man's coat. "Are you a ship's captain?"

"I am. I've been a sailor since I was no bigger than you. And a captain for years and years. But just this winter I felt I should come in to land. And now I see why."

"Why?"

"To rescue you."

Vasko was sure he was joking, but Cappy just looked steadily at him. The fire crackled.

"Why?"

"Because a long, long time ago, someone rescued me."

Vasko could not imagine this hale man with brass upon him needing to be rescued. And for a third time, he said, "Why?"

The man leaned back and smiled. "Because I was in need. Like you."

Vasko felt a little prick of pride. He was able to take care of himself. Hadn't he done so for years now?

"I know what you're thinking," Cappy said, and Vasko jumped. "I was proud once myself. But when you get past that, you can be rescued. The man who found me—though not in a barrel, mind you—taught me that. And how to sail and how to be a captain."

Vasko finished the bread and stared into his cup.

The captain said, "You like ships?"

"My grandfather was a ship's captain," said Vasko. "He died when I was very small. My father, too, in a storm."

"Ah. The sea is the sea, is she not? I'm sorry." Vasko said

nothing. "So you would have salt in your blood then, I guess."

Vasko looked up and smiled a small smile. His grandmother used to say that about his grandfather—and he was not displeased to hear it said of himself.

"My grandfather was captain of the *Midnight Sun,* the finest ship on open water."

The captain looked at him so directly that Vasko set his cup down and slid back a bit on the hearth. "I-I'm sure your ship is fine, too, sir. I meant no disrespect."

Cappy broke into a smile. "None taken." Still he looked curiously at Vasko. "It's Christmas, Vasko. What did you wish for?"

"Nothing. Really. I am just glad to be warm and full."

"Nothing?"

Vasko hesitated. "Well, I did wish my captain grandfather were here to see to me."

Cappy came to sit on the hearth. "I have a Christmas gift for you, Vasko." Vasko tilted his head. "Was your grandfather's name . . . Antonin?"

"Yes! My middle name is Antonin, after him. How did you know?"

"It would appear, my boy, that your grandfather rescued you as well as me, when he took me aboard the *Midnight Sun* some forty years ago this very day."

In that instant Vasko knew he would never again have to try to think of something warm. His grandfather had seen to that.

4

CREATURES GREAT and SMALL

Mijbil—Iraq to London

from The Otter's Tale
by Gavin Maxwell

illustrated by Sam Laterza

Simply Aloof

Mijbil's story begins where the Tigris joins the Euphrates. A few years ago I traveled with Wilfred Thesiger, the explorer, to spend two months or so among the Marsh Arabs who live there. It had crossed my mind that I should like to keep an otter. I had mentioned this to Wilfred soon after the start of our journey, and he had replied that I had better get one in the Tigris marshes before I came home, for there they were as common as mosquitoes, and were often tamed by the Arabs.

I returned to the Consulate General, where I was living, late in the afternoon, having been out for several hours, to find that my mail had arrived. I carried it to my bedroom to read, and there squatting on the floor were two Marsh Arabs; beside them lay a sack that squirmed from time to time.

With the opening of that sack began a phase of my life that has not yet ended, and may, for all I know, not end before I do, because I can't any longer imagine being without an otter in the household.

The creature that emerged from this sack onto the tiled floor of the Consulate bedroom did not at that moment look like anything so much as a very small dragon. From the head to the tail he was coated with pointed scales of mud armor between whose tips you could see a soft velvet fur like that of a chocolate-brown mole. He shook himself, and I half expected a cloud of dust, but the mud stayed where it was, and in fact, it was not for another month that I managed to remove the last of it and see him, so to speak, in his true colors.

For the first twenty-four hours Mijbil was neither friendly nor unfriendly; he was simply aloof and indifferent, choosing to sleep on the floor as far from my bed as possible, and to accept food and water as though they were things that had appeared before him without human help. He ate small reddish fish from the Tigris, holding them upright between his forepaws, tail end uppermost, and eating them, always with five crunches of the left-hand side of the jaw alternating with five crunches on the right.

The second night Mijbil came on to my bed in the small hours and remained asleep in the crook of my knees until the servant brought tea in the morning, and during that day he began to lose his sulks and take a keen, much too keen, interest in his surroundings. I made a collar, or rather a body belt, for him and took him on a lead to the bathroom, where for half an hour he went wild with joy in the water, plunging and rolling in it, shooting up and down the length of the bath underwater, and making enough slosh and splash for a hippo. This, I was to learn, is what otters do; every drop of water must be spread about the place; a bowl must at once be upset, or, if it will not overturn, be sat in and splashed in until it overflows. Water must be kept on the move and made to do things.

It was only two days later that he escaped from my bedroom as I entered it, and I turned to see his tail disappearing around the bend of the corridor that led to the bathroom. By the time I had caught up with him, he was up on the end of the bath and fumbling at the chromium taps with his paws. I watched, amazed; in less than a minute he had turned the tap far enough to produce a dribble of water, and, after a moment or two, the full flow. (He had, in fact, been lucky to turn the tap the right way; later he would as often as not try with great violence to screw it up still tighter, chittering with annoyance and disappointment at his failure.)

After a few days he would follow me without a lead and come to me when I called his name. By the end of a week he had accepted me completely, and then he began to play. Very few species of animals play much after they are grown up; but otters are one of the exceptions to this rule; right through their lives they spend much of their time in play that does not even need a partner. In the wild state they will play alone for hours with some floating object in the water, pulling it down to let it bob up again, or throwing it with a jerk of the head so that it lands with a splash and becomes something to be chased. No doubt in their holts they lie on their backs and play too, as my otters have, with small objects that they can roll between their paws and pass from palm to palm, for at Camusfeàrna all the sea holts contain small shells and round stones that can only have been carried in for toys.

Mij would spend hours shuffling a rubber ball around the room like a four-footed soccer player using all four feet to dribble the ball, and he could also throw it, with a powerful flick of the neck, to a surprising height and distance. These games he would play either by himself or with me, but the really steady play of an otter, the time-filling play born of a sense of well-being and a full stomach, seems to be when the otter lies on its back and juggles small objects between its paws. Marbles became Mij's favorite toys for this pastime, and he would lie on his back rolling two or more of them up and down his wide, flat belly without ever dropping one to the floor or, with forepaws upstretched, rolling them between his palms for minutes on end.

Even during those first two weeks in Basra I learned a lot of Mij's language. The sounds are widely different in range. The simplest is the call note, which has been much the same in all the otters I have come across; it is a short, anxious mixture between a whistle and a chirp, and it can be heard for a long way. There is also a query, used at closer quarters; Mij would enter a room, for instance, and ask whether there was anyone in it by the word "Ha!" in a loud, harsh whisper. But it was the chirp, high or low, from a single note to a continuous flow of chitter, that was Mij's main means of talk.

An otter's jaws are, of course, very strong, and those jaws have teeth meant to crunch into pulp fish heads that seem as hard as stone. Like a puppy that nibbles and gnaws one's hands, otters seem to find the use of their mouths the most natural thing; knowing as I do their enormous crushing power, I can see how hard my otters have tried to be gentle in play, but perhaps they think a human skin is as thick as an otter's. Mij used to look hurt and surprised when scolded for what must have seemed to him real gentleness, and though after a time he learned to be softmouthed with me, he remained all his life somewhat over-excitably good-humored with strangers.

The days passed peacefully at Basra, but I dreaded the prospect of transporting Mij to England. The airline insisted that Mij should be packed into a box of not more than eighteen inches square and that this box must be carried on the floor at my feet.

The box was delivered on the afternoon before my departure on a 9:15 P.M. flight. It was zinc lined, and it seemed to me as nearly ideal as could be.

Dinner was at eight, and I thought that it would be as well to put Mij into the box an hour before we left, so that he would become accustomed to it before the jolting of the journey began to upset him. I got him into it, not without difficulty, and he seemed peaceful when I left him in the dark for a hurried meal.

But when I came back, with only barely time for the Consulate car to reach the airport for flight, I saw an awful sight. There was complete silence from inside the box, but from its air holes and the chinks around the hinged lid blood had trickled and dried on the white wood. I whipped off the padlock and tore open the lid, and Mij, exhausted and blood-spattered, whimpered and tried to climb up my leg. He had torn the zinc lining to shreds, scratching his mouth, his nose, and his paws, and had left it jutting in spiky ribbons all around the walls and the floor of the box. When I had removed the last of it, so that there were no cutting edges left, it was just ten minutes until the time of the flight, and the airport was five miles distant. It was hard to bring myself to put the miserable Mij back into that box, that now seemed to him a torture chamber, but I forced myself to do it, slamming the lid down on my fingers as I closed it before he could make his escape. Then began a journey the like of which I hope I shall never know again.

Otter Frenzy

I sat in the back of the car with the box beside me as the Arab driver tore through the streets of Basra like a bullet. Donkeys reared, bicycles swerved wildly, out in the suburbs goats stampeded, and poultry found unguessed powers of flight. Mij cried in the box, and both of us were hurled to and fro and up and down. Exactly as

256

we drew to a screeching stop before the airport entrance, I heard a splintering sound from the box beside me, and saw Mij's nose force up the lid. He had summoned all the strength in his small body and torn one of the hinges clean out of the wood.

The aircraft was waiting to take off; as I was rushed through the customs by infuriated officials, I was trying all the time to hold down the lid of the box with one hand, and with the other to force back the screws into the splintered wood.

The seat booked for me was at the extreme front of the aircraft, so that I had a bulkhead before me instead of another seat.

The port engines roared, and then the starboard, and the aircraft trembled and teetered against the tug of her propellers, and then we were taxiing out to take off. Ten minutes later we were flying westward over the great marshes that had been Mij's home, and peering downward into the dark I could see the glint of their waters beneath the moon.

I had brought a briefcase full of old newspapers and a parcel of fish, and with these scant resources I prepared myself to withstand a siege. I unlocked the padlock and opened the lid, and Mij was out like a flash. He dodged my fumbling hands with an eel-like wriggle and disappeared at high speed down the aircraft. As I tried to get into the gangway I could follow his progress among the passengers by a wave of disturbance among them not unlike that caused by the passage of a weasel through a hen run. There were squawks and shrieks and a flapping of traveling coats, and halfway down the fuselage a woman stood up on her seat screaming out, "A rat! A rat!"

I ran down the gangway and, catching sight of Mij's tail disappearing beneath the legs of a portly white-turbaned Indian, I tried a flying tackle, landing flat on my face. I missed Mij's tail, but found myself grasping the sandaled foot of the Indian's companion; furthermore, my face was inexplicably covered in curry. I staggered up babbling apology, and the Indian gave me a long, silent stare. I was, however, glad to see that something, possibly the curry, had won over my fellow passengers, and that they were regarding me now as a harmless clown rather than as a dangerous lunatic. The stewardess stepped into the breach.

"Perhaps," she said with the most charming smile, "it would be better if you resumed your seat, and I will find the animal and bring it to you." I explained that Mij, being lost and frightened, might bite a stranger, but she did not think so. I returned to my seat.

I heard the ripple of flight and pursuit passing up and down the body of the aircraft behind me, but I could see little. I was craning my neck back over the seat trying to follow the hunt when suddenly I heard from my feet a distressed chitter of recognition and welcome, and Mij bounded onto my knee and began to nuzzle my face and neck. In all the strange world of the aircraft I was the only familiar thing to be found, and in that first return to me was sown the seed of the absolute trust he gave me for the rest of his life.

Otters are extremely bad at doing nothing. That is to say that they cannot, as a dog does, lie still and awake; they are either asleep or entirely absorbed in play. If there is no toy, or if they are bored, they will set about laying the land waste. There is, I am convinced, something positively provoking to an otter about order and tidiness in any form; and the greater the un-tidiness that they can make, the more contented they feel. A room does not seem right to them until they have turned everything upside down; cushions must be thrown to the floor from sofas, books pulled out of bookcases, wastepaper basket overturned, and the rubbish spread as widely as possible, drawers opened, and contents shoveled out and scattered. An otter must find out everything and have a hand in everything; but most of all he must know what lies inside any man-made container or beyond any man-made obstruction.

We had been flying for perhaps five hours, when one of these moods descended upon Mijbil. It opened fairly harmlessly, with an attack upon the newspapers spread carefully around my feet, and in a minute or two the place looked like a street upon which royalty has been given a tickertape welcome. Then he turned his attention to the box, where his sleeping compartment was filled with fine wood shavings. First he put his head and shoulders in and began to throw these out backward at enormous speed; then he got in bodily and lay on his back, using all four feet in a pedaling motion to hoist out the rest. I was doing my best to cope with the litter, but I was hopelessly behind in the race when

he turned his attention to my neighbor's canvas TWA travel bag on the floor beside him. The zipper gave him pause for no more than seconds; by chance, probably, he yanked it back and was in head first throwing out magazines, handkerchiefs, gloves, bottles of pills and tins of ear plugs. My neighbor was asleep; I managed, unobserved, to haul Mij out by the tail and cram the things back.

My troubles really began at Paris, a long time later. Mij had slept from time to time, but I had not closed an eye, and it was by now more than thirty-six hours since I had even dozed. I had to change airports, and since I knew that Mij could slip his body strap with the least struggle, there was nothing else to do but put him back in his box. In its present form, however, the box was useless, for one hinge was dangling unattached from the lid.

I explained my predicament to the stewardess. She went forward to the crew's quarters and returned after a few minutes saying that one of the crew would come and nail down the box and rope it for me. She warned me at the same time that Air France's rule differed from this of TWA's, and that from Paris onward the box would have to travel freight and not in the passenger portion of the aircraft.

Mij was sleeping on his back inside my jacket, and I had to steel myself to force him back into that hateful prison and listen to his pathetic cries as he was nailed in what now seems to me like a coffin.

It was the small hours of the morning when we reached London Airport at last. Mij, who had slept ever since the box was nailed up, was wide-awake once more by the time we reached my studio, and when I pried open the lid of the box, Mij clambered out into my arms to greet me with a frenzy of affection that I felt I had hardly deserved.

MAN'S NEXT-BEST FRIEND

Michael Garrett Deas
illustrated by Sam Laterza

Wouldn't it be fun to have a friend ready to play outdoors whenever you are? How about a friend that's outgoing, good looking, and loyal, besides being funny and talented? Any of us would like to meet someone like that—but few would think to look for such a likable personality in a river otter.

The Perfect Pet

It may be that a dog is man's best friend, but the otter runs a close second. Even though it is very similar to the weasel, an otter resembles a dachshund in quite a few ways. Both animals have sleek, dark brown fur, a whiskered muzzle, a long, low, "hot dog" body, and four short legs. Beyond that, the otter is also extremely friendly—it will even approach animals that are strangers to it. An otter, especially a young one, makes a great pet. It is easy to train, clean, smart, and faithful—almost better than a dog!

The Otter's Habitat

But of course, you won't find many otters for sale in pet stores. This is because a river otter, as the name suggests, needs to live near fresh water. Although this remarkable swimmer is at home just about anywhere in the United States and Canada, its ideal habitat is a lake in a forest in the hilly midwestern regions. The coves and embankments around a lake meet the otter's need for "playground area." But more essential than these is the underbrush on the bank, for this is where the otter couple will build their den, or *holt.* You can't spot the den from the outside. It is like a cave hollowed out deep within the thicket, comfortably lined with ferns and leaves. The only entrance to the den is a secret underwater tunnel, opening on the side of the lake. This hidden passage keeps the otters from being seen coming and going and protects the otter pups from predators.

An otter den is built near fresh water.

Special features make the otter an extraordinary swimmer.

Family Life

The mother otter may give birth to two or three pups in each litter. Once the pups' eyes have opened, the family will dig out of the holt. They avoid the underwater passageway because young otters are not born knowing how to swim. The pups ride "piggy-back" on their mother and father until they overcome their fear of water and can swim on their own. Soon they learn not only to maneuver as gracefully as their parents but also to stay underwater for long periods of time. Can you imagine swimming the length of four football fields before coming up for breath?

After about a year of close, affectionate family life, the young otters will travel on, abandoning their den and exploring new waters. But the mother and father usually remain intensely loyal to each other. In fact, when one mate dies, the other may seem to grieve for days, staying close by the body and mourning aloud. This ability to react to loss is uncommon among animals.

A Champion Swimmer

Of course, family life for the otter involves much more than just learning new skills and being together. The adult male has the job of keeping his family fed. He is mainly a fisherman, but instead of using hook and line, he chases and corners his prey in the water.

An otter can out-swim just about any fish in the lake—an amazing feat for a land animal. Its "scuba gear" surpasses anything humans have ever invented. Two coats of hair cover everything but its eyes and nose. The outside coat, made of long, coarse, oily hairs, keeps an otter dry no matter how long it stays in the water. The inside coat of short, soft fur keeps the otter comfortable whether it's nine or ninety degrees outside. For its uncovered ear and nose holes, the otter has special membranes that seal water out. The skin between the five toes on its paws is called webbing, just like that on a duck's foot. Webbed paws allow an otter to steer underwater in any direction. To propel itself through the water at speeds up to seven miles per hour, an otter swishes its muscular, foot-long tail.

What's for Lunch?

Sharp hearing, short-range vision, and a good sense of balance help the otter hunt, but its real food-finding devices are its whiskers, which grow on its nose and—of all places—its elbows. Like television antennas picking up broadcast signals in the air, these fine-tuned whiskers tell the otter exactly where a fish or other likely prey is in the water. Breakfast for an otter may consist of turtles and eels, then snakes or crabs for lunch. It may snack in the afternoon on insects and snails and then possibly for supper try something really different, like frogs or birds. But dessert must be crayfish, the otter's favorite. All this it will catch itself by darting, circling, or jumping around its prey as if it enjoyed playing with its food before eating it.

To Live Is to Play . . .

Most of the otter's time isn't spent in raising a family or in hunting food, but in playing. Unlike other animals, otters would rather have fun than do almost anything else. They excel in water sports, whether summer or winter. In summertime they do everything you love to do at the swimming

In any season, otters excel in extraordinary playfulness.

pool—swim, dive, do belly flops, splash and chase each other, play tag or tug-of-war, and frolic about. Otters even make their own slides. They clear a path down an embankment that leads to deep water. Then for hours they slip, slide, and roll down their slick pathway again and again. Wintertime doesn't stop any of their activities. The mud slide becomes a snow slide; but instead of splashing into water, they go sliding across the frozen lake. When they find a break in the ice, otters dive in and continue their usual antics, not the least bit hin-

dered by the cold. To catch a breath of air, they'll stick their flat noses into air pockets trapped beneath the ice. In this way they can keep on playing without having to rush back constantly to an ice hole for air.

Add to the otter's special abilities extraordinary playfulness, and you can see why it stands out from others in the animal kingdom. If you ever have an opportunity, get to know an otter at a river or lake in the woods. You may find yourself a next-best friend!

Research and Writing

Researching and writing about a topic does not have to be a hard or long process. When done correctly, researching can be fun! To remember the right process, think of the acronym CROWN.

Choose a Topic

The first step in research and writing is to choose a topic. Robert's teacher wanted the class to write reports on the theme "Creatures." If you were to write a report about "Creatures," what animal would you choose? Perhaps you would like to find out more about a certain type of dog, cat, or horse. Maybe you would like to write about a specific wild animal. Spiders fascinated Robert, so he chose the topic of spiders for his report.

Research the Topic

Check to see what guidelines you are to follow. The teacher may require a certain number and variety of sources such as books, encyclopedias, or magazines. You will also need to find out what information is needed. This will help you focus your research on specific information.

Let's see what Robert found out about the topic of spiders. His teacher required that Robert tell the class what spiders eat and where they make their homes. Given these guidelines, Robert knew that he didn't need to learn about how spiders spin webs.

Now you are ready to read and take notes. To *take notes* means to select the needed information and write it down as briefly as possible. Robert began to investigate his sources of information. He had note cards to write down the discoveries—one idea per card. Robert headed his first note card with the question "What do spiders eat?" in the upper left-hand corner.

To answer the question, Robert first checked an encyclopedia on the topic of spiders.

The encyclopedia article told Robert about different kinds of spiders and how spiders spin webs, but as he scanned the headings he found a paragraph entitled "The Spider's Diet." He carefully read the following paragraph.

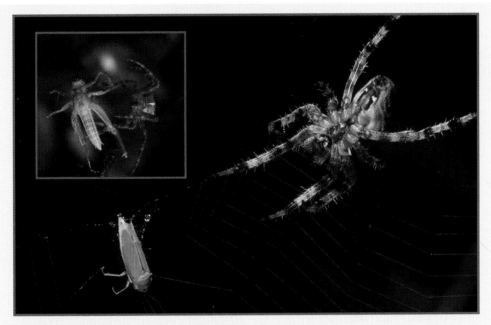

The Spider's Diet. Most spiders eat small insects, especially flies. But larger spiders will catch and eat insects bigger than themselves. Pirate spiders eat only other spiders. Fisher spiders live near water and eat small fish and tadpoles. The biggest spiders, tarantulas, sometimes attack and eat rodents. One type of tarantula, the bird spider, lives in trees and eats small birds.

Under the question "What do spiders eat?" Robert made a short list from what he had read. Then he recorded the source and page number(s) in the upper right-hand corner of the card.

Robert decided that he might want to include some more facts, just in case some of his classmates didn't believe that a spider could eat a bird. He added explanations to his list, as shown below. Checking another book and a magazine also helped Robert to verify that his information was accurate.

Robert went on to read and take notes about his next question: "Where do spiders live?"

Organize an Outline

An outline helps you organize your thoughts before you begin writing. Each main point includes specific examples. Robert arranged the note cards by using his questions. The beginning stages of Robert's outline looked like this:

> 1. What do spiders eat?
>   A. Insects and spiders
>   B. Fish and birds
>   C. Rodents
> 11. Where do spiders live?
>   A. In burrows
>   B. Under debris
>   C. Near water

What do spiders eat?   Encyclopedia of Animals
                            Page 312

Large and small insects —most spiders

Other spiders —pirate spider

Small fish —fisher spider

Rodents —tarantula

Small birds —bird spider (tarantula)

Headings for notes or an outline do not have to be in question form. Instead of questions, Robert could just as easily have written headings like "Food for spiders" and "Homes for spiders." As long as he captured the correct ideas for his headings, he could use either questions or phrases for taking notes.

Write a Rough Draft

Use your note cards and outline to write a first draft of your paper. Present your own ideas as well, but use your research information to back up your thinking.

Robert expected his rough draft to need improvement. A rough draft is a way to begin putting ideas in writing. The teacher's comments let Robert know what to improve.

Nail Down the Final Presentation

Rethink, revise, and edit your paper so that it is organized and free of errors. Reading his report aloud helped Robert notice incomplete sentences and missing punctuation.

Allow time for a fresh look at the paper. It is best to let your words rest at least a day or two between writing and revising.

Look carefully for spelling and punctuation errors. Be sure to follow any special instructions from your teacher.

You should then have a well-written and neatly organized paper. Others may also want to expand their interests by reading your discoveries.

The Silent Witness

adapted from a true story by Milly Howard
illustrated by Mary Ann Lumm

Fishing as Usual

Cato lay still in his hammock and listened to the whisper of early morning waves on the beach. Closer by came the whirr of night insects and the fluttering of the birds that roosted in the thicket outside the hut. Turning his head, Cato could see the pale rectangle that framed the dawning light.

Outside, the sky would be flaming pink and orange over the sea, but inside the hut, night shadows still cloaked familiar objects. Something stirred in the darkness. Cato's eyes followed the movement, knowing it had been made by his wife's black and tan short-haired dog.

There had been no children to bless his marriage to Mera. Years ago, when Cato had brought home the fuzzy, roly-poly puppy, the dog had changed Mera's heart. Now, old and silver-muzzled, the dog she called Punik seldom moved more than a few feet from his mistress, still returning her love with devotion and protection.

Cato's eyes moved upward from the dog, seeking the sleeping form of his wife. As he watched, her hammock swayed. The shadows shifted as Mera's feet sought the floor, gently sliding over the dog to rest on the dirt floor.

The pale light touched her face and silvered the gray in her hair as she bent down to pat the old dog on the head. Punik's thin tail happily thumped the floor. Then,

270

wrapping her shawl around her shoulders, Mera left the hut. Punik got up and padded after her. Cato stirred restlessly. Mera would be gathering driftwood to start a cook-fire. By the time the fire burned hot, others in the village would be awakening. The smoke from the cookfires would drift through the thicket, and the deep, rich smell of corn cakes would bring the men from their hammocks.

Cato took a deep breath of the sea air. "A good day for fishing," he thought, and sighed. For six days of the week, his friend Tali fished with him. Today was the seventh day and today was different. Today was the day Tali, his wife, Belee, and Mera called Sunday. On Sunday they went to the mission church outside the village. And every Sunday Cato fished alone. Not that they didn't

ask him to join them. No, even good-natured and easy-going Tali was often persistent in trying to persuade Cato to go to the church and hear the missionary.

Outside, the fire crackled and blazed up. The roosting birds screeched and beat the air with their wings as they left the thicket. Cato swung his feet over the hammock and stood up in one easy motion. He left the hut and walked to the fire. When he stopped beside Mera, she fanned the smoke out of her eyes and smiled up at him.

"Will you go with us today, Cato?" she asked.

Cato looked away. "There will be many redfish today. Perhaps some other time."

The smile left Mera's eyes but she nodded. "We will be ready to eat soon," she said.

Cato strode down the sandy path to the beach and leaned down to check his boat. Light and long, it lay on the sand beside the boats of the other villagers. Satisfied, Cato walked to the edge of the sea and looked out over the water. As always, he marveled at the brilliance of the sun as it rose from the night, paling the dark water to pink and silver, then to blazing gold and blue green. The waves crashed on the sand, spinning the shining foam almost to Cato's feet, then breathing the foam back into the water. Cato breathed with the ocean, feeling its pull in his own body. Impatient to be skimming over its surface, he turned away and hurried back up the path to the hut.

Punik looked up and wagged his tail as Cato climbed over the ridge of sand and rock that separated the village from the open beach. When he reached the hut, Mera took the last corn cake from the cookfire. Cato ate hungrily, enjoying the crisp texture of the fried cakes.

"Where will you fish today?" Mera asked.

Cato swallowed his last bite. "There'll be some redfish near the lagoon," he said, knowing she worried about him when he went out without Tali. "I'll fish there. Maybe get some lobster," he added with a smile. "You can take some to Pastor Sam."

Mera smiled too. All the villagers knew of Mr. Sam's love for the sweet meat of the lobster. Even those who didn't attend the church would sometimes bring the missionary his favorite treat, for the missionary was well liked in the village.

He had often visited Mera and Cato, but he had been unsuccessful in his efforts to get Cato to accept Jesus Christ. However, the two men respected each other, and Mera still believed that one day

272

Cato would walk with her down the road to the little mission church. But for years now, she had gone with Tali and Belee, with Cato's permission, but without Cato. Even Punik went to church with her, obediently curling up by her feet and nobly refraining from joining in with the singing of the small congregation. Tali, always merry, often told Cato of how Punik would lift his head at the first note of music, his throat trembling with restrained howls. Punik had always enjoyed singing, but he behaved himself in the church.

Mera watched her husband as he reached for his battered straw hat and gathered up his fishing net. Although age and the sun had burned wrinkles deep into his skin, his movements were still swift and sure.

His years of fishing had kept him supple and strong, and his knowledge of the sea gave him a wisdom that made the young men of the village seek him out for advice. "A natural leader," the missionary had told her once. "What a witness he would be for Christ in the village!" But despite the testimony of Mera, Tali, and others in the village, Cato held back. And so did most of the young men.

Mera put her hand to her head and rubbed it, a motion she had been repeating often lately. Cato frowned as he stopped beside her. "What's wrong?" he asked.

"Only a little headache," Mera answered. "It'll go away soon."

Cato hesitated. "Shall I stay with you today?"

Mera shook her head. "I'll be all right. Punik is here, and Tali and Belee are nearby. You go ahead."

"Well—" Cato bent down to rub Punik's head. "You take care of Mera for me, Punik."

Punik thumped the sand with his tail. He and Mera watched as Cato disappeared down the path to the beach. Then Mera went back inside the hut, hoping its coolness would ease the throbbing of her head. Punik whined as she lay back down in the hammock. Then he curled up below her and put his head on his paws. He looked up and wagged his tail when Tali and Belee stopped by for Mera. Belee touched Mera's hot forehead.

"She's sick, Tali," Belee said. "You go on to church and I'll stay with her."

"Should I get Cato?" Tali asked quietly.

Belee hesitated and Mera spoke from the hammock. "No," she said,

"It's only a headache. I've had them before. Just ask Mr. Sam to pray for me."

Tali nodded and left the hut.

After church Mr. Sam came with Tali to see Mera, carrying his bag of medicine and his Bible.

"She's worse," Belee told them. "And she's calling for Cato."

"I'll take my boat and go for him," Tali said, hurrying from the hut.

By the time the two men returned, shadows had crept into the hut. Mera lay quiet in the hammock, pale and weak. When she heard Cato, she opened her eyes and spoke to him. He leaned closer to listen, but when he tried to speak, her eyes closed and she was still. Punik stirred underneath the hammock and whined.

Mr. Sam touched Cato's shoulder. "She has gone to be with the Lord, Cato."

"You mean she's dead!" Cato exclaimed. He stared at the still form of his wife, then back at the missionary, as though expecting him to do something.

"Yes," the missionary replied quietly. "To us, she's dead; to Christ, she's alive."

"Don't talk riddles to me," Cato cried. "Just leave us alone!" He pointed to the door. "Go. All of you. Leave us alone." Again, Punik whined and pushed his head against Cato's knee as the others silently walked out.

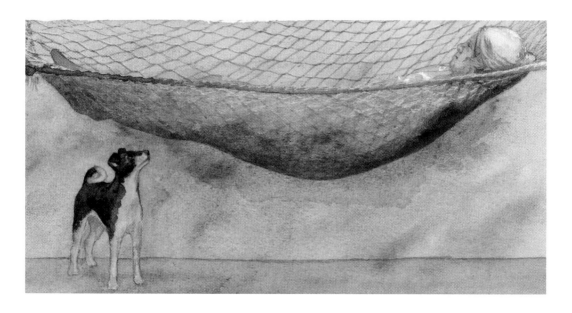

Footsteps for Following

Weeks later, long after the funeral, Cato was still alone. He refused to see Mr. Sam. He avoided Tali and Belee and he left Punik alone at the hut. Cato spent his days on the ocean, returning home late at night.

One day when Mr. Sam and Tali came to visit, Cato saw them coming. Grabbing his net, he hurried down to the beach. His two friends watched him leave.

"He has a great anger," Tali told Mr. Sam. "And a great hurt. It will take time to heal."

"I understand," Mr. Sam answered. "He has no faith that he will see her again. If only we could reach him with the gospel!"

On the ocean the sun still burned down as brightly as ever. Its rays sparkled over the surface of the water in an ever changing pattern of light and dark. Cato lay in his long boat, cocooned in the heat, bobbing gently on the swells of the ocean. But inside him the ice left by Mera's death still lingered, cold and sharp. It had been a Sunday, just like this Sunday, when she had died, he thought. When he closed his eyes to sleep, her last whispered words seemed to drift on the sea breeze, "I'm going home, Cato. I'm going home." Sighing, Cato sat up and began to paddle toward the shore. It was still early—Tali would not be back from church yet—but Cato was tired of fishing alone.

When he reached the empty hut, Cato stopped. He stood for a moment in the door, remembering the warm welcome Mera had always given him. Cato turned away from the dark doorway and walked out into the thicket, calling for Punik. No answering bark broke the quiet of the hot afternoon. Cato rubbed his face in a tired motion, then walked stiffly back into the hut. He climbed into the hammock and put his arm over his eyes to shut out the light. He let his other arm dangle over the edge of the hammock.

He awoke when something touched his hand. Opening his eyes, he looked down and saw Punik.

"Where have you been, Punik?" Cato asked, puzzled. The dog looked at him with his sparkling dark eyes and lay down beneath Mera's hammock. Cato drifted back to sleep.

For a week, Cato remained at the house. Tali came by, and Mr. Sam. This time Cato let them in. They talked for a long time.

Still, when Tali stopped the next Sunday and asked if Cato wanted to go to church, Cato shook his head, wanting only to lie in the hammock and listen to the sounds around him. But just as Tali left, Punik got up and trotted to the door. At the door he stopped and looked back into the hut. Then he barked, looking at Cato. Cato looked up, surprised, but when he didn't move, Punik trotted outside.

The dog didn't come back. Cato lay without moving, watching the door. Later when he heard the sounds of villagers arriving from the mission church, Punik trotted into the hut. Cato swung his feet over the hammock and sat up. "Punik, where have you been all this time?" he asked.

The next Sunday Punik followed the same pattern. Tali stopped to visit, then Punik disappeared. Cato got up and followed the dog through the thicket and out onto the dusty road.

At the mission church, the dog entered the open door without looking back. Cato followed slowly and stopped in the doorway. In amazement he watched as Punik trotted down the aisle and curled up underneath an empty space on the bench beside Tali and Belee. As the singing began, Mr. Sam saw Cato and motioned him inside. Cato went in slowly and sat beside Belee. Punik shifted to rest his muzzle on Cato's foot.

Cato listened as Mr. Sam preached about Jesus and how He died on the cross for the sins of the world. After the service, Cato asked his friends why Punik came to the church.

"He always came with Mera," Belee explained. "She always sat there, and he lay beneath her seat through the whole service."

"Yes," Tali added, "you know he was never far from her."

Cato nodded. The bond between Punik and Mera had been strong. Punik had felt the loneliness too.

When the villagers stopped to speak to Cato, he responded with relief. He had missed their companionship more than he had thought.

The next Sunday Cato dressed carefully. He and Punik left the hut together. Punik trotted along beside Cato, stopping occasionally to look up at him. Mr. Sam met them at the door of the mission church.

"Hello, Cato," Mr. Sam said. "Welcome."

Cato nodded, shaking the missionary's hand. "I enjoy your sermons, Mr. Sam, but I have some questions. There are some things I don't understand."

"Why not wait after the service?" Mr. Sam asked. "You can eat with me, and we can talk then."

Cato greeted a few young men who had not been at the service the last Sunday and walked up the aisle to sit beside Tali.

After the service he and Punik went to the missionary's house. Punik lay down on the porch as Cato and Mr. Sam went into the kitchen. Cato helped Mr. Sam boil shrimp and cook rice, marveling at the refrigerator that kept the food cold and at the electric stove that cooked so much faster than the fires.

When the last shrimp was eaten and only crumbs remained on the bread plate, Mr. Sam took out his Bible and spread it open. For hours they sat at the little table, searching the Word of God for the answers to Cato's questions. The first one he asked was why Mera said she was going home. The last one he asked was how he could be saved.

When the moon lit up the evening sky, Cato left the missionary's house a new creature in Christ. As Cato stepped off the porch, Punik stretched and yawned. Then he padded down the steps and followed Cato home.

EAGLE on a LEASH

Milly Howard
illustrated by Del Thompson

The Predator

Brent Thompson finished cleaning Rama's cage and carefully shut the door. When the golden eagle gave a protesting screech, he laughed. "Now, Rama, take it easy. Dad is going to let you fly today. He promised. I'll be back in a little while."

Rama tilted her head to one side and made a twittering sound deep in her throat. "I promise, Rama. Dad said before noon." Brent latched the door of Rama's eight-by-twenty-foot cage and picked up his tools. Rama's cage was located behind the house on the canyon rim with a clear view of the canyon below.

The high canyon walls cast early-morning shadows on the green of the canyon floor. A moving wave of white caught Brent's eye. A flock of sheep was being herded into the Culpeppers' sheepfold. Brent was surprised. It was too early for the sheep to come back from the pastures. He watched as a small figure stopped at the Culpeppers' ranch house. A taller figure came out on the porch, listened to the younger one for a minute, and disappeared inside. When he reappeared, both figures went around the side of the ranch house. A few seconds later, a jeep left the Culpeppers' ranch, spinning a cloud of trailing dust as it churned up the dirt road toward the Thompsons' house.

When the jeep screeched into the front yard, Brent was waiting. The Thompsons had bought the canyon-rim house just before school had let out for summer vacation. Although they had stopped at their nearest neighbor's house several times, there had been little response. The older Culpeppers kept to themselves, responding curtly to the friendly advances of the newcomers up on the rim. However, their thin, sun-browned boy about Brent's age seemed shy but cheerful. Although the interest in his clear gray eyes hinted at friendship, the boys had spent little time together. The Culpeppers were sheepherders and Jasper was often away with the sheep.

But now, as the man and boy strode toward him, Brent realized this was no friendly visit. Brent looked from Jasper to the tall, dark man beside him. Jasper's face was as tense as his father's. Brent's startled gaze took in the rifle in Barlow Culpepper's hands.

"Dad!" Brent called.

The screen door opened behind him. "I'm here, Brent."

"My boy lost a lamb this morning, carried off by an eagle." Barlow's voice was harsh. "Folks say you got an eagle up here."

"Yes sir, we do," Noel Thompson said. "We have a license to keep a golden eagle for research. But this territory is new to Rama, so we haven't flown her free yet. She's still on jesses and a leash. Are you sure it was an eagle?"

"It was an eagle all right." Mr. Culpepper thrust out an object he had been holding in his hand. The light glinted on a feather—the white-splashed tail feather of a young golden eagle.

"It sure looks like one of Rama's." Mr. Thompson took the feather and turned it slowly in his hands. "But she's still in her cage. I assure you, Barlow, it's a strong cage. It's impossible for her to get out by herself."

Mr. Culpepper's cold eyes turned on Brent, and the boy felt a shiver run down his spine. "Perhaps your boy here let her out."

"I never—"

"Brent has been responsible for Rama ever since we got her, under my supervision, of course." Mr. Thompson put his hand on Brent's shoulder. "He would never let her out without permission. I'm sure she's still in her cage."

Jasper stood half behind his father, scuffing the toe of his boot in the dirt. His troubled gray eyes left the ground for just a moment and met Brent's; then he stared down again at his dusty boots.

"Mind if we take a look?" Barlow Culpepper shifted his rifle slightly.

"Not at all. The cage is behind the house." Mr. Thompson stepped off the porch. "Follow me, please."

The Culpeppers followed as Mr. Thompson led the way to the cage. Rama was perched inside on a branch of gnarled pine, preening her feathers. When she caught sight of the procession of men and boys, her head lifted. Her beak opened slightly. Slowly the golden feathers on the back of her neck lifted; the rest of her feathers flattened tightly. Her eyes glittered.

Shifting his grip on the rifle, Mr. Culpepper stepped forward to check the construction of the cage. He inspected the latch and rattled the cage door. With a wild screech, Rama flung herself across the cage, talons first. Her weight thrust the mesh net cage wall a full two feet out from the side. Brent smothered a grin as both Barlow Culpepper and his son leaped back.

"Don't be alarmed." His father moved between the Culpeppers and the cage. "She can't get out."

"She'll be a goner if she does." Barlow shook his rifle menacingly. "There's something attacking my lambs. If it turns out to be your eagle, her flying days are done, and that's no idle threat!"

He turned on his heel and stalked around the house.

Jasper followed him slowly. Suddenly he stopped, took off his hat and began turning it around and around in his hands. He swung around and faced Brent.

"I'm sorry—"

"Jasper!" Mr. Culpepper's voice could be heard from the front of the house.

Jasper looked over his shoulder, then turned and disappeared after his father. The jeep roared out of the driveway down the dirt road toward the canyon.

"What's he blaming Rama for anyway?" Brent could feel his anger rising inside him like the cloud of dust rising from the canyon below. "He doesn't know it was Rama who killed his lamb. One little feather was all he had and I don't see how anyone can prove anything with just one little feather. It couldn't be Rama." Brent kicked a loose rock over the rim of the canyon. "Just because we happen to live above the canyon and happen to have a golden eagle, he has to blame his dead lamb on us. Besides, Rama wouldn't hurt a lamb. Would she, Dad?"

"She could, Son, if she weren't well-fed and well-trained." Mr. Thompson stood beside him staring in the same direction. "And a sheep man will shoot anything that attacks his sheep, and he would be within his legal rights to do it, too. Barlow Culpepper is doing what he thinks is right to protect his flock. To him, an eagle is a predator that could cost him his livelihood." He looked at Rama thoughtfully. She stared back, the wild glitter in her eyes gone, the perfect example of a gentle bird. "I wonder if there is another eagle in this territory."

"Wouldn't we have seen it by now?"

"Maybe not." Mr. Thompson scanned the sky and the canyon. "But Rama should have. If there were another bird, it would want to defend its territory. We'd better wait a little longer before letting Rama fly free."

"But Dad, you promised she would get to fly," Brent protested.

"I told her this morning she could fly today!"

"Not today, Son." Mr. Thompson shook his head. "Let's let things simmer down a little."

For the next few weeks, Rama was exercised only on the jesses and leash. But the tethered flights were unsatisfactory, not only to Rama, but to her trainers also.

"She's ready to fly, Dad," Brent insisted.

"We need to wait just a little longer, Son," his father replied. "I know you're impatient, but it's better to be safe than sorry."

Rama, perched on Brent's fist, tensed when they approached the cage. Brent stopped. "Maybe we could make a perch out here on the rim and tie her to it. She'd feel more free at least."

Mr. Thompson thought a moment. "That's a good idea. We'll have to keep an eye on her, though." Brent raced to get the materials to build another perch. "If there is another eagle and it discovers Rama, she would be helpless against an attack."

Team Plan

Saturday dawned hot and dry. Brent made sure Rama was secure in her cage before he joined his parents for a ride to town. On the weekend, the small town of Cottonwood overflowed with farmers, ranchers, women, and children. They came from miles around to buy the week's groceries and visit with each other. The Thompsons were no exception. While Mrs. Thompson shopped for groceries, Mr. Thompson and Brent headed for the hardware store to pick up some fencing. Across the road Jasper was sitting on the soft-drink box outside the gas station, drinking an orange soda. His tanned face turned away as he saw Brent. In a lot of ways Jasper Culpepper was just like his father.

He slid off the box and silently pushed back the lid. Mr. Thompson smiled at Jasper and handed Brent some change before crossing the street to the hardware store. Brent leaned over the box, letting the blast of cold air cool his face.

"Hot as a firecracker and it's only July." He carefully pulled out a chocolate drink, dropped his money into the coin box, and pried the cap off the drink. He looked at Jasper. "Aren't you hot?"

Jasper grinned. "I'm used to it, I guess. You'll get used to it, too, if you stay." He looked at Brent shyly. "It gets pretty lonesome out here. There aren't any other boys close by."

"I'd like to be friends," Brent said, "but what would your father say?"

"Pop hasn't always been like this," Jasper slid his empty bottle into the rack. "He's just worried about money lately. We've lost a lot of lambs, one way or another. Now, the eagle—"

"It wasn't Rama!"

"Maybe not," Jasper replied uneasily, "but you'd better keep her penned up good. Pop'll shoot any eagle he sees without checking to see who it belongs to. He told me once that ranchers used to hunt eagles from airplanes. Pop's been fussing ever since he found out you had an eagle."

"Maybe we could prove it isn't Rama that killed the lamb." Brent slid his empty drink bottle into the rack next to Jasper's.

"How?"

"Catch the other eagle!"

"You know how to catch an eagle?" Jasper stared at Brent.

"Sure. I helped Dad catch Rama," Brent replied. "Course, she

was just a fledgling and we got her from a nest. But I've read lots of books about eagles. We can use Dad's bow net and a lure. It won't hurt to try, anyway. We've got to help Rama."

"Okay," Jasper said. "Pop always takes the sheep to the far pasture on Thursdays and he gives me the day off. Why don't you meet me at the ranch then? We'll have the whole day."

"Sounds great!" Brent stuck out his hand. "We'll be a team."

The next Thursday, Brent was up early. He finished his chores and made sure Rama had water and food. Then he gathered up the bow net and a dead squirrel for bait. After fastening them to his bicycle, he pedaled down the dirt road. The unwieldy net made Brent's progress slow and clumsy. When he finally reached the ranch, Jasper was waiting on the porch.

"Let's go!" Jasper jumped down and reached for his bike.

The two boys rode northwest to Sunset Crag. Brent finally stopped and looked up. "This looks high enough," Brent said in satisfaction. "We should be able to see every direction from the top."

"Yeah, and the eagle can see us." Jasper followed Brent's gaze. "Are you sure this is all right?"

"Sure," Brent said with more confidence than he felt. "It's done all the time. Besides, we've got to do something to prove to your father that Rama isn't a killer. She can't stay in that cage forever."

The boys scrambled up the crag. By the time they reached the top, they were out of breath. Brent wiped his face. "Just look at the view!"

Sunset Crag was higher than the canyon rim. To the east Brent could see his house clearly. He and Jasper watched as Mr. Thompson took Rama from her cage, tied her to the perch outside, and went back into her cage.

"He's going to build another section onto Rama's cage," Brent told Jasper. "That'll give her a little more room if she does have to stay cooped up."

"They look like dolls," Jasper said. He walked over to the north edge of the crag. "I wonder if I can see Pop from here. Yep, there he is!"

Far below, in a box canyon, the boys could see sheep milling around a pool. Barlow Culpepper moved along the edge of the flock, herding them up the canyon to the grassy floor. The sun glinted off the rifle in his hand.

Brent looked away and scanned the sky for some movement. To the left, a hawk circled lazily in the heat. Nothing else moved. "Well, let's set it up," he told Jasper.

The boys struggled with the bow net, trying to get it just right. "It looked a lot easier in the book," Brent grumbled as the net collapsed for the third time. Jasper just shook his head and stopped to watch a bird in the sky. "See anything?" Brent asked as he spread the net again.

"Just a hawk," Jasper said.

Brent released the net slowly. This time it stayed. He tied the squirrel inside the net and looked at it doubtfully. "It'll have to do," he said wearily.

He straightened up. "Are you sure that was a hawk? Where'd you see it?"

Jasper pointed to the bird still circling in the sky. "There."

Brent watched as the large bird spiraled in the sky, riding an updraft. He caught his breath. "That's not a hawk! It's an eagle!"

The wild bird banked and swept toward them. "Get down!" Brent pulled Jasper down beside him. Just over the crag, the eagle swung and circled again, its wings outspread. "Look at the size of those wings!" Brent shivered. The eagle was big, bigger than Rama. Its wingspan must have been at least eight feet. Brent grabbed Jasper's arm. "It's seen the lure!"

The eagle tightened its circle, then—folding its wings—it dived. Straight down it came, right on target. The boys scrambled behind the rocks as the whistle of air through its feathers became a roar. Then, talons outstretched, the eagle struck. The net sprang together sharply, slinging itself sideways. The eagle's wings spread, beating the air fiercely. With a wild shriek, it rose into the air.

"Missed!" Brent could have cried from disappointment.

"It missed the squirrel, too." Jasper shrunk back against Brent. "And it's mad!"

Jasper was right. The eagle flew back over the crag, shrieking. Suddenly from the east came an answering shriek.

Brent jumped to his feet. "Rama!"

He saw his father reach the cage door just as Rama flung herself into the air. She hit the full length of the leash with all her strength. The leash snapped. Rama was loose!

Noel Thompson dropped his tools and ran for the truck as Rama launched herself from the canyon rim. Riding the updraft, she soared upward, seeking height to attack. The other eagle quickly closed the gap between them.

Brent groaned. "They're going to fight!" Grabbing the squirrel from the net, he swung the lure, trying to attract Rama and bring her down. It was no use. The birds had no thought for anything except each other.

Wounded Eagle

With a sudden dive, Rama attacked. The wild eagle rolled over in the air, warding off the attack with out-thrust talons. The two birds broke away. Again they circled, each trying to gain altitude over the other. Again a sharp dive, a breaking away, and another dive. This time, with a flurry of wings and talons, they closed together.

For one wild moment, they tumbled over and over in the air, falling. Angry screeches and harsh challenges vibrated through the hot air.

Desperately, Brent and Jasper scrambled down the crag. At the bottom Brent's father had just arrived in the pickup. White-faced, Brent explained what had happened. Mr. Thompson listened grimly, keeping his attention on the battle in the sky.

Huge wings beat the air as the birds, one wild and one tame, fought for a killing hold. Feathers drifted downward. Tumbling end over end, they released their holds only when the ground rushed up to meet them.

This time they circled higher and to the north. Jasper pointed down at the canyon floor. "They're flying over the box canyon where Pop is!"

Brent and his father looked at each other. "If they don't kill each other, Barlow will! Let's go!" Mr. Thompson motioned both boys into the pickup. A cloud of dust rose behind them as they raced toward the north pastures.

They found Barlow Culpepper standing with his rifle ready. His eyes didn't leave the fighting eagles as the pickup pulled up and the man and boys leaped out. He took aim. His finger tightened on the trigger.

"Pop! No!"

Mr. Thompson caught Jasper's arm and held him back. Brent held his breath. The birds broke apart. Rama's jesses and leash showed clearly against the blue sky as she turned to attack again. She and her enemy plunged into each other and tumbled behind the sturdy stone peaks that closed off the deeper part of the canyon.

Barlow lowered the rifle.

"Pop," Jasper ran to his father. "You didn't shoot."

Mr. Culpepper shook his head. "They were right. There are two eagles and I can't be sure which one did the killing."

Noel Thompson sighed. "Rama broke her leash when she saw the wild eagle. I'm afraid they'll fight to the death."

"Then that wild eagle's the one that killed our lamb, I guess."

Noel nodded, turning to scan the empty sky. "It's a young female, too. This must be her territory. She looks pretty big and certainly has the advantage, but Rama is giving her a good fight. Rama must feel like she has to protect us. Nothing else would give her the confidence to invade another bird's territory."

"Brent and I tried to capture the wild one." Jasper kicked at a rock with his boot. "So you would know that Rama didn't kill the lamb."

Brent stepped up beside Jasper. "Dad explained why you don't like eagles and I do understand. But now what I did may cost Rama her life."

"Let's just wait, Son," his father said quietly. "What's done is done. There would have been a fight sooner or later anyway. We were just postponing the time by keeping Rama penned up."

"But what do we do now?"

Mr. Thompson shook his head. "Nothing. It's up to Rama now."

By late afternoon, neither bird had returned. Mr. Thompson and the two boys helped herd the sheep back to the ranch. Then Brent and his father returned to the house.

Early the next morning Brent and his dad went out to Rama's cage. They stood looking out over the canyon rim. The rising sun edged the ridges in deep red and spilled golden light into the night-darkened canyons. Night shadows faded into the purple and pink of a new day. There was still no sign of Rama.

Down below, Brent could see Jasper and his father out by the corral, also watching the morning sky. At last they turned away and entered the ranch house. "We might as well go in," Mr. Thompson said. Silently, Brent followed him to the house.

The sun had been up several hours before Brent started down the dirt road to the Culpepper ranch. As he rode around the bend in the road, he could see Jasper ahead, shouting and pointing excitedly. Brent looked up at the sky. A large bird was approaching, flying low. He watched closely. The bird was moving too slowly and too low to be an eagle. The bird came on, wings pumping up and down, up and down. Brent's heart thudded. It was Rama. She was flying with pure determination, too tired to fly any higher. Her line of flight was taking her to the ranch at the bottom of the cliffs, not high enough to reach the house on the rim.

Brent began to pedal. He reached Jasper just as Rama reached the ranch. She landed at their feet, exhausted. Mr. Culpepper ran from the house, shaking his head in amazement.

"I'll call your dad." Without another word, he went back into the house.

When Brent's father arrived, Barlow helped load the wounded eagle into the back of the pickup.

"Is she going to be all right?" Barlow stepped back from the truck.

"The fact she's made it this far gives us hope. I think we can nurse her back to health." Mr. Thompson held out his hand. "I want to thank you . . ."

Mr. Culpepper shook the offered hand but dropped it quickly. "Don't mention it." He turned to Brent. "Always thought of eagles as being nothing but trouble. Never thought they could be somebody's pet. Maybe when Rama is well, you can show me and Jasper how those jesses and stuff work."

Brent looked from Jasper to his dad and then back to Mr. Culpepper. He smiled and held out his hand. "I'd be happy to, Mr. Culpepper. I'd be happy to."

EAGLE: KING *of* BIRDS

Marilyn Elmer

High above the earth the eagle soars majestically in strength and beauty. With its magnificent wingspan, the eagle is powerful in flight. With its speed and keen vision, it is a fierce hunter. With patient tenderness, the eagle feeds and cares for its young. The eagle—large, swift, powerful, fierce, and faithful—deserves to be known as king of the birds.

Bald eagles view their territory from tall trees.

Types

There are forty-eight kinds of eagles in the world, but the best known in the United States are the golden eagle and the bald eagle. The bald eagle was named years ago by early settlers, who used "bald" to mean white. A bald eagle is distinguished by the white feathers covering its head, while the golden eagle displays golden brown feathers at the back of the neck. Because of its strength and splendor, the bald eagle was chosen to be the symbol of our country.

Characteristics

Eagles are mentioned in the Bible over thirty times. From Genesis to Revelation, the writers of Scripture described characteristics of the eagle that we can still see today.

Job, Jeremiah, and other biblical writers described eagles as swift. Both bald eagles and golden eagles have been found to travel at almost 120 miles per hour in a dive after prey. Birdwatchers have seen these masters of flight almost ten thousand feet above the earth.

Eagles can spot their prey from great distances. This ability inspired the expression "eagle eye."

Once, a bald eagle was observed to detect a fish three miles from where it was soaring and to capture it after one long, slanting dive.

Moses lived in the desert and the wilderness for eighty years. He probably viewed eagles at close range many times. In Deuteronomy 32:11-12, he compared God's care of the Israelites to an eagle's care for its young: "As an eagle stirreth up her nest, fluttereth over her young, spreadeth abroad her wings, taketh them, beareth them on her wings: So the Lord alone did lead him." Both golden eagle and bald eagle parents mate for life. The male and female stay together throughout

the year instead of just in the breeding season as many other types of birds do. They arrange and rearrange their nesting materials. They spread their wings to protect their young from the rain, the burning sun, and the biting wind. Occasionally an adult bird will let a faltering eaglet rest on its back as the youngster is learning to fly.

Nesting

Bald eagles build their nests in tall trees; golden eagles prefer high cliffs. The nests, called *aeries,* are built mainly of sticks. They are lined with leaves, grass, feathers, moss, and other soft materials.

294

At the time it hatches, the eaglet is not much bigger than a farm chick.

Eagle nests, enlarged for use each year, can weigh up to two tons.

Eagles use the same nesting site year after year. They build each new nest on top of the others. Since these birds can live from thirty to fifty years, the nests become enormous. One nest in a tree blown down near Lake Erie weighed over four thousand pounds, or two tons.

The female eagle lays two or three white eggs each year. The eggs are not much bigger than chicken eggs. Over the next thirty-five to forty days, the parents take turns sitting in the nest until the eaglets hatch. At birth the eaglets are covered with fuzzy, grayish-white down until the feathers begin to grow.

When the babies are first hatched, the adults put food directly into their mouths. Soon, however, the parents show the youngsters how to tear the food into pieces and feed themselves.

Growing to Adulthood

Eaglets spend much of the first few weeks of their lives preparing to hunt and fly. They learn to grasp objects with their talons. They exercise by flapping their wings, jumping up and down, and stamping about. When they are about

Because it is swift and powerful, the bald eagle is a symbol of strength.

three months old, they are finally ready to take their first shaky flight from the edge of the nest. If they delay starting to fly, the parents coax them with pieces of food held just beyond their reach. As they become more skillful in flight, the growing birds spend less and less time in the aerie. However, the parents supply food until the youngsters are about a year old.

Eagles as Hunters

Eagles are carnivorous, or meat-eating. Eagles are called predators because they kill their own food. An eagle's diet can include small birds and mammals, fish, and snakes. The bald eagle seems to prefer fish. Eagles are also scavengers because they eat animals that have been killed by cars or have died from other causes.

Eagles need to consume a certain amount of fur, feathers, and bones to remain healthy. These indigestible items roll up into a ball in the bird's *crop* (a pouch in the throat). The ball is called a *casting*. It acts like a brush to clean the crop. Each morning the eagle regurgitates the casting. Scientists collect eagle castings, pull them apart, and study them to find out what the bird has been eating.

The eagle's weapons are his beak and talons. The hooked beak is from two to three inches long. The razor-sharp claws may be the same length. The talons continue to grow throughout life as our fingernails do. The eagle sharpens and trims them by constant use.

Human Responsibility

Mankind must be wise in his care of these birds. As farmers and ranchers well know, eagles present a threat to young livestock, and in certain areas the number of eagles has to be controlled. But hunters and eagle-egg collectors have greatly reduced the overall eagle population. Some pesticides caused the female eagles to lay eggs with thin shells that were easily broken. This too caused a decrease in the number of eagles in our country.

Laws now protect these magnificent birds. It is against the law to kill, shoot, or capture an eagle for sport. It is also illegal to molest eggs or take them from a nest. These laws are strictly enforced to protect the eagle from extinction.

Isaiah 40:31 says, "But they that wait upon the Lord shall renew their strength; they shall mount up with wings as eagles; they shall run, and not be weary; and they shall walk, and not faint." This promise that God made to his people centuries ago is for us today too. Whenever you think of an eagle, remember that God will strengthen you as you look to Him.

THE EAGLE

Alfred, Lord Tennyson

illustrated by Paula Cheadle

He clasps the crag with crooked hands;

Close to the sun in lonely lands,

Ring'd with the azure world, he stands.

The wrinkled sea beneath him crawls;

He watches from his mountain walls,

And like a thunderbolt he falls.

One in a Million

written and illustrated by Tim Davis

Of course the Mobsters were the best football team in the league. All of Boston was proud of them, especially Coach Wilson. But one million dollars apiece? Nobody was worth that much, and the owner of the team knew it.

"We simply can't afford to pay them that much, Wilson. It's outrageous!" Mr. Libscomb, the owner, stood up behind his large desk. Then he turned and stared out the window. "They already make more than anybody else in the league."

Coach Wilson, sitting in Mr. Libscomb's office, heaved a long sigh. "It's just all gone to their heads," he said finally. "Those two undefeated seasons in a row just went to their heads."

"I know, I know," said Mr. Libscomb. "But what are we going to do about it? The season starts in one week, and if we don't agree to their outrageous demands, they're all going on strike tomorrow!"

After a long pause, Coach Wilson replied, "Maybe we could take out a loan?" Mr. Libscomb turned toward the coach with his teeth clenched. "A loan for forty million dollars?" he shouted. "Tell me, Wilson, who's going to pay it back? You?"

"Just kidding, Boss." Coach Wilson smiled weakly and wiped the perspiration from his face.

Mr. Libscomb bent over his desk and stared Coach Wilson right in the eye. "Listen, Wilson, we can't pay them that much. If they won't play, we'll get somebody else to play instead."

"B-but, Mr. Libscomb, sir, there's only one week left before the season starts," replied the coach. "We could never get a good team together in that time. Besides, the Mobster fans are so used to winning that they'd boo us off the field if we lost."

"Wilson!" Mr. Libscomb scowled and leaned even closer to the coach. "Everybody thinks you're a good coach. Now you get a team together, anyhow, anyway—and make them win! If you don't, you won't be a good coach. You won't even *be* a coach. Understand?"

Coach Wilson understood all right. After a long, hard swallow, he politely excused himself and went home. Needless to say, he didn't sleep very well that night.

The next day disaster struck. All the sports pages proclaimed the bad news: "MOBSTERS GO ON STRIKE! Players Say No Season Without Million-Dollar Salaries."

Coach Wilson sat in his little office watching the news. As bad as the strike itself was for him, it was even worse when he saw a reporter interviewing some of his players.

Reporter: Why is that, Flex?

Flex: Because anybody that signs up has a good chance of getting injured.

Reporter: Is that because he'll have so little time to get ready for the season?

Flex: No, that's not it.

Ace Spence, the quarterback, only bragged about how good he was. However, Flex Bulk, the Mobsters' towering defenseman, really got everyone's attention.

Reporter: Flex, how about leaning down a little bit so both of our faces can be on the screen at once?

Flex: I don't think we need your face on the screen.

Reporter: Oh . . . uh . . . sure. So, Mr. Bulk, what do you think of the rumor that your team owner, Harry Libscomb, might hire players to replace you for this season?

Flex: I don't think that would be wise.

Reporter: Why then?

Flex: Because I'll be paying him a visit.

"Oh, no," thought Coach Wilson, "now nobody will play for me. Everybody in Boston is afraid of Flex Bulk."

Coach Wilson felt very much discouraged. He was just about ready to turn off the TV and start typing his resignation when a news story came on about the city zoo. Looking at the bulky rhinos, the swift gazelles, and the agile monkeys, Coach Wilson came up with an idea. It was a crazy idea—even outrageous—but maybe it would work.

"Animals on a football team!" Mr. Libscomb couldn't believe his ears.

"I think it's our best shot, Mr. Libscomb," answered Coach Wilson. "I've read the league's rules thoroughly and it's completely legal."

"But animals?"

"Yes, sir."

"But, Wilson, they don't even know how to play the game," snorted Mr. Libscomb. "And the season's only one week away!"

"I'll be working closely with some of the zoo's animal trainers, sir," replied the coach. "They're willing to cooperate with us fully."

"But animals?"

"I know it will take a while, sir, but just think of the potential!" A smile crept onto Wilson's face. "How would *you* like to tackle a rhinoceros?"

"Well, I . . . uh . . . but animals, Wilson? It's outrageous!"

"The zoo is only asking for a reasonable contribution to improve the grounds—one *half* of what we paid in salaries *last* year, sir."

With that remark, Mr. Libscomb quieted down. "Yes." He smiled. "Heh, heh. Yes, Wilson, you're a genius. Let's do it!"

The next morning all the animals and a couple of trainers were delivered to the stadium for Coach Wilson to start his one-week training camp. Everyone got along well. The animals seemed to take a special liking to their new coach. He was delighted to find out that many of the animals had already been trained to respond to a number of hand and voice signals.

Throughout the day Coach Wilson tested the animals' abilities in passing, running, blocking, and kicking. He was exceptionally pleased. And many of the animals seemed to be really enjoying themselves.

The rhinoceros seemed to especially enjoy charging toward the ball—or toward whoever had the ball, for that matter. "I can't wait to see him on defense," thought Coach Wilson.

The ostrich was particularly excited about running around the field with the football in his mouth. In fact, it was rather difficult to get it away from him. He was quite unpredictable. "A star if I ever saw one," thought the coach.

Then there was the orangutan. What an arm! And the gazelle made a terrific receiver! It seemed as though he could catch almost anything between his horns. Actually, it took several minutes to

pry the football loose if the orang-utan threw it too hard.

Coach Wilson was so excited he was jumping around on the field like a cheerleader.

"What a team!" he thought. "If only . . ." Then his smile faded a little. "If only they can learn the rules."

The next day Coach Wilson tried to teach the animals some plays. Before long he had a terrible headache. It wasn't that they couldn't perform. But almost every play was offside, illegal procedure, illegal this, or illegal that. Sometimes they even ran in the wrong direction!

"It's going to take time," Coach Wilson reminded himself. "Too bad the season starts this Saturday."

In just a few more days he would find out whether his outrageous idea would really work. If it did, it would be one in a million.

Saturday arrived. The whole team sat in the locker room. Each animal wore his own custom-made jersey. There was an uneasy silence in the air. Coach Wilson and the trainers stepped out of the office.

"I've never seen these animals so quiet," whispered one of the trainers.

It's just a case of pre-game jitters," remarked the coach. "They'll get over it . . . I hope."

"Let's go!" he yelled suddenly, running out to the hallway leading to the stadium. He led the stampede of enthusiastic animals onto the field.

Amid the cheers of the crowd, Coach Wilson detected several screams. Apparently some people hadn't believed the reports that real animals would be playing. There were also some loud boos coming from one particular section. It was the old Mobster team. Ace, Flex, and many others were hissing and booing as loudly as they could. The coach tried to ignore them. He also ignored the chuckles of the opposing coach and his team, the San Francisco Golden Gators.

The Mobsters got the ball first. On the very first play they were called offside: a penalty. (The giraffe had leaned his neck over the line.) The next play was a penalty similar to the first. Then on their third play, the ostrich got the ball. He dodged right. He dodged left. He hopped right over a defender. Before the San Francisco players knew what was happening, the ostrich was running straight toward the end zone.

"He's going to score!" yelled Coach Wilson, jumping up and down. But then something went wrong. The ostrich suddenly dodged right—right off the field! Right up into the stands!

Up and up he went to the top row. Then he ran around the top edge of the stadium. As you might guess, it took several minutes to catch him, and the Mobsters were penalized for delaying the game.

One in a Million   305

When the other team got the ball, things didn't go much better. The Mobsters gave up so many yards in penalties that San Francisco had to gain only one yard on their own. The score became Gators 7, Mobsters 0. By half time it was Gators 21, Mobsters 3. The Mobsters' only score had come when the giraffe stumbled and accidentally kicked the ball through the goalposts. Coach Wilson was not discouraged, though. Each time the Mobsters made a play, they did it a little bit better.

In the second half it was the San Francisco coach's turn to get uneasy. Not only were the Mobsters playing better, but they were also catching up! The gazelle made a leaping catch in the end zone for one touchdown. Having had his fling for the day, the ostrich ran straight for the end zone for the Mobsters' second touchdown. The score stood at Gators 21, Mobsters 17 with only two minutes left in the game.

The Gators had the ball. They wanted to hold on to it for only two minutes to finish the game and win. Now they were afraid of the Mobsters' defense. No longer was Coach Wilson's team making silly mistakes and being penalized. Now

they were charging and tackling like—well, like animals!

On the next play, the hippo opened his mouth and let out a tremendous roar just as the Gators snapped the ball. It startled the San Francisco quarterback so much that he dropped the ball. It bounced on the grass. About half the players on both teams tried to jump on it at once.

The pile of men, gorilla, hippo, and baboons collided with a mighty "THUD!" The ball shot high up into the air. Down, down it

came, right down on the rhino's horn.

"Go, rhino, go!" shouted Coach Wilson above the wildly cheering crowd. And the rhino did go—as fast as he could toward the end zone. Three—four—five San Francisco players tried to bring him down. He dragged them all into the end zone with him.

"Touchdown!" yelled the referee, just as the gun sounded to end the game. The crowd went crazy. The Mobsters had won, 24 to 21.

Each Saturday following that first game, the Mobsters seemed to get better and better. They beat Rochester, 31 to 14. Pittsburgh was defeated, 44 to 3, and Tallahassee lost by 52 points. And that was only the beginning.

Nowadays not many people can remember the names of the old Boston Mobsters players. But the fans at Wilson Stadium do know one thing for sure. The team they have now is one in a million.

a Spear for Omar

Heddy Rado
illustrated by Preston Gravely

Omar knelt at the bottom of the small dugout canoe and let his hand drift in the balmy water of the Red Sea. He loved this hour of the day, heading homeward with the keel of the canoe deep in the water, heavy with a day's catch of fish. It usually made him feel peaceful to watch the sun sink slowly behind the jagged mountains that lined the dry, hot desert.

Today, however, there was no peace in Omar for he had failed again. As if in answer to his shame came his father's soothing voice, "Do not worry too much, my Son. Tomorrow you will be able to hold your breath underwater longer than you did today."

Omar's father was known to be the best spearfisherman from Suez all the way down to Port Sudan. He was a big man with strong muscles rippling underneath his tanned skin. Clad only in a loincloth, he squatted in the canoe and paddled homeward with even, powerful strokes.

Omar's brother Gomez, who knelt in the stern of the canoe, cleaning and drying his underwater goggles with the tail of his galabia shirt, started to laugh. "Tomorrow Omar will be bobbing up for air every few seconds just like he did today," Gomez mocked. "How can he ever be a spearfisherman if he is afraid he might drown

308

as soon as he is underwater for more than a few seconds?"

"Tomorrow I will stay underwater for hours, you will see!" cried Omar. Deep inside he was thoroughly ashamed of his fear of drowning.

With an angry motion Omar's father jarred the paddle against the canoe. "There will be no more fighting between you two," he said. "And as for you," he added, turning around to Gomez, "it would not harm you to exercise some more caution. It is not well to show fear, but also it is not wise to disregard danger altogether as you so often do. The sea is full of danger for the reckless spearfisherman." After

that he took up his paddle, and no one spoke again.

Omar sighed and looked with deep longing at the spears at the bottom of the canoe. His father had promised him a spear of his own as soon as he had conquered his fear. The spears were slender, long shafts of smooth wood with metal points that gleamed dark red in the last rays of the sinking sun. To Omar the spears looked beautiful and well worth the effort he silently promised to make.

The next morning Omar's father announced that he would stay behind. "I want you two to go to sea alone today," he said. "Gomez is well able to do some spear fishing alone, providing he will be careful. And as for you, Omar," he continued. "I expect you to keep your promise and do some real diving today."

Omar respected his father too much to argue, although he did not want to go without him. Silently he nodded, and then the two boys went on their way.

Gomez smirked at Omar and said, "Let's go. I'll race you to the beach."

The minute the two brothers jumped into the crystal-clear water Omar forgot his disappointment that his brother had won the race over the burning sand. As much as Omar resented his brother's teasing, he felt great admiration for him. Now he admired the way Gomez gripped the heavy spear and shot downward with the ease and grace of a dolphin. It took only a few seconds until he bobbed up again with his first catch. He threw the fish into the canoe and grinned at Omar.

"How about coming down yourself?" he asked.

Omar held onto the canoe, "I will, I will," he said hastily. "But Gomez, please don't take any chances and stay down too long. You know that father warned you yesterday."

"You worry about yourself," Gomez called. Then he flipped back his hair, took a few deep breaths, and down he went again.

Now came the big moment for Omar to dive himself, and he was determined to dive well today. He let go of the canoe and submerged quickly.

A few feet below the surface the very water seemed to be alive with fish. The trembling rays of the sun penetrated the clear water and illuminated the colorful fish in a soft, mysterious light. Yet the whole scene seemed almost unreal because no sound broke the deep silence.

By now Omar's breath began to give out and he felt like darting to the surface. However, he forced himself to overcome his panic and swam deeper toward the pink coral reef. It was covered with flaming red sponges and the curiously nodding heads of purple worms. Scattered over the coral like precious diamonds were thousands and thousands of sparkling sea gems.

But the sight of numerous clams half hidden in the reef dampened Omar's enthusiasm a little. With their wide-open jaws they seemed to be just waiting for Omar. If he swam too near, they would close their shells as quick as a flash over a finger or an arm. Omar kept well away from the gaping jaws of the clams, swimming with smooth, careful strokes.

When he finally came to the surface he was very happy. His father would be proud of him when he heard how well Omar had dived today.

Gomez emerged a few feet away with another catch. He was panting for air but nevertheless didn't linger long. After treading water for a few moments, he took a deep breath and went down again.

A slight breeze had come up and sent gusts of hot air from across the desert. The water, however, was still as cool and smooth as flowing silk.

Omar turned on his back and paddled slowly to the canoe. He held on to the crudely carved wood which gave him a funny, tickling feeling in his palms. Then as he hung on to the canoe he suddenly went limp all over. The water around him became cold as ice.

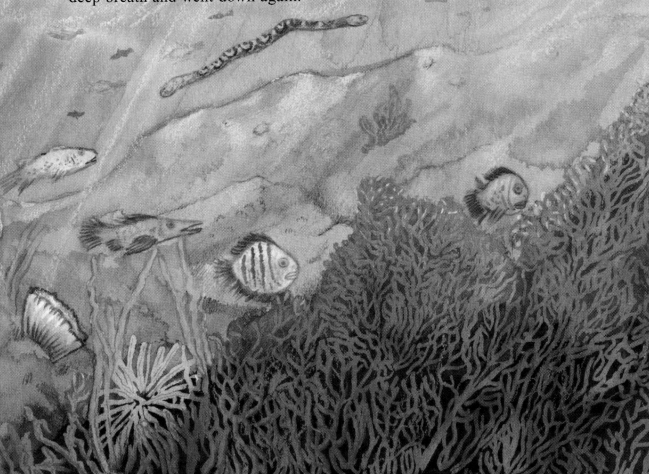

Before Omar even saw the motionless shadow he knew that a shark must be near. With a quick glance he scanned the water below him and saw that most of the fish had disappeared into the countless alcoves of the reef. That was all he needed to know. In one smooth motion he slipped into the canoe.

The shark slowly emerged from the deep water and started circling the boat. He had a huge, silvery, streamlined body, small, murderous eyes, and a set of teeth that made Omar shudder. The boy leaned over the side of the canoe and looked frantically for his brother. The water was almost deserted. Only a few herring fish darted about.

There was no sign of Gomez.

Omar scanned the water from the other side of the boat. About fifteen feet below, half hidden by the protruding ridge of a deep alcove in the reef, he saw his brother.

Omar's hand went to his mouth to stifle a cry. He saw that his brother's hand had been caught in one of the many clams and he was desperately trying to free himself. But he was already weakened by lack of air and seemed unable to pry his hand loose.

"Oh, how could he have been so careless," moaned Omar. He knew that he had only a few precious seconds in which to save his brother.

There was a slim chance that the shark might not attack if Omar could disregard him completely. He felt his mouth go dry as he lowered himself into the water. He did not turn his head when the shark moved in closer. Without any outward sign of his deadly fear he went straight down.

Never before had Omar dived as deep as that, and he felt as if his lungs would burst. For a second everything went black before his eyes.

But then he saw his brother in front of him. His body was swaying, helpless from the terrible lack of air. His hand was caught in the closed jaws of the clam. If he had not stayed underwater until there was hardly any breath left in him,

he might have been able to free himself somehow. The cocky expression Gomez usually wore was gone. He looked at Omar with horror in his eyes.

Omar acted quickly. With deft fingers he pried the clam loose from the coral. He left it attached to Gomez's hand because he didn't want to waste precious time. He could attend to the clam when they were safe in the canoe, if they ever reached it.

The shark, whose giant shadow had been hovering above their heads, swam toward them. Omar tried to ignore the shark as he grabbed Gomez by the armpits and started upward. Suddenly the shark seemed to look directly at Omar with his murderous, yellow eyes. He came in closer, almost brushing against him with his powerful, fan-like fins. Omar's fingers began to loosen their grip on his brother, and they started to sink. The water around them had grown murky with waves churned by the shark.

If it was true that a shark might not attack if his victim showed no sign of fear, then Omar knew what he had to do. He tightened his fingers around his brother's arm until he could feel his nails sinking into the soft flesh. Then he turned his back on the shark and began to swim upward in calm, slow motions.

The effort took all Omar's strength and courage. Only a few feet more and they would be safe. A few feet more was all they needed.

When their heads broke the surface the shark came in for attack. He made a sharp turn and shot directly at Omar through the boiling waves. For a split second they were face to face, the shark a dreadful sight with his huge set of razor-sharp teeth.

In desperation, Omar took the last measure his father had taught him in an emergency like this. He let go of Gomez, raised his right arm and slapped the shark across its pointed nose. Then he struck again and again and again.

For a long moment the shark seemed stunned and motionless. Then he churned about, brushing against Omar's face with his rough fins as he turned toward the deep water.

Omar grabbed Gomez and pulled him into the canoe. Gomez sank to the floor, too exhausted to move, while Omar fell forward on his knees. His breath came in painful gasps and his eyes felt as if they would burst from their sockets. For a moment he gave way to the wave of faintness that washed over him, and supported his head against his arms on the seat in the boat's stern.

But only for a moment. Then he felt for his brother's arm. He took a knife and with its strong handle chipped away part of the shell. Although Gomez winced with pain, Omar worked fast until he could press the knife in and pry the clam open.

"It's only a flesh wound and will heal fast," Omar said after he had examined the wrist. He wrapped his dry shirt around it to stop the bleeding.

His brother opened his eyes weakly. He smiled at Omar and his smile was full of love and admiration. "Thank you, my brother," he said, "thank you."

Omar gave the makeshift bandage a last tug. "Shhh," he said, "do not speak now. You must rest."

Suddenly he felt very weary. His whole body ached and his right hand was bruised from fighting off the shark. However, it was not time for him to rest yet. Slowly he took the paddle and brought the boat in safely to the dock.

The next morning when Omar awoke he found a spear next to his sleeping mat. His father stood looking down at him, warm approval in his eyes. Omar jumped to his feet, gripping the spear tightly in his hand.

"You will be a fine spear-fisherman, my Son," his father said, and Omar lowered his head, a great surge of happiness rushing through him.

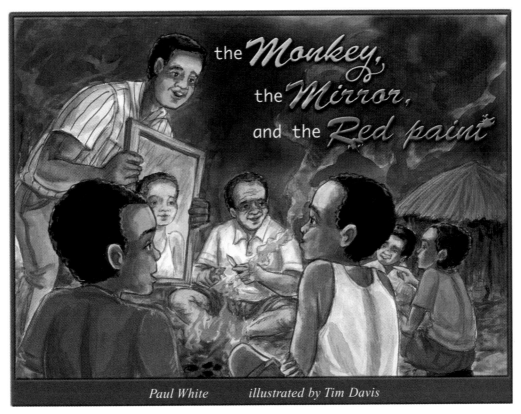

the **Monkey,** the **Mirror,** and the **Red paint**

Paul White   *illustrated by Tim Davis*

Daudi held a great mirror before him. Those who came to the camp-fire crowded round to see themselves in it.

"Mirrors are things of wisdom," said Yohanna, who had just finished carving a small wooden dog.

M'gogo looked from the little large-eyed puppy at his feet to the wooden miniature in Yohanna's hand.

"There is another mirror which makes it possible for you to see inside your skin. The four-legged ones of the jungle will help you to understand it."

'Vumbe was a tan-coloured monkey who was interested in everything and who spent much of his time both in mischief and in rummaging in the rubbish-heap near the Jungle Hospital.

One morning he found an object that gave him no little joy. It was a nearly empty pot of red paint.

He sped through the thornbush, clutching his treasure and chuckling with glee.

Twiga the giraffe saw it all and thought thoughts of alarm. He bent his neck gently as 'Vumbe chattered importantly. Monkey wisdom and his strong curiosity urged him to wrench off the lid and investigate.

Giraffe knew the worst had happened when he saw 'Vumbe's head disappear into the pot as far as his ears.

Slowly, an oddly decorated monkey face appeared. 'Vumbe could smell oil, but no matter how he rolled his eyes he could not see his face.

Twiga coughed a gentle cough and with difficulty kept laughter from entering his neck.

"*'Vumbe,*" he said huskily, "your face will cause your family no amusement. You yourself will have no joy in the hard work of your uncle's paw in the way you know so well."

The corners of 'Vumbe's mouth moved up and down and a tear ran uncomfortably down his nose. He dropped the pot.

In a small voice he said, "What shall I do then?"

Giraffe nibbled at the thorntree shoots and thought deep thoughts. He turned to 'Vumbe:

"O ball of mischief, if you go carefully to the paw-paw tree at the hospital and look through the door you will see a small shining sort of window. Look into it and you will look back at yourself. This useful object is called 'mirror.' It is a

thing of true wisdom. With it you will be able to see your trouble and remove it. That is the special and most valuable use of this shining thing."

Little monkey waited for no more. He scuttled towards the hospital, going more cautiously as he came closer.

He peered through the fence, climbed it, looked this way and that. There was the paw-paw tree, there was the door, and there was the window of wisdom.

He took a deep breath, bolted through the door. There was the mirror, but before he could look into it, voices came from outside.

'Vumbe grabbed the mirror and scuttled through the window, up the pomegranate tree and on to the roof.

"Stop, thief!" someone shouted, and a large stone whizzed through the air.

Over the wall, through a hedge, round trees he rushed, till he stopped, panting, under a jifu bush.

He was about to look at himself when jackal passed. 'Vumbe was pleased to see the way hyaena's partner looked at the mirror under his arm. Even the wife of Simba the lion stopped and looked at him—a thing she had never done before. Monkey then made a tour

of the larger buyu trees to impress both friends and relations. He felt warm in his inner monkey as he saw eyes turn towards him and mouths that moved behind hands.

'Vumbe made self-satisfied noises which stopped suddenly when he saw Twiga looking at him rather queerly.

"Have you looked at yourself, small monkey?"

'Vumbe shook his head, and in so doing he noticed something dancing along in front of him. As he moved the mirror to and fro he noticed how it threw a handful of bright light.

Curiosity welled up in his mind. He flicked the shining patch into the questioning eyes of Twiga who blinked and swung his neck sharply away.

The Monkey, the Mirror, and the Red Paint 317

'Vumbe somersaulted with monkey glee and dashed farther into the jungle.

In the deep green coolness he saw Lwa-lwa the tortoise. The flying blob of light flashed blindingly in his beady eyes. Tortoise's head disappeared quickly under his shell and his voice came shrilly:

"Stop it at once, or I shall inform the senior members of your family tree."

'Vumbe swung by his tail and applauded his own sense of humour. He laughed till his ribs ached when he found that the light flashing in hippo's eyes made him sneeze in a way that reminded him of thunderstorms.

Twiga walked over to where mischievous monkey still swung by his tail and said very gently:

"Small one, you are so intent on mischief that you have forgotten the condition of your nose. A mirror is made to look in, not to play with. The light it reflects opens up the dark places. It helps you to see and avoid things of danger like pythons and leopards."

But 'Vumbe made a rude face and scuttled on to the top of an ant hill, where he saw Mbisi the hyaena winking at him.

'Vumbe came down to hyaena's level and heard his sinister whisper.

"O monkey, take no notice of giraffe. Do not look in that thing, or you will have fear."

'Vumbe shuddered and his mouth went dry.

"Wrap it in a banana leaf and hide it," advised Mbisi, slinking off towards the rubbish-heap.

Mischievous monkey decided to use it just once more when he saw his uncle Nyani comfortably and happily eating bananas.

The mirror moved in mischievous monkey's hand. Nyani blinked as the blinding light flickered into his face. He shaded his eyes and peered round to see what was producing the trouble.

Vaguely through the irritating glare he saw 'Vumbe with something dazzling in his hand.

Twiga saw that trouble was near and came closer.

Nyani continued to screw up his eyes and blink as the patch of light hovered round his face. Monkey words of horrid violence came through his clenched teeth, and threats that would turn monkey blood to water were directed towards gleeful little 'Vumbe.

With the skill of years, Nyani peeled an over-ripe banana, his hairy arms shot out and—*Wham!*—'Vumbe staggered back, tripped and fell, clutching the mirror over his head. His features were now decorated not only with red paint but with over-ripe banana.

Mbisi the hyaena laughed his evil laugh as he heard sounds of monkey misery mixed with the noise of hard paws striking with enthusiasm.

Twiga waited a suitable time and then came close to the tree where small monkey stood, for it was more comfortable that way, letting the cool wind from the jungle blow caressingly on his less comfortable portions.

Twiga said, "Small monkey, what is the use of a mirror unless you use it for its proper purposes? It is not a toy or an ornament or a charm."

But such are the ways of monkey wisdom that little mischievous monkey turned his back on giraffe, wrapped the mirror in a long strip of buyu bark and stuffed it in a convenient hollow in his family tree.

"The Bible is the Great Mirror," said Daudi. "Read it and you see yourself exactly as God sees you. It is to be read, not merely carried. A closed Bible on a shelf does little for its owner.

"To make light of the Bible, to misquote it, to twist its words to suit your convenience are certain ways of producing trouble.

"Its own words are, 'The man who looks into the perfect mirror of God's Law, the law of liberty, and makes a habit of so doing, is not the man who sees and forgets. He puts the Law into practice and wins true happiness.'"

Conflict in Stories

"A Spear for Omar" has something in common with almost every story ever written. It has a main character who struggles for something—and either wins or loses.

What does Omar struggle against? First, he fights his own fear, then his brother's mocking, then the shark. And why does he struggle? He wants to prove himself worthy, not only to his father, but also to himself.

A struggle almost always comes from a character's wanting something. Omar wants to be brave like his brother and father; he wants his brother to stop making fun of him. He wants to rescue Gomez from the shark.

Internal and External Conflicts

Struggles in stories are called *conflicts*. Sometimes the character has a conflict inside himself. Which of Omar's struggles are inside? His struggle with his fear of drowning is clearly inside his own mind. Can you think of something you wanted to do but were afraid of doing? Do you remember how you felt? You had an *internal conflict.*

Other conflicts are with people or things outside the character— *external conflicts.* Which of Omar's struggles are external? The one with his brother and the one with the shark. One conflict is more physical than the other, but both are with forces outside himself.

Other Conflicts

Omar's conflict with his fear is the *main conflict.* But others in the story have conflicts too. Gomez and his father have a conflict. Can you find it on page 309? And Gomez has a conflict with a clam. But these are *secondary conflicts,* which mostly help to intensify the main conflict. They never concern the reader as much as the main conflict.

The Need for Conflict

Why do you think every story has conflict? Primarily, it makes the story a story. Think how different "A Spear for Omar" would be if Omar had been given his spear at the beginning and were as good at fishing as Gomez. The unusual setting and the action of spearing fish would still be interesting. But without any conflict, the writing would be *informative* or *descriptive;* that is, it would be perhaps a report or an essay.

To have a story, a *narrative,* there must be conflict. Narratives have beginnings and middles and ends. The beginning lets the reader see what the character wants. Can you find where Omar states his innermost desire on the second page of the story? Where does the author introduce Omar's desire to stop his brother's teasing?

The middle of a story presents the struggle. In Omar's story, the middle is the longest part. Do you think that is true of most stories? Why do you think the middle tends to be longer? It takes more time to show how a character responds to his problems than it does to show he has them. If the middle is too hurried or short, the story is not satisfying. It does not let us feel with the character or imagine how *we* might respond.

The ending of a story is the *resolution,* the outcome. How a conflict turns out is most important; it gives the story its meaning. Take Omar's struggle with fear, for example. Suppose Omar had not overcome his fear in time to save Gomez. "A Spear for Omar" would then be a far different story, wouldn't it? Instead of teaching that fear can be mastered, the story would suggest that fear will always be the master.

When you read a story, find the character who most wants something. Follow his struggle to the end—and then ask, "What does that ending make the story say?"

5

ENDEAVORS

MOSES AND JOSHUA

Henry Becker

No Small Parts

Everybody knew that of all the teachers at Riverside Christian School, Mrs. Morrison did the best job putting on plays, even if she was kind of old. I had been in plays in the third and fourth grades, but they weren't anything compared to this. Now I was in Mrs. Morrison's fifth-grade class, trying out for the part of Joshua. Crossing the Jordan River and fighting the battle of Jericho—this play was definitely the thing!

It probably wasn't as exciting for the sixth graders since they'd gotten to be in a play the year before, but when you come right down to it, there

wasn't a sixth grader who said he'd rather not.

Everybody got a script to learn a part for tryouts. Mrs. Morrison gave me a big smile. "Here's a script for you, Mark. Choose a character and memorize some of the lines for the tryouts."

I figured I would probably get the main part. Most other people thought I would too. Just about everybody knew I was one of the best speakers. Some of the sixth-grade boys said they thought I was too little, but I figured they were just jealous because they knew I

could do a better job than they could.

When I got home that night, I ran up to my room to start learning my lines. I highlighted them with my yellow marker—fifty-seven of them. I might as well learn all of them, not just a few for the tryouts.

I worked on my lines every spare minute for days. While I set the table I shouted, "Prepare food! For within three days you shall pass over this Jordan to possess the land that the Lord your God gives to you!" While I carried out the trash I said, "Go. View the land of Jericho. Tell us what sort of people inhabit this land and whether they stand in fear of our almighty God." While I mowed the lawn I yelled, "Listen to me! This is how you will know that the living God is among you. As soon as the priests' feet touch the edge of the mighty Jordan River, the waters shall part and stand up

in a heap." My sisters even had to come ask me to be quiet one night because I was saying my lines in my sleep.

After two weeks, long enough for everybody to practice the part he wanted to try out for, we had tryouts. The principal and all the fifth- and sixth-grade teachers were there.

When it was finally my turn, I saw Mrs. Morrison smile before she called my name. "Mark Whitmore," she said. Then she leaned over to say something to the principal. That made me stand up even taller and say my lines even louder. "She must think I'm pretty good," I thought. But then the principal started to frown a little, and he waved his hand around. That made it a little hard to concentrate. Mrs. Morrison looked worried, and she leaned back and whispered something to the principal.

And he whispered to her again and pointed somewhere on stage, and she whispered to him again and looked even more worried. And I was starting to get a little nervous.

I had to leave before the next person tried out, but I kind of hung around Mrs. Morrison for a minute wondering if she would go ahead and tell me something terrible. But she was too busy taking notes on the tryouts. She just said, "Goodbye, Mark. I'll see you in class in the morning."

After school the next day Mrs. Morrison asked all the people who had tried out to sit in the reading circle. The reading circle was the most cramped it had ever been. First she said the little speech that the sixth graders remembered from the year before. "You young folk are all so good that it was very hard for me to decide who would play which part. But, as always, some people will have more lines to say than others. Now, I don't want you to think that just because you may have gotten a smaller part, you're not good. After all, every part in this play is important. Every one of you is important. There are no small parts, just small actors."

Well, everybody knew that if Joshua got sick it would be a whole lot worse than if one of the Israelites who just marches around the wall did. We were all kind of squirming in our seats waiting for her to assign the parts, but she kept on going. "Now, one thing that we have to remember is that we have some unsaved parents who will be coming to see some of you in this play. All through our rehearsals and other preparations we have to remember to honor the Lord above all. Maybe some of them will come to know the Lord through our play."

Well, wouldn't you know it, she started with the smallest parts and worked up to assigning the big ones. I could tell that some people were happy and some were disappointed. I guess it was always that way. But I was starting to get a little worried about me. Maybe I was losing my nerve, but suddenly I wasn't as sure of myself as I had been.

Finally, when she had assigned all the way up through Caleb and I still had not been named, she stopped for a long, long time. Everybody started to get nervous, and I think I might have been the most nervous of all. Then she said, "I'll be assigning the part of Joshua tomorrow. All of you who have your parts, go home and learn them well so we can honor the Lord with this play."

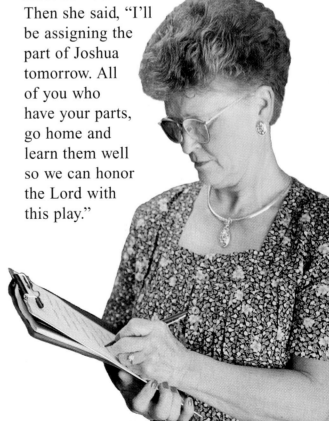

Everybody else was leaving and a bunch of them whispered to me that they thought I would get the part, but Mrs. Morrison asked me to stay and talk to her. I stood around until everybody else had left.

As soon as the rest were all gone, Mrs. Morrison said, "Mark, I didn't get a lot of sleep last night—worrying and praying. More worrying than praying, I'm afraid."

Now I could hardly stand it. "Well, what is it?" I asked.

She stopped a little, and then she said, "I'm afraid we can't give you the part of Joshua—"

"You mean I don't do a good job with Joshua's lines?" I could hardly believe it.

"Oh, no, it isn't that. It's just that we need someone a little different for this part. Well, Mark, I'm just going to put this to you straight—I'm afraid we need someone a bit bigger than you. Mr. Alexander and the other teachers and I all talked about it after tryouts last night. You're an excellent speaker, Mark, excellent! But since you are smaller than most of the other boys, and your voice is . . . well, quite a bit higher . . ."

"Yes, ma'am." My eyes stung some, but I wasn't going to let her see me cry.

"And after talking, the other teachers and I decided that we should use Randy Ortega from the sixth grade—"

"Randy Ortega!" I said it so loudly I almost scared myself. "I never hear him say anything! How could he do all the shouting Joshua has to do?"

"Well," she said in a quiet voice, "Randy is a big boy with a deeper voice, and I think he could do a good job with some help. I know he's shy, but this might be just what he needs."

"But what about me?" I asked. "I mean, what part do I get now? Can I at least be Caleb or somebody like that?"

"Well . . ." she hesitated. "We would rather you be an understudy and a coach. I wasn't sure Randy could learn his lines well without a good coach—"

"I'll say," I said.

"Mark, I won't tolerate that kind of spirit."

"Yes, ma'am."

"And we thought you could do the job," she went on. "You can also be an Israelite. Since you'll be an understudy, you'll have to have a nonspeaking part."

328

"Mrs. Morrison, I can't," I said. "I just can't help Randy when he took my part away from me—please don't ask me to do that."

"Well, Mark," she said slowly, "first of all, let me say that Randy didn't take your part away from you—that was a part you were never promised. And let me say furthermore that before you say you can't, you should ask the Lord if He wants you to. Because if He does, He will give you the strength to do it."

"Yes, ma'am." I turned slowly and left.

Well, I didn't pray about it. Not really. I put off helping Randy on purpose, and he was too shy to ask me. When the first rehearsal came, we hadn't gotten together even once. I sneaked into the back to see the first rehearsal. It was only for people with speaking parts. Randy was still reading his part from the paper. He didn't have any expression, and he couldn't pro-nounce a bunch of the words. He wasn't into the character at all. Mrs. Morrison was pretty patient with him, but I could tell she was kind of frustrated. Deep down inside, I felt smug. "I tried to warn her," I thought.

question. Did you even pray about working with Randy?"

I just looked down.

She sighed, but she still sounded patient and still kept her voice soft so the rest of the class couldn't hear what she was saying. "Maybe you *will* pray about it tonight. But before you do, read some verses—I'll find the reference and give it to you before you leave today."

I didn't much care anymore. I'd gotten plenty of verses in my life. She put a piece of paper on my desk later while she was checking homework. All it said was, "Read Deuteronomy 3:23-28 tonight." I stuck the paper away in my math book.

I was just opening that book to do my homework when Dad called us all for devotions. There was the paper with the note on it, so I grabbed it and took it with me.

"Can we read this for devotions tonight, Dad?" I asked. And I explained how Mrs. Morrison had said I should read that before praying about helping Randy with his lines.

So Dad read it in his quiet voice.

Behind the Scenes

The next day Mrs. Morrison called me up to her desk again. "I was hoping I wouldn't have to talk to you about the play again, Mark," she said. "But it looks as if you haven't been willing to help Randy as I asked you. Let me ask you a

And I besought the Lord at that time, saying, O Lord God, thou hast begun to shew thy servant thy greatness, and thy mighty hand: for what God is there in heaven or in earth, that can do according to thy works, and according to thy might? I pray thee, let me go over, and see the good land that is beyond Jordan, that goodly mountain, and Lebanon. But the Lord was wroth with me for your sakes, and would not hear me: and the Lord said unto me, Let it suffice thee; speak no more unto me of this matter. Get thee up into the top of Pisgah, and lift up thine eyes westward, and northward, and southward, and eastward, and behold it with thine eyes: for thou shalt not go over this Jordan. But charge Joshua, and encourage him, and strengthen him: for he shall go over before this people, and he shall cause them to inherit the land which thou shalt see.

When he was done I said, "I don't get it. I mean, I know that Moses is talking there, and I know that story about how Moses didn't get to go into the Promised Land, but I don't see why Mrs. Morrison wanted me to read that before I prayed about it. I mean, except that it has Joshua in it, and Randy's going to be Joshua now."

Dad looked down for a moment and then asked, "How did Moses respond when he was asked to train Joshua?"

Sandy, my older sister, thought for a moment before she spoke. "Moses obeyed and was content to train Joshua or to do whatever the Lord asked him to do."

Dad then looked at me. "How did you respond when asked to help Randy? Maybe you should consider Moses' example in his reactions and then consider your reactions to the task before you."

So Dad read it again all the way through.

"Now, Mark," Mom said, "Why don't you take some time to pray about it right now? We'll pray for you too and ask the Lord to show you just what He wants you to do."

But even before we prayed I knew what the Lord wanted me to do.

It was pretty rough helping Randy. He wasn't exactly what I would call a quick learner. It seemed like a million times that I had to say, "All right, say that line again." And he would say, just the same way, "Pass through the hosts—" and I would stop him. "Randy! Joshua is talking to all the officers, and he's excited. Say 'PASS THROUGH THE HOSTS!!'" And Randy would say, "PASS THROUGH THE HOSTS!!" And over and over again we did it.

And he started to get a little better. We got to talk some after we worked, too, and he seemed to be a pretty nice guy, and not so shy when you got to know him. I found out he was really funny sometimes. And he didn't try to act big and tough like a lot of the sixth graders do. In fact, one time he said to me, "Mark, I know you were supposed to be Joshua." He hadn't ever said anything about it before. Then he said, "It was really nice of you to help me. I was pretty scared when Mrs. Morrison told me she wanted me to be Joshua. But I feel like I can do a lot better now."

I was about to say something like, "Well, I'm glad to do it," because I couldn't stand to think about what he would have sounded like if I hadn't helped him. But he interrupted me. He said, "A lot of the other guys made fun of me because a fifth grader was going to help me learn my lines. But I told them to get lost, and they did." He laughed a little. "After all, I am the biggest boy in sixth grade."

Well, I'd never thought about it from his side of things. I didn't say what I was going to say.

Randy was a little better every day we worked together. I could tell he was really trying hard. And I tried hard to remember how Moses helped Joshua, and how he did a lot of work behind the scenes—just like me, Mark Whitmore.

I liked Mrs. Morrison better now than I had for a while, and sometimes she called me Moses, like a private joke.

Then dress rehearsal night came, and I got to dress up like an Israelite. I guess it was fun. I got to watch Randy the whole time, and he did a great job. He messed up only a couple of times. At the end I heard Mr. Alexander joke to Mrs. Morrison, "They say that if the dress rehearsal goes well, the performance night will be a flop."

But Mrs. Morrison said, "I don't believe in any of that superstitious nonsense. We've always had good dress rehearsals, and we've always had outstanding plays."

Her words reminded me of stories I'd heard, stories about opening nights of plays when one of the lead players got sick and the director had to find a stand-in at the last minute. That's what understudies are for.

I couldn't help thinking . . . What if Randy gets sick at the last minute and they need somebody? . . . I'm the only other person who knows the lines.

I thought about it a lot, and I know I shouldn't have. Especially because Randy didn't get sick, and he was right there ready to be Joshua on performance night. Just before Mrs. Morrison called us all together for prayer, he pulled me into a corner.

"Mark, it's great! I've been praying for this for months!" he said.

I wanted to say, "What? You want me to be Joshua after all?" But I just waited.

He said, "My mother is here, Mark! She came! She isn't a Christian, and she would never come to anything at this school. She never would really say whether she was going to come to this play, even though I was going to be Joshua. So I prayed and prayed, and tonight she came! I just peeked out and saw her sitting in the second row!"

I was really glad, but I didn't get a chance to say anything because Mrs. Morrison was calling us together. "I know we have some parents here who are not saved," she said. "Let's especially pray that they will see the Lord in our performance tonight."

Randy really did do a great job being Joshua. I mean, he really sounded like he was Joshua! I did a pretty good job of being an Israelite too. Whenever I got a chance, I peeked out into the second row and

tried to figure out who Randy's mother was. I finally decided she was the lady with the dark hair who kept smiling a lot and couldn't stop looking at Randy.

When it was all over, everybody applauded, especially for Randy. I couldn't help thinking how if I had been where he was, they would have been applauding for me. But I had helped behind the scenes, so maybe they were applauding for me a little bit. And besides, what difference did it make? Changing my attitude about helping Randy pleased the Lord, and that's what matters most.

Everybody's family came backstage to congratulate all of us, and of course my family told me that I

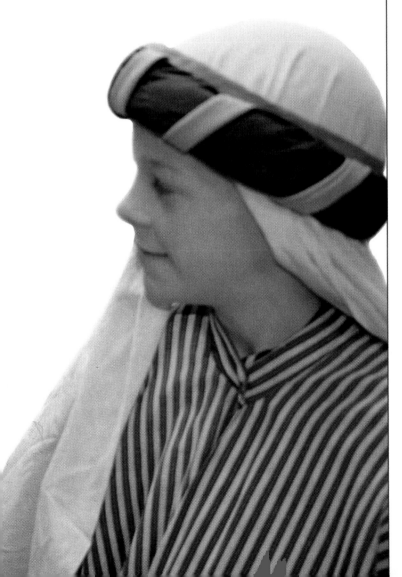

was the best Israelite of all. But when Randy got a chance he ran over to me and whispered, "Thanks, Moses."

I was pretty surprised. "How did you know about that?" I asked. "I never told you."

"No, but Mrs. Morrison did." His face was all lit up like I had never seen it. "Have you seen a program?" I hadn't yet, and he handed it to me. Right there at the bottom of the first page it said, "Director: Linda Morrison. Assistant Director: Mark Whitmore." "Wow!" I shouted. That was almost as good as getting a speaking part! But Randy was pulling on my arm. "Come on, Moses," he said. "I want you to meet my mother."

David's Endeavor

I Samuel 17:1-54

illustrated by Del Thompson

1 Now the Philistines gathered together their armies to battle. . . .

2 And Saul and the men of Israel were gathered together . . . and set the battle in array against the Philistines.

3 And the Philistines stood on a mountain on the one side, and Israel stood on a mountain on the other side: and there was a valley between them.

4 And there went out a champion out of the camp of the Philistines, named Goliath, of Gath, whose height was six cubits and a span.

5 And he had an helmet of brass upon his head, and he was armed with a coat of mail; and the weight of the coat was five thousand shekels of brass.

6 And he had greaves of brass upon his legs, and a target of brass between his shoulders.

7 And the staff of his spear was like a weaver's beam; and his spear's head weighed six hundred shekels of iron: and one bearing a shield went before him.

8 And he stood and cried unto the armies of Israel, and said unto them, Why are ye come out to set your battle in array? am not I a Philistine, and ye servants to Saul? choose you a man for you, and let him come down to me.

9 If he be able to fight with me, and to kill me, then will we be your servants: but if I prevail against him, and kill him, then shall ye be our servants, and serve us.

10 And the Philistine said, I defy the armies of Israel this day; give me a man, that we may fight together.

11 When Saul and all Israel heard those words of the Philistine, they were dismayed, and greatly afraid.

12 Now David was the son of that Ephrathite of Bethlehem-judah, whose name was Jesse; and he had eight sons: and the man went among men for an old man in the days of Saul.

13 And the three eldest sons of Jesse went and followed Saul to the battle: and the names of his three sons that went to the battle were Eliab the firstborn, and next unto him Abinadab, and the third Shammah.

14 And David was the youngest: and the three eldest followed Saul.

15 But David went and returned from Saul to feed his father's sheep at Bethlehem.

16 And the Philistine drew near morning and evening, and presented himself forty days.

17 And Jesse said unto David his son, Take now for thy brethren an ephah of this parched corn, and these ten loaves, and run to the camp to thy brethren;

18 And carry these ten cheeses unto the captain of their thousand, and look how thy brethren fare, and take their pledge.

19 Now Saul, and they, and all the men of Israel, were in the valley of Elah, fighting with the Philistines.

20 And David rose up early in the morning, and left the sheep with a keeper, and took, and went, as Jesse had commanded him; and he came to the trench, as the host was going forth to the fight, and shouted for the battle.

21 For Israel and the Philistines had put the battle in array, army against army.

22 And David left his carriage in the hand of the keeper of the carriage, and ran into the army, and came and saluted his brethren.

23 And as he talked with them, behold, there came up the champion, the Philistine of Gath, Goliath by name, out of the armies of the Philistines, and spake according to the same words: and David heard them.

24 And all the men of Israel, when they saw the man, fled from him, and were sore afraid.

25 And the men of Israel said, Have ye seen this man that is come up? surely to defy Israel is he come up: and it shall be, that the man who killeth him, the king will enrich him with great riches, and will give him his daughter, and make his father's house free in Israel.

26 And David spake to the men that stood by him, saying, What shall be done to the man that killeth this Philistine, and taketh away the reproach from Israel? for who is this uncircumcised Philistine, that he should defy the armies of the living God?

27 And the people answered him after this manner, saying, So shall it be done to the man that killeth him.

28 And Eliab his eldest brother heard when he spake unto the men; and Eliab's anger was kindled against David, and he said, Why camest thou down hither? and with

whom hast thou left those few sheep in the wilderness? I know thy pride, and the naughtiness of thine heart; for thou art come down that thou mightest see the battle.

29 And David said, What have I now done? Is there not a cause?

30 And he turned from him toward another, and spake after the same manner: and the people answered him again after the former manner.

31 And when the words were heard which David spake, they rehearsed them before Saul: and he sent for him.

32 And David said to Saul, Let no man's heart fail because of him; thy servant will go and fight with this Philistine.

33 And Saul said to David, Thou art not able to go against this Philistine to fight with him: for thou art but a youth, and he a man of war from his youth.

34 And David said unto Saul, Thy servant kept his father's sheep, and there came a lion, and a bear, and took a lamb out of the flock:

35 And I went out after him, and smote him, and delivered it out of his mouth: and when he arose against me, I caught him by his beard, and smote him, and slew him.

36 Thy servant slew both the lion and the bear: and this uncircumcised Philistine shall be as one of them, seeing he hath defied the armies of the living God.

37 David said moreover, The Lord that delivered me out of the paw of the lion, and out of the paw of the bear, he will deliver me out of the hand of this Philistine. And Saul said unto David, Go, and the Lord be with thee.

38 And Saul armed David with his armour, and he put an helmet of brass upon his head; also he armed him with a coat of mail.

39 And David girded his sword upon his armour, and he assayed to go; for he had not proved it. And David said unto Saul, I cannot go with these; for I have not proved them. And David put them off him.

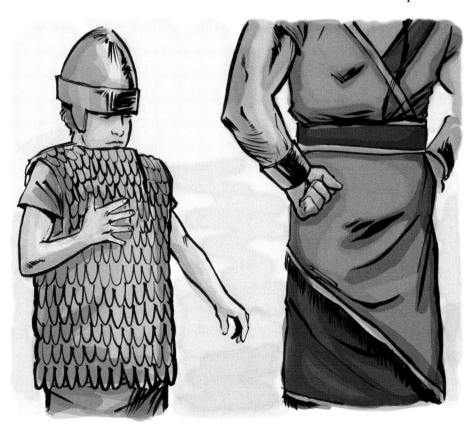

40 And he took his staff in his hand, and chose him five smooth stones out of the brook, and put them in a shepherd's bag which he had, even in a scrip; and his sling was in his hand: and he drew near to the Philistine.

41 And the Philistine came on and drew near unto David; and the man that bare the shield went before him.

42 And when the Philistine looked about, and saw David, he disdained him: for he was but a youth, and ruddy, and of a fair countenance.

43 And the Philistine said unto David, Am I a dog, that thou comest to me with staves? And the Philistine cursed David by his gods.

44 And the Philistine said to David, Come to me, and I will give thy flesh unto the fowls of the air, and to the beasts of the field.

45 Then said David to the Philistine, Thou comest to me with a sword, and with a spear, and with a shield: but I come to thee in the name of the Lord of hosts, the God of the armies of Israel, whom thou hast defied.

46 This day will the Lord deliver thee into mine hand; and I will smite thee, and take thine head from thee; and I will give

the carcases of the host of the Philistines this day unto the fowls of the air, and to the wild beasts of the earth; that all the earth may know that there is a God in Israel.

47 And all this assembly shall know that the Lord saveth not with sword and spear: for the battle is the Lord's, and he will give you into our hands.

48 And it came to pass, when the Philistine arose, and came and drew nigh to meet David, that David hasted, and ran toward the army to meet the Philistine.

49 And David put his hand in his bag, and took thence a stone, and slang it, and smote the Philistine in his forehead, that the stone sunk into his forehead; and he fell upon his face to the earth.

50 So David prevailed over the Philistine with a sling and with a stone, and smote the Philistine, and slew him; but there was no sword in the hand of David.

51 Therefore David ran, and stood upon the Philistine, and took his sword, and drew it out of the sheath thereof, and slew him, and cut off his head therewith. And when the Philistines saw their champion was dead, they fled.

52 And the men of Israel and of Judah arose, and shouted, and pursued the Philistines, until thou

come to the valley, and to the gates of Ekron. And the wounded of the Philistines fell down by the way to Shaaraim, even unto Gath, and unto Ekron.

53 And the children of Israel returned from chasing after the Philistines, and they spoiled their tents.

54 And David took the head of the Philistine, and brought it to Jerusalem; but he put his armour in his tent.

BIBLE STUDY
CLIMBING HIGHER

A mountaineer's goal is to climb higher and higher. There are special tools designed to help the mountaineer reach his goal. *Crampons* are spikes attached to boots to keep them from slipping. *Pitons* are spikes that can be driven into rock or ice to secure a rope. These are only two of the tools that make the mountaineer's climb easier and safer.

The goal of a Christian should be to increase daily in spiritual strength through prayer and Bible study. Some special tools can help accomplish this goal.

Cross-references

One Scripture can often help a reader to understand another Scripture. Many Bibles have additional references listed down the center or sides of the page or across the bottom. Such references are called *cross-references* because they *cross* from one Scripture to another, joining the same words, stories, or ideas. Look at the first sample Bible page. In I Samuel 17:4 there is a cross-reference to I Samuel 21:9 where Goliath is also mentioned. On the page with I Samuel 21:9, there is a cross reference to I Samuel 22:10 where Goliath is again mentioned.

> *A small letter in the verse matches the cross-reference.*

a I Sam. 17:51

b I Sam. 21:9

c I Sam. 16:21-23

d Gen. 37:13-14

4 And there went out a *a*champion out of the camp of the Philistines, named *b*Goliath, of Gath, whose height *was* six cubits and a span.

5 And *he had* an helmet of brass upon his head, and he was armed with a coat of mail; and the weight of the coat *was* five thousand shekels of brass.

6 And *he had* greaves of brass upon his legs, and a target of brass between his shoulders.

7 And the staff of his spear *was* like a weaver's beam; and his spear's head *weighed* six hundred shekels of iron: and one bearing a shield went before him.

8 And he stood and cried unto the armies of Israel, and said unto them, Why are ye come out to set *your* battle in array? *am* not I a Philistine, and ye servants to Saul? choose you a man for you, and let him come down to me.

9 If he be able to fight with me, and to kill me, then will

15 *c*But David went and returned from Saul to feed his father's sheep at Beth-lehem.

16 And the Philistine drew near morning and evening, and presented himself forty days.

17 And Jesse said unto David his son, Take now for thy brethren an ephah of this parched *corn,* and these ten loaves, and run to the camp to thy brethren;

18 And carry these ten cheeses unto the captain of *their* thousand, *d*and look how thy brethren fare, and take their pledge.

19 Now Saul, and they, and all the men of Israel, *were* in the valley of Elah, fighting with the Philistines.

20 And David rose up early in the morning, and left the sheep with a keeper, and took, and went, as Jesse had commanded him; and he came to the trench, as the host was going forth to the fight, and shouted for the battle.

21 For Israel and the Philistines had put the battle

Concordance

A *concordance* is an alphabetical list of key words that are found in the Scriptures, along with the references where they may be found. Many Bibles have a small concordance in the back. More complete concordances are available in separate volumes.

A person who reads the story of David and Goliath in I Samuel 17 might like to know if there are other giants mentioned in the Bible. Look at the sample concordance page. There are a number of other Scriptures where the word *giant* may be found.

The first part of the entry in a concordance often tells the meaning of the word.

A list of references tells where in Scripture the word can be found as part of a main idea.

The key word, in this case, gin, *is abbreviated with the first letter.*

Gethsemane—*A garden in which Jesus prayed just before his death*

Matthew 26:36 Then cometh Jesus . . . unto a place called G.

Mark 14:32 they came to a place which was named G.

Gezrites—*inhabitants of Gezer*

I Samuel 27:8 David . . . invaded . . . the G.

giant—*fearful one*

Deuteronomy 2:11 Which also were accounted g.

Joshua 12:4 Og . . . of the remnant of the giants

18:16 in the valley of the giants on the north

II Samuel 21:16 g. . . . thought to have slain David

I Chronicles 20:4 Sippai, . . . of the children of the g.

20:6 he . . . was the son of the g.

20:8 These were born unto the g.

Gideon—*One of the judges of Israel*

Judges 6:11 his son G. threshed wheat

7:1 G. and all the people . . . rose up early

8:4 G. came to Jordan and passed over

8:35 shewed they kindness to . . . Jerubbaal, namely, G.

gin—*A snare*

Job 18:9 The g. shall take him by the heel

Psalm 140:5 they have set gins for me

141:9 the gins of the workers of iniquity

Isaiah 8:14 for a g. . . . to the inhabitants

Amos 3:5 Can a bird fall . . . where no g. is for him?

Topical Study

Once a person knows how to use a concordance and cross-references, it is possible to do a *topical study.* A topical study can give a full picture of one idea or topic throughout the Bible. In doing a topical study of the word *giant,* it would become clear that Israel's trouble with giants did not begin with Goliath. Ever since their journey brought them to the Promised Land, the Israelites had met with giants. A topical study would also reveal that later in David's life he was almost killed by another Philistine giant named Ishbi-Benob, but God gave the victory to David and his fighting men.

God speaks through His Word, and those who love and serve Him want to know what He says. Prayer and Bible study are the sources of a Christian's daily strength and growth.

Today's Swordsmen

Andy Thomson

Gleaming swords dance under the lights. Two armed men leap back and forth at each other. A crowd looks on in respectful silence. The air is charged with tense expectation.

Perhaps this scene reminds you of the Three Musketeers or the famous sword fighters from another century. But it could describe one form of sword fighting that is still practiced today—the sport of fencing.

We usually think of sword fighters as men who fearlessly swing their swords while hanging from chandeliers or striding across tabletops. But today, fencing matches take place in narrow, taped-off lanes called fencing strips. Contests are supervised by judges and a director. Good fencers rely less on brute strength and more on skill and quick reflexes.

The Uniform

Unlike the deadly sword fighting of the past, modern fencing is carried out with concern for personal safety. Fencers wear helmets made of finely woven wire mesh. The fencing jacket is padded. The collar of the jacket and a heavy canvas bib attached to the mask protect the fencer's neck. A sturdy glove covers the fencer's sword hand.

One type of fencing sword is called a *foil*. It weighs a little more than one pound and is about three and a half feet long. A curving handguard protects the handgrip. The blade tapers to a flexible point, and a heavy plastic coating covers the blunted tip. A fencing foil cannot pierce the protective jacket of a fencer, but it can still inflict a nasty bruise if used improperly. Good fencers avoid hurting each

other with the foil. Since the goal of fencing is speed and skill, "muscling" a foil into an opponent is poor sportsmanship.

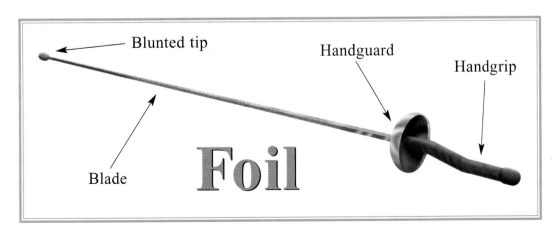

Blunted tip

Handguard

Handgrip

Blade

Foil

Competition

Fencers observe many rules of etiquette while competing. Opponents salute each other by standing at attention with their heels at right angles. The fencers do not face each other squarely. Rather, each turns his head slightly over his left or right shoulder to eye his opponent. He points his foil straight down. Then he snaps it upright so that the handguard is level with his chin. With the same brisk motion he returns the foil to its original position.

After a match, fencers remove their masks and shake hands. Fencers always shake hands with the hand that is not holding the foil. That means that a right-handed fencer will hold his foil in his right hand and shake hands with the left.

The fencer's stance is low. His feet are almost two shoulder widths apart. He holds his back arm above his head, with the wrist and hand relaxed. Every step takes coordination and poise; the fencer knows that he can use his stance to gain distance and power. He advances by stepping forward first with the front foot and then with the back. He retreats by moving the back foot first and following it with the front foot. The fencer lunges by leaping forward with the front foot. An effective lunge may cover a distance of six feet, yet the fencer is able to pull back quickly to retreat.

Salute

Lunge

Fencers also observe strict rules to score during the match. A fencer must claim his "right of attack." He does this by being the first one to make a threatening action. Usually he will simply thrust his foil forward. He may follow the thrust with any of several complicated moves. His opponent must first *parry,* or block, the attack or evade it. The opponent can then *riposte,* or counterattack. Then the first person must parry or evade. This back-and-forth type of attacking and defending continues until both persons draw back or one of them scores a point. A fencer scores a point by striking at his

Thrust

Parry

opponent's torso (chest and back). Hits directed elsewhere are against the rules.

A fencing match can be compared to a conversation. In conversation one person speaks, and the other replies. In fencing one person attacks and the other parries and counterattacks. It is impolite to interrupt one person's attack with a counterattack. Instead, the defender parries, ending the attack, and then has the chance to counterattack.

Riposte

Traditional fencing matches are supervised by four judges. The judges form a square around the fencers. They follow the fencers up and down the fencing strip. A fifth

350

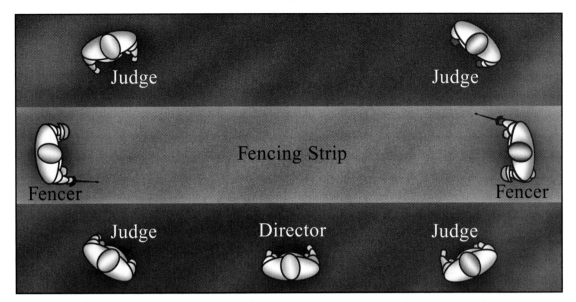

Judge   Judge

Fencing Strip

Fencer   Fencer

Judge   Director   Judge

person, called the director or president, governs the match. When a judge sees a point, he will call it, and the director recognizes him and consults quickly with the other judges. In recent years electronic equipment has replaced the judges in some matches, leaving only the director to decide on points. Electronic equipment is more accurate than judges, but is also expensive.

Although skill is the key to good fencing, the fencer can use his strength in some attacking techniques. He can *beat* his opponent's foil with a single sharp blow to the blade. This will knock it aside and allow him to *strike,* that is, to aim the tip of his foil at the opponent's mid-section. Or he can execute a *press* to force his opponent's blade down or away. A strong fencer can

also use the *glide,* pushing so hard against his opponent's blade that he forces it down, sliding his own blade across it to score a point.

Occasionally one fencer will try to block another fencer's glide by strength alone. When this happens, their foils will slide up

Corps-à-corps

against each other all the way to the handguards. The result is that they stand pushing against each other at the handguards. Such an encounter is called a *corps-à-corps*. It literally means "body-to-body." Although it looks dramatic, a *corps-à-corps* may mean that one or both opponents are using strength instead of skill.

Another basic technique is the *disengage*. In a disengage, a fencer quickly circles his blade under his

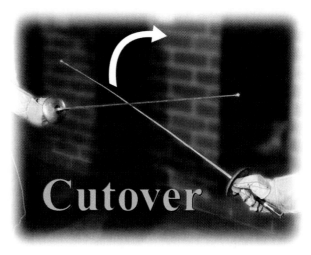

opponent's blade. A disengage can prevent a contest of strength. The fencer can also use a *cutover,* in which he circles his blade over the blade of his opponent. Although modern fencing does require strength, it is designed so that a person cannot win by strength alone but must develop speed, coordination, and strategy. As is true in any sport, fencers develop their skills with practice and hard work.

—Corps-à-Corps—

Jeri Massi

illustrated by Mary Ann Lumm

Blade to Blade

"Six . . . four . . . six—four—six!"

We thrust our foils back and forth, repeating the parries at Mr. LeBlanc's commands.

"Aha! Sloppy defense! Rest!"

Perspiring, we dropped our arms and stood up straight while he corrected Robert. "The power is here!" he exclaimed, straightening Robert's gloved wrist. "Don't bend it so!" He clapped his hands. "Come, come!"

We all lined up before him like soldiers. "Ah, Jack, you will preside. My four judges will be Bruce, Rick, Harry, Sid. Ah, now, let me see." He deliberately ran his eyes up and down the line of us. "You, Patrick." He pointed at me and then at Robert. "And you, Robert."

Inside, I groaned. Robert! Yes, he held his wrist wrong, but that didn't matter. He outweighed me by at least thirty pounds. I had never beaten him. Nobody had ever beaten him.

He took his position, the light fencing foil pointed down to the ground as he prepared for the salute.

I took my position; we saluted smartly. Yes, that one dramatic part of the game—the snapping of the foil straight up and then snapping it back down—he had mastered that. We slipped our masks on.

"Are you ready?" Jack asked him. Robert grunted. I sensed his excitement. Another victory for him.

"Are you ready?" Jack asked me.

"Yes," I replied.

"Commence!"

I sprang from my place with a leap. He hesitated. I feinted to his outside, slipped the point under his blade, and neatly scored against him, tapping him in the chest.

All four judges agreed to the score, and Jack nodded. For once I was winning, but I knew it wouldn't last long.

He slapped his foil against mine, beating the blade. The blow knocked my foil aside. Effortlessly, he pressed his blade against my foil and slid it straight across until the red protective button nipped me in the chest. The judges called it.

Beating and pressing the blade were Robert's techniques. He could overpower anybody in the class. He quickly scored on me three more times.

It went on until my right hand could barely grip the hilt. He made me retreat, and I gave ground as far as I could, even beyond the white warning line on the fencing strip.

Once when he executed a straight lunge, I ducked low, bending at the waist and dropping my back leg as though in a split. The

point went over my head. As he retreated, trying to pull out of too deep a stance, I pushed myself forward and caught him again, square in the chest. But the judges argued over my move. In fencing a man must have the right of attack. They were accustomed to somebody's parrying a thrust before counterattacking. They argued about my ducking, for they had never seen anybody avoid a hit in that way.

I knew that behind his mask Robert was sneering, for he already had four points on me, and the match was nearly over.

For once, Mr. LeBlanc interfered with the boys in a class match.

"The technique was masterful. Award the point, Jack."

"Yes, sir."

"The time is up," he said. "I want to get another match in."

Grateful to my teacher, I slipped the mask off and went up to shake hands with Robert. He gripped my hand and ground my knuckles together. I gasped and winced.

"Masterful!" he exclaimed sarcastically and strode away.

Holding my left hand in my right, I walked off the strip.

"Ah, masterful!" Mr. LeBlanc exclaimed much later to my parents. Mom smiled, and Dad glanced over at me.

"Next month is your first tournament, Patrick," Mom said.

Mr. LeBlanc rubbed his hands together. "What a day that will be! There will be spectators there from the Olympic Committee—" He stopped short. "Pardon me, Julio," he said to my father.

Dad waved it away. He glanced down at his bad leg a little wistfully but without pain in his eyes. "Once it hurt to think of it, but not any more." He glanced at me fondly. "Not with Patrick here. Come here, Son."

I came and sat on the arm of his chair. Before my birth my father had been diagnosed with bone cancer, and the doctors had amputated his right leg just above the knee. No longer could he fence back and forth on the strip, high on the balls of his feet, ready to leap or lunge. In his prime he had been an Olympic contender, but now he was just my father, Dad instead of Poppa, for he and my mother wanted me to grow up thoroughly American.

But I had seen film clips of him, and ever since I had been able to walk he had shown me his foils and equipment. Fencing, I had always thought, was the finest sport in the world.

"Mr. LeBlanc, do you think I can win next month?" I asked.

"Of course I do!"

"But Robert—"

"But Robert! But Robert!" LeBlanc threw his hands into the air. "He has strength, but no style. Look what you did to him tonight!"

"I lost to him tonight."

"Yes, but the way you scored!" He turned to my parents. "The big boy comes in, so—" He imitated Robert's powerful lunge. "What does the little one do—" He imitated the way I had ducked. To my surprise it did look graceful. Mom and Dad looked pleased. "And then so—he comes up and thrusts the boy right on the chest." Mr. LeBlanc demonstrated the lunge, a little bit of sweat gleaming in his silver hair. "Where have I seen such technique?" he asked, smiling at my father. He had been my father's coach.

"Where indeed?" Dad asked, laughing.

Mr. LeBlanc stood up to leave. Dad gripped his crutch and stood up, shaking hands with him. "Good night, good night, LeBlanc. Thank you."

"Good night, Julio, and you, Marie. Good night, Patrick."

"Good night, sir. Thank you."

That night I lay awake in bed, watching the triangles of light from the highway play across the ceiling of my narrow room. Our house bordered the highway, but the traffic had become my lullaby. I went to sleep thinking of the tournament, of Robert, of Mr. LeBlanc. "Masterful," they had said, but what was it to be a master? What good are thinking and practice and style if, with one strong blow from his blade, Robert could sweep away my defense?

At breakfast I was still sleepy. "Patrick, you are dragging. Your mind is on the tournament, eh?" Dad asked, smiling. For the first time I noticed how his eyes crinkled up when he smiled. "But for now you have to eat and think about schoolwork, right?" He rubbed his big, rough hand over my hair. I tried to smile.

"I must go," he said. "The guys will be here soon." He drained his coffee, pulled himself up, and stumped away to get his briefcase. During the mornings my father worked as a law clerk. In the after-noons and evenings he went to law school. He would not be depend-ent, he said. Ever since I could re-member, Dad had been in school, but soon, I knew, he would be tak-ing his bar examinations.

"We must go too," Mom said. "Finish, Patrick. Will you do the dishes this afternoon?"

"Yes."

"Mrs. Strand will drop in after school to check on you and put the roast in."

We hurriedly cleared up break-fast in the cramped kitchen and then left for school.

"Are you nervous about the tournament?" she asked me as we pulled out.

"Robert is undefeated in the class. Mr. LeBlanc did not tell you that."

"Hmm." She frowned at the road. "Mr. LeBlanc says only what he thinks is important," she replied at last. "So he must not think that Robert's strength is that important."

"Mr. LeBlanc doesn't get beaten by Robert every week."

She smiled. "Strength alone guarantees nothing, Patrick. If this Robert boy has no style, then it is only a matter of time until you defeat him."

I shrugged.

"I will help you," she said at last. "Yes." She nodded, suddenly resolute. "I will help you."

Then she said no more. That afternoon I came home and did the breakfast dishes, and Mrs. Strand came and helped start dinner, then left. At 5:00 Mom came in. "Patrick, what's this?" she asked. "Put on your gear, quickly. We only have an hour!"

"But Mom—"

"Do it, Patrick! Hurry down!"

I ran upstairs and put on my gear. When I came down, she had pulled most of the furniture out of the living room and into the dining room and the small hallway.

"This is not a big room," she said. I saw to my astonishment that she was wearing a fencing outfit. "But it is almost regulation length. We shall practice as best as we can."

"You fenced?"

"The jacket is mine. The rest is your father's. Yes, for a while I fenced. But more important, I watched your father when he fenced, and I can judge you correctly and test your strength."

We slipped our helmets on and saluted each other. Hesitant, I took the offensive and lunged at her. She parried with a clack of foil against foil and tapped me on the chest.

"We cannot fence nonstop for an hour," she said. "You will let me attack. Defend as best as you can."

"All right."

She beat my blade and knocked it away just enough so that she slipped in and hit me again. "Ah! That is where you are weak. Hold your foil closer. Do not extend the arm so much. Better," she said as she tried it again. "Be ready, Patrick, to slip under my foil with your own if you see that I am about to beat my blade against yours. Avoid it if you cannot parry."

She thrust at me again and again, varying her attacks, sometimes beating, sometimes pressing or gliding on my foil. We sparred until my hand was numb. Only a half-hour had gone by.

"Wait," I gasped, pulling off my mask. She pulled off her mask and collapsed into one of the chairs that she had pulled to the side. "Perhaps," she said, puffing, "a half-hour is enough for the first day, eh?"

Dad came home a little later. He had just enough time to eat and talk a little, and then it was back to class until nine o'clock.

"You seem tired out, Son," he said.

"Patrick and I have been practicing for the tournament," Mom said.

"Ah!" he raised his eyebrows at her. "And how does your mother fence, Son?" he asked without looking at me.

"Very well, Dad."

He glanced at me. "If you don't want to be in the tournament, Patrick, you should tell us," he said sternly.

"I want to fence," I said.

"It's just that fencing meant so much to me, Son. I don't want you to think that you must fence to please me." He nodded. "Well, then, back to class for me. I will be home later."

Champion at Heart

The next day I went to class, but I did not fence with Robert. On Saturday Mom and I practiced for an hour while Dad studied upstairs at his desk in their tiny bedroom.

Again on Monday we practiced. Tuesday night at class I fenced with Robert, and he beat me, 5-1.

"You are tired," Mr. LeBlanc told me as he drove me home. "But I see new things in your defense. You are practicing at home?"

"Yes."

"Good. You will improve."

I doubted him that night, but then on Thursday when I fenced with Robert, I began to feel more confident. I saw that when he struck at my blade he would pull his hand up a little, barely an inch. But it was enough warning for me to drop my blade. Once when I did it, he missed it entirely, and I thrust at him. Twice he still struck my blade, but not where he intended to, not as strongly, and I kept him from gliding up or pressing.

Yet I was not perfect. He scored three times on me, and I scored only once on him—I was still wearing myself out against his strength. The other boys congratulated me on holding him off so well. But next time, I thought, he will be ready for my defenses. He will know what to do to wear me out more quickly.

Mom and I worked with each other every day. Sometimes Dad came home and asked me to put on my gear. Then Mom and I worked together in front of him, with all the furniture pulled back except one tiny chair where he sat and directed us.

For two weeks Mr. LeBlanc kept Robert and me apart. The other boys I defeated easily enough, for they never practiced in their spare time.

At last I again met Robert on the strip. He had not forgotten our last match, and he was not ignorant of my latest victories.

He fenced carefully at first, and I began to think that he had been polishing his style. But then when I lunged at him, he suddenly drove his foil straight into me. The red button drilled into my chest as I met it full force, unable to stop myself. I gasped as I saw the foil bend and then snap in two, and I was thrown back a pace on the strip. My own foil dropped to the ground, and I clutched my right shoulder and chest.

"Leave the floor! Leave the floor!" Mr. LeBlanc barked. I

looked up, thinking he was talking to me. But no. Red-faced, Robert was walking toward the dressing room, his eyes bitter. So he had not fooled Mr. LeBlanc. "Help that boy up," Mr. LeBlanc said.

Jack and Bruce pulled me up and helped me out of the fencing jacket. I could barely move my right arm. The other boys were arguing over whether Robert had done it purposely or not. Simultaneous attacks happen in fencing, and I had known of men to snap their foils in half while they were fencing. Yet I was sure that Robert had deliberately broken the rules and attacked me before defending himself, knowing that my attack had been declared first by my out-thrust blade.

There was a black bruise with a red spot in the middle on my chest. It glistened as though it weren't a bruise at all but a puddle of ink somebody had spilled on me. The sight turned my stomach. Mr. LeBlanc was in the dressing room, and I could hear him shouting. I sank down onto a bench against the wall. The other boys crowded around, curious and awed. Nobody had ever been hurt before in class.

Mr. LeBlanc suspended Robert until the tournament. He dismissed the class early and drove me home.

In the car I saw that his hands were shaking as he gripped the wheel.

"Never! Never!" he kept murmuring. "Never in my class! What possessed the boy? Never has this happened—not with two Olympic trainees! Never before!"

Dad looked shocked when Mr. LeBlanc told him. With some difficulty I showed him the bruise.

"Get into your pajamas, Patrick. Come down and I will put something on it for you," Mom said.

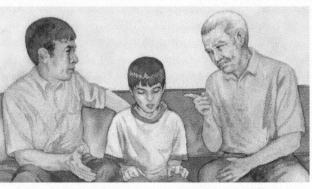

As I went upstairs, I heard Dad's voice. "I will not let him fence in the tournament, LeBlanc. Why did you not suspend that other boy from competing?"

"What, and protect a champion? Should I add that insult to Patrick's injury?" Mr. LeBlanc replied.

Mom put hot compresses on the bruise. "They will draw the blood and you will heal more quickly," she said. "Let your right arm rest."

Mr. LeBlanc looked at me gravely. "Your father does not want you to compete next week," he said.

"Fencing is not sword fighting," Dad added. "You do not have to be a swashbuckler, though that other boy is."

"You told me yourself that we win by style, not by brute strength," I replied. "If that is true, then I can beat him."

"The boy is right," Mr. LeBlanc said. "You know he is right, Julio."

"You have to grow yet, Son," Dad said. "You can fence Robert again later."

"It will be worse than losing a match to him if I allow him to frighten me away."

He hesitated, then nodded. "I would not have you think of yourself as a coward. I will not forbid you to fence him if you think that your heart is ready for such a contest."

"A champion at heart can never be defeated. When a fencer has his courage, he is a champion," Mr. LeBlanc added. "Patrick will yet defeat Robert."

"I will compete," I said, and Dad nodded gravely.

As the days ran out, Mom made me build up more strength in my right arm. Sometimes in the evenings when Dad came home, he would let me arm-wrestle with him. We were in dead earnest when we did it. He never budged his great muscular forearm, and I would push and push against it for twenty seconds at a time, never moving it, but building my own muscle against it. Then twenty seconds of rest, and then I would start pushing again while he encouraged me or said nothing, only watching me steadily.

At last the Saturday of the tournament came. We had steak for breakfast. Mom ate silently while Dad told me to relax and chew carefully.

There was little conversation as we drove to the gym. I was already registered, so I went into the dressing rooms while they found seats.

The pledge was over quickly, the salutes exchanged. Several schools had come to compete, so for several bouts I did not fence with anybody I knew.

Mr. LeBlanc was beside himself with pride, and I was surprised at myself. It seemed so easy—ridiculously easy. "Is this what I have been so nervous about?" I thought. Again and again I fenced, and again and again I won.

"You are doing splendidly!" Mom exclaimed during a break.

"Marie!" Dad retorted. He looked at me. "You win so easily, Son, because these are the first eliminations. These are the boys who do not practice. It gets harder in the second eliminations. Do not get overconfident."

He was right. As the judges filled in the double elimination chart and my name went lower and lower, the matches became harder. Fewer of us were competing, and the judges conducted the matches one at a time.

I examined the chart and saw that Robert also was undefeated. Yes, his huge size and unusual strength were coming to his aid. Perhaps he had even been practicing during his suspension. Mr. LeBlanc had been careful to keep us scheduled apart, perhaps hoping that somehow Robert would be eliminated by somebody else.

But no. The clusters of names around his name grew smaller and smaller, as did the cluster of names around mine. Several of the spectators strolled over to my parents and shook hands with my father. They looked at ease in the gym. Perhaps they were from the Committee. They pulled up folding chairs and sat by my parents while I fenced again.

Again I won, and the judges called a ten-minute recess, and I checked the chart again. Robert and I were the only ones left. We would have to fence each other at least twice because we were both undefeated.

"Give me your hand," Dad said. He pulled off my fencing glove and massaged the tendons and knuckles of my hand with hard short rubs. "Do not play his game, Patrick. Take the offensive. Use speed and style. You must rely on evasion. I

have been watching him, and he is quite strong."

The judges called my name, and I felt afraid.

I slipped on the mask, saluted Robert, and went to work.

Dad had been right. When he took the offensive, he beat my blade or tried to glide on it, using his strength. I evaded him and quickly gained the lead on him by two points, but I was tired. At last he thrust aside my foil long enough to score on me. Then I scored on him, so that he had three points against him. Two more, I thought, and I would win.

I thrust out, and he quickly swept his foil up, catching my blade as it came in. Next thing I

364

knew he was almost on top of me, with our foils locked. I leaped back, and he scored on me. Somehow when he came in again, we were locked in a corps-à-corps position; only this time he bore down on me with his foil, and I resisted with mine the best I could. But he was too strong. He was pushing me back, the handguard of his foil pushing on the handguard of mine, for our blades were crossed right at their bases.

He has been practicing, I said to myself quite calmly. I managed to break away, but he scored on me again.

My hand was numb. While the judges discussed the point, I quickly rubbed it with my other hand.

He defeated me in our first match. As the president declared him the winner of the bout, I returned to my parents.

"What can I do?" I asked my father while he rubbed out the cramps in my right hand. "Every time we lock together he gets a point."

"Watch his blade!" Mr. LeBlanc exclaimed. "You are taking your eyes off his blade!"

"When I watch his blade he uses his feet."

"You must try," Dad said.

"You think I will lose!" I exclaimed.

"Perfection of style will come with time. But if you let him defeat your heart—if you quit, then you are truly defeated. I have always believed that, and I feared that you were too young for such a contest."

I had tears in my eyes, and I rubbed them on the back of my hand.

"For some, the contest comes in fencing," he said. "For others, the fight lasts all their lives to keep their hearts from defeat." He looked down at his leg and then back up at me. And then I understood. "Now this contest has come to you, and you must fight. There is more at stake here than a fencing match."

The president called my name, and I went back to the strip.

I saluted Robert and leaped to the attack, taking the first point as usual. But my hand would not obey me. It was too tired. I saw him come in to beat my blade, to press on it, to glide on it, yet my reactions were clumsy. I evaded him too slowly, and he scored on me. He had worn me out in the last match.

Again he took the offensive. Something savage surged through me. I discarded style and poise and

smashed his foil close to the tip, where the blade is most flexible. It knocked his attack aside, and I lunged in, scoring on the riposte.

Again we clashed, and again he slid his blade up mine until we met hilt to hilt and chest to chest, one knee straight and one bent as we strained against each other. His mask hid his face completely under the gym lights, but I felt his gasping breath as he pushed against me.

I pushed and resisted until I heard myself grunting, but still he was more powerful. My hand quickly grew numb, and the numbness started up my wrist. We broke apart, and he scored on me.

After the judges conferred, he smashed his blade against mine, and this time the foil flew out of my hand.

One of the judges retrieved it for me. Even in that brief space some feeling had returned to my fingers. I grasped the hilt and tried to take the offensive, but again found myself locked into a corps-à-corps with him.

I grunted and gritted my teeth as I pushed against him. Tears rolled out of the corners of my eyes, but when I lifted my eyes to that faceless mask, the tears stopped. Perhaps he would defeat me. Perhaps he would knock me right off the strip, but I would never stop resisting him. I had fenced him for months and never won, but each time I got better, and suddenly I knew—as my father knew—that his time of victory was limited. Let him win this match— there would always be another, and another beyond that. I would never stop trying. That was the reason he had disliked me so much. He had known all along that someday I would defeat him.

The thoughts gave me courage, and I pushed against him more heartily than before, but then the buzzer went off, and the match was over.

I pulled off the mask with my left hand and suddenly found myself in my dad's arms with Mr. LeBlanc and the visitors and the boys from the school all around me, pounding me on the back and congratulating me. The silver medal was thrust into my hands, and I saw that Dad was crying and one crutch was thrown down on the floor as he hugged me. I looked from him to the medal, and I realized that, when the contest goes beyond fencing, a silver medal can be better than a gold.

100-Meter Dash

Morgan Reed Persun
illustrated by Kathy Pflug

Searing crack! of thunder,
The starter's pistol that sent
    Me leaping from daydreams
To challenge black clouds,
Rolling engines of rain,
(World champions
    in this event).

Big drops splat the dust,
    Drum on barn roofs, pummel under
        The trees, slick down grass
        Beneath my very heels, it seems.

A lightning surge, if I can just—
Hot breath on my neck again,

Then a sound around, like great crowds
Cheering me as I pass,
Thundering applause as I slam in,
Shut rattling rain out and—win!

The All-American Game

Henry Becker
Although there are many team sports that Americans enjoy, there is only one official team game that can trace its roots back to no other country but America. This is the story of the invention of that game, which took place in 1891.

"OOOF! Dr. Naismith, did you see that last soccer ball? It almost knocked me out!"

"Yes, and the one before that just about smashed a window. Another inch and we would've been collecting broken glass."

"I know, I know, boys." James Naismith shook his head sadly. "I guess soccer is just too rough a game to try to play inside a gymnasium. But so is Rugby and so is football. And baseball would be impossible! What other team games are there?"

No one had an answer. The young men slowly gathered their

belongings and trooped out of the YMCA. James Naismith shook his head and trudged back to his office. The YMCA had given the coaches two weeks to invent a new indoor game—one that would not cost so much in broken windows as indoor soccer did. The time limit was almost up, and Dr. Naismith had been determined to submit the best idea. But so far none of his ideas had been practical. Somehow he still had to find an answer.

He sat down at his desk and mulled over the problem again. The young men had several wonderful rough-and-tumble games to play outside when the weather was pretty. But in the wintertime they had to stay inside the gymnasium, so all there was to do was calisthenics, marching, and weightlifting. But the fellows didn't want this routine day after day. They just didn't see any point to any of those activities. They needed teamwork and the excitement of competition. It was obvious that what they needed was a game.

But it seemed that none of the games the men were familiar with could be modified for playing inside. What in the world could he do? Once more he racked his brain, trying to think of some game that could be modified. But the problem with all those games was that they were just too rough! He had to find a different game, one that would require more skill than brute strength. But there simply wasn't one.

"Well!" Dr. Naismith whispered to himself. "Why, how foolish I've been! All along I've been trying to modify a game when what I really need to do is invent one that is completely new." He grabbed a piece of paper and began to scribble furiously.

"Now," he muttered while he scribbled, "we want it to be simple so that all the young men can understand it easily. We want the ball to be big enough to maneuver with the hands instead of some other instrument—it's too dangerous to be swinging bats or mallets in a gymnasium. We don't want the young men to have to tackle each other, because that's too rough. But they could get the ball away from the other team a different way—instead of running with the ball, they could pass it to each other. That would give everyone a sporting chance.

"And what about a goal? If we had a goal as big as a soccer goal, they'd just throw the ball and possibly break out a window. Hmm. That's what almost happened today. Well, why not have a small goal, like a box? And why not put it up high so that they have to have even more skill? Yes, a box mounted up on a post—they pass the ball to their teammates and shoot for the box. That's it! That's our new game!"

Dr. Naismith couldn't wait to try out his new invention. He asked the janitor to nail a couple of boxes to the walls at either end of the gymnasium. As it happened, the janitor couldn't find any boxes and used two peach baskets instead.

Once again the young men gathered in the gymnasium. They were a little discouraged by now, because none of Dr. Naismith's experiments had worked so far. But when they saw the baskets nailed up high and heard the rumor that they were going to try out a brand-new game, their interest perked up.

Dr. Naismith read the thirteen simple rules to the young men and watched them grow more and more excited as they listened. This sounded like a game that could really work—a game of skill that even the smaller and skinnier young men could play as well as the big brawny ones!

The young men grabbed the Rugby ball and went at it.

"Here, throw it here, Jim!"

"I can get it in the basket!"

"No, you missed! Ha!"

"Wait, there goes William!"

"William did it! He got it in the basket! YEA!"

And William Chase scored the one and only point of the first historic game. Teammates cheered as one person ran up to the balcony to get the ball out of the basket. Even the opposing team had to admit that it was a pretty good game.

"Hey, Dr. Naismith, what do you call this game?" one boy hollered.

"Well, I haven't got a name for it yet. What do you boys suggest?"

"I know," one offered. "Why don't we call it *basketball?*"

"Well, we have a basket and a ball," Dr. Naismith said with a grin. "Basketball seems as good a name as any!"

So basketball it was. It soon became a favorite sport at the YMCA.

Basketball was fifteen years old before someone finally got the idea of using a basket with no bottom so that the ball could fall through easily. The game went on to become popular all over the nation. The rules changed again and again until they were finalized at last in the mid-1900s. Dr. Naismith lived to see the game he invented become the most popular indoor sport in the world.

The Little Things of Sissa

an East Indian folktale retold by Dawn L. Watkins • illustrated by Dana Thompson

It is written in the records of ancient India that a small old man named Sissa was more famous than the kings. It is also written there that Sissa did not seek this fame, but it came to him anyway, a little at a time.

Sissa had been advisor to the king (and to the king's father before that) as long as anyone could remember. Umbar, Behut, and Pune, the other advisors on the council, yawned when Sissa took a long time to think about what he would say. They had winked at each other when Sissa had refused to help the youngest prince prepare his lessons.

"Ah," said Behut, "Prince Jalna will tell the king how Sissa treated him, and then we will be free of this old man for good!"

Umbar nodded. "Indeed. Does the old fool think he can refuse a prince and nothing will happen to him?"

But nothing did happen. Prince Jalna did not tell his father anything, and he still smiled at Sissa and sat with him in the garden every morning.

"How he does get away with things!" Behut said.

Umbar said, "We will never have the king's ear until this old man is gone. And from the looks of it, he will never die."

Pune said, "Perhaps we will not have to wait until he dies."

"What?" said Umbar, stopping midstride.

"Perhaps," said Pune, "it will be enough if his wit dies."

They smiled, for they all knew that one thing the king liked about Sissa was his clever wit.

The next day, Umbar, Pune, and Behut approached the king. "Great King of the Ghaggar River Province, we seek only your good," said Behut.

"What do you want?" the king said, resting, as a servant fanned him. It was the hot season, and the king did not like to have problems in the hot season.

The three advisors bowed, and Pune said, "We wish to warn you of a danger to your kingdom, Great King."

The king now looked directly at them. "You have new word of Moradabad, King of the North?"

Behut said, "No, Sire. This danger is somewhat smaller. I speak of Sissa."

"Sissa?" said the king.

Umbar said, "His mind is getting old, Sire. We fear he is doing your rule harm."

Behut said, "If it please you, Great King, let us show you what we mean."

The king considered this request for a moment and then nodded.

Behut asked Sissa, "Where were you yesterday while the council was meeting?"

At length Sissa said, "I was helping a boy find his chickens."

Behut turned to the king with a look of triumph. "There, Sire," he said, "you see."

"What is it that I see?" said the king.

Behut said, "Begging Your Majesty's pardon, Great King, but you see that Sissa serves your servants rather than you."

Sissa looked at the advisors, all grinning at him. Then he looked at the king. "By serving your subjects, I serve you, Sire."

"Come, come," said Pune, "how is that?"

Sissa tilted his head. "I mind the small things for the king. Thus they do not become big things for *him* to mind."

"Posh-tosh," said Behut, "how does finding chickens save the king?"

Sissa said, "If a boy and his family go hungry, they will blame the king. They will speak ill of the king to others. And soon the king will be blamed for hunger everywhere."

The advisors burst into laughing. They laughed heartily until they saw that the king was not laughing. They bowed low and retreated from the hall.

"Sissa made a fool of all of us," said Umbar.

"We made fools of ourselves," said Pune. "We must be more clever if we are to prove that this old man, who still has his wits, has lost his wits."

"And what do you propose?" said Umbar.

"I think we must set a trap. Now, what can we be sure of about Sissa?"

"That he will be able to outwit us no matter what we do," Behut said.

"Agreed," said Pune. "We were not wise to strike him there. We must strike him elsewhere."

"And where might that be?" said Behut.

"In his honesty."

"Ah," Behut and Umbar said. For they all knew one thing the king liked about Sissa was his honesty.

The next day, at the council meeting, Behut said, "Great King, we think it best that anyone who suggests that Moradabad is a greater fighter than you should be banished from the kingdom."

The king snorted. "There is no need for this rule."

"But Your Majesty," said Pune, "Moradabad may have sent spies among us to say things secretly about you. They will make the people fear Moradabad, and so undermine you."

The king had never thought of this possibility before. "Well," he said, "perhaps you are right."

The advisors pressed the king with all their reasons, and before long the rule was made. Sissa, who had missed another council meeting to chink up a small hole in the palace garden wall, arrived just in time to see the king sign the new law.

Sissa did not say anything, but he looked a long time at the other three advisors. The king said, "Do you think this law will protect me, Sissa?"

"I think," Sissa said, "the law will do what it was meant to do."

The following day, the three advisors talked together where many people could hear them.

"Yes," said Pune, "our king is the greatest war maker and we have nothing to fear from this Moradabad."

"Indeed," said Behut, "how silly people are to believe the reports of Moradabad's skills as a great warrior. Ha! Why should that worry us?"

And just as they had wanted, their words stirred up the people to worry. The people went to Sissa, as they often did, to get advice.

"Is Moradabad, King of the North, truly better at war than our king?" they asked.

Sissa sat quietly for a long, long time. Then he said, "It is difficult to answer that. Since our king and this king have never fought, we have no way of knowing for sure who would win."

The crowd gasped, and Behut said, "That is good enough!"

Within minutes, the three advisors had dragged Sissa before the king and made their accusations.

"Sissa," the king said, "can you not say I would have the edge at least?"

"It would not be good to speak without proof, Sire." Sissa smiled at the king, kindly. "And as I love the king, I cannot lie to him."

Prince Jalna, who had been learning to think through his lessons by himself, spoke up. "Father, if I may? I think, sir, that Sissa should make a test that proves you are a better warrior. One that does not require real war."

"Impossible!" said Pune.

But the king looked with surprise and joy at Jalna and said to Sissa, "Do it. Return by the rainy season."

Sissa left the court and was gone all the hot season. Rumor said that he lived by himself by the river and that a boy brought him eggs to eat every day. Rumor also said that he only sat under the trees and thought and carved little figures from ivory day after day.

When the rainy season began, Sissa appeared in the king's hall. Without a word, he opened flat a wooden box. It made a board with red and black squares. Upon that board he placed two sets—one

white, one black—of finely carved miniature elephants, soldiers, footmen, kings, and queens.

"What's this?" asked the king.

"A little battlefield," said Sissa. "Upon this checkered board Your Majesty may engage his enemy Moradabad and see who is the better maker of war without really going to war."

The king was intrigued. He said to his oldest son, "Go. Invite Moradabad here to play this new game with me. To be fair I will not study it until he arrives."

Moradabad indeed came. Sissa taught the kings the rules of Chess, which were very like the methods of war. And both kings being brilliant men, they soon caught the idea and set to playing.

The game went on for three days and nights. But at last, the Great King of the Ghaggar River Province won. Moradabad said graciously, "You are a great maker of war. But next year, you must come and play this little war at my palace." And so it was agreed.

"What reward would you like, Sissa?" said the king, beaming, after Moradabad left.

"One grain of rice from Pune," said Sissa. "And the next day, two grains from Umbar. And the next four grains from Behut. And so on, doubling every day, until sixty-four days have passed."

"That is so small a reward!" said the king. But he decreed that it should be so, for one of the things he liked about Sissa was his humility.

Pune laughingly paid his debt the first day. And Umbar the next. And Behut the next. But by the tenth day, Pune was paying 512 grains. The eleventh day Umbar paid 1024 grains. On the twenty-first day, Behut had to bring a million grains. None of them laughed now. And by the sixty-fourth day, Pune had to bring ninety-nine wagonloads to meet his debt of 18,466,744,073,709,551,615 grains.

Sissa gave all the rice to the people in the name of the king and said nothing more of the matter.

The ancient records show that Jalna became the greatest of all the ancient kings by minding the little things, as he had learned to do from his famous and beloved teacher, Sissa of the Ghaggar River Province.

Coronation Day

Taken from False Coin, True Coin
by Lois Hoadley Dick

illustrated by Steve Mitchell and Julie Bunner

Cissy Nidd's story takes place in seventeenth-century England. The country is in much tumult as the Stuart kings try to force the people into state-regulated worship. Many devout men form dissenting groups or leave England to seek freedom elsewhere. One well-known dissenter, John Bunyan, is thrown into jail for the crime of preaching the Word of God. Although Bunyan is a prisoner, he often finds himself outside the jailer's door, preaching truth to those who will listen. His privilege is maintained as long as he returns to the damp jailhouse by his own free will.

Cissy's father earns a living as the jailer where Bunyan is imprisoned, but her family also earns a few extra shillings by spending counterfeit coins and receiving back genuine money in change. It is at this jail that Cissy meets the kind John Bunyan and begins to wonder about the truth of the gospel he preaches.

Hidden Purse

April 23, 1661, Coronation Day. The great noisy splashing water wheel of London Bridge had awakened Cissy early. She looked out of the window just in time to see the drawbridge part in two and rise to let a ship pass. The gears ground and the drawbridge lowered itself with a thud that shook the house.

A most fair day, she thought, and I shall see a king crowned! Ostrich feathers of smoke floated down from the neighboring chimney tops and partly blurred her view.

"New clothes for the young gentlemen!" Peg entered the room, holding up two suits, shirts, and plumed hats. "This way you and Frank can shop in the best of shops and spend that false coin without being suspected."

Cissy pulled on dark blue breeches and a silk shirt and slung a man's purse over one arm. The dark cloak lined in red would make her look like a brother to Frank.

"Braid your hair and pin it up under this cap," Peg said. "Pull some loose hair down over your ears. There, the cap covers your head down to your eyebrows. Too bad I can't trim those long curly eyelashes; mayhap they will give away your secret."

Cissy ate heartily at breakfast and finished with a hot drink. She could hear the river traffic growing louder, and outside, a hurdy-gurdy woman was whacking out a shrill tune on her instrument.

"Trig and I will bide here," said Peg. "The Black Pot will do a grand bit of business today, what with serving meals and giving change in our new coin." She winked at Cissy. "Next time, you stay a little longer with old Peg. She'll dress you up like a fine lady, and we'll go to the theater in Southwark."

"Cissy's to wed Paul Cobb, Pa says." Frank smoothed his shoulder-length hair and cocked his hat at an angle. "Hurry on, Cis."

"Don't ever say that again!" Cissy flared at him. "You be a bubble-headed dunce to think I'd wed with that man. I'll see me a spinster or in my grave afore that!"

"Tush, tush, children." Peg soothed them both. "Have you each two purses? Put one on display under your right arm, the other hidden on the left. Pay out from the right-side purse with the false coin. Put the true coin into the hidden purse. Now then, you look fine; a pair of brave young gentlemen, off to see the Coronation."

"Much we'll see of it." Cissy tossed the cloak over her shoulder. "Thousands of other people will be ahead of us, and the best seats on the scaffolding are given to the rich."

"Never mind the scaffolding," Peg told them. "Creep around the crowd, closer and closer to Westminster Abbey. Say, 'Pray let us through; we are part of the procession.' "

Trig came into the dining room carrying two fancy walking canes for them. "You be here to pass the coin, not to see the Coronation," he grumbled.

Peg shooed Cissy and Frank outside. "You have yourselves a good time. Buy, buy! Pay in false and bring back true! God save the king!"

Even at seven o'clock in the morning London Bridge was alive with people in holiday clothes, and excitement spread from one person to another.

The Thames was at low tide, and Cissy saw homeless children and crippled old folks poking in the muck for nails or coins or pieces of coal to sell. "They're called *mudlarks*," Frank explained. "They live in the big sewers and make as much as a half penny a day. They find bones and rope and spoons and things folk drop what got washed down the sewer."

"Isn't it dangerous?"

"Of course. Aren't you glad you live in a better place?"

Do I live in a better place? Cissy asked herself. Am I glad? She didn't have an answer.

"Move along now; we have a long walk." Frank guided her off the Bridge and toward St. Paul's in the distance. They passed the Temple Bar where lawyers worked. The streets were clogged with people, off to see the Coronation. Cissy felt she was drowning in a sea of people. Twice Frank had to seize her arm and pull her along. "We will never get to see a thing," she mourned aloud. "Why don't we stay on the outskirts of the crowd and pass coin only inside the shops?"

"We are going to see the king," Frank replied stubbornly. "I have a plan."

They reached a street corner and stopped under a shop awning.

"Look here." Frank unrolled two long silver ribbons from his pocket.

He pinned one across Cissy's chest from her left shoulder down to her right hip. The ribbon was decorated with pearl buttons spelling out the initials CS—Charles Stuart, the king's legal name.

Frank pinned the other ribbon on himself. "Now we're venders. And venders can go anywhere."

Cissy pointed out sellers of cheap bracelets and ear bobs, toys and candy. "Shall we deal in goodies?"

"No. Programs, that's what we want. I say, sir!" Frank hailed two old men. "How much will you take for your trays with the scrolls on them? We mean to play at peddling today for a lark."

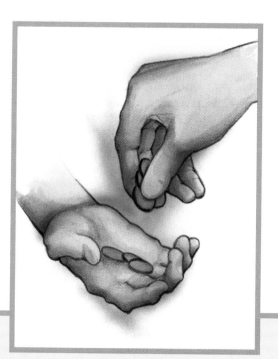

Unbelief spread over one man's face. "It's me livin'; I can't part with me livin'."

"I'm going to pay you more than you'd earn, my good man, and you can go off and enjoy the Coronation without any bother."

Both old men hung back. "I'd make near five shilling today," the taller one said.

"I'll give you ten shillings each."

"The tray is handmade by me brother what is a carpenter on the quay," the tall one added.

Frank pulled open his purse of false coin. "A pound for each of you, only because I have a rich uncle in Parliament."

The men slipped the leather straps off their shoulders and laid down the trays. "It's our bounden dooty to go off and pick pockets in the crowd so's the rich won't be heavy laden," said the first.

"Thank you kindly, young gentlemen, and may you have a good day," ventured the second.

Cissy's heart felt heavy. Should the old men be caught with false coin, it would go hard with them, and all because of us, she thought.

Priceless Treasure

"Carry your tray and follow me." Frank headed for the scaffolding, where nobles and wealthy families had been waiting for hours to see the king.

Cissy looked up at the balconies and windows jammed with people. Along the procession way, a blue carpet stretched from the Abbey to Westminster Hall, where the king would banquet with the House of Lords. Cissy knew the ceremony by heart from hearing the talk of Bedford townfolk.

First, the Knights of the Bath would bear the heavy platters of food to the king's table, escorted by servants. Then the King's Champion, a knight in armor, would ride in on a splendid steed to throw down the gauntlet, challenging any man to step forward and say why Charles II should not be king.

"Why are we standing here so long? My back aches." Cissy leaned against the bottom of the scaffolding and waited for Frank to tell her what to do.

Finally, when the first sound of trumpets could be heard in the distance, Frank jolted her alert. "Now, follow me," he said. "Do what I do! We are going to the top of that scaffolding."

He stepped out from under the stand and began to push his way through the mob, shouting, "Make way! Free programs for the ladies!"

A few women heard the call and stretched out their hands. Others heard and made way for the venders. "Let us pass!" shouted Frank. "Free programs, compliments of His Majesty!"

Cissy shouldered her way through the people, following Frank. In a short time they were on the scaffolding. Slowly they climbed up the narrow aisle, distributing the scrolls as they went. The sound of trumpets grew louder. Cissy reached the very top row and eagerly looked down upon the scene.

All the buildings were hung with rich tapestries. The ladies showered posies onto the street. "Oh, isn't it splendid?" Cissy laughed aloud. "The finest parade I ever did see! The coaches look like bulging pumpkins from our garden! See the lace round the coachmen's necks? That's handmade bobbin lace, or I'm not Cissy Nidd!"

The flashing, gem-studded armor and helmets so dazzled her eyes that she had to blink. Next in the procession marched the Duke of York's Horse Guards and Knights of the Bath, all in cloth of gold and emeralds.

At last Cissy saw the king. He was robed in ermine, riding on a white horse under a canopy of silver cloth carried by six barons. His wavy black hair fell below his shoulders, and his full lips smiled at the crowd. He rode straight into Westminster Abbey. There, a brief service was held that those outside could not see. Cissy heard the anthem sung by combined choirs of all the churches in London. Most likely in heaven they hear singing like this every single blessed day, she thought in awe.

Suddenly all the bells of all the churches in London struck the noon hour. Though Cissy could not see it, she knew the crown of England now rested on the head of their lawful king. When he reappeared on the street with the Archbishop of Canterbury beside him, a shout went up from ten thousand throats. "God save the king!"

Cissy felt the scaffold tremble and sway. Now the bells pealed like divine thunder, and the sound clanged in her head until she felt giddy and leaned against Frank lest she faint. "Long live His Majesty, King Charles II!" She wanted to join in the cry, but she could only whisper.

Would England be happy now after all her trouble? Would there be a better life for all, as her father predicted? And what of Cissy Nidd?

She stood unmoving on the scaffolding as the frock-coated gentlemen and their ladies began to depart, going off to dine or ride in

the country as was the custom. The golden music of the bells died away. Still Cissy didn't move.

"Well, now!" Frank shook her arm. "You have seen a king. Throw that ribbon away and drop the tray. We're off to buy with false and get change in true. While you were gawking like a stage-silly, I have cut two purses with my sharp little scissors; and well paid we'll be, for they were rare gentlemen."

Cissy stared at him in alarm. "Frank! You, a cutpurse? They didn't see you, did they?"

"Never even missed the purses, so set were they on bellowing and bawling greetings down to the king. The purses are chock full of large gold and silver pieces. I tied them under my arm next to my shirt."

Climbing slowly down the scaffolding, Cissy remembered something. "I didn't buy any souvenirs to remind me of this day. Though I vow I'll never—no I'll never—forget the parade and the bells. I fancy a silver thimble or a new pattern book and a bolt of cloth."

"Fine noise it was," Frank agreed. "Buy whatever you like. Mayhap you'll see combs and such from a far country."

Further down the street, people crowded around a farmer who was flourishing a whip and selling books that were piled on his cart next to bales of hay. "I can read fair well," Cissy said wistfully. "Frank, don't you ever wonder what's in the big books in the stalls near St. Paul's? The books rich people have. Can we walk over to Bookseller's Row sometime?"

"Not today." Frank stopped, took a few steps, stopped again and shaded his eyes with one hand.

"What is it?"

"Look yonder! Don't you recognize him?"

They walked closer to the farmer selling books, and Cissy looked up at him closely. His hair was covered with a rough cap and he wore hobnail boots, but there was no hiding the orangy moustache nor the deep preacher's voice.

"Master Bunyan!" Cissy exclaimed, shocked. "He's here, preaching in London! And selling Bibles!"

"Don't let him see us like this!" Frank grasped her hand, but it was too late. Master Bunyan pointed at them with his whip. "Ah, friends from back home! Now I know you'll want a Geneva Bible, only three shillings, as a proper sou-venir of Coronation Day. Step closer, gentlemen. . . ."

Cissy thought a smile twinkled in his eyes for a moment, but she couldn't be sure.

"He knows us, Frank. Pa must have left his jail door unlocked on purpose like he sometimes does. But to stand up *here* and preach! Oh, I want a Bible for a souvenir, I do! I never saw a Bible save the big one chained to the pulpit in church. They say it be words from God! Frank, I must have a Bible!"

"No! What do you think Pa would say? Only Dissenters have Bibles."

"I have a right to some of the money, and I will spend it the way I please! Pa doesn't have to know."

"A Bible! Do you fancy you'll preach too?"

"A Bible for the gentleman, a wise choice." Master Bunyan smiled widely and held out the book to Cissy. "And if you are short of coin today, this shall be a gift," he said to her in a gentler tone.

"Pay in true, lest he discover us," Frank said in her ear.

"I can pay, sir." Cissy handed up three shillings. "I thank you for your kindness."

He laughed heartily and turned his attention to other folk who

were holding out their money for Bibles. Cissy wrapped the book in a handkerchief and hid it under one arm. "Don't you tell," she said. "I'll only look at it when Pa is downstairs collecting tolls. Wait a bit; I want to hear what he has to say."

Master Bunyan seemed satisfied that his street congregation was large enough. Opening one of the Bibles, he began to preach.

"You say this Book be only paper and ink," he began. "But it is a Book that is alive! The proof that this is the Word of God lies in its power to change a person's life. It changed me. Once I went to Divine Service twice a day, and every Sabbath Sunday. I loved the music, the incense, the rituals and play-acting. Yet it did not change me.

"I led a most wicked life. I could outcurse the meanest jacktar from off the ships. One day while playing ball on the green, I seemed to hear God saying, 'Will you have your sins, or will you have heaven?'

"The call awakened my soul, and I saw what a priceless treasure was my soul, that it would spend eternity with its Maker, or without Him."

Cissy listened, and a horror of great loss began to seep into her mind. My soul, she thought. I have a soul that will live forever, that will outlive even my body. My soul may be kept or lost, as he says.

Master Bunyan went on, his powerful voice drawing in people from all around and holding them silent. "Then I tried to make myself righteous. I gave up everything, even dessert at mealtime. I thought that in the whole of England no man pleased God better than I did. I was fair pleased with myself. I was a painted hypocrite, though men called me godly. I was like a counterfeit coin!"

Now even Frank was interested, his eye fastened on the farmer with hay sticking out of his boots.

"That wasn't the way to salvation!" cried Master Bunyan. "For I fell into worse sin than before. When temptations came, I couldn't stand. I was like a pig that washed itself and then returned to the mud. *Because I wasn't any different within!*"

Aye, he speaks true and looks right into my own life, thought Cissy. For if I were good within and in favor with God, I would have the courage to say no to law-breaking.

Bunyan went on: "One day I saw a toad croaking in a puddle, and I thought he was happier than I. For three years I was up and down, up and down; quiet in my soul one day, then in fear the next. I had no peace.

"One day as I walked in the field, this sentence flashed into my mind: *Thy righteousness is in heaven.* Then I saw that Jesus Christ at God's right hand was my righteousness—no matter how I felt.

"Jesus, only Jesus. Not myself. In Him I stand at God's right hand. Jesus Christ, the same yesterday, today, forever. He is calling you today. Will you follow Him?"

Cissy stood silent as a statue. Righteous. Pure and holy. Could that be said of her? Though the air was warm and her vest heavy, she shuddered.

Frank put his arm around her shoulder. "Pay him no mind—frightening good churchgoing people so's he can sell them Bibles. He should stick to tinkering. We must dispose of this coin quickly, so let's have a bite to eat down the block at the Poets and Writers Nook."

They paid for their meal in false and received change in true. They bought a side of meat from a butcher for Peg, paid in false, pocketed the true. Cissy picked out three bolts of cloth and a new set of bobbins from Flanders, carved and decorated with beads. They hired a small boy to carry all the bundles.

"Here's a penny for yourself, boy." Frank grinned at the small urchin and handed him the parcels.

Cissy bought a pearl pin and a pair of silver buckles from one merchant, scissors and colored threads from a seamstress.

"Buy a small item; give a large coin," Frank instructed her. "Degrooter has people in all the English towns passing his coin. Don't forget to get everything on the list Peg gave you."

Cissy nodded unhappily. "Do we ride back tomorrow?"

"Up before dawn to get a good start."

She walked along mechanically, the happiness gone out of her day. Jesus was calling, Master Bunyan said—he that was willing to lie in cold, damp Bedford Jail rather than in a feather bed in his own home. Jesus was calling. The only Jesus she knew had a crown of thorns and mournful eyes with circles underneath them. Jesus, ascending to heaven on a pink-edged cloud, as she'd seen him once in a painting. Jesus had somehow called to Master Bunyan, and Master Bunyan had become a new man. The Prayer Book spoke of Jesus' love, but it didn't explain anything.

Cissy went through the motions of buying, paying, and handing the bundles to the errand boy, but one great yearning swelled in her heart and repeated itself over and over: *Oh, if only He would call me—how gladly would I run after Him!*

Cissy dreaded returning to Bedford Jail. The only thing that helped her feel better was the thought of seeing Master Bunyan again. And the Bible hidden in her saddlebag.

Cissy must face choosing between doing what she knows to be right, risking her father's wrath and an unwelcome marriage to Paul Cobb, or continuing to deal in false coin, risking not only being caught but struggling against the truth she finds in Bunyan's message. As Cissy endures the horrors of the plague and the Great Fire of London, she learns the difference between deceit and righteousness, between the false and the true.

John Bunyan: Prisoner with a Pen

Bea Ward
illustrated by Paula Cheadle

Frivolous Ways

"Mommy, Mommy! Help me! He's going to get me! Come quickly!"

For the third night in a row, little John's cries pierced the quiet night. His mother quickly lighted a candle, slid on her slippers, and hurried to comfort the fitful sleeper.

"John, John, wake up." She gently shook him as she sat on the edge of his bed. "It's only a dream, Son, wake up," she said, kissing his forehead.

"Mommy," he panted, wide-eyed and frightened, "the jugglers were chasing me, and the puppets were laughing because I couldn't run fast enough!"

"John Bunyan," his mother said sternly, "I knew I shouldn't have taken you to the fair. Too much excitement always stirs up your imagination."

Truly the Stourbridge Fair was the most exciting event of the year. Those living in the small village of Elstow looked forward to it all year

long. For three weeks in September, merchants and entertainers from all over England—and from other countries as well—set up stalls to sell goods of every kind.

Farmers and their wives bought tools, furniture, cloth, and other household items. But children had the best time watching jugglers, puppet shows, performing animals, and musicians. For a ha'penny they could buy delicious sweets like gingerbread and peppermint drops. Children with extra money could choose from a delightful array of toys such as dolls, drums, hobby-horses, popguns, kites, hoops, shuttlecocks, and much more.

An imaginative child like John Bunyan would always remember the sights and sounds of the fair.

Except for his visits to the fair, John's boyhood was uneventful. He lived in a small village in the countryside and learned to read and write at a school for poor farmers' children. When he was still young, he left school to become a tinker like his father, repairing pots and pans and other metal utensils.

Though John didn't have much schooling, he heard and read many tales and saw plays of medieval romance. These experiences filled his mind with visions of knights, dragons, and giants. He also heard many sermons and read the Bible. But the Bible reading in the Bunyan family did not indicate that the family had a saving faith in Jesus Christ. The Bunyans were religious people, members of the Church of

England. But John was not saved during his boyhood in the church his family attended.

In 1644 when John was sixteen, his secure and happy home life came to an end. In June his mother died, in July his younger sister Margaret died, and in November he was mustered—that is, drafted— into the army of Lord Oliver Cromwell.

For two years England had been fighting a civil war. The English Parliament (like our Congress) had many disagreements with the king, Charles I. They wanted the king to change many things in government. Parliament usually argued with the king about money—harsh taxes and foolish spending. Many members of Parliament were also concerned with the religious condition of the country.

One member, Oliver Cromwell, was a leader of the Puritans (those who wanted to purify the Church of England). He especially wanted freedom for personal religion in England. The Church of England controlled every church in the land and the ways in which the worship services were conducted. Cromwell believed that groups of

Christians should be able to follow their own methods of worship. In 1642 the House of Commons, one of the houses of Parliament, appointed Oliver Cromwell to help command an army to fight the king.

When John Bunyan came into Cromwell's army, he had many new experiences. Besides gathering his soldiers around campfires at night for prayer meetings, Cromwell made sure his army had good treatment and regular pay, but he exercised strict discipline.

A soldier who swore had to pay a fine. A soldier who got drunk was put in stocks. If he deserted, he was whipped. All this discipline made good soldiers, and Cromwell was able to win many battles, ultimately defeating the king.

Although John Bunyan didn't become a Christian in the army, the prayers and actions of Christian soldiers greatly impressed him. One particular event made a lasting impression on him. One day John was pulled out of his regular troop and ordered to fight at a nearby town. While he was away, a friend who took his place was shot and killed. Later when John became a preacher, he gave God the glory for sparing his life.

After leaving the army, John married a girl whose name we do not know. She was an orphan, and she and John were so poor that they didn't have one dish or spoon between them. But his wife did bring to their little home two Christian books, which they read together over and over.

John had not been a particularly naughty boy or a wicked young man, but he had been lively and sometimes mischievous, and his imagination often ran away with him. As he became a man, John was confused and restless in his search for God. The people of Elstow knew him as a carefree fellow who spent Sundays with rowdy friends and whose main vice was his constant swearing. But since he was pleasant and hard working, most folks liked him.

However, in his soul John was tormented with doubts and guilt. He thought that God was a terrible Judge who would send him to hell for all his frivolous ways. He had nightmares, just as he had experienced as a boy, dreaming he was in everlasting fire. Often, though, to shake off these fears, he became even rowdier in his attempts to forget about God.

Tinker-Preacher

One day John was walking to the town of Bedford on business. It was a beautiful day—gardens and orchards in bloom, a little river flowing under stone bridges. As he walked past the churches, stores, and thatched-roof cottages, he saw a group of women, their housework done, sitting in the sun spinning and talking. They weren't talking about families or neighbors but about religion.

"I'll join them," John thought, "for I like a good conversation, and I know something of religion too."

Yet when he listened for a moment, he heard them speaking of a joyous Christian life, of a loving God, and of Jesus as their friend! John's casual friendliness turned to deep interest and concern.

"Please," he begged them, "how can I know this great happiness that you have? My religion fills me only with dread and terror." Explaining that they knew little of theology, the good women urged him to speak to their pastor, John Gifford, at St. John's Church.

He left directly to find this man they called pastor, the leader of a little church, not part of the

Church of England. But knowing himself to be only an ignorant tinker, he hesitated to speak to so godly a gentleman. "Sir," he said after having introduced himself, "can God save so wretched a sinner as I?"

"As you?" the preacher smiled. "Let me tell you what I was before God saved me. Then you'll worry no more about your own sins." And he told John Bunyan of his years in the army.

"I served with King Charles's army and was taken prisoner in battle and condemned to die. The night before I was to be hanged, my sister came to bid me farewell. Believe it or not, she found all the guards asleep and all my fellow prisoners in a drunken stupor. Only I was awake, for I had wanted to talk to my sister. So she whispered to me, 'Now's your chance to escape. Get as far away as you can.' So, like St. Peter, I escaped from my jailers.

"For three days I hid in a ditch until the search for me died down; then I went to friends in London. Finally, I came here to Bedford, where no one knew me. Since I'd had some training in medicine, I set up as a doctor.

"You would think I would have been grateful to God for my escape,

but I was not. I was not even a good doctor, for I spent all my time drinking, gambling, and swearing. One day I read a little book. The message of the writer spoke to my soul and made me consider my sinful ways and turn to Jesus Christ as my Savior. How surprised my neighbors were to see their wicked doctor so soon changed into a God-fearing preacher!"

John Bunyan was amazed to hear a story so similar to that of his own life. Then and there he found a friend and counselor in this fervent preacher. John moved his family to Bedford, partly to gain more work in a larger town and partly to join Mr. Gifford's congregation. With good Bible preaching and counseling, Bunyan turned from his sins and put his trust in Jesus Christ. Soon he too was eager to tell friends and neighbors of this wonderful Savior. John Bunyan was a fine preacher, and many townspeople came to hear about Jesus from him.

Not long after he became a Christian, trouble came to John Bunyan. His wife became sick and died, leaving him with four small children, the oldest a blind daughter. Not long afterward, his good friend John Gifford also died, leaving the congregation in Bedford without a pastor.

Then in 1658 Oliver Cromwell died. Two years later King Charles II was invited to rule England, but when he came to the throne, he no longer allowed religious freedom for the people. All Englishmen had to return to the Church of England, even those in the little Bedford congregation, or be punished.

By this time John Bunyan was a leader of the Bedford church. One cold night, November 12, 1660, a group of men and women, their dark cloaks wrapped tightly about them, quietly but quickly walked in small groups to a large farmhouse. They carried no lanterns, for they did not want the king's soldiers to know of their meeting. Once inside, they nervously whispered to each other, waiting for one other member to arrive.

Finally, John Bunyan's broad shoulders appeared in the doorway. "Peace to you, brethren," he greeted them warmly.

"Brother Bunyan," said one who stepped quickly toward him, closing the door, "we have bad news. We think you should not preach tonight."

"What's that? What have you heard?"

"The magistrates know you have been preaching. They are sending men here to arrest you tonight. Please flee to safety!"

Everyone in the crowded room looked at John Bunyan, wondering what he would do. They had come to love this tinker-preacher and did not want him in jail.

After a long silence Bunyan spoke cheerfully, "Come, let us have our meeting. I will preach. Nothing can happen to me unless it is God's will. First, let us pray."

So these poor country folks, many of whom could not read but could recite from memory long passages of Scripture, settled onto chairs or benches or stood about the room to pray and then listen to their bold preacher.

Then came a heavy tramping on the doorstep, and a rough voice called, "Open, in the king's name!" Two men pushed to the front of the quiet room. "John Bunyan, tinker?"

"I am John Bunyan."

"You are under arrest for preaching unlawfully. Come with us."

So it was that he left the care of his family to his little congregation and to his new wife, Elizabeth.

Bunyan had not been in prison many months before his pious ways and joyous attitude won the respect and confidence of his jailer. Talking kindly to his fellow prisoners, praying with them, and teaching them the Bible, he soon had an influence over them as well. So when a member of Bunyan's congregation was on her deathbed asking for him, the jailer let him out to see her, only warning, "Be back before night."

By and by the jailer allowed Bunyan some freedom to go away to preach and to visit his family.

One day, however, a man on horseback rode to the jail to speak to his friend, the jailer. "Ho, friend," he called out. "I hope all your prisoners are safe in their rooms. You are to have visitors this afternoon."

"What? What's this you say?" he asked in alarm.

"Someone has been telling tales of you to the magistrates, and they are coming to check on John Bunyan."

"Oh, I am ruined then!"

"Do you not know where he is to send for him?"

"Yes, I know. But he is in London to preach and not due back until tomorrow."

"My dear friend, then you are in trouble. The magistrates will surely lock you in your own jail."

The jailer dropped his head to his hands, thinking all was lost, when John Bunyan stepped around the corner. "What's the trouble, my good man?"

"John Bunyan!" the jailer cried, his arms outstretched, a smile on his face. "What brings you home a day early?"

"I'm not sure," Bunyan answered, "but I just felt I must come back."

"Then up to your room quickly. And you're welcome to leave whenever you please, for you know better than I when to come back."

But after that, the magistrates had Bunyan watched closely, and he could not leave nearly as often.

For twelve long years Bunyan stayed in prison. Often he had the comfort of visits from his family and friends. Often he kept busy writing or making shoelaces to support his family. Sometimes, though, he was unhappy; sometimes he doubted God's love and promises. He would sometimes brood over his sins for days and wonder if such a sinner could really be right with God. But

God was faithful and comforted Bunyan when he got discouraged. And Bunyan learned to love the promises of God in Scripture. Eventually his faith in God's ability to save him and keep him became stronger as he studied these promises and claimed them for himself.

When he was finally freed from prison, the congregation at Bedford voted to have him as their pastor, and Bunyan was happy to be home with his family.

He was put in prison later for a short time. At that time, he thought about all the experiences he had had as a Christian.

He remembered how miserable he had been before he trusted Jesus as his Savior, and he wrote about a man named Christian who also carried a great burden until it rolled off him at the cross.

He remembered the Stourbridge Fair that had both excited and terrified him as a child, and he wrote about Vanity Fair, where the worldly townspeople could not understand a Christian who did not crave all the pleasures and temptations of the world.

He remembered the doubts he had suffered in prison before and wrote about Doubting Castle and the Giant Despair.

Many more experiences he thought about and described so that every Christian could recognize his own journey to the Celestial City, heaven.

As soon as it was published, *Pilgrim's Progress,* as he named the book, became popular. People, rich and poor, saw themselves as Christian and enjoyed reading the story of his journey. Before long

Through the years, John Bunyan's Pilgrim's Progress *has become a treasured book.*

nearly every home in England had a copy of John Bunyan's *Pilgrim's Progress.* In many homes it could be found alongside a well-worn Bible.

Soon Bunyan wrote other books. Remembering his experiences as a soldier in Cromwell's army, he wrote *The Holy War* about troops of Diabolus trying to capture the town of Mansoul.

When his wife and children became curious about the family of the pilgrim Christian, Bunyan wrote a second part to *Pilgrim's Progress.* It tells the story of Christian's wife, Christiana, and their children on their way to the Celestial City.

As John Bunyan grew old, he spent his time preaching and writing. He was well known in England and well loved.

One evening when Bunyan was nearly sixty years old, a young man came to see him. Bunyan recognized the caller as the son of an old acquaintance.

"Mr. Bunyan, I wish to ask a great favor of you, please."

"Certainly. I'm always glad to be of help."

"My father and I have quarreled," the young man began. "I know it was my fault, and since he is old, I wish to apologize, but he refuses to see me."

"What would you like me to do?"

"Mr. Bunyan," he pleaded, "I know my father lives a long way off, but he greatly respects you. If you would kindly see him and talk to him, I know he would soon forgive me."

"I'll be glad to do what I can. I leave tomorrow to preach, and your father's house is not too far out of my way."

"Thank you, Mr. Bunyan, and Godspeed to you."

When the young man had left, Mrs. Bunyan looked up from her mending and said to her husband, "John, why must you go there? You are not well, and you could easily write a letter to the man."

"No, I know the boy's father. He must have a visit. But don't worry about me; I am in God's care."

The next day John Bunyan saddled his horse, kissed his good wife, and set off on his journey.

What he said to the angry father we do not know, but soon the man and his son were reconciled.

He went on to visit friends and to preach, but as he rode through the rainy countryside, he caught a chill. After several days he became too ill to preach and knew that he too was about to enter the Celestial City.

"I'll be glad to go," he told his friends gathered at his bedside. "My affairs on earth are in order, and I shall be with my Lord."

Thus, like the Christian he wrote of, John Bunyan entered the gate to hear the Shining One say, "Enter thou into the joy of thy Lord."

Biography

John Bunyan wrote The Pilgrim's Progress *to show Christian's travels and trials while on his way to the Celestial City.*

John Bunyan had a great ability to understand the sorrows and joys of other people. He understood the Christian's fight against the world. Bunyan's understanding enabled him to write a book that Christians have read through more than three hundred years of change. Even though our world today is much different from Bunyan's world, we can still see ourselves in *The Pilgrim's Progress.*

Bunyan's ability to understand people was a gift from God. Today we have an opportunity that he didn't have to understand other people. Biographies can help us understand exactly how people in the past encountered some of the same problems and enjoyed some of the same pleasures that we enjoy today.

A *biography* is the story of a real person's life. Most biographies are written about people who lived in the past. Authors write about people whose fame or accomplishments will attract readers.

Enjoying Biographies

If you have ever wondered what it was like to be the first president of the United States, then perhaps you have read a biography of George Washington. Or if you've wondered how the man who ended slavery felt, then you might have decided to read about Abraham Lincoln. People read biographies out of curiosity. They also read them to understand a certain time in history or the meaning behind one person's accomplishments.

Consider John Bunyan. While it is interesting to read selections from *The Pilgrim's Progress,* the book becomes more important when you realize that he wrote it from prison, trying to comfort the members of his church who themselves were in danger of going to prison. We know that Bunyan was suffering for his beliefs. This knowledge helps us to see that his book expresses his enduring faith. We also can understand how he used his own long periods of doubt and despair to write the episode about Doubting Castle. When we see how Bunyan overcame his struggles, we can better know the meaning of his book. This is one way that his biography helps us.

Biographies help us to understand history better. It may seem dull to learn that Cromwell died in 1658 and that Charles II replaced him and took away religious liberty. But it isn't dull to read that armed soldiers of the king broke into a small church and took John Bunyan to jail for his religious beliefs.

The Range of Biographies

A biography should be based on fact. Some biographies are completely factual. They are made up of quotations from diaries and other documents, along with the author's comments and explanations. Other biographies, such as the biography of John Bunyan in this book, are written in story form. The author researched a person's life, found out as many exact details as possible, and then made it easier to understand by writing it as a story. The difference between these two types of biography can be compared to the difference between a photograph and a portrait. The first captures the exact details of a person, and the second tries to bring out the personality and character of the person to make others interested in him.

But a biography, whether in report form or story form, should always be true to facts. The author must be willing to admit that the person he is writing about had faults as well as virtues. It would not be honest for the author of the biographical story on John Bunyan to lead the reader to think that Bunyan never felt depressed while imprisoned. The author should let us know that Bunyan was often in despair while in prison. Bunyan sometimes wondered if God had deserted him. Despair and doubt were the greatest problems in Bunyan's life. If the author had never told us about these problems, Bunyan would have seemed too perfect and too different from his readers. Readers have to know they have something in common with the people they read about.

Not every biography you might read is about a Christian. And not every biography has a Christian author. Some authors might think that a person's actions are good, even though you know that those actions are contrary to Scripture. It is important to remember, especially while reading a biography, that some authors may use facts to serve their own purposes. The reader has to think about what he is reading and decide whether all the facts are being presented fairly. Using good judgment is part of a reader's job.

THE PILGRIM'S PROGRESS

John Bunyan

illustrated by Jim Hargis

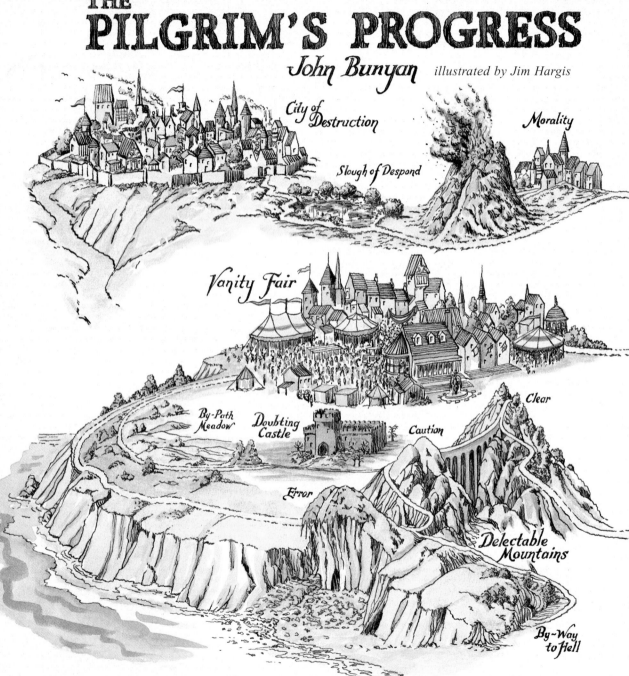

City of Destruction

Morality

Slough of Despond

Vanity Fair

Clear

By-Path Meadow

Doubting Castle

Caution

Error

Delectable Mountains

By-Way to Hell

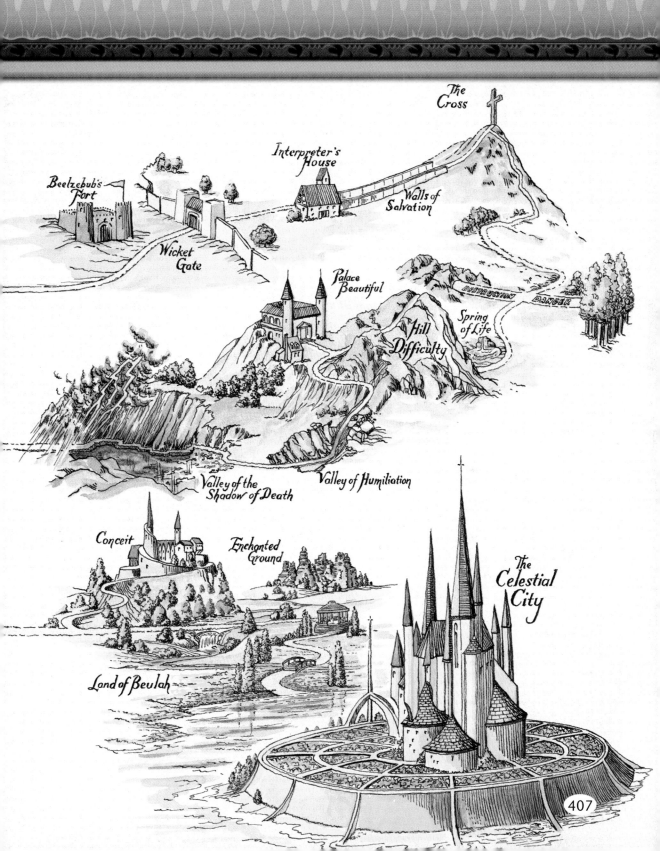

The Cross

Interpreter's House

Beelzebub's Fort

Walls of Salvation

Wicket Gate

Palace Beautiful

DESTRUCTION   DANGER

Hill Difficulty

Spring of Life

Valley of the Shadow of Death

Valley of Humiliation

Conceit

Enchanted Ground

The Celestial City

Land of Beulah

Vanity Fair

from The Pilgrim's Progress *by John Bunyan, adapted by Karen Duncan*
illustrated by Stephanie True

John Bunyan tells the story of The Pilgrim's Progress *to show the Christian's journey along the path of life. Although the book was written over three hundred years ago, the story shows the same trials and enemies that a Christian faces today. Written as an allegory, the book helps us clearly see a godly example of faith and hope in the promises of God's Word.*

The Pilgrim's Progress is written as if it were a dream about a man called Christian. First, he turns from the City of Destruction and comes to the Cross. It is here that Christian's burden of sin is removed. Now his feet are on the King's highway, and he travels on toward the Celestial City. Along the way, Christian must fight against the enemy, Apollyon, and travel through the Valley of the Shadow of Death. Coming out of the valley, Christian meets another pilgrim whose name is Faithful. They walk on until at last they come to Vanity Fair. They stay there longer than they intend to and suffer together.

Business at the Fair

Then I saw in my dream that Christian and Faithful saw a town before them. The name of that town is Vanity, and at the town there is a fair called Vanity Fair. It is called Vanity Fair because all that is sold there and all who come there are worthless and empty.

This fair is no new business, but an ancient thing. Almost five thousand years ago, pilgrims began walking to the Celestial City. Beelzebub, Apollyon, and Legion saw that the pilgrims' road led through this town of Vanity. The evil ones decided to set up a fair there. At that fair would be sold all sorts of vanities, everything empty and worthless. That is why these things are found at this fair: houses, lands, businesses, silver, gold, privileges, countries, kingdoms, honors, lusts, pleasures, cheats, and all delights that belong only to this world. Here one can see also, for no extra charge, many thefts, murders, and terrible lies. Indeed, this fair has people from all the countries of the world, and the goods that belong to them are arranged in rows on its streets.

Now, as I said, the way to the Celestial City lies just through this town where the fair is kept. The Prince of princes himself passed through this town on the way to His own country. Beelzebub, the chief lord of the fair, invited Him to buy of the vanities. He took Him from street to street and showed Him all the kingdoms of the world in a little time, hoping to tempt the Blessed One to cheapen Himself and buy some of the worthless things. The Prince did not want what Beelzebub had to sell and left the town without buying a single vanity. As you can see, this fair is an ancient thing.

Now Christian and Faithful had to travel through this fair. Well, so they did; but even as they entered the fair, all the people there and in the town itself were thrown into a hubbub for these three reasons:

First, the pilgrims dressed differently from any who did business at the fair. (They still wore the armor that their Lord had given them for the journey.) The people therefore stared at them, and some said that they were fools or madmen or strangers from some other country.

Second, few of the people there could understand what they said. The pilgrims spoke the language of the Promised Land, but the merchants at the fair were men of this present world. From one end of the fair to the other, they sounded like foreigners to the merchants.

Third, these pilgrims paid very little attention to the things that were for sale. They would not even look at them. If a shopkeeper called to them to buy, they would put their fingers in their ears and say, "Turn away mine eyes from beholding vanity." Then they would look upward to show that their business was in heaven.

One citizen who was mocking them happened to say, "Come, will you buy nothing?" But they answered him seriously, "We buy the truth." This made the people hate them even more. At last almost everyone was mocking and ridiculing and speaking cruelly and calling on others to beat the pilgrims. The entire fair fell into confusion.

Soon the master of the fair sent some of his most trusted friends to find these men who had almost turned the fair upside down. So they questioned the pilgrims, and when they found out who they were and where they were going, they would not believe them. They thought they must be madmen or troublemakers. Therefore, they took the two travelers and beat them and smeared them with dirt and then put them into a cage so that all the men of the fair could come and stare at them.

There the two men stayed for some time. Anyone who passed could make fun of them or hurt them as he wished. The master of the fair only laughed at anything that happened to them. But the pilgrims were patient and did not give back evil for evil. Instead they gave good words for cruel ones and returned kindness for injuries.

Some of the men there who were more fair-minded watched them carefully. After a while, these men tried to stop the others from treating the prisoners so cruelly. This interference made the abusers angry. "You are as bad as the men in the cage," they cried. "You are plotting with them, and you should have the same treatment."

The others replied, "For all we can see, the men were quiet and sober and meant nobody any harm. There are many who do business in the fair who deserve punishment more than these you have abused."

After they had argued for some time, they began to fight among themselves and hurt one another. Then, even though the pilgrims had behaved wisely and quietly through it all, they were blamed for the new trouble at the fair. The citizens of Vanity Fair beat them and put chains on them.

Then they led them up and down the streets to warn other people from joining them.

But Christian and Faithful took all this treatment with so much meekness and patience that it won to their side several more men of the fair. This threw the cruel men into a rage.

"You two shall die for what you have done," they shouted. "Neither a cage nor chains will do. You will die for deceiving the men of Vanity Fair!"

The pilgrims then were sent back to the cage again to wait with their feet fastened in the stocks. They were not afraid to suffer but put themselves in the care of the all-wise God who rules all things.

Testimony of the Truth

When the time came for the trial, they were brought before their enemies and charged with their crimes. The judge's name was Lord Hategood, and here is the charge read against them:

"They are enemies to the fair and disturbers of trade. They have caused unrest and rioting in the town, and have won other people to their dangerous ideas. This is all against the law of our king."

Then Faithful answered, "I spoke only against those who oppose the God Most High. And I made no disturbance, for I am a man of peace. The men who joined us were won by seeing our truth and innocence. And as for the king you talk of, since he is Beelzebub, the enemy of our Lord, I defy him and all his angels."

When he had finished, the judge called for any who wanted to give evidence to step forward. Three witnesses came: Envy, Superstition, and Pickthank.

Envy spoke first, and said, "My Lord Judge, this man is one of the worst men in our country. He does not obey any of our laws or customs. Instead he tries to persuade all men with his evil notions, which he calls principles of holiness and faith.

"And I myself once heard him claim that Christianity and the customs of our fine town were exactly opposite, and that they never could agree. By saying that, my Lord, he condemns all our good efforts and us as well."

Then the judge said to him, "Have you any more to say?"

"My Lord," he said, "I do not wish to bore the court. Yet if the court needs more evidence to convict him, I will think of more to say."

Then they called Superstition and asked him what he had to say against the prisoner.

"My Lord Judge," he began, "I do not know this man well, and I do not wish to know him better. However, this I do know: he is a very bothersome fellow. I heard him say that our religion was nothing, and that a man could not please God with it. When he says this, my Lord Judge, he means that we worship in vain, we are still in our sins, and shall finally die without hope. That is what I have to say."

Then Pickthank was brought to testify.

"My Lord Judge," said he, "I have heard this fellow speak things that should not be said. He has scorned our noble prince Beelzebub and all the rest of our important men. He has said, besides, that none of these men live according to the truth. He has not been afraid to call even you, his judge, an ungodly villain. I have told my tale."

When Pickthank finished, the judge spoke to Faithful, saying, "You renegade, heretic, and traitor—have you heard what these honest men have witnessed against you?"

"May I speak a few words in my own defense?" asked Faithful.

"You deserve to be killed this moment," answered the judge. "But so that all men may see our kindness to you, we will hear what you have to say."

Faithful began to speak. "I say only this to them: The worship of God requires faith and must agree with the Word of God. Any law or custom or rule that is against the Word of God, or is added to the Word of God, is error; it cannot lead to eternal life. As for the prince Beelzebub and his gentlemen, they are more fit to live in hell than in this country. The Lord have mercy upon me."

Then the judge called to the jury (who had heard and seen all this): "Gentlemen of the jury, you see this man who has made such an uproar in this town. You have also heard what these gentlemen have witnessed against him. Also you have heard his reply and confession. Now it is up to you to hang him or save his life.

"Remember our ancient laws," he continued, "the same laws by which Pharaoh killed the Hebrew male children and Nebuchadnezzar threw the men who would not worship his golden image into the fiery furnace. By the same laws of our land, Darius cast Daniel into the lions' den. This rebel has broken these laws in both word and deed. For the treason he has confessed, he deserves to die the death."

Then the jury went out to discuss the verdict, even though each of them had already decided for himself to condemn him.

Mr. Blind Man, who was in charge, said, "I see clearly that this man is a heretic."

Then said Mr. No-good, "Away with such a fellow from the earth."

"Ay," said Mr. Hurtful, "for I hate the very sight of him."

"Hang him, hang him," said Mr. Headstrong.

"Hanging is too good for him," said Mr. Cruelty.

Then said Mr. Unforgiving, "If the whole world were given to me, I could not stand to have him live. Let us find him guilty and condemn him to death."

All the others spoke in the same way, and so they did find him guilty. Then was Faithful condemned to the most cruel death that could be invented.

When they brought him out to carry out his sentence, first they scourged him, then they struck him, and then they cut him with knives. After that they stoned him with stones and stabbed him with swords. Finally, they burned him to ashes at the stake.

Now I saw that there were nearby a chariot and a pair of horses waiting for Faithful. As soon as his enemies had killed him, he was taken up into the chariot, and carried up through the clouds with the sound of a trumpet. He went by the shortest way to the Celestial City.

But Christian was sent back to prison instead of killed. There he stayed for a time; but He who rules all things gave Christian a way to escape. He went on his way singing, thankful that Faithful was still alive and with God.

Now I saw in my dream that Christian did not leave the town alone. A man named Hopeful, who had seen the testimony of Christian and Faithful at the fair, joined him on his journey. Thus one died to bear testimony of the truth, and another came as a result to walk with Christian on the King's highway. Even more, in the time to come, would follow in the way because of them.

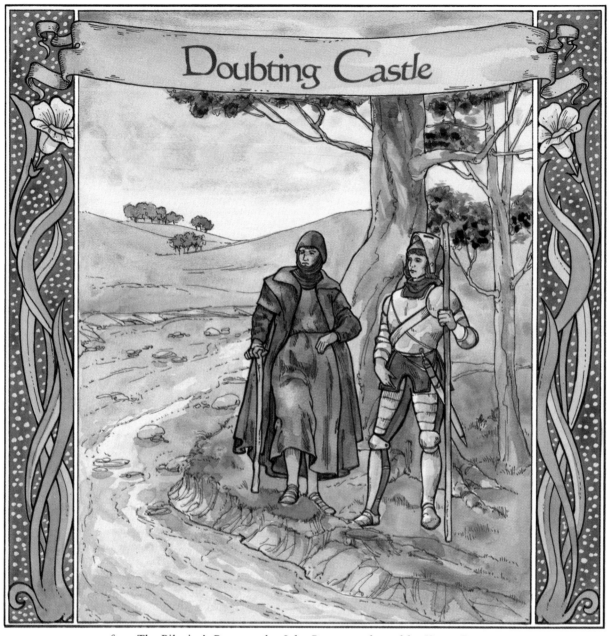

Doubting Castle

from The Pilgrim's Progress *by John Bunyan, adapted by Karen Duncan*
illustrated by Stephanie True

Christian and Hopeful become friends, but Hopeful is the younger man. Often on the path to the Celestial City, Christian has to watch out for Hopeful and warn him of danger. Hopeful always listens willingly, and he loves Christian as a brother.

By-path Meadow

I saw then that Christian and Hopeful came to a pleasant river. David the king had called this river "the river of God"; but John, "the river of the water of life."

Here the King's highway went along the bank of the river. Christian and his companion walked along it with great delight. They also drank the water from the river, which was pleasant and lifted their weary spirits. Besides this, on the banks of this river were green trees that bore all sorts of fruit and also leaves that were good for medicine. They were delighted with the fruit of these trees, and they ate the leaves to prevent illnesses. On either side of the river there was a meadow beautifully carpeted with lilies. It stayed green all year long.

In this meadow they lay down and slept, for they knew they would be safe in this place. When they awoke, they gathered more fruit from the trees and drank more water from the river and then lay down again to sleep. This they did several days and nights. They felt so happy and comfortable that they sang songs in praise of the sweet crystal water and pleasant fruit.

At last they knew they must continue on their way. They ate again a meal of the fruit and drank from the river, and then they started down the road.

They had not journeyed far when their path led away from the river. They were sorry to leave the pleasant bank, but they dared not leave the road that they were traveling. Now the road away from the river was rough, and their feet were already tender from walking so far on their journey. As they went on, they wished for an easier way and began to be much discouraged.

Now a little before them they saw, on the left side of the road, a meadow and a stile to go over the wall into it. Christian and Hopeful did not know it, but that meadow is called the By-path Meadow.

Then said Christian to his friend, "If this meadow goes alongside our road, let us cross over and walk there." He went to the stile to see and found a path lying along the way on the other side of the fence.

"It is as I hoped," said Christian. "Here is an easier way to walk. Come, good Hopeful, and let us go over the stile."

"But what if this path should take us the wrong way?" asked Hopeful.

"That is not likely," said the other. "Look, does it not follow the highway?"

So Hopeful, being persuaded by his companion, followed him over the stile. The path on the other side was very easy for their feet, and they began to enjoy their walk. Suddenly the night came on, and it grew very dark. When they could no more see the path before them, Hopeful stopped and said, "Where are we now?" But Christian was silent, because he feared that he had led them in the wrong way.

Now it began to rain and thunder, and lightning flashed around them, and the water in the river rose and rushed against the banks.

Then Hopeful groaned, "Oh, I wish that I had kept on the King's highway!"

Christian answered, "Who could have thought that this path would lead us out of the way?"

"I was afraid of it at the very first," said Hopeful. "But you are older than I, and I thought that you would know best."

"Good brother, I am sorry I have led you out of the way, and that I have brought you into this place of danger. Please, my brother, forgive me; I meant to do no evil to you."

"Be comforted, my brother; I forgive you," Hopeful replied, "and believe that this shall work out for our good."

Then said Christian, "I am thankful for your kindness, brother; but we must not stay here. Let us try to go back to the right way again."

By this time the waters were high and made the way back by the river dangerous. (You know that it is easier going out of the right way when we are in it than going back when we are out.) Still, they tried to go back, but the night was so dark, and the water was so high that they probably would have been drowned nine or ten times before they reached the highway.

Try as they might, they could not reach the stile that night. At last they found a sheltered spot beside some trees. They sat down to wait for day to break, but were too weary and fell asleep.

Now there was nearby a castle called Doubting Castle, which was owned by Giant Despair. It was on his property that the pilgrims now were sleeping. The giant, getting up early in the morning, went walking in his fields and caught Christian and Hopeful there asleep. Then with a grim, loud voice he told them to awake and asked them where they came from and what they were doing in that place. Trembling, they told him that they were pilgrims and that they had lost their way.

Then said the giant, "You have this night trespassed on my prop-erty, and therefore you must come with me."

They were forced to go because he was stronger than they were, and besides, they knew that they were in the wrong. The giant took them then into his castle and put them into a dark dungeon, nasty and stinking to their spirits. There they lay from Wednesday morning until Saturday night, without one bit of bread or drop of drink or any light, and far from friends or any-one who knew them. Christian was doubly sorry, because he knew his eagerness for the easy way had brought them to this trouble.

Dungeon of Despair

Now Giant Despair had a wife, and her name was Distrust. That night the giant told his wife what he had done and asked her what else he should do with them now. She counseled him that he should beat them the next morning without mercy.

So when he arose, he found a heavy crab-tree club and went down into the dungeon where the pilgrims were. He first began to scold them as if they were dogs, although they never said a word to offend him. Then he beat them fearfully with the club until they were not able even to turn over on the floor. This done, Giant Despair left them there to comfort each other and to mourn about their distress.

So all that day the pilgrims did nothing but sigh and lament. The next night Distrust and her husband talked further of the prisoners and decided he would counsel them to end their own lives.

When morning came he went to the dungeon and saw that they were sore from their beating the day before. He told them that since they would never leave that place, their only hope was to end their own lives quickly, either with knife or poison, or by hanging themselves. "For why," said he, "should you choose life, seeing that living is so painful?"

Still they begged him to let them go. That angered him, and he rushed at them to kill them. But at that moment he fell into one of his fits. (Sometimes sunshiny weather made him lose the use of his hands or legs for a time.) Since he could not hurt them at that time, he left them again to consider what to do.

"Brother," said Christian, "what shall we do? The life that we now live is miserable. I know not whether it is best to live this way or simply to die. The grave would be more easy for me than this dungeon. Shall we live and be ruled by the giant?"

"Indeed," answered Hopeful, "death would be far more welcome to me than to live for ever in this place. But consider this: the Lord of the country we seek hath said, 'Thou shalt do no murder.' If we are not to murder others, we are much more forbidden to obey Despair and kill ourselves. And remember, too, that all the power does not belong to Giant Despair. Others, I think, have escaped from him before. Who knows? God who made the world may cause Giant Despair to die, or at some time the giant may forget to lock us in. He may soon have another of his fits and altogether lose the use of his limbs. And if ever that should happen again, I am resolved to try my utmost to get away from him. My brother, let us be patient and endure a while. The time may come when we can get away. Let us not be our own murderers."

With these words Hopeful comforted the mind of his brother.

Well, toward evening the giant went down into the dungeon again to see whether his prisoners had done what he said. He found them alive; and truly, alive was all. For now, from hunger and thirst and the wounds he had given them, they could do little but breathe. Even so, finding them alive sent him into a terrible rage.

"Since you will not do what I say," he howled, "you'll wish you had never been born, you will!" And he slammed the bars behind him.

At this they trembled greatly, and began to talk about the giant's order. Christian again seemed to be for doing it.

"My brother," said Hopeful, "do you not remember how brave you have been until now? That evil fiend Apollyon could not crush you, nor could all the things you heard, or saw, or felt in the Valley of the Shadow of Death. I am a far weaker man than you are, yet I am in the dungeon with you, and also wounded and hungry and thirsty, and like you I mourn without the light. But let us be a little more patient. Remember how brave you were at Vanity Fair, and were afraid of neither chains nor cage, nor even of death. Therefore let us be patient as well as we can.

That night, Distrust asked her husband if the prisoners still lived. He replied, "They are sturdy rogues. They choose to bear all hardship rather than to kill themselves."

Then said she, "Take them into the castle yard tomorrow, and show them the bones and skulls of those that you have already destroyed, and make them believe that you will tear them in pieces also before the week comes to an end."

So when the morning came, the giant went to them again, and took them into the castle yard, and showed them the bones, as his wife had told him to.

"These," said he, "were pilgrims once, and they trespassed in my grounds, as you have done. When I saw fit, I tore them in pieces, and within ten days I will do the same with you. Go, get down to your dungeon." With that he beat them all the way there.

They lay all day Saturday recovering from their wounds.

Now when night came, Mrs. Distrust and her husband the giant began to talk again about their prisoners. The old giant wondered why he could not bring them to an end.

With that his wife replied, "I fear that they live in hope that some help will come, or that they have with them some means of escape."

"Think you so, my dear?" said the giant. "I will search them in the morning."

Well, on Saturday about midnight the two pilgrims began to pray and continued in prayer till almost daybreak.

Then suddenly Christian jumped to his feet and shouted aloud. "What a fool am I," said he, "to lie in a stinking dungeon when I can easily have liberty! I was given a key called Promise. It will, I am certain, open any lock in Doubting Castle."

"That is good news, good brother," said Hopeful. "Take it out quickly and try."

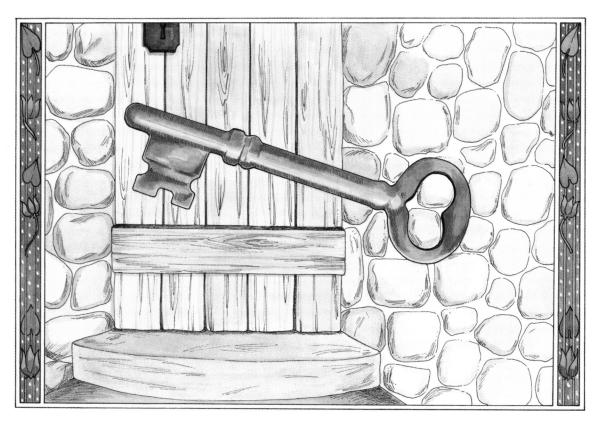

Then Christian pulled out the key and began to try the lock on the dungeon door. The bolt shot back, the door flew open, and Christian and Hopeful hurried out. They opened yet another door and came to the iron gate. Although the lock was terribly stiff, the key did open it. But that gate, as they pushed on it, made such a creaking that it woke Giant Despair. He jumped up to go after his prisoners, but one of his fits came upon him, and he fell down helpless in the sunshine. Christian and Hopeful went on until they came to the King's highway. There at last they were safe from the giant.

Now when they had climbed back over the stile, they began to plan what they should do to prevent others from falling into the hands of Giant Despair. So they made there a stone marker, and wrote upon the side of it this sentence: "Over this stile is the way to Doubting Castle, which belongs to Giant Despair. He hates the King of heaven and tries to kill His holy pil-grims." (Many who came later read the warning and escaped the danger.)

When they had finished, the two pilgrims began to sing, and went on their way to the Celestial City.

To their joy, Christian and Hopeful saw that they were coming closer to the Celestial City. Several times friends along the way took them to high mountains where they could see their destination. Yet as they came closer,

the perils that they faced became subtler and more dangerous. Now enemies of the King dressed as His own Shining Ones to lead the pilgrims away. More and more frequently they saw handsome travelers who tried to persuade them of new ways to reach the city.

But there were watchers on duty, and these servants of the King helped or rescued the travelers when they were in trouble. At last through all their difficulties, they came to a deep river. It was

the last step of their journey, and then they would be safe in the city, which they could see from the riverbank.

But there was no bridge on this river and no ferry. A man had to cross it by going through it, and it was deep or shallow according to a man's faith in the King. As they stepped in, Christian sank and called for help. He could feel no bottom, and he was afraid of the cold waters of the river.

But Hopeful, the younger and weaker of the two, held on to Christian to help him. "I feel the bottom and it is good," he urged Christian, trying to keep his friend's head up out of the water. But all his life Christian had been afraid of this river, and now such a horror fell on him that he even forgot how his sins had been forgiven, how he had overcome Apollyon, and how he had walked through the terrible Valley of the Shadow of Death.

"Brother, I see the gate and men standing by to receive us," Hopeful called to him, but Christian only answered,

" 'Tis you, 'tis you they wait for."
He would have forgotten everything, but suddenly his heart was
revived. He remembered the promises of the King, and he took
courage again. "I see Him again!"
he exclaimed, "And He tells me,
'When thou passest through the
waters, I will be with thee.'"

Then Christian's feet felt the
bottom, and he and Hopeful
walked on and were received into
the city with trumpets and joy.
There they rejoined their friends
who had come before them, and
they were given the rewards of all
their journeying, suffering, and
mourning. Yet for their sins they
were pardoned and fully recovered,
for they were given shining
clothes, and they would never sin
again. So they lived happily in the
presence of their King from that
day forward.

6
REFLECTIONS

The Base Stealer

Robert Francis

Poised between going on and back, pulled
Both ways taut like a tightrope-walker,
Fingertips pointing the opposites,
Now bouncing tiptoe like a dropped ball
Or a kid skipping rope, come on, come on,
Running a scattering of steps sidewise,
How he teeters, skitters, tingles, teases,
Taunts them, hovers like an ecstatic bird,
He's only flirting, crowd him, crowd him,
Delicate, delicate, delicate, delicate—now!

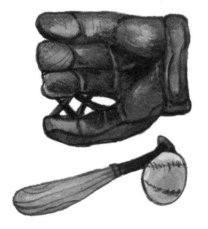

Rufus & the Fatal Four

Eleanor Estes   *illustrated by Tim Banks*

The following story comes from Rufus M., a book from the Moffat series, about a family of four children who grew up in the early 1900s. Athough they were poor, their family was happy, held together by their own strong sense of family unity. The Moffat children did everything they could to entertain themselves, and the stories of their adventures have entertained readers for forty years. In this story, ten-year-old Janey Moffat and her younger brother Rufus, who is left-handed, take up baseball.

Not Just Practice

For some time Rufus had been seeing "The F. F." on all of Janey's notebooks and on the brown covers of her grammar and arithmetic books. He asked Jane what it meant. Jane said it was a secret. However, if Rufus would not tell anybody, the initials stood for the Fatal Four. More than that she would not say. Rufus assumed it had something to do with pirates. Therefore he was really surprised when Jane, in a mood of confidence, further enlightened him to the extent of revealing that the Fatal Four was the name of a baseball team she belonged to that could beat anybody.

"Then," she went on to explain, "if the Fatal Four gets tired of baseball, oh, not gets tired 'cause they'll never do that, but if it should snow, and they couldn't play any more, they'll still be the Fatal Four because it's a good name the members can keep always. Baseball . . . football . . . no matter what. Or it could just be a club to eat cookies and drink punch made out of jelly and water."

This all sounded good to Rufus, particularly the punch. He asked if he could join. Did it cost anything? Jane said she was sorry but the Fatal Four was all girls. However, she would try to bring him a cookie if they ever decided on punch and cookies instead of baseball. So for a time Rufus was not allowed to have anything to do with this team. But sometimes he went across the street to the big empty lot behind the library, sat down on a log, and watched them practice. There were a half-dozen or so silvery gray old telephone poles piled up in one part of the lot. Bleachers, Rufus called them, and that was where he sat to watch the Fatal Four.

Jane and Nancy had organized the Fatal Four baseball team. At first Jane was worried that they were playing baseball in October when the time for baseball is spring. She thought it would be better if the Fatal Four started right in with punch and cookies on Tuesdays. But once they had begun playing baseball she wondered how she could ever have been so foolish. She loved baseball and could not understand how anybody was happy who did not play it every day.

Naturally, since Jane and Nancy had thought up this whole team, there was no reason why they should not take the two most important roles, the pitcher and the catcher, for themselves. Jane was the catcher. She accepted this position because she thought the name alone would automatically make her a good one. "Yes," she said, "I'll be catcher." And she put her trust in the power of the title and the mitt to enable her to catch anything. Nancy was the pitcher. For a time they were the only members of the team, so they had to be the pitcher and the catcher, for in baseball that is the very least you can get along with. Soon, however, other girls in the neighborhood joined up.

"I'll be the captain," said Nancy. "Let's take a vote."

They took a vote and elected Nancy. Clara Pringle was the outfield to catch all flies. She never really had very much to do because there weren't many flies hit and she sat in the long grass and waited for business. A girl named Hattie Wood was first base. That made four girls they had on the team and that was when they decided to call themselves the Fatal Four.

So far Rufus had had nothing to do with this team except to sit and watch. He did this gladly however, for he considered that anything that called itself the Fatal Four was worthy of being watched, especially if there was that vague possibility of pink punch and cookies in the offing. He used to sit there pounding his fist into one of Joey's old mitts, hoping they'd take him into the Four.

At first the Fatal Four baseball team practiced ardently every day. However, after a week or so Jane grew tired of chasing balls, since she rarely caught one. The mitt and the title of catcher had not produced the desired results.

"A back-stop is what we need," she told Nancy.

None of the girls was willing to be a back-stop. Moreover, they were all needed where they were. Take Hattie Wood off first base and what kind of a team would they have, they asked themselves. An amateur team. The Fatal Four was anything but that, Nancy assured them. "But if you want a back-stop, why not ask Rufus?" she suggested.

Now there was much arguing back and forth as to whether or not they should invite Rufus to be the back-stop. He was not a girl and this team was supposed to be composed of girls only. But then everybody thought how nice it would be to have Rufus chasing balls for them, so they enthusiastically assented.

"After all," said Jane, "a back-stop is not really part of the team. It's part of the grounds."

So that clinched it and that was how Rufus came to be back-stop for the Fatal Four baseball team. Rufus was happy over the arrangement. When they abandoned baseball for punch and cookies, he might be an accepted member. Moreover, the more practice he had, the sooner the big boys would take him into their team, he thought. Certainly if the pitcher of the boys' baseball team had the same tendencies as Nancy, left-handed Rufus would be a tremendous asset.

Nancy used to be a rather good pitcher. But ever since the girls' baseball team had been organized, Nancy had taken to practicing curves. Somehow these curves always shot the ball way to the left of the batter. The batter would move farther and farther to the left, hoping to catch up with Nancy's curves. But it was no use. No matter how far to the left the batter edged, the farther to the left flew Nancy's balls. Often the bases had to be moved several times during the game to catch up with the home plate. Frequently, by the end of the game, home plate was where the pitcher's box originally had been, and vice versa. Nancy realized there was a flaw in her pitching which she would have to correct.

Meanwhile, it certainly was lucky the team now had a left-handed back-stop, for Jane had a hard enough time catching just straight pitches, let alone these curves of Nancy's that veered off to the left all the time. But Rufus had only to reach out his left arm farther and farther, and he caught most of them. What he didn't catch he cheerfully ran for, over Mr. Buckle's hen coop or in Mrs. Wood's asparagus patch that had gone to seed, or he hunted between the long silvery logs that lay lined up in a corner of the field.

As a reward for his back-stop duties Nancy pitched Rufus some curves, and since he was a left-handed batter, her balls that veered to the left were just perfect for him and it was only when Rufus was at the bat that Clara Pringle, picking goldenrod in the outfield, had anything to do in the game.

This convinced Nancy that there was nothing wrong with her pitching after all. The trouble lay with the material she was working

Rufus and the Fatal Four 433

with. "Slug at 'em, fellas," she said, "Rufe hits 'em all." And the girls, feeling rather ashamed, now tried harder, sometimes even turning around and batting left-handed as Rufus did, hoping to hit Nancy's balls.

One Saturday morning Rufus was sitting in the driver's seat of the old abandoned sleigh that was in the Moffats' barn. He was thinking that if he had a pony next winter he could harness it to this old sleigh and go for a ride. Suddenly Nancy and Janey burst around from the front yard. Nancy was swinging her bat. She had her pitcher's mitt on. Jane was pounding the baseball into Joey's big catcher's mitt, limbering it up.

"Come on, Rufe," they yelled. "This is the day!"

"What! Punch and cookies?" exclaimed Rufus.

"No, we're having a real game today. Not just practice," they said.

For a long time Jane and Nancy had thought they were the only girls' baseball team in Cranbury, in the world in fact. Then one day a girl accosted them after school. She said her name was Joyce Allen and that she was the captain of the Busy Bee baseball team, a team composed entirely of girls on the other side of town. She wanted to know whether or not Nancy, the captain of the F. F. team, would accept a challenge from her, the captain of the Busy Bee team, to play next Saturday. Nancy consulted with Jane and said "Yes."

Batter Up!

So now today was the day. Rufus climbed off the sleigh, found his old pitcher's mitt that he used to catch Nancy's curves, and they all marched across the street to the big lot behind the library where the game was going to be held. While they waited for the teams to show up, Rufus spit in his mitt, rubbed sand in it, and got it into condition to play.

"I hope we don't have to go all over town and round everybody up," said Jane impatiently.

The Fatal Four had added another team member, Nancy's sister Beatrice, but they still called themselves the Fatal Four because it sounded better than fatal anything else. Since this team had such an excellent name, the F. F., it had plenty of applicants to join. Nancy and Jane were particular, however, saying to join the F. F. you really had to know something about baseball. Most applicants backed away apologetically when Nancy stated this firmly.

At last here came somebody across the lot. It was Joyce Allen, the captain of the Busy Bees.

"The others will be here soon," she said cheerfully. "Some of them hadn't finished washing the breakfast dishes, but they'll be here soon."

"While we're waitin'," said Jane, "since both the captains are here, we can see who's up at the bat first."

Rufus took the bat, threw it, and Nancy caught it. She put her right fist around the end of it, then the other captain put her fist above Nancy's and swiftly placing one fist above the other they measured the length of the bat. The visiting captain's left fist was the last one to fit the bat. It was a tight squeeze but fair, and Rufus said that the visiting team was first up at the bat. Rufus sometimes had to act in the capacity of umpire as well as back-stop.

But where was the visiting team? Or Nancy's, for that matter?

Rufus began to feel impatient. Here were the captains. All right. Let the teams come then. "Why not have the punch instead?" he asked. But nobody paid any attention to him. It seemed to Rufus as though the game were off, and he decided, Fatal Four or no, to go and find something else to do. Over in a corner of the field some men had started to dig a cellar to a new house. This activity looked interesting to Rufus and he was about to investigate it when along came two girls, arms linked together. So Rufus stayed. There was always the possibility that the Fatal Four might switch from baseball to punch and cookies. Either was worth staying for in Rufus's opinion.

"These girls must be Busy Bees," said Nancy.

They were Busy Bees. They both admitted it. However, they said they wished they could join the F. F. instead. They liked the name of it. They had heard many rumors as to what it stood for. Most people thought it stood for Funny Fellows. Did it?

"Of course not!" said Nancy, and Jane clapped her hand over Rufus's mouth before he could say the Fatal Four and give away the secret. No matter what it stood for, the girls wanted to join it and be able to write the F. F. on all their red notebooks.

While the discussion was going on three more girls arrived, three more Busy Bees. It seemed they too wanted to join the F. F., so they could write the F. F. on their note-books also. Nancy and Jane looked at the captain. She must feel very badly at this desertion. But she didn't. She said she wished she could join the F. F. too.

"Oh, no," said Nancy. "You all better stay Busy Bees. What team would there be for us to beat if we let you join ours?"

So that settled the matter and Busy Bees remained Busy Bees. Now they lined up at the home plate for they were to be the first at the bat. At last the game began. "Thank goodness, Rufus is here behind me," thought Jane, pound-ing her fist into the big catcher's mitt. For it really took two Moffats to make one good catcher. If one of them was she, that is.

Nancy's team did not get off to a good start. Nancy had been prac-ticing her curves more than ever, and they swung more and more sharply to the left. If they had not had such a good left-handed back-stop as Rufus, goodness knows where the balls would have landed. In order that they would not crash through a window of the library, the girls rearranged the bases many times.

Of course there was no danger of the balls crashing through the li-brary windows from hits. The dan-ger lay in Nancy's curves. So far she had not been able to strike the Busy Bees out. They were all walk-ing to base on balls. And the balls were flying wild now. Rufus had dashed across the lot to take a look at the men who were digging the cellar to the new house and he was sorely missed. Jane, who had had enough trouble catching in the old days before Nancy cultivated her curves, was becoming desperate.

Right now happened to be a very tense moment. The captain of the Busy Bees was at the bat. There were men on all bases. They'd gotten there on walks. The captain had two strikes against her, however. She had been striking at anything, for she evidently had grown tired of just walking to base. If Nancy could strike her out, it would break the charm and maybe the Fatal Four team would have a chance at the bat. So far the Bees had been at the bat the entire game. The score must be big. They had lost track of it.

Beside wanting to strike Captain Allen out, Nancy was trying especially hard to impress her. She came over to Jane and said in a low voice, "They'll think they have a better team than we have, and I bet that pitcher can't even throw curves! I've just got to strike her out!"

"Yes," agreed Jane, who was anxious to bat herself for a change.

"Watch for a certain signal," Nancy said. "When I hold my two middle fingers up, it means I'm going to throw a curve, a real one. It'll curve out there by the library, and then it will veer back, right plunk over the home plate. She won't strike at it because she'll think it's going over the library. But it won't, and she'll miss it and that's the way I'll put her out."

Jane nodded her head. Another curve! Of course curves made it real baseball and not amateur. She knew that much. All the same she wished she had said, "Why don't you pitch 'em straight for a change?" But she didn't have the courage. Nancy was the captain and the pitcher. She certainly should know how to pitch if she was the pitcher. Nancy wasn't telling Jane how to catch. She expected Jane to know how to catch since she was the catcher. She didn't tell her anything. So neither did Jane tell Nancy anything, and she waited for the signal and wished that Rufus would return and back-stop for this very important pitch.

Now Nancy was winding her arm around and around. Then she stopped. She held up her middle two fingers. The signal! Jane edged over to the left but Nancy frowned her back. Oh, of course. This curve was really going to fly over home plate. Nancy crooked her wrist and threw! The girl at the bat just dropped to the ground when she saw the ball coming and she let it go. And the ball really did come right over home plate only it was up in the air, way, way up in the air and spinning swiftly toward the library window, for it did its veering

later than calculated. Jane leapt in the air in an effort to catch it but she missed.

"Rufus! Rufus!" she yelled, and she closed her eyes and stuck her fingers in her ears, waiting for the crash.

Just in the nick of time Rufus jumped for the ball. He caught it in his left hand before it could crash through the window. He sprinted over with the ball.

"We'd better move the bases again," said Nancy. And they all moved farther away from the library.

"Stay here," said Jane to Rufus, pleadingly. So Rufus stayed and he said since he had caught the ball the girl was out, and why not have punch now? Jane gave him a nudge. This was real baseball and he mustn't think about anything else. The girl said it didn't count that Rufus caught the ball, for he was the back-stop and not on the team. Even so, she graciously permitted Nancy's team a turn at the bat now, because the Busy Bees had had a long enough inning. They had run up such a big score she was sure the F. F. could never come up to it.

"That's the way with baseball," thought Jane. "Whoever is first at the bat usually wins."

Nancy was the first one up of the Fatal Four. The captain of the Busy Bee baseball team did not throw curves. Nancy struck at the first ball. It was a hit. She easily made first base. Now Jane was at the bat. Rufus, who decided to play back-stop for the foreign team as well as Jane's, was pounding his fist into his mitt to get some real atmosphere into this game.

While the pitcher was winding her arm around and around, Jane was busy too. She was swinging the bat, limbering up. At last, she thought. At last she was at the bat. That's all she liked to do in baseball. Bat! And so far she hadn't had a chance. And she swung herself completely around in her enthusiasm. Unfortunately the bat flew out of her hand and it hit Rufus on the forehead.

Rufus was staggered and saw stars. However, he tossed it off saying, "Aw, it didn't hurt," even though a lump began to show. Jane rubbed his forehead, and thereafter she swung with more restraint. Even so, the catcher and Rufus automatically stepped back a few paces whenever Jane was at the bat, taking no chances with another wallop.

But now the pitcher pitched. Jane, still subdued and repressed, merely held the bat before her. Bang! The ball just came up and hit it and rolled halfway toward the pitcher. Both the pitcher and the catcher thought the other was going to run for the ball. Therefore neither one ran, and Jane made first base easily, putting Nancy on second. Now the bases were full because that's all the bases they had. And it was Clara Pringle at the bat.

The situation was too grave for Clara. She did not want to bat. How could she ever face Nancy if she struck out? Nancy and Jane might never speak to her again if she struck out. Besides, she had hurt her wrist pulling up a stubborn pie-weed when she was in outfield. She looked at Jane, who was dancing toward second, and Nancy, who was dancing toward home, impatiently waiting for the hit that would send them in. Clara gulped at her position of unexpected responsibility. When she joined the Fatal Four she had never envisioned being in a spot like this. She raised her hand to make a request.

"Can Rufus pinch hit for me because I hurt my wrist?" she asked timidly.

Rufus did not wait for anybody to say yes or no. He threw his mitt at Clara and seized the bat, pounding the ground, the home plate, and an old bottle. That's the way he warmed up, and if Jane had been vociferous at the bat, Rufus was nothing short of a tornado.

"Stand still!" yelled the pitcher. "You make me dizzy."

Rufus swung at imaginary balls.

"Hey!" exclaimed the pitcher. "He's left-handed."

"Sure," said Jane. "Why not?"

"You call 'em southpaws," said Nancy. "I pitch good to him myself."

"Well, here goes," said the pitcher. "It just looks funny if you're not used to 'em." And she swung her arm around and around again.

While she was warming up and while Rufus was stomping around, swinging the bat, waiting for the ball, Spec Cullom, the ice-man, came along Elm Street. Evidently he saw in an instant that this was a real game and not just practice, for he stopped his team, threw down the iron weight to anchor his horse, Charlie, and strode into the lot and straddled the nearest log in the bleachers to watch. Rufus saw him and became even more animated with the bat.

At the same moment the twelve o'clock whistle blew. Now all the children were supposed to go home to lunch. The Busy Bees were in favor of stopping, but the Fatal Four protested. Here they were with all bases full and they should certainly play the inning out at least.

So the pitcher pitched and Rufus struck. Crack! He hit the

ball! Up and up it sailed, trailing the black tape it was wound with behind it like the tail of a kite!

As it disappeared from sight in the pine grove, Nancy ran to home plate and Jane ran to second base, and then home, and Rufus tore to first, and then to second and then home. And so it was a home run that had been hit.

"A home run!" everybody yelled in excitement. It was surprising that that hit had not broken a window, and the outfielder of the visiting team ran in search of the ball. But she couldn't find it and Clara joined her, for she was an experienced outfielder, but she couldn't find it either. Then the whole Busy Bee baseball team ran and looked for the ball, but they couldn't find it. So they all went home. The captain, impressed by the home run, yelled to Nancy that the score must have been a tie and they'd come back in a week or so to see who was the champ.

Jane and Nancy ran over to the pine grove to look for the ball. They hunted in the corner of the lot where skunk cabbage grew thick and melon vines covered a dump, covered even the sign that said DO NOT DUMP. They searched through the long field grass on this side of the library,

trying not to get the thick bubbly-looking dew on their bare legs. Was this really snake spit as Joey and Rufus claimed, Jane wondered. If it was, where were all the snakes? She'd never seen a single snake. But where was the ball? That was some home run!

"You don't suppose he batted it clear across Elm Street into that lot, do you?" asked Nancy incredulously.

"Might have," said Jane, not knowing whether to be proud or ashamed. And the two girls crossed the street to take a look, just in case Rufus had swung as mighty an arm as that.

Rufus did not join in the search. He ran around from base to base to home plate, again and again, in ever widening circles until his course led him to the iceman. The ice-man was one of his favorite people in Cranbury.

"Here," said Spec, "catch." And he threw the missing baseball to Rufus. "I yelled to the team that I caught the ball, but they couldn't hear me, I guess, what with whistles blowing and all the cheers. Some batter!" he said. "Keep it up, fella, and maybe next spring you can be bat boy for the South End baseball team."

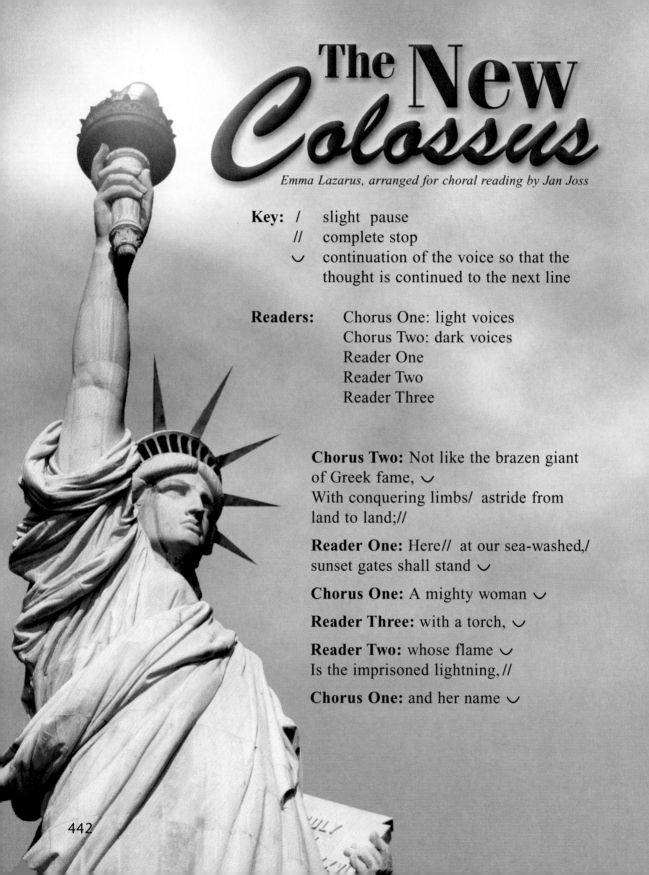

The New Colossus

Emma Lazarus, arranged for choral reading by Jan Joss

Key: / slight pause
// complete stop
⌣ continuation of the voice so that the thought is continued to the next line

Readers: Chorus One: light voices
Chorus Two: dark voices
Reader One
Reader Two
Reader Three

Chorus Two: Not like the brazen giant of Greek fame, ⌣
With conquering limbs/ astride from land to land;//

Reader One: Here// at our sea-washed,/ sunset gates shall stand ⌣

Chorus One: A mighty woman ⌣

Reader Three: with a torch, ⌣

Reader Two: whose flame ⌣
Is the imprisoned lightning,//

Chorus One: and her name ⌣

442

Chorus Two: Mother of Exiles.//
From her beacon-hand ⌣
Glows world-wide welcome;//

Chorus One: her mild eyes command ⌣
The air-bridged harbor that twin cities frame.//

Chorus Two: "Keep ancient lands,/ your storied pomp!"//

Reader One: cries she ⌣
With silent lips.//

Reader Two: "Give me your tired,/

Reader Three: your poor,/

Chorus One: Your huddled masses/ yearning to breathe free,/
The wretched refuse of your teeming shore."//

Reader One: cries she ⌣
With silent lips.//

Reader Two: "Give me your tired,/

Reader Three: your poor./

Chorus Two: Send these,/
the homeless,/
tempest-tost to me,"//

Reader One: cries she ⌣
With silent lips./

Reader Two: "Give me your tired,/

Reader Three: your poor . . . // to breathe free.//

Chorus Two: I lift my lamp// beside ⌣

All: the golden door!"//

Reader One: cries she ⌣
With silent lips./

All: "Give me your tired,/

Reader Three: your poor."//

May the Plum Tree Always Blossom

Milly Howard   *illustrated by Steve Mitchell*

The following story takes place when the Japanese were invading China just before the beginning of World War II. The setting is Hangchow, a city in occupied China. Refugees from other parts of China where the battles were still raging had to travel through city after city, searching for some place to settle and begin their lives again. As the Japanese army pushed farther into China, the stream of homeless people increased every day. When the city gates of Hangchow opened in the morning, the streets swelled with refugee families. Those who chose to remain in the city went about their business as usual. They tried to ignore the foreign soldiers who occupied their city and the flood of strangers that flowed from the east gate to the west gate.

Silent Vigil

High summer pressed down on the city of Hangchow with the heat of a thousand feather blankets. Only the slightest of all breezes made its way through the open gates of the orphanage. Just inside the gates, Seventh Plumblossom crouched behind an empty willow basket. Only her straight-cut bangs showed above the pale willow. Unwaveringly her eyes watched the steady stream of people that moved along the dusty street outside the open gates.

As Seventh Plumblossom watched, old women tottered by the orphanage on their way to market, balancing on tiny feet that had been bound in their childhood to prevent growth. Shop workers hurried about on errands, threading their way through the crowd. A peddler pushed his cart, calling for people to stop and eat. The blue smoke of his fire teased Seventh Plumblossom with memories of crisp shrimp and crystallized fruits. She rubbed her nose and swallowed. Blinking her eyes, she renewed her silent watch for her brother, Luang.

At the edge of the mass of people, a gray-bearded man walked along slowly, holding a brightly painted bamboo birdcage. A group of boys rushed by, shouting something. Brushing past the startled old man, they leaped over rubble left by the bombs of December and disappeared into the crowd. The old man lost his balance and fell, dropping the bamboo cage. It rolled under the peddler's cart and splintered. A flash of red and yellow blurred into the air as the freed bird swept upward into the sky. Muttering, the old man struggled to his feet. Without even brushing off his black silk robe, he thrust his way into the midst of the crowd.

Down the street in the direction from which the boys had come marched a squad of Japanese

May the Plum Tree Always Blossom 445

soldiers. The people glanced backwards over their shoulders and then hurried silently on.

Seventh Plumblossom's eyes widened as the soldiers' strong legs scissored a path through the stream of people and headed for the orphanage gate. She shouted a warning to the children playing behind her and shrank backward into the shadow between the basket and the wall. With sharp, frightened shrieks, the children fled into the buildings. Still, the gathering of the boys old enough to fight took little time. Seventh Plumblossom heard the pounding on the doors, the harsh orders, and the quick shouts. Then seven boys were marched from the orphanage that had been their home—Chang, Lin, Ling Yo, Tau, Dai, Fu, Chin Lo. All of the fifteen-year-old boys marched past the willow basket that hid the frightened Seventh Plumblossom. All of the fifteen-year-olds except her brother Luang.

Seventh Plumblossom trembled. Her movement drew a soldier's attention to the willow basket. Calling sharply in Japanese, he knocked the basket aside, yanking the frightened girl up and thrusting her against the wall. Eyes huge in her pale face, she crouched there, waiting.

"It's only a girl-child. Leave her alone."

The words were spoken quietly but firmly. The soldier who held Seventh Plumblossom released her with a grunt of disgust and turned away.

The one who had spoken knelt beside Seventh Plumblossom. He didn't touch her but looked at her kindly. Still trembling, she stared back into the face of the hated conqueror. Fear shook her as she remembered the men who had stormed into her home at Peking, leaving death and destruction behind them.

"It has passed; you will not be hurt," the man said gently. "What is your name?"

Surprised at his Chinese, she opened her mouth, but no sound came. She tried again. "Seventh Plumblossom," she whispered and swallowed to ease her dry throat.

He looked surprised. "Seventh? Why seventh?"

"Many girls named Plumblossom have come to the orphanage since the war began. We were numbered as we came," she answered falteringly. "I am the seventh."

"How many are here now?"

446

"Thirteen."

The soldier sat back on his heels, a strange look on his face. If she had not known the conquerors to be unfeeling monsters, she would have said it was a look of sorrow and pity. The years had taught her differently. She and Luang . . .

Her eyes flicked toward the gate. If Luang should return now— the thought filled her with terror. He would be forced to join the ragged line of boys. Like the others, he would be taken to fight in the Japanese army, to fight against his own people. Go! Go! Silently she turned her face away from the soldier and willed him to leave. Go!

"I have a daughter—" he began, but before he could finish, a harsh command from the gates brought him to his feet. A moment later the soldiers and boys were gone.

The other children gathered hesitantly in the yard. For a while they moved aimlessly from group to group and then slowly returned to their games. Seventh Plumblossom stayed at her post, watching the street.

Another hour passed before she saw Luang. Her fear turned to relief and pride as she watched her tall brother move up the street with an easy stride, stopping to help an overburdened mother with her child. The Japanese invasion of their country had thrust him into responsibility before his time. After the death of their parents, he had become mother and father to Seventh Plumblossom. He was her strength, her hope of life, her only thread to the peaceful existence before the war began.

"Luang! Luang!" she cried, running to meet him. "They came! They came!"

"The soldiers?" Luang understood her fear. For a moment he didn't ask the question that was in his mind. He knew the answer.

"What happened?"

"They took the boys—Chang, Lin, Ling Yo, Tau—"

Luang's face darkened. He struggled not to speak in front of his sister. When he had regained control, he said quietly, "It will pass. It will pass."

"No, they will come again," Seventh Plumblossom said urgently. "And again, and again. We must hide. We must go away from here!"

Luang frowned, thinking. "You are safer here in the orphanage than you would be on the streets. We must stay here, Plumblossom."

"No! We must go!"

Luang gave her a troubled look. "We will talk to Madame Kai. She will advise us."

Luang knew what Madame Kai's advice would be. It would be safer for Luang to go, for Seventh Plumblossom to stay. But Luang also knew that his sister would never stay in the orphanage without him. He was all she had left, and she clung to him fiercely. Luang felt strongly too. If they were separated, all of their careful planning to stay together would be lost. Each of them would be alone—perhaps never knowing if the other was still alive. He sighed. It was a decision that could not be made quickly.

Unexpected Ally

The weeks went by and the raids on the orphanages increased. No amount of prayers on the prayer wheels, no amount of burning incense could protect Luang forever. Finally even Madame Kai suggested that the two children leave together.

"If you stay, it is certain what will happen. If you go," she hesitated, then continued, "perhaps you will be safe."

Luang and Seventh Plumblossom packed their few belongings—a small ivory fan, a jade hair ornament that had belonged to their mother, a tiny carved figure that had been one of their father's treasures, two bowls, chopsticks, and bedrolls. Saying good-bye took longer. They had been at the orphanage over two years. Luang was a respected older one. Seventh Plumblossom was loved for both her tenderness and her fierceness in protecting the younger ones. The tiny Eleventh Plumblossom had been a special favorite of hers. She took the little orphan in her arms and wiped away the tears.

"I must go," she whispered. "I cannot lose Luang, not to the soldiers, not to time." Luang motioned for her to come. The sun was low in the sky. Soon the gates would close for the night. The two children left the orphanage and joined the stream of refugees that pushed toward the open gates of the city. Afraid to be seen alone, they walked close to another family. They were accepted quietly, without question. As they neared the big gates, the people in the crowd began to hurry, jostling against each other. Seventh Plumblossom was swept away from Luang. She struggled against the tide of people, crying out frantically. She was pushed aside, and she stumbled, falling against the curb. Dodging the hurrying feet, she scrambled across to one of the wooden stalls that edged the road. She huddled against the side of the stall and waited.

The crowd flowed out the gates, leaving only Seventh Plumblossom and the slow, aged stragglers behind. Then across the street, just inside the gate, she saw Luang. He was anxiously searching the street. She leaped to her feet, but before she could cry out, he saw her. At a quick motion from him to stay away, she moved back against the stall. She watched in disbelief as Luang disappeared down a side street, leaving her alone.

Then a commotion to her right told her why he had gone. A troop of soldiers hurried to the gate, shouting orders to the gatekeepers. Slowly the huge carved gates began to close. Seventh Plumblossom began to weep silently. Through her tears she saw the soldiers separate and begin to search the stalls and buildings along the street. They were looking for someone—who? Frightened shopkeepers were herded outside and lined up.

Seventh Plumblossom backed slowly along the side of the stall, trying to move without attracting attention. Once she thought a soldier looked her way, but he made no move toward her. She continued inching her way backwards. She reached the shadow of the buildings and turned to run. A darker shadow stirred, then slid silently behind her. Suddenly a hand covered her mouth, smothering her startled scream.

"Sh! It is I, Luang," the shadow whispered.

Seventh Plumblossom went limp with relief. Silently Luang guided her down the alley toward an old discarded peddler's cart.

"Under here," he said quietly. He scrambled underneath. Seventh Plumblossom followed. Underneath the cart there was only enough room for the two thin bodies to crouch close together. Shattered wood hung low over the cart, shielding them from sight. They peered through cracks, watching the half-shadowed entrance to the alley. Minutes passed and the street sounds faded. Seventh Plumblossom relaxed and looked up at Luang. Before she could speak, he caught her arm. Fearfully she looked back at the entrance. The shadowy bulk of a soldier, outlined in the red glow of the setting sun, blocked the entrance. Rifle in hand, the soldier entered the alley. Debris crunched under his boots as he walked slowly toward the cart. He stopped in front of the cart. Seventh Plumblossom felt Luang tense beside her and knew that he too was holding his breath.

The listening silence that descended on the alley seemed unbearable. Seventh Plumblossom was suddenly seized by the desire to stand and run. Then one of the broken planks was ripped away, and she shrank back against Luang. He let his breath out in an agonized hiss of defeat as a shadowed face looked down at them.

"Ah, so it is the Seventh Plumblossom from the orphanage," the man said softly. "I thought I recognized you."

Seventh Plumblossom stared blankly. Then the man knelt, and she recognized the soldier who had come to her aid weeks ago. Her heart began to beat again, but her voice was still frozen within her throat.

He looked past her at Luang, who was trapped behind Seventh Plumblossom and could do nothing. Luang said in a thin voice, "I am the one you want. Let Plumblossom go. My sister will return to the orphanage. I will go with you."

The soldier shook his head. "You are not the one we seek," he answered, "We are searching for a spy, not children. But it is not safe for you to move about now. It is past curfew and the streets are empty, except for soldiers. You have chosen a good hiding place. Stay here for now. I will return later and take you to safety."

The board scraped as he lowered it back into place. Stepping back, he paused. Then with a soft sound of satisfaction, he turned and strode away.

"Who was that?" Luang whispered. "Why did a soldier help us?"

"He is one of the soldiers who came to take the boys away," Seventh Plumblossom whispered back. "He helped me then. I don't know why."

"I don't like it. He has gone to get the others."

"No." Seventh Plumblossom shook her head. "He is different. He is kind." She hesitated, then spoke again. "I do not fear him."

Surprised, Luang stayed where he was. For Plumblossom not to fear—this man must be different indeed. They would wait.

Darkness crept into the alley and settled around the cart like an old familiar blanket. Hot and tired, brother and sister slept fitfully. When the light came, they were caught unaware. It blinded their eyes, causing them to blink and stare blankly at the dark forms behind it.

"Come."

It was the Japanese soldier. Someone else was with him. Hope died as they climbed stiffly out and stood up. Luang stepped in front of Seventh Plumblossom.

They could not see the smile on the soldier's face, but they heard it in his voice. "Do not worry. This is Ping, a brother in Christ from your own land. I cannot leave my post to take you to safety. Ping will guide you in my place."

"Where will we go?" Luang asked, distrust still clouding his mind.

"You can trust me," the soldier said earnestly. "I am a Christian. Several months ago our troop was fighting in the mountains to the west. While there, I attended

services in which a foreign missionary woman talked. Some of the villagers told me she also runs an orphanage. Ping will take you to her. You will be safe, and she will teach you about Christ. She will take good care of you."

"But why do you want to help us?"

"You would not understand now, but I hope you will in time." The soldier knelt beside Seventh Plumblossom. "I have a daughter about your age," he said gently. "She is safe in Japan. She was born in the spring when the plum tree bears its blossoms. She, too, is called Plumblossom. I would not like to see fear in her eyes as it is in yours, little sister."

He stood up and placed a hand on Luang's shoulder. "There is much I cannot do, for I am loyal to my country, as you are to yours. But for the sake of my Lord, I can help two children survive the pains of war. You must hurry. Ping will take you to his friends. Tomorrow you will go through the outer gates to the mountains. Now go."

Bewildered, Seventh Plumblossom and Luang followed Ping. The soldier stood still, watching them for a moment. Then he called softly, "Seventh Plumblossom!"

Startled, she turned.

"You no longer need answer to that name," the soldier said quietly. "From now on you are not numbered. Go with God, Plumblossom."

A smile lifted the corners of Plumblossom's lips. "Thank you," she said and turned back to the others.

As the soldier watched, three shadows crossed the entrance to the alley and disappeared around the corner to the street. For a moment the soldier remained in the dark, silently watching. Then his hand went to the pocket that held pictures of his wife and daughter, and he said softly, "May the plum tree always blossom, little one, in your land and in mine."

Making Judgments in Reading

Can you think of a story you've read that made you laugh? Well-written stories always affect our emotions—making us laugh or feel pity or gasp with surprise. Even when we know that the story is entirely made up, we can react as though the characters were real people and as though the events were happening right then.

Reading a story that way stretches our understanding. It helps us experience what others experience. Reading is one way that we can become "wise as serpents" while remaining "harmless as doves." We don't have to make the mistakes that the characters in a story make to be able to learn from them.

God wants us to be sensitive to the joys and sufferings of others, and sometimes fiction can help a reader understand other people—and truth—better than nonfiction can. Christ the Lord taught His listeners about themselves, their neighbors, and Himself with parables, some of which are recorded in the Bible for all time.

Reading with Wisdom

When a story is written well, it can easily carry us along with the gripping adventure or the funny dialogue or the outrageous characters. And in being carried along, we may not notice other things the author is trying to give us as well. For example, if a character is clever and likeable and always making jokes, we might enjoy his company so much that we find ourselves laughing when he makes fun of going to church.

Most authors who do not believe in God do not write stories in which the characters come right out and say, for instance, "God does not hear our prayers." Rather, they usually write stories with characters that heartily believe in God and prayer. The stories then show the characters praying diligently and those prayers never being answered. At the end of the story, the characters might even still believe in prayer, but the reader will begin to have some doubts.

Sometimes authors want us to accept their view of things as *the only* view of things. If an author is bitter and unhappy, he may write stories that say life is hopeless and unfair. And if he writes with great power and beauty, many readers will accept his view as truth. But he is giving a false picture of life and of God, who allows all things to happen for His ultimate glory and who knows the end from the beginning.

But, you ask, don't sad things happen, and can't authors write about them? Of course! The difference is in the meaning that the story represents. "May the Plum

Tree Always Blossom," for example, shows the pain of war. But the characters, and the readers, realize in the end that a holy and loving God is in command of everything that happens. Rather than pretending that war never happens or that good people never suffer, the author uses grim events to encourage faith in God.

Looking for Help

Sometimes when you are reading a story, you may come upon ideas that seem wrong, or actions that are too violent or ugly, or a character that is hopeless. What can you do? You can just stop reading. But it's a better idea to take the book to someone you trust and talk about it.

Your parents, your teacher, your Sunday school teacher, or some other Christian adult can look at the story with you and help you understand how the author is making something look. Does the "bad guy" seem likeable and trustworthy? Do characters "get away with" doing wrong? Then the story is not good. Or do wrong actions look bad? Are good characters respected in the story? Would God approve of the style and meaning? Then the story, even if about hard times or unhappy events, is probably good.

Getting some help on thinking such ideas through will help make you a stronger reader. You will be growing into an adult who can judge what he reads. You will be someone who can't be tricked into accepting wrong information. You will be someone who can decide for himself that a story is good or bad, based on how it makes good and evil look. And then you can laugh and feel pity and gasp with surprise for all the right reasons.

ROUNDING UP THE SHEEP

Elizabeth Yates
illustrated by Kathy Pflug

Iceland, an island in the North Atlantic Ocean about the size of the state of New York, lies midway between Europe and America. Its northern coast fringes the Arctic Circle, but the Gulf Stream, flowing near, moderates the climate. During good weather, Iceland possesses crisp, clear days with an average temperature of fifty degrees. Iceland's far north location gives it twenty-four hours of light during summer days but only a few hours of light during winter days.

A dramatic beauty offsets Iceland's stony land. Volcanic rock reflects fantastic colors in the brilliant sunlight. The distant silver glaciers set off the bright green of meadows and the blue of mountain ranges.

Gudrun set off with her cousin Finnur, Uncle Tomas, and their friend Hans to help Cousin Olaf gather the sheep from the high mountains of Iceland at the end of summer.

460

TO THE HIGH MOUNTAINS

"Stoppa!" Uncle Tomas called, after they had been riding an hour on the trail that led up to the mountains. He tucked into his belt the silver-handled whip, which he never used except to snap it in the air. Tossing the reins over his pony's neck, he slid off the saddle.

Finnur, Gudrun, and Hans slipped from their saddles and stood quietly while the ponies moved away to feed where the grass was green.

"How big the world is!" Gudrun exclaimed.

"It's not the world," Finnur reminded her. "It's just a part of Iceland."

Soon it was time to journey on again, and after tightening the strap of a saddlebag here and a blanket roll there, they mounted. Leaning low over the heavy manes, they patted their ponies and whispered in their ears, for everyone knew that ponies went better if you loved them. The ponies pressed their noses forward and pricked their ears as if answering the call of the mountains. Then they were off, single file, over the stony trail.

The time for the in-gathering of the sheep had come, and Uncle Tomas was taking the three children to Cousin Olaf's farm to help

with the work. Next to fish, sheep are the most important product in Iceland. They furnish food, wool for warm clothes, hides for shoes, horns for implements, and bones for toys.

When Uncle Tomas called "Stoppa!" again, they halted by a tumbling brook where the ponies could drink, pushing their soft noses around in the cool water.

"The sandwiches are in your saddlebag," Finnur said to Gudrun, "and here's the milk." He took from his bag a bottle wrapped in layers of wet newspaper to keep it cool.

"I'm as hungry as a pony," Hans exclaimed.

"Then eat as well as one," Uncle Tomas said with a smile, "for there is a long way yet to go."

It was late afternoon when they reached the great rift that led down to the Plains of Thingvellir. They reined up their ponies and surveyed the historic scene while Uncle Tomas told them that it was in this very spot, over a thousand years ago, that the first parliament in the world had met.

"If I had a hat on, I'd take it off," Hans commented, for there was something noble in the scene. The great open plain was bounded

by snow-streaked mountains, with a lake at one end and a river filling the silence with sound.

Even the ponies stepped softly as they reached the shore of the lake where they were to camp for the night. Two little tents were quickly erected, and Gudrun was instructed to build a small fire. She gathered sticks and dried moss to keep the fire going and the others

went to the lake to see what they could catch for their supper.

"The fish are certainly in a hurry to be eaten," Finnur shouted to Gudrun. They came back to the camp with four salmon trout between them.

When there were only piles of clean bones remaining on their plates, Gudrun said, "This is the best kind of supper ever." Then she yawned, and Uncle Tomas said it was time for everyone to go to bed.

The ponies were hobbled so they could not stray. The fire was put out. Blankets were unrolled, and one tired traveler after another rolled up in them. The ground might be hard and the night far from dark, but sleep came quickly to them all.

The next day, the country grew wilder and rockier. The rivers were deeper, and some of the ponies could not wade. They had to swim, their riders clinging to them. Of course the riders got wet, but people could shake themselves as well as ponies; and the wind, keenly blowing, soon dried them off.

"We're getting into the high mountains now," said Uncle Tomas, looking around. "See how much greener the grazing is than farther south!"

"Don't the sheep get lonely way up here?" Hans wondered.

"They keep each other quite good company from early spring till summer's end," Uncle Tomas said. "They get fatter and fatter, and their long coats grow heavier."

They reached Cousin Olaf's farm by noon, and Cousin Sigrid had a hot luncheon ready for them—mutton stew and boiled potatoes—and for dessert, rhubarb jam with bread. Then, with Olaf leading and the two sheepdogs winding in and out among the ponies, they started up to where the pasture land stretched high and far and the sheep were grazing.

"We part here," Cousin Olaf cried out when they reached a certain point, and taking Finnur and Hans with him, he went up one trail while Uncle Tomas and Gudrun took the other.

"Bless!" they called to each other in parting.

Up in these high meadows there were more than three hundred sheep with their lambs. Cousin Olaf thought that he and the two boys would round up the larger portion of the flock. He figured that only a hundred sheep, or even fewer, would be found where Uncle Tomas and Gudrun were going. Then, if all went well and they located the sheep, they would meet again the next afternoon in the valley.

GUDRUN'S RAM

"We've got ninety-nine," Uncle Tomas said near evening when he made his count, "and I don't believe there are any more to be found."

"It's been very easy," Gudrun said almost regretfully. "The sheep have all come together so well."

They herded them into a small enclosure between the rocks, with Bruni, the sharp-eyed dog, standing guard at the opening. Then they built their tiny campfire and heated some soup and sipped it slowly before rolling up in their blankets for the night.

"Good night, Uncle Tomas," Gudrun said softly.

"Good night, my child, and don't count sheep in your dreams."

Gudrun had heard bleating so much of the day that she was not surprised to hear it at night. She was not surprised until she woke up and found that the short night was over. On the far peaks, the sun was glinting. At hand, the sheep in their enclosure were lying so close that they looked like a rough woolen rug that had been left out all night and was sparkling with dew. Bruni lay stretched across the opening, his nose between his paws, but Gudrun knew he was alert.

There was such stillness everywhere that Gudrun began to think she had been very silly to let a dream awaken her. Then she heard the bleating again, far away. One

sheep in the flock gave answer, hoarsely, sadly.

Bruni, sensing that Gudrun was awake, looked around at her. He was troubled. He knew there was a lamb left on the mountain; but he had been told to guard the flock, so he could not go in search of it.

"Never mind, Bruni, we'll find the lamb," Gudrun said, and Bruni's tail wagged feebly.

She scanned the mountainside. Trained to see the minute speck of a cormorant's egg on a cliff-face or to spot the tiny sail of a boat on the shimmering horizon, she used her sharp eyes. There, high, high up, in a place that seemed part of the world of clouds and sunshine, was the lamb.

Once Gudrun had seen the lamb, there was only one thing to do—go after it. She never thought about how it could be done. She knew only that it must be done.

"Uncle Tomas." She nudged him as she spoke. He turned and opened his eyes slowly.

"Will you take Bruni's place watching the sheep so that I may have him to go up the mountain? There's a lost lamb."

Her uncle nodded slowly, sleepily, hardly realizing what she had said. He saw Gudrun unroll herself from her blanket and give a shake

to her body and a toss to her head, like a pony coming out of its stable. She started off, Bruni bounding to her heels at a word.

"Gudrun, where are you going?"

"Up there," she pointed.

"But the rocks are slippery, it's too early—" her uncle shook himself from his blanket.

Gudrun's swift feet had already carried her beyond the reach of his words. The sheep, knowing Bruni had left them, began to move around in their enclosure and would have been all over the mountain again if Uncle Tomas had not turned to them.

The wall of the mountain rose above rocks and crumbling stone that slipped and slid as Gudrun's feet tried to trace a way on them. She knew that her hope of ascent was to find the way the lamb had gone. Bruni was doing everything to help her, sniffing back and forth, trying to pick up one trail from a dozen intercrossing ones. Suddenly Bruni looked back at Gudrun, then he started up the mountain.

She followed quickly, up, almost straight up. Bruni was soon a long way ahead, but his excited yelps were a good guide up the steep slope. Now the tone of his barking changed. He was cross. The sharp tone dropped again to a wail. Something had happened to make Bruni very angry, then very sad.

Higher and higher up the steep face of the mountain, Gudrun climbed until she reached Bruni and saw what the trouble was. Crouching on a ledge, ears laid back and tail pressed between his legs, Bruni had reached the point where he must stop. There was no way up, no way sideways. But the lamb had come that way, for there was the imprint of its hoof on a patch of earth.

"Good, Bruni, it was clever of you to find the way," Gudrun said consolingly, her arms around the dog.

There was another ledge near them, only a little more than out of reach, and on it was the lamb, looking at them with curious eyes, so interested that it had forgotten to bleat.

A strange stillness hung in the air. Then from far below in the valley came Uncle Tomas's voice, "Please be careful, Gudrun."

At that moment, the sun came over the mountains and lit up the whole valley. It shone brightly on the rock walls, and in that new light, the distance from ledge to ledge looked greater. Gudrun's heart felt heavy. Then a shadow moved across the mountain and Gudrun looked up. It was an eagle hovering in the sky. It was waiting for the moment when it might descend on the lamb.

466

"I'll be careful, Uncle Tomas," she shouted down to the valley.

Putting her face to the mountain, she counted the cracks between the ledges where her fingers might go, the places where her feet might lodge. Not for nothing had she scaled the cliffs of her island ever since she could walk.

Slowly she eased herself along the rock. There was no sound anywhere, not from her uncle or the sheep below, not from Bruni or the lamb she was approaching—no sound save the dull thumping of stones as they became loosened. But there was always the black shadow of the eagle drawing nearer and nearer.

Gudrun reached the lamb and comforted it, then she waved her arms to free the air of the swooping bird. Picking up a stone from the ledge, she hurled it toward the eagle, which flapped its wings and soared skyward.

"How will I ever get you back, you poor little thing?" Gudrun murmured softly to the lamb.

Then she remembered a picture in a book at home, a picture of a man who went out to find a lost sheep and returned with it over his shoulders. She hunched her back and pushed the lamb up over her shoulders, gripping its legs. Quickly she tied them together around her neck with her scarf.

The lamb was safe now, and her arms were free.

She faced the mountain again, seeking the familiar crevices for her hands and, because of the added weight she was carrying, making her feet doubly secure in each niche they fumbled after. The eagle still flew above them, but its circular flight was winging higher and higher. Back on the ledge with Bruni, Gudrun looked across at the spot where the lamb had been. How easy everything seemed, now that it had all been done.

Bruni led the way down the mountain, the lamb following and Gudrun behind them both. As they approached the enclosure, the sheep began to bleat joyously; the ponies were neighing; Uncle Tomas was cheering.

"It's just like the story!" Gudrun smiled to herself, for it was fun when stories came to life, and this was so much like the one in the Bible. Because one lost lamb was being returned, there was great rejoicing, as if only the lost one mattered.

The afternoon sun was lengthening over the valley when they joined the others at the farm, driving the sheep before them. Uncle Tomas told proudly of how the lamb had been brought down the cliff, and Cousin Olaf thanked Gudrun warmly.

"Such a fine little ram he is, too," he said, running his fingers around the curve of one small horn. "He shall be the head ram of our flock, and all the rest of his days he shall walk the mountain land like one who has done great things."

"And he shall always be called 'Gudrun's ram,'" Cousin Sigrid said, smiling.

Finnur and Hans had been busy rounding up the two hundred sheep that were their charge, but they had had no great adventures. They were proud of Gudrun and shook hands with her as the best way of showing how they felt.

Cousin Sigrid called them in from the sheepfold to their meal. Spread around the table were bowls of *skyr,* a bowl for each one.

In the center of the table were plenty of sugar and rich yellow cream to pour over the *skyr.* It was good, this dish that had been a favorite in their land for so many centuries. It was made from curdled milk that was beaten and then eaten like a pudding, and nothing could have pleased them more.

"It's the Icelandic *skyr* that makes us strong," Cousin Olaf said, and he winked at Gudrun as they took up their spoons.

MAP PROJECTIONS

Locate Iceland on a globe. Which direction would you travel if you were to visit Iceland? Globes and maps are important tools for planning a voyage. Globes are accurate because they match the spherical shape of the earth. Flat maps can give more detail and are easy to carry.

Maps are not as accurate as globes because it is impossible for a flat piece of paper to be a correct copy of the surface of a sphere. Compare the earth to an orange with its skin on. The oceans and continents could be drawn on this skin to make the orange a small globe.

But it would be difficult to convert the orange globe to a flat map. Even if it were possible to open the orange skin with only one cut all the way around, you couldn't lay it out flat like a map. You would have two half spheres, forming two "mounds" or "bowls." If you flattened them, the edge of each half sphere would split in several places. You could make the half spheres into square maps only if you stretched them.

Mapmakers draw torn or stretched figures to depict parts of the earth. The many methods they use to cut, stretch, or reduce the areas of land on their maps are called *map projections.*

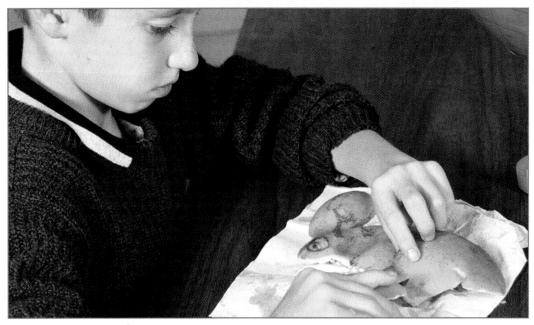

Interrupted projection

When a mapmaker uses an *interrupted projection,* he draws the map with several cuts through the oceans. These cuts break the map into a strange shape, but they leave the size and shape of the continents fairly accurate. Look at the map to see how you would travel to Iceland. This type of map would not be a good travel guide to Iceland because your route might be through one of the map's cuts.

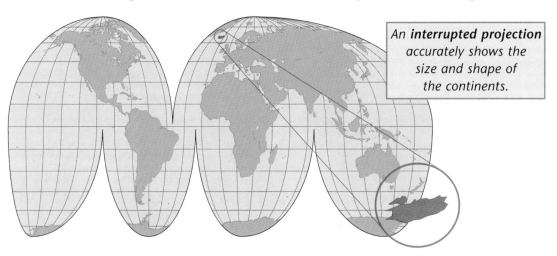

An **interrupted projection** accurately shows the size and shape of the continents.

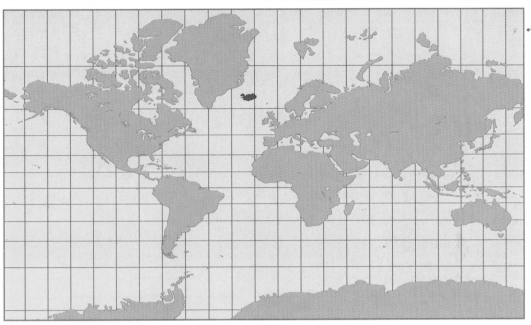

*Navigators use a **Mercator projection** and a compass to accurately plan a course.*

Mercator projection

Another projection is called the *Mercator projection.* This depiction stretches the earth's surface instead of cutting it. On a Mercator map, the land along the equator is accurate in size and shape. The lands at the top and bottom of the map, however, have been stretched to enormous sizes in comparison.

A Mercator projection is better than an interrupted projection for tracing ocean voyages. Lines of latitude and longitude are parallel on a Mercator projection. This means you can navigate between two points in a straight line without changing the compass setting. You would want to use this type of map when traveling to Iceland.

If you were comparing the size of two countries, however, a Mercator projection would not be as helpful as an interrupted projection. Land areas on an interrupted projection map are more accurate than on a Mercator projection.

Remember that map projections are another way to show the spherical shape of the earth. You need to choose the type of map that best fits your purpose, whether for travel or comparison.

The Store-Bought Dress

Milly Howard   *illustrated by Preston Gravely*

In the 1950s the Palmers were sharecroppers on Evan Grant's farm. By late fall of every year, the ripe cotton stretched in long rows of white across the Alabama hills. Gathering the fluffy cotton became important to the Palmers and to most of the county; even schools let out so the children could help in the final weeks of picking. In this way the children could earn money for the luxuries their families might not be able to afford otherwise.

Fluffy White Cotton

Merrilee Palmer put her hand on her back as she straightened wearily. She tugged at the strap of her half-filled cotton sack and groaned.

"Only ten o'clock and I'm already tired," she said aloud.

Her older sister looked across the two rows of cotton plants that separated them. "You only have three weeks to earn enough money to buy that bike you want," she warned. "It takes a lot of cotton to make that much money."

Merrilee sighed. Josie was right, of course. Not having a bike meant that she had to walk everywhere. And Alice, her best friend in the whole fifth grade, had a shiny new bike.

Josie was pulling ahead of her, moving slowly but steadily. Merrilee watched her slender fingers pull the fluffy white cotton balls from the dry plants and stuff them into the sack trailing behind her.

"What are you going to buy with your money, Josie?"

Josie looked back at Merrilee. "More than you are, if you don't come on," she answered, smiling.

"Here, I'll help you catch up, and then we'll go empty these sacks into the ones by the cotton wagon."

472

She let her sack fall to the ground and stepped over the low rows. The two sisters worked up the row, stuffing the cotton into Merrilee's sack.

"Thanks, Josie," Merrilee said as they reached Josie's sack.

"It will be strange, not riding together on the same bus this year," Merrilee said as she walked to the wagon with her sister. Josie was four years older than Merrilee, and this was her first year in high school.

"I know," Josie said. "I'm half of one mind, half of another about moving up. At least I know most of the kids in the ninth grade."

"You wouldn't have any trouble even if you didn't know any of them," Merrilee said affectionately. "You don't have trouble talking to people."

Daddy said that Josie was a word spinner, weaving words like Mama wove cloth. He was right, too. That was Josie's gift. No one had been surprised when she was chosen to give a speech at the Thanksgiving fair this year.

After returning, Merrilee pushed her straggling hair out of her eyes. Right now she wished she could grow a little and move as fast as the older pickers. Behind her the younger children were strung out across the field. Ahead of her the boys worked, shouting back and forth across the rows. The men had already pulled out of sight over the hill, and a group of slower-moving women were reaching the top now. Merrilee shaded her eyes, looking for her mother's pink-flowered sunbonnet. Yes, it was there, the one closest to them.

"Reckon Mama's going to be okay?" she asked Josie.

"It appears so," Josie replied, casting an anxious look in her mother's direction. "She's keeping up, but just barely."

"Doc said she was well," Merrilee said.

"Doc didn't say anything about picking cotton," Josie said. "Daddy wanted her to stay at home, but she convinced him she was all right. I think Mama's worried about all the doctor bills that piled up when she was sick. Mr. Grant says cotton's not selling too high this year."

"Aw, Mr. Grant always says that," Merrilee scoffed. Josie smiled. That was true. If prices were higher, Mr. Grant was well pleased. If they were low, he said, "I told you."

"He's a fair man, though," Josie said. "He always gives Daddy his rightful share."

"Mm-hmm," Merrilee mumbled, keeping a wary eye on the boys picking a couple of yards ahead of her. They were slowing down now that the adults were out of sight. Slowly Merrilee and Josie drew closer to the boys. A boy from Merrilee's class was on her right. He had quit picking and was lying on his sack, watching a hawk circle in the blue sky.

"Travis Benton," Merrilee warned as she passed him, "you'd better not!"

"Not what?" he said innocently.

"Throw that hairy caterpillar on me!" Merrilee snapped.

"Me?" Travis exclaimed indignantly.

Merrilee frowned and reached behind to yank her sack closer. The boy behind Travis flipped something across the rows. Her fingers touched the fat worm that landed on the shoulder strap. "Yuck!" she muttered under her breath. She knew that one satisfactory scream could bring on a flock of practical jokes. Steeling herself, Merrilee flicked the caterpillar away and continued to pick.

"Aw, you're no fun," Travis grumbled.

"Too bad," Merrilee sniffed. She grinned as the boys lagged behind them, waiting for the next group of girls to come closer.

Only Randall Farley and Josie kept working. He was picking the rows next to Josie. Picking at the same pace, they began to pull ahead of Merrilee. She heard the quiet murmur of Randall's voice and Josie's silvery laughter. After seeing them together, Merrilee first thought about teasing her older sister. Then she saw how happy Josie was as she talked with Randall. She forgot her mischievous thoughts and suddenly feared that Josie would grow up and leave her behind. The four years between them had widened suddenly into a gulf.

Then she shook her head. "She's only thirteen," Merrilee told herself. "She's not going anywhere yet."

The noontime sun drove the pickers into the shade of the cotton wagon. A dipper from the barrel of cool water was passed around. Merrilee drank deeply and sat down beside her mother.

"You okay?" she said, looking at her mother's pale face.

"Just a little hot," Mrs. Palmer answered. "You wouldn't think it would be this hot in October." She fanned herself with the pink sunbonnet and smiled at Merrilee. "They're weighing now."

Merrilee looked at the group clustered around the scale. Sack after sack was weighed and recorded in Mr. Grant's little book. She watched eagerly as her sack was lifted to the scale. "Merrilee Palmer," Mr. Grant called out. "Eighty pounds."

Merrilee flushed with pleasure. That was fifteen pounds more than she had been able to pick in one morning last year. Mrs. Palmer patted her hand.

"You're doing great, honey," she said. "Keep it up, and you'll have that bike."

Mr. Palmer grinned at Merrilee as he stopped beside them. "A hundred pounds next year, maybe?"

Merrilee grinned back. Suddenly the morning's work didn't seem so hard.

Mr. Palmer looked at his wife's face. "You're going back to the house this minute," he said sternly. "Merrilee, Josie, I'm going to take your mother home. Go back to the field after you eat lunch. I'll be back in a little while."

The girls nodded and settled down with their paper bags. Josie unfolded her napkin as Merrilee hungrily bit into a chicken leg.

"Slow down, Merrilee," Josie said, "you're going to get sick."

Merrilee swallowed carefully. "I hope Mama isn't going to get sick again."

"I think she's still tired. We can help her do the housework when we get home," Josie said.

"Mm-hmm," Merrilee nodded, mouth full again. It didn't seem long before one of the pickers called, "Let's go!"

Groaning, Merrilee crawled to her feet. The afternoon stretched on, hot and dry. The children often sought the shade of nearby trees, trying to keep cool. Every trip back to the wagon to empty the full sacks was a relief. In the late afternoon a cool breeze sprang up, making work easier. Everyone began to pick a little faster. By the time the setting sun had turned the sky pink, the wagon was full.

"The first day is always hard," Daddy said, looking at the tired girls. "How about a ride home?"

"On the wagon?"

"On the wagon."

"Whoopee," Merrilee yelled, swinging herself over the sideboard.

Josie landed beside her on the soft cotton, bouncing slightly, then rolling over to look at the reddening sky.

"This is the best part of the day," Josie said dreamily. "Look, Merrilee, there's the evening star."

"Where?" Merrilee popped out from under the cotton she had piled over herself. "Where?"

Josie took one look at the cotton stuck to Merrilee's flushed face and laughed. Evening star forgotten, the girls began to sing.

Crisp, Green Bills

When Mr. Palmer stopped the wagon outside the barn, the girls slid off and raced into the house.

Mrs. Palmer was sitting up, leaning against the pillows and reading.

"Are you feeling better, Mama?" Merrilee asked.

Her mother put down the book and held out her arms. "I'm much better," she said hugging her and starting to get up. "I was just a little tired."

"Don't get up, Mama," Josie said. "We're going to fix supper."

"That's right," Daddy said from the doorway. "And I'm going to help."

Mama threw up her hands and began to laugh. "All right, you three, I know when I'm beaten."

Sounds of running water and clattering pots soon came from the kitchen, along with giggling as Daddy sang his favorite songs loudly and more than slightly off-key.

After supper the girls did the dishes and went off to take their baths. "I feel better," Merrilee said, bouncing on the bed and shaking her wet hair.

"Don't get water on the bed," Josie said absently. She was standing in front of the window, brush-ing her hair and looking out at the brilliant stars. The breeze lifted her hair and spread it across her shoulders.

Merrilee lay watching for a moment. "I bet I know what you are going to buy," she said suddenly.

Josie smiled.

"That dress in Carlson's win-dow," Merrilee said triumphantly.

Josie's smiled faded, and she swung around to look at Merrilee. "How did you know? I didn't tell anyone."

"You stand outside that window every Saturday when we go to town," Merrilee replied. "It had to be something in the window, and I knew it wasn't the furniture."

"Well, what do you think?" Josie asked. "Isn't it beautiful?"

"Yes," Merrilee answered, re-membering the swirls of white eye-let embroidered in a green the exact color of Josie's eyes. "But a store-bought dress? All that money for just a dress?"

Josie flinched. "Well, I need shoes, too." She hesitated for just a moment. "I know Mama could make me one, but she's not feeling well—and when I saw this one . . . ."

Merrilee nodded, thinking of the speech Josie was going to make at the fair. Half the county would be there, and that dress would look beautiful on Josie.

"Uh-huh. It's a pretty dress, Josie. You'll look nice in it."

Josie brightened. "You don't think I'm wasting my money?"

"Well," Merrilee teased, "you'd be better off with a basketball, or a rope."

She broke off as Josie jumped for the bed. Giggling, Merrilee slid off the other side, hitting the floor with a bump.

"Get to sleep in there, girls. Tomorrow's another day of hard work," their father called.

"Yes sir," the girls called back, straightening the bed. Then the only sound was night noises stealing in the open windows.

The next day was easier. Merrilee began to catch the rhythm of the other workers. Dragging behind her, the sack became less of a burden. Then too, whenever she began to drop behind, Josie stopped and helped her catch up.

"You're losing money," Merrilee said. "You could have emptied your sack twice more today if you hadn't helped me."

"A bike costs a lot of money," Josie smiled. "We'll do all right together."

And so the days passed by, clear and beautiful. None seemed as hot as that first day had, and the chatter back and forth among the workers made the picking seem easier. Mr. Palmer didn't let his wife pick again, but she was soon up working around the house. The days melted into weeks. November arrived, and Merrilee was half surprised when the last field was picked.

Josie and Merrilee stood in line with the others to get their brown pay envelopes. Merrilee ripped hers open to count the crisp green bills. Hugging herself in delight, she looked over at Josie. Josie had already resealed her envelope, but the brightness of her eyes told Merrilee that the dress and shoes were as good as bought.

After the picking was finished, Mr. Grant always gave a wiener roast for the workers. That night they roasted hot dogs and marshmallows over a bonfire. Afterward the children played hide-and-seek in the dark, and Mr. Grant settled the accounts with Mr. Palmer.

Merrilee was racing wildly around a bush when Josie suddenly reached out and grabbed her arm. "You scared me!" Merrilee yelled.

"Hush," Josie said sharply. "I just heard Mr. Grant talking. The cotton did sell for less this year. I don't think Daddy made enough money."

"What are we going to do?" Merrilee said, startled.

"We can give him ours," Josie said. "You know he'd never ask for it."

Merrilee gave a fleeting thought to her disappearing bike before nodding. "Okay."

The next morning the girls put their pay envelopes on the breakfast table. "We want you to have these, Daddy," Josie said.

Mr. Palmer's eyes misted as he looked at his daughters. "Thanks, girls. Every bit helps. I'll give as much as I can back to you."

The next day was Saturday. Josie and Merrilee finished their chores early and were waiting beside the old Ford when their mother and father came out. Money or no money, they weren't going to miss a trip to town.

"Ready, girls?" Mr. Palmer asked as Josie reached up to straighten his tie.

When they reached town, Mr. Palmer parked in front of the doctor's office. "We'll meet you girls at Watkins's Drugstore in about an

480

hour. Everything should be settled by then, and we can get some hamburgers."

The girls walked down the street to the dime store. Merrilee noticed that Josie didn't look across the street to Carlson's Department Store. They looked at just about everything in the dime store before Josie said, "It's time."

When they reached the drugstore, Mr. and Mrs. Palmer were just driving up. "Let's eat, girls," he said.

Merrilee had finished her hamburger and was gently blowing bubbles through her straw when Mr. Palmer put two envelopes on the table. "We had some left. I thought you two would like to go shopping."

"Oh, boy!" Merrilee said, reaching for her envelope. "Can we go now?"

He grinned and said, "Take off!"

Merrilee was the first one out the door. She waved at her mother and father and turned toward the department store. Josie followed more slowly. Inside the store Merrilee headed for the sporting goods department, counting her money as she went. "Enough for a volleyball," she thought, "and a net and maybe something else."

Merrilee found the ball and balanced it in her hands. "I wonder if Josie likes volleyball," she thought. Putting the ball down, she walked back to the door. Josie stood outside on the sidewalk, looking at the dress in the window.

Merrilee stood for a moment watching her. She twisted the envelope in her hands, thinking of how Josie had helped her. Josie couldn't have more than Merrilee had. If Josie had worked on her own, she might have had enough money left over for the dress. Merrilee took one last look at the sporting goods section and walked outside.

"Well, come on in! Someone may buy that dress while you're looking," she said.

Josie just shook her head. "I don't have enough money. I can't get the dress."

"Sure you can," Merrilee said, handing Josie her pay envelope. "It'll be our dress. After all, I get it next, don't I?"

And she did. Josie wore the white dress with the pretty shoes to the Thanksgiving fair. Merrilee sat on the grass below the platform, listening to her sister with pride. Three years later, an older, taller Merrilee stood on another platform wearing the same dress. She looked across at Josie, seated with the others who had come to the eighth-grade graduation, and knew that she was remembering too.

The Store-Bought Dress   481

Eli Whitney's Big Idea

Beki Gorham

Cotton, cotton! Even at the Greenes' dinner party, cotton was the main topic of conversation. The women stopped to listen as the men discussed the problems of getting their valuable crops to market.

"Just about every family in the South grows cotton in their back yard. After all, cotton fiber can be made into strong cloth for clothing. But planting whole plantations in cotton! Foolish, gentlemen, foolish!" Dr. Ashley tapped his glass with his fork to emphasize his remark.

Two chairs down from him, Evangeline Charles murmured in agreement. "Just think about picking all that cotton in the hot sun. Then it has to be stored until the seeds can be picked out. Why, it takes a small family all winter to clean enough cotton to weave their own clothes and stockings!"

Mr. Tremayne coughed. "Some large plantations *do* invest chiefly in cotton, but the workers have to pick out the seeds by hand, Evangeline. The longer it takes, the less prof-

itable it is. We need something to make the work go faster."

Mrs. Greene leaned forward. "Gentlemen," she exclaimed, "you simply must meet the young man from New York who has been staying with our family. He's extremely intelligent, and he is always working on better ways to do things. He'll be an inventor someday, I'm sure. In fact, he made me a beautiful loom after mine broke."

She put down her napkin and motioned to the servant at the door. "Louisa, set up the loom that Mr. Whitney made for me in the parlor." Turning back to her guests, she said, "If you are all finished, please join me in the parlor, and we will take a look at the loom."

The ladies and gentlemen gathered in the parlor. As they admired the workmanship of the loom, Mrs. Greene slipped out of the room. She returned shortly with a lanky young man.

"Ladies and gentlemen," she said, motioning toward her companion, "I'd like you to meet Mr. Eli Whitney."

Mr. Whitney was besieged with questions about the loom; then he and the men talked about cotton and the difficulty of removing the seeds.

"If we could only process the cotton more quickly," Mr. Tremayne said, "we could increase our production and exportation to other countries. Why, cotton could become the moneymaker of the South!"

Interested, Mr. Whitney nodded. "I'll see what I can do," he said. "I'll have to give it some thought first."

He went out to the field to look at the small crop and took some of the cotton with him when he went back to the house. When he asked for a place to work, Mrs. Greene had a workshop set up for him in the basement. For ten days he worked behind the closed doors of the basement workshop. The banging and squeaking drew curious people from all over the plantation. As rumors of the secret project spread, people from all over Savannah came to see what the young Northerner was making. Eli turned everyone away from the door—servants, visitors, even his hostess. "It's a machine that will remove seeds from cotton," he told them. "That's all you need to know. The rest will remain secret until it is finished."

And no one knew any more until ten days later. Eli had completed a small model. He showed it to a few people, but they still kept the secret. Then six months later his invention was ready. Eli obtained a patent for his machine in March of 1794. The secret was finally out. Eli Whitney had changed cotton growing forever.

Eli Whitney's invention consisted of a roller with wire teeth that projected through slits of an iron guard. The slits were smaller than the cottonseeds. When the roller turned, it pulled cotton fibers through the slits, leaving the seeds to fall into a box. The one-horsepower machine could separate seeds from the cotton fibers faster than fifty men working by hand. The machine increased cotton exportation twentyfold and made cotton the staple crop of the South.

The Proving of a Hero

Jamie Turner
illustrated by Sanela Tutaris

Thousands of American heroes never get their names in the history books. Andrew Carnegie knew this when, in 1904, he established a system of rewarding special acts of heroism. Most of the recipients of Carnegie Hero medals are largely unknown outside their families and hometowns, but their courage is no less than that of a Paul Revere or a John Paul Jones. To honor the ordinary citizen who performs a deed of bravery at the risk of personal safety, the Carnegie Hero Fund awards a silver medal inscribed with the hero's name and a brief citation of his act of heroism. Also engraved on the medal are the words from John 15:13: "Greater love hath no man than this, that a man lay down his life for his friends."

Fourteen-year-old Ethel Bundy gathered up the red-checkered tablecloth and stepped outside to shake out the crumbs. It was a crisp, sunny November day in Cherry, Illinois, and the Bundy family had just finished their noon meal. Ethel looked forward to the rest of the day, for it was a perfect Saturday afternoon to spend outdoors. Besides that, other pleasures were in store. Ethel's older sister Amy was visiting from Chicago with her three-year-old daughter. A visit from Amy was always a special time for the family. That evening they would all gather in the kitchen and eat their mother's chewy taffy and pop corn on the big cook stove. Playing their favorite games of Flinch, Authors, and dominoes, they were sure to have a lively time of fun. As Ethel flapped the tablecloth briskly, she looked across the field toward the mine where her father worked. Suddenly she gasped. Billows of black smoke from the mineshaft were clouding the clear autumn sky. Ethel immediately sensed danger. Heart pounding, she ran inside.

"Mother! Mother! There's a fire at the mine!"

The Cherry coal mine had begun operating in 1905. It was a rich, productive mine providing employment for hundreds of men, many of them foreigners seeking a new life in America. The coal was extracted and hauled by mules to cages that traveled up and down the shaft. These mules, sixty-five of them in all, lived in stables within the mine.

John Bundy, the mine manager, lived with his wife, Sarah, and five of their children in one of the company houses located near the mine. Three more children were grown and living away from home. A short, broad-shouldered man with keen blue eyes, a mustache, and brown hair streaked with gray, John Bundy took his job seriously. He was a hard worker during the day and even spent many nights at home poring over the account books or studying a ponderous magazine entitled *Mine and Minerals.* On that Saturday he had eaten an early lunch and hurried back to the mine.

As John Bundy worked within the interior of the mine that day, a mine car holding several bales of hay was lowered into the main shaft to be sent to the mule stables below. Hundreds of bales had followed this same route many times before with no mishap. Baled hay, because of its high density, ordinarily does not burn easily; but on this day the load of hay, stopping temporarily at the mine's second level, somehow became saturated with kerosene from a large torch hanging nearby and began to burn slowly. At first the small fire was ignored as more loads of coal were raised to ground level. One miner who left work early that day and passed right by the smoldering hay said later that the fire was so small he could have easily put it out with his coat. But because he was in a hurry to leave, he did not stop to tend to it. Someone else would take care of it, he was sure.

When the seemingly insignificant fire erupted into a frightening blaze, nearby workers hastened to push the car toward a sump. But before they were able to move the burning hay to the water hole, it had ignited the supporting timbers of the mine. The powerful ventilation fan increased the danger by feeding and spreading the flames.

News of the raging fire spread quickly, and men began crowding into the escape stairway. As the townspeople heard of the fire, they began hurrying toward the mine.

Ethel Bundy wanted to join the others at the mine. But one of the cardinal rules in the Bundy home was that the children were to remain at home with their mother in case of an emergency at the mines. John Bundy wanted the assurance that his family would be safe even if his own life was in danger. On that grim day, Ethel's mother remembered his wishes and gathered her children about her to await further news of the disaster.

out of the main shaft and into the airshaft. The rescuers then descended into the interior of the mine. The cage operator, John Cowley, was instructed to follow their signals exactly.

Six times the thirteen volunteers rode into the heart of the fire and helped fellow workers into the cage. The system was working smoothly. The operator lowered the cage until he received the signal to halt. He waited breathlessly until receiving the signal to raise them and then lifted the men to safety.

Cowley lowered the cage for the seventh time and stopped it when he received the halt signal. Soon he received the next signal and began to raise the cage slowly. But in the process of raising, he suddenly received a signal to halt and then to raise, followed quickly by a signal to lower. Bewildered by the conflicting signals, Cowley froze.

"Hoist it!" shouted several bystanders.

Seventeen-year-old Herbert Bundy, employed as a blacksmith's apprentice on the surface of the mine, turned his eyes away in grief as the cage emerged from the depths of the mine. He slowly

Back at the mine, John Bundy was greatly alarmed when he learned of the fire. He quickly made his way with the others to the surface. But his first thoughts were not for his own safety.

"There are hundreds of men down there! We can't let them die! Who will volunteer to go with me?" he shouted as he climbed into a cage. Twelve brave men responded to his plea and joined him in the cage.

"Reverse the fan!" Bundy called, noting the tremendous draft of heat and smoke pouring up the main shaft. The direction of airflow was reversed, pulling the flames started home to tell his mother the sorrowful news.

Silently watching the window, Sarah Bundy and her children waited at home for news of John. At last they saw Herbert approaching with his head hung low. No words were necessary to tell them that Sarah's husband—and their father—was dead.

But John Bundy's courage did not die with him. He had implanted that same staunch spirit in the lives of his family. Though small and slender, Sarah Bundy possessed an inner strength that carried her through the following days with quietness and dignity. Now the mainstay of the family, she stepped into her husband's place with courage and assurance. Although she was a shy woman with outsiders, she instilled a sense of confidence and purpose within the lives of her children. She wisely managed the limited income and taught her children the value of honest work. When asked later how she had managed to raise such a fine family all alone, she replied, "Well, it took a lot of prayer."

The story of the Cherry mine disaster is riddled with many *ifs*. *If* the electricity in the mine had not shorted out some days earlier, the kerosene torch that ignited the bales of hay would not have been in use. *If* the fan had not shut down, more men could have been rescued. *If* the cage operator had acted more swiftly, the thirteen rescuers might have been spared. But perhaps the biggest *if* implies human carelessness. *If* the men who saw the fire in its earliest stages had taken only a few minutes to put it out, the whole tragedy would never have occurred.

John Bundy's name never appeared in a history book or an encyclopedia, yet he is an American hero. He was a man of small stature, yet he set a towering example. He left his children fatherless, yet the memory of his life guided them to success.

Courage is not born in a moment of crisis. John Bundy had the makings of a hero all along. He followed principles of right behavior in his conduct. He tackled every responsibility with diligence, whether it was singing in the male quartet or organizing the local church, school board, and bank. When others came to him for counsel, he gave of his wisdom freely. It was his desire to do right and to think of others that led John Bundy to act with bravery on that day, just as on any other day.

The Cherry mine fire of November 13, 1909, that claimed the lives of over two hundred men did not make John Bundy a hero. He had the character of a hero long before that.

The Carnegie Hero Fund awarded Bundy and his twelve helpers medals of bravery. Though they were not alive to receive the honor, their acts of love and valor inspired their friends and families to live as selflessly and courageously as the heroes died.

We, the People

Elizabeth Yates

illustrated by Nora Unwin

Who were "the people"?

They were the Founding Fathers who framed and signed the Declaration of Independence, the statesmen who inflamed and inspired public opinion, the patriots whose names and deeds live in history books.

And they were those who lived in small towns and villages and on distant farms, who thought and talked about events and made their feelings known: men who left their stock and crops and marched off to fight because they were convinced of the rightness of the stand that had been made and women who took over the work of the farms along with the care of their homes and families.

Their names made no news. They did no particular acts of heroism, except as the living of each day was heroic in itself. Hard work they knew well, and hardship they could endure. Giving their lives or living their lives, they were as much the foundation of the new nation as were those whose names have long been known.

Learning to Do Without

Early April 1775

It was a fair evening. Jess and Jonas sat on the doorstone before their house with a good feeling. The work of the day was done and the children tucked up to sleep, Matthew and Mark in the trundle bed and baby Liberty in the cradle.

"Five years." Jess sighed happily. "Five years since we've been living on this land, and you've made a farm out of a piece of the wild."

"I couldn't have done it without you."

Jess smiled. It was like Jonas to put it that way.

Silent again, her thoughts went back over the years. Six years ago, in 1769, they had been married in

490

Exeter where they had grown up. Jonas had been nineteen, blue-eyed and broad-shouldered. When he spoke, his words were deliberate. His movements were those of a man who worked with the land and knew what it was to wait for the seasons to bring their yield. Jess had been seventeen, sturdy and spirited, with hair as dark as her eyes.

A month after their wedding, Jonas had gone to the newly incorporated township of Temple where he had been promised land for the clearing, high land with a good supply of water. He had spent a year there alone except for his dog, Spy. Helped by other settlers and giving help in return, he had made a clearing, built a small hut with a stout chimney, and dug a well.

When he brought Jess to Temple, they had signed their names in the Town Book kept in the recently-built Meeting House, to which the Reverend Samuel Webster had been settled as minister. Under their names, Jonas had written those of their twin sons, Matthew and Mark. The blue-eyed, dark-haired babies looked in their way as robust as their parents, and Mr. Webster welcomed them all to the township.

Then Jess and Jonas had started up the long hill to their land, leaving behind them the settlement with its houses clustered near a small green. Their possessions were in a cart drawn by a red-brown horse; two sheep followed the cart, and Spy followed the sheep.

Jess smiled at the memory. During the years that followed, they had worked hard. The children had grown, and another had been born. The hut had become a house with board sides and shakes on the roof instead of bark. The windows

at the south were glazed, but those on the three other sides were still covered with sheets of oiled paper. Fields enclosed by stone walls served for pasture and tillage; other land still had stumps in it. There were more sheep now, a rooster, and several hens; but the horse was gone, and the cow Jess longed for was in their future.

"I miss Big Red," Jess said.

"He was a help," Jonas agreed. He remembered how the horse had twitched logs from the forest, drawn the plow, and shortened the time when they went to the village. "But we may miss more than a horse if things go as they're going."

Jess nodded.

It had been only a month ago, on a March day as much like winter as this April evening was like summer, that Jonas had placed a sack of grain on Big Red's back and gone to the mill to have it ground. He had returned without the horse, with the meal slung in a bag across his shoulders. At the mill he had heard talk of the need for horses, some to get stores of powder and cannon into Boston, others to be used as remounts for officers of the Continental Army. He told Jess that he had been paid for Big Red and that with the money he would get a young steer to train for work.

So they had got on without the horse as they had got on without tea, drying leaves of mint or blueberry and telling themselves that the flavor was better. A useful animal like Big Red could be replaced, a luxury like tea had substitutes, but there were many things they were learning to do without. The people of Temple, like the people in other villages and towns, had voted to buy no more goods from Britain, preferring to go without rather than pay taxes they felt were unjustly levied.

Jess repeated Jonas's words, "If things go as they're going," and brought them both into the present.

As a child in Exeter, she had grown up to the talk of Parliament's refusal to consider the claims of the Colonies; now, as a farm wife in Temple, she heard the talk continue.

Jonas looked at her. "We're still loyal subjects of the Crown, Jess, but we'll not be slaves, and we'll not be taxed unfairly. We've our right to a voice and a vote, and until we have both we'll not be quiet."

"You sound like Mr. Webster!"

"And why not? Those of us who heard him speak to the Minute Men of Groton at their muster are not apt to forget what he said: 'subjects though we are, we're free men and as such we have a duty to God.'"

A small cry coming from the house reminded Jess of a duty she had. She stood up and placed her hand on Jonas's shoulder. He lifted his head, and their eyes met.

"We'll be fine," Jess said with a smile, "as long as we have each other."

She went into the house and Jonas sat alone in the twilight. "How long will that be?" he asked himself. Shortly after Samuel Webster had addressed the militia at Groton, the men of Temple had organized their own. Thereafter, on three evenings a week, no matter what the roads were like or how heavy the day's work had been, they met for muster on the village green. Farmers, millers, tanners, smiths, each shouldered his musket and became a soldier.

"But I'd rather work with the land," Jonas thought, and he looked across his fields.

It's Time

Mid-April 1775

That spring brought good weather. Fair day had followed fair day with just the right moistening of rain. Men who had wrestled with weather as they had with boulders were aware and thankful. Plowing was done earlier than anyone could remember; the planting of some crops was made the first week in April. Peas were now well above the ground. Turnip seed had sprouted; buckwheat was like a green carpet.

The day Jess planted Indian corn, helped by the two little boys, was the same day that Jonas came back from a trip to the mill leading a young steer.

"Can we ride him, Pa?" The boys shouted excitedly.

"You can sit on him," Jonas said, lifting first Mark, then Matthew up onto the thin, bony back, "but he's too ornery to ride."

"He needs good grazing," Jess commented, running her hand down the steer's rump.

Jonas agreed. "And he needs training, but he's young and it's in him to be strong and willing."

Next morning Jonas took the steer to the woods while Jess and the boys planted potatoes among the stumps in the newly cleared field. The baby, Liberty, slept in her cradle that swung from a nearby tree. From the partly-built barn came the sound of ewes bleating.

Later, when Jonas came out of the woods at the field's edge, Jess looked up as he brought the steer to a halt. She cried out in dismay at the size of the welt on Jonas's forehead.

Jonas laughed ruefully. "Can you do something to make it go down?"

Jess sent the boys scurrying for moss and a jug of cold water.

"He balked," Jonas explained. "The logs jolted and one of them caught me on the head."

"Jonas, it might have cracked your skull or bashed your eyes!"

"And it might have missed me altogether!"

Her gaze rebuked him, but he said, "A man has to take his chances, Jess, whatever he does."

She made him sit back against the stone wall, then she placed damp moss on his brow and dampened it constantly. By the time they ate their afternoon meal, the swelling had gone down, leaving only a yellowing mark on the skin. An hour later, Jonas went off to muster.

News had been traveling quickly once the roads had dried; now that the days were lengthening, it spread even more rapidly. It came by peddlers, with as many stories to tell as they had wares to sell; it came by drovers getting their cattle up to summer pasture; and it came by courier, often with a news sheet to be tacked on the board by the door of the Meeting House. News of the Battle at the Bridge reached Temple on the night of April 21 when a rider pounded up the hill and into the village. The black mare was white with lather, her heavy breathing almost drowning the messenger's words.

"They're fighting—the bridge at Concord—the green at

Lexington. Get your men off. Get me a fresh horse."

There was time for a few more words while another horse was saddled and bridled, then the rider cantered off toward Peterborough.

Those who had heard the news rode to alert the men on the hill farms, telling them to be ready to march at daybreak.

When the first light came over the hills, fifty-six men wearing buckskin jerkins and homespun trousers and carrying their muskets met on the green where they had been drilling. They were ready to do what needed to be done, and they knew why they were doing it. They stood at ease while Mr. Webster spoke to them, reminding them that though none knew what the horrors of war might be, no one could doubt what the horrors of slavery would be. They cheered, then marched away singing. The sound of their voices could be heard in the village long after the men had disappeared from sight down the road that led to Boston.

Jonas was back in a week, for most of the fighting was over when the men from New Hampshire arrived.

"Yes, we routed the Redcoats," he replied in answer to Jess's questioning. "Yes, we made it clear that we're ready to defend our rights." He hung up his musket, picked up the hoe, and went to cultivate the cabbages that were growing between the potato hills.

Later, when they were sitting on the doorstone with the boys playing at soldiers nearby, Jess said, "You're different."

"You don't see the things I've seen without becoming different."

"What things?"

"Men dead. Men wounded. Horses squealing until someone has a bullet to spare for them. Houses burned. Fields trampled." He could have said much more.

"Did you see Big Red?"

Jonas shook his head.

"What will happen now?"

Jonas opened his hands and held them with the palms up. "There's time, Jess, for Parliament to know it's dealing with free men and act accordingly." He closed his hands. "And there's time, Jess, for the Colonies to gather their strength." His gaze turned to the land that was being brought to bear, then to the family so near he could have scooped them all into one embrace. He looked up and caught sight of the first star. "And it's time for us to go to bed so we can get on with our work tomorrow."

What News?

The battle that had started at the bridge in Concord and ended when the British regulars retreated to Boston showed the town of Temple that, whatever the outcome, present events were to be taken in all seriousness.

In addition to the stock of powder and ball held by the town, it was voted that salt be secured and kept on hand. Among other votes passed at the Town Meeting held in mid-May was one "to enlist 12 men to march immediately at the rate of Two Pounds per month," and another "to raise 15 or 20 men to stand at a minute's warning, and to pay them at the rate of one shilling per half-day, training one half-day in a week, omitting six weeks in hay-time and six weeks in the winter season." And a committee was appointed to care for the wives and families of the men who answered an alarm.

The month of May meant shearing, and farmers helped their neighbors on the next hill or across the valley. As the fleeces piled up, Jonas looked ahead to using them to purchase what the land could not raise. Jess, seeing them, looked ahead to the blankets and clothes she could make once she had the wool carded and spun and ready for her loom.

As often as he could spare the time, Jonas worked to make more cleared land, felling trees, lopping off branches, and rolling logs for the steer to haul down to the barn he hoped to get finished by winter. As often as she could, Jess worked beside him.

Jonas chided her for her zeal. "Not so fast, Jess, not so hard at it. What we don't do this year we will do next."

"It's such slow work." Jess leaned back against a tree, breathing hard.

"Yes, but a few feet a day and we'll have another acre in a month." Jonas looked up to where the crown of a great tree had waved. "It's a pretty sight to see blue sky instead of leaves."

Jess gazed at the land littered with brush, at the stumps oozing sap. "This will make fine pasture for the cow."

On Sunday, only the necessary chores were done. The family prepared to spend the day at the Meeting House with other families of the township. Liberty was wrapped in a cocoon of blankets, Matthew and Mark put on their hobnail boots, Jess packed food in a basket, and they started down the hill. Jonas carried his musket, and his knapsack swung over one shoulder. As a member of the militia, he had to be ready to march at a minute's notice.

At the spring, halfway down the long hill, Jonas stopped to fill the leather flask that hung from his belt.

"Pa, that water's going to be warm before we get to the village," Mark said.

"So it will. But if we march, I want to have our own water to drink as long as it will last."

Then they all drank from the wooden cup that hung near the pool made by the spring. It was even offered to Liberty, but she made it clear that she preferred other refreshment.

One Sunday, Mr. Webster had just commenced his second sermon of the day when the sound of galloping hoofs could be heard. A courier, riding posthaste, came to a halt at the open door of the Meeting House. People turned to face him.

"What news?" Mr. Webster called from the pulpit.

The courier, not taking time to dismount, shouted, "Ticonderoga! Crown Point! Send as many men as you can. The country behind me is on fire with excitement and all are marching!"

"Let us go immediately," Mr. Webster said. He closed the large Bible over the many papers of his sermon.

The courier rode off, and the people in the Meeting House began to move. Women gathered their children around them. Men went for their muskets: some guns had been stood against the pulpit, others were lined up along the walls.

A voice filled the Meeting House. It was that of Priest Trowbridge, a man old when the town was young whose kindly but unctuous manner had earned him the name by which he was known. With a gesture that encircled the men holding muskets, he said, "I'll be bondsman for every man of them."

Some smiled, wondering how he could take on such a task, but all were warmed by his offer.

A deacon spoke up. "You shall see to the committee to take care of the women and children whose men are away."

At that the men cheered, knowing their families could not be in safer hands.

The Sunday quiet was now marked by such a commotion as

had not been seen before in the village. Men who lived near went to their barns to ready them; others went to fill their powder horns from the town's store. A wagon and team, prepared for just such a moment, was brought up to the Meeting House and loaded with

supplies—blankets, dried meat and peas, sugar, a hogshead of salt. Other provisions would be obtained along the way. Every man was equipped with a generous supply of balls and flints to go with the powder. Reserves were carried in the wagon.

Within an hour, the men were ready to leave.

"You'll write to us," Jess said. "You'll get a message through somehow?"

"If I have to find a carrier pigeon, you shall have word." Then Jonas looked at his sons. "You're the men of the family now. You have your work to do."

They nodded solemnly, each one standing straighter because of the trust their father had in them.

Mr. Webster moved among the men, speaking to each in turn, then he gave the word and the small army started off. Only a third rode, but during the long march to Lake Champlain they would use the ride-and-tie method. One man on a horse would ride a distance of five or six miles, dismount, tie the horse to a tree, and go ahead on foot. A man following on foot, when he came up to the horse, would untie it, mount, and ride on until he overtook his companion.

The women and children, gathered near the steps of the Meeting House, watched their men go. Lean and straight-standing, hardened by work on their own land and trained by muster practice, they were free men.

Jess was proud of Jonas as she watched him go up the road and disappear from sight at the bend.

"There's not a coward among them," Mr. Webster said as the last of the line was lost in the distance and the rumble of wheels, the thud of marching feet, the sound of hoofs could no longer be heard. He turned to the women. "Nor among you, either."

Soon the women went their separate ways, some to houses and farms close to the village, others back to the hills. Priest Trowbridge spoke to each one, promising an early visit, assuring help from the town if ever it should be needed.

When Jess and the children got back to their home, Spy came to meet them, wagging his tail; then he stopped short and his tail dropped. He looked at Jess questioningly.

"He'll be back, never fear," Jess said as she fondled the dog. Sending the boys to gather eggs, she went into the house and made Liberty ready for the night.

Surprise Attack

Mid-May 1775

The days that followed were alike except as the weather gave them showers or shines, both of which brought the growing things along and gave promise of good yields. Jess hoed the corn for the first time, telling herself that when it was ready for the second hoeing Jonas would be back. The boys had charge of the potatoes. Collecting potato bugs in a pannikin, they took them to a flat stone and squashed them as if the success of the rebellion depended on their work alone.

Jess took the scythe to the near field and made an early cut of clover to encourage later growth. With an iron bar she worked stones loose that the boys rolled to the edge of the clearing so that some-day a wall could be built. She led the steer to the woods and brought out the seasoned logs to be sawn and split into burning lengths for the hearth. When the day's work was done and the children bedded, she returned to her own tasks at spinning wheel and loom.

One day was like another, except Sunday, when they went to the village, or the day Priest Trowbridge came by.

His offer was always the same, and her answer was always that, with the boys' help, Jonas's work was being done. "We thank you kindly, Mr. Priest Trowbridge."

Often in the brief time when light faded and before the first star appeared, she sat on the doorstone with Liberty in her arms, rocking her and singing to her.

She kept her voice low. The boys were asleep, and she had no wish to wake them. Liberty needed only a croon to keep her sleeping, a croon and the gentle motion of her mother's arms.

One day might be like another, but no day was the same after Jonas's letter came.

It was the boys who heard the horse coming up the hill and ran to get their mother. By the time Priest Trowbridge reached the house, the family was gathered on the door-stone to welcome him.

"I saw the smoke from your chimney and knew you were home," he said in greeting.

"And where else would we be?" Jess asked, feeling mirthful because of the folded paper she glimpsed in his hand.

" 'Tis a letter, Jess, brought by a courier on his way to Boston, and it's the first news to reach Temple since the men left."

She took it from him with eager hands and a smile that lighted her face. There was her name in Jonas's own script. She could hear the sound of his voice behind it.

"What's he say, lass? They'll all be wanting to know when I get back."

She opened it. It was not overlong, and even at a glance she knew that much of it she would keep to herself.

"He says . . ." She went slowly so the words skipped would not be noticed. "He says that the march was fatiguing, and much of it made in rain, but that they got there on the fourth day."

"Read the words."

"*Some men got colds,*" she read, "*some were bothered with the quickstep, but thanks to our wool and your fashioning, my trousers kept me warm and my jerkin shed the rain.*" She paused, then went on, "*Captain Allen greeted us and soon was calling us by our names. Every man ready to fight for his country was just as ready to fight for him. He says we'll seize the Fort tomorrow . . .*" Jess gasped and looked over the edge of the paper at Priest Trowbridge, who was leaning from his saddle so he would not miss a word.

"Then they've won, sure as my name is Trowbridge!"

"He can't say, this was written before the attack." Her glance went back to the page and she read, "*This is the only news you will get from me till I embrace you all, for Captain Allen says when we take Ticonderoga and Crown Point and lay our hands on all the powder stored in them we can go home. Tell the boys—nay, I'll soon tell them myself,—I . . .*" Jess had no intention of sharing the next two

502

lines. Reading them to herself, she folded the paper and slipped it into her pocket.

"They've taken the Forts, praise the Lord!" Priest Trowbridge sat up in his saddle and raised his hat.

"Jonas wrote this before the battle."

"No matter. The outcome is clear. Ethan Allen is not one for defeat."

That evening, when Jess sat on the stone with the letter, it was almost as if she had Jonas beside her. The apple tree he had planted the year he spent alone on the hill was in bloom. Its fragrance surrounded her. She breathed deeply and read the letter again, savoring it. To have it in her hand was like having Jonas's hand in hers. Soon she would have his hand, for the letter had been written on the ninth of May, and more than a week had already gone by.

Three days later, when the sun had just passed the noon mark on the south wall of the house, Jonas came up the hill. Soon he was doing what he had said in his letter he would do, wrapping all four of them in one embrace.

"That's a mean rent in your jerkin!" Jess exclaimed.

"Better tear buckskin than flesh."

"I'll soon have it mended, and washed too."

Jonas laughed. "A man needs to get back to his home. I've not been out of these garments since I left, and that was a long time ago."

"Three weeks and three days," Jess said, pointing to the nicks the boys had made under the noon mark.

"It seemed longer."

While they sat at the trestle table eating hasty pudding and drinking cold spring water, Jonas told them how the fighting had gone.

"Fort Ti and Crown Point were taken without a shot fired or a man lost, but it wouldn't have been so without Captain Allen."

The small force of Green Mountain Boys, augmented by men from Massachusetts and New Hampshire, had been loaded into two boats and ferried across the water. Knowing that the attack would be a surprise one and aided by the light of a waning moon, they were as stealthy as men on a wolf hunt, yet ready for anything. A sleeping sentry had been roused and taken prisoner. Once inside the Fort, Captain Allen had roared out to the commander, "You old rat, come out!" The room echoed as Jonas's voice roared in it.

The boys shouted gleefully, and even Liberty gurgled with excitement. "Did he come out, Pa?" the boys asked.

"He did, and like a mouse! Then he asked Captain Allen by whose authority he was there, and the Captain answered in words that will ring across the land for years to come, 'In the name of the Great Jehovah and the Continental Congress!' How we men cheered! Crown Point was fifteen miles down the lake, but it fell in the same way. Many prisoners were taken, but more important were the stocks of powder and cannon and flints. Maybe enough to win the war."

"So it's war now," Jess said, "not rebellion."

"It could still be rebellion, but if they don't soon believe us, it will be war."

The musket was cleaned and oiled, then hung in its place. Jonas took the hoe and went to the field for the second hoeing of the corn.

Jess picked up the strands of her loom, idle now for too long. She gazed around her at the other tasks awaiting her—the board floor to be scrubbed with sand, the kernels of grain to be pounded into hominy. With time remaining, she would set about dressing some of her flax. Linen was in demand with the need for men's shirts growing, and it fetched a good price; but it was a long process to hatchel the slender stalks and ready them for the loom.

Sounds Like Thunder

Bunker Hill, June 1775

Whenever Jonas went to the edge of the woods to continue clearing, he never went without his musket. There might be game that would mean a meal for his family; there might be varmints. Walking through one stone-walled field to another, Jonas was pleased at what he saw—buckwheat tall enough to wave in a breeze, wheat with a tinge of color, corn ready to be thinned and transplanted, potatoes and cabbages higher than the stumps among which they grew. The grass in the pasture looked thrifty. He stood for a moment to watch the lambs frolicking, the ewes nibbling. This was his fortune; with it and what it meant for the future he felt himself rich.

A boulder marked the place where he had stopped. He leaned his musket against the stone and shifted the ax he had been carrying to his right hand. An oak had been blazed earlier as the next tree to go, and Jonas started his work. Less than halfway into the massive trunk, he was aware of a commotion coming from the direction of the house, and he turned to see what was causing it. Leaving his ax in the tree, he reached instinctively for his musket.

Spy was barking. Jess was shouting. The rooster was crowing as if a dozen dawns had burst on the world. Jonas slipped some powder in the pan, cocked the hammer and held himself ready.

Coming out from under the barn and running toward the woods was a fox with one of the hens in its jaws.

"Pa!" Matthew screamed.

"Where's Pa?" Mark cried.

Jonas aimed, waiting the fraction of a second, then fired. The fox rolled over, kicking convulsively before it lay still. The hen flapped its wings, squawked loudly, and flew back to her chicks. Matthew and Mark came running to see the dead fox.

"Will we eat him for our dinner, Pa?"

Jonas shook his head. "He's vermin, but we'll skin him and cure his hide. It will make a warm cover for Liberty's cradle when winter comes around." He cleaned the musket as he spoke, then slipped another ball down the muzzle and leaned it against the boulder. "Now, where's my ax?" he said, more to himself than the boys.

"Look what we've got, Ma!" the boys shouted as they dragged the animal back to the barn to await their father's attention.

Jonas went back to work on the tree, and before long he had hitched up the steer to drag the logs out of the forest. But once again Jonas found that he was struggling as much for cooperation as the steer struggled against it.

"He'll do well enough when I get another one to work with him," Jonas said to Jess. "A pair always behaves better."

"When will that be?"

"Could be next week when I take him down to the smith to get him some shoes. There'll likely be someone there willing to sell or trade one of his beasts."

But when Jonas went to the village with the steer, he came back alone.

"What happened?"

It was no easier for Jonas to say than it was for Jess to hear.

"It's the Port-Bill the British have put on Boston," Jonas explained, "and there's little food getting into the city. People are in dire straits, Jess. They're hungry. There was a news sheet on the Meeting House board telling about it. Men who read it wanted to do what they could. Some had grain to send, others had root crops. Meat on the

hoof was as welcome as a warm day in winter. The steer may have been ornery, Jess, but he was grass fed and that makes for good quality beef. I'll get another one when I get back. Maybe I'll even have some bounty money to get us a cow."

Jess smiled at the thought, then her tone sharpened. "Get back? Are you marching again?"

He nodded. "Tomorrow."

"Where?"

"Two hills near Boston, Breed's and Bunker's. The Redcoats have a large force assembling and it's up to the Minute Men to make a stand. We've got the powder, Jess, and much of it is what came from Fort Ti."

"So! You'll give them a taste of their own medicine."

"That's the nub of it," Jonas said.

The June night was soft around them when they sat on the door-stone. Jonas gave Jess some advice about the crops and the breeding of the four ewes that were to be taken a mile to the farm with a ram. He urged her to acquire a suckling pig so they could fatten it for later use. "I'll be back in time to dig the potatoes."

"First ones will be ready soon." Jess said. "The boys have been poking the earth around them and say they're already the size of small apples."

"Potatoes relish well when a man's hungry; they'll relish even better next winter with smoked pork." Taking Liberty from Jess's arms, he cradled her awkwardly but tenderly. "We gave her the right name."

"We did, indeed."

The moon rose full over the eastern hills, and they sat for a long time in its light.

Next morning early, Jess stood in the doorway, the boys beside her, the baby in her arms. Together they watched Jonas go down the road.

Spy brushed against her, his tail moving slowly, his eyes searching her face.

She touched his head, then waved him away. "Go see to the sheep."

He was off with a bound. Matthew and Mark ran after him to let down the bars from the night pen so the flock might graze in the near pasture. Jess set Liberty in her cradle. She turned to the fire to uncover the coals and have heat for the day's cooking. Picking up the hourglass, she turned it and watched the sands start to flow.

Swallows chuckled around the house; birds chattered as they went about their affairs; bleats and baas mingled with the shouts and laughter of the boys. Back of them all, Jess heard the marching feet and saw the brave line of men on its way from the village. Their destination was not so important as their task. Likewise for her, she thought. It was the work to be done that mattered, her work and Jonas's.

The wind blew from the south almost constantly during the next three days, and the sound it brought reached even to the hill towns of southern New Hampshire.

"Is it thunder, Ma?" Matthew asked.

"Thunder?" Mark echoed, for the sky was clear.

"No, it's not thunder. It's the guns."

"Where Pa is?"

"Yes, but your Pa is lying low by a stone wall. When he fires he'll be as sure of his aim as he was when he got that fox."

The boys raced off with whoops and shouts, knowing that wherever their Pa was, the enemy would fare badly.

Jess took the baby and held her against one shoulder; with her free hand she carried her tools and went to the woods. There was no way now of getting logs easily down to the house without an animal, but logs were needed for the hearth. She would have to work on them where they were with ax and saw. Once she had them in manageable lengths she could drag or carry them, and the boys would help.

It was always the same when Jonas was away: the work was harder and it took longer, but it got done. Liberty, placed close to a boulder on a bed of hay, cooed happily; Matthew and Mark could be heard at their work and at their play of being Minute Men. At a point between the two groups, Spy settled himself, restful but watchful.

At day's end, when the children had been tucked in trundle bed and cradle, the chickens gone to roost, the sheep penned, the fire covered, Jess gave herself to the comfort of thinking. Sitting on the doorstone, she watched while the dusk became night, even blotting out the small blooms from the laurel that grew where pasture and woodland met. The lights from fireflies pricked the darkness around her as stars did the sky above her. She listened to the trees talking as the wind moved through them. The sound of Jonas's voice was with her, and the words he had said when they had last watched the night come down.

"So long as a man has a life to give or a fortune to spend, he owes it to his country." Perhaps she remembered the words clearly because it was the first time Jonas had ever spoken of his life.

From somewhere between the far pasture and even more distant pond, a whippoorwill started calling. Jess got up and went into the house, shutting the night out as she closed the door behind her.

But there were times when comfort was not to be found.

One evening, after the children had been tucked up for sleep, Jess went to the near pasture. Wearied from her work that never ended, taut from waiting for the news that never came, she threw herself down on the ground. Tears filled her eyes, overflowed, and ran down her cheeks. She pressed one cheek then another against the earth, wondering if anything would ever grow again in soil where salt had soaked.

"Jonas, Jonas . . ." She had no other words, no other thought.

Into her tumult, or across it, or through it, there came a sound. Gradually she stilled her weeping the better to hear it. It was from the house, and the house was not a stone's throw distant. Jess sat up and rubbed her eyes with her hands. Then she stiffened. It was Liberty, crying shrilly as if her need was great.

Jess stood up, swayed for a moment, then started running toward the house. Grateful for the darkness that had come down while she was in despair, she was grateful for something else that she did not fully realize until she knelt by the cradle. Taking the baby in her arms, Jess knew that she was needed.

Spy padded across the floor and looked up at her. He leaned against her, his tail moving slowly. Jess felt the swish of it against her skirt. When the baby had been led into contentment and Jess had a free hand, she placed it on Spy's head.

The Beginning of the End

Mid-June 1775

Three days later, as Jess was tending her flax in the garden plot south of the house, Priest Trowbridge came up the road with news. The men were on their way home and should be in the village by sunset. The courier who brought the news said they had been on their way for some hours but with only three horses, and those needed for the wounded, they were making slow time.

"What was the outcome?" Jess asked.

"The British took the hills, but at a terrible cost. Our men withdrew because they had used up all their powder." At the disappointment in Jess's face, Priest added hastily, "Wait and see, lass, if this is not the beginning of the end for the British and the beginning of independence for the Colonies."

"Then it is war?"

"Yes, from now on. No doubt about that."

"Are all the men from Temple coming home?"

"A goodly lot, but some have their heads bandaged, and others have an arm in a sling or walk with a crutch." Priest Trowbridge nudged the horse to move forward. "I'll be on my way now."

Jess took no time to watch him go. Calling to the boys, then to Spy, she made ready for the walk to the village and Jonas's return.

From farm to farm the news spread, as it had from house to house within the village. Long before sunset, the women and children had gathered near the Meeting House to be on hand when their men arrived. Mr. Webster stood with them, his usual flow of words reduced to a trickle.

At the first glimpse of men coming up the road from New Ipswich, older boys and girls raced off to greet fathers and brothers, shoulder knapsacks, and ask about the battle. The wounded were on the horses, two to a horse, in one case, three. Women strained their eyes to see who rode and who walked, and to count. Twenty men had answered the alarm. There were not that many on the road, but word soon got around that the badly wounded were following in a wagon at ox pace.

Jess, searching the group, at last caught sight of Jonas. He was near the end of the line, and he was limping. Once she saw that he stopped and leaned against a tree as if he had little strength to go farther. He lifted his head, then, and looked toward the village. Jess waved and cried out his name. At the sight of him, lame though he was, she felt she had no more to ask of Heaven.

"There's Pa, near to the end," she said to the boys, giving them a push as she spoke. "He can use your help."

They ran down the road. She could see them weaving through the crowd until they reached their father.

There was a great hubbub around the Meeting House when the men finally arrived: laughter and tears, questions that could not then be answered, sobs and huzzas.

When Jess and Jonas moved away from the crowd and faced the long hill, Jess took Jonas's knapsack and gave the boys the care of the basket in which Liberty was sleeping. "Up the hill with you now, and walk so your sister won't waken." Then she offered her free arm for Jonas to lean upon.

He settled his musket into its leather sling across his shoulders and gripped her arm.

"We'll take it slowly," she said.

"We'll make it." The smile he gave her had even more certainty than his words.

They had not gone a rod up the road when they heard the clipclop of hoofs behind them. Jess turned to see Priest Trowbridge.

"Got a bit of pasture up your way for this nag?" he asked. "I'm not planning to use her until wheat harvest."

"We've got the best high grazing in all of Temple Township," Jess answered.

"Take her then." Heaving his right leg over the saddle, Priest eased himself to the ground. "My wife asked me why I wanted four legs under me when I had two good ones." He gave Jonas a hand in mounting, then slapped the white rump. "Get along with you."

So Jonas rode up the hill, and when they got to the spring where the boys had stopped to change arms on the basket, the horse came to a natural standstill. Jess took the wooden cup that hung by the spring and filled it with water for Jonas. Three times she filled it for him, then they all drank in turn. Finally the old horse snuffled in the pool and blew out more than she swallowed.

"You don't know how I dreamed of this spring," Jonas said, "those days we were lying in the sun, crouching behind stone walls, crawling to better positions. What little water we had was needed to clean our guns, fouled from firing. Yes," he added softly. "I thought of this spring, of the cool water flowing out of the hillside and of its sweet, clean taste."

"Oh, Jonas!" Jess leaned her head against the horse. She wanted to cry. Why now? she asked herself. He was home, he was alive, and if not well, she would care for him until he got well.

"Matthew, Mark," she said swiftly, "go along up the hill with Liberty. When you get to the house, stir up the fire so there'll be coals to roast those potatoes you dug this morning."

"Yes, Ma," they chorused, then they started up the hill with the basket swinging between them.

Jonas leaned down and put his arms around Jess. She gave a little jump and was on the mare's broad back. "The two of us aren't much more than the weight of Priest Trowbridge," Jonas said as he gave the horse a touch of heel.

Another Beginning

Late July 1776

It was a hot evening, hay harvest was over, wheat harvest had not commenced. After the day's work, Jess and Jonas sat on the doorstone, tired but content. Matthew and Mark were building a dam in the brook to divert water into a sluiceway so the small wheel they had constructed could be turned. Liberty was crawling between house and garden plot, but she was kept from mishap by the watchful eye and quick moves of Spy. A dozen chickens pecked around for tasty tidbits before the night's long fast. From the near pasture came bleats and baas, an occasional whinny, a long-drawn moo-oo.

Jess and Jonas knew what their next day's work would be; they knew, too, what was ahead for their country. However long or bitter the years might prove, there was no uncertainty in their minds, nor in the minds of any of the people of the United Colonies. They were all free men and women, whoever they were, wherever they lived, and they were the nation that had been born. Skirmishes were over; battle lines had been drawn. There was no need to bestir patriotism; from hill farms to villages to towns and cities, people were imbued with its spirit, ready to devote their lives and property to a cause that involved them and their children.

In April of that year, 1776, the Committee of Safety had sent to the selectmen of every town a paper known as the Association Test. With it was the request that it be signed by all men over twenty-one. Few there were who did not sign it:

We, the subscribers, do solemnly engage and promise that we will to the utmost of our powers at the risque of our lives and fortunes, with arms oppose the hostile proceedings of the British fleets and armies against the United Colonies.

By the time a few months had passed, in Philadelphia the members of the Continental Congress had put their names to a longer document, the Declaration of Independence, that concluded with the words

We mutually pledge to each other our lives, our fortunes, and our sacred honour.

Each man who signed the Test or the Declaration knew that when he wrote his name he put his life with it.

Jonas pointed to the star that had just become visible in the evening sky. "It's another beginning, Jess."

"I know it is, Jonas," she said, and she closed her hand over his.

Glossary

This glossary has information about selected words found in this reader. You can find meanings of words as they are used in the stories. Certain unusual words such as foreign names are included so that you can pronounce them correctly when you read.

The pronunciation symbols below show how to pronounce each vowel and several of the less familiar consonants.

ă	pat	ĕ	pet	îr	fierce
ā	pay	ē	be	ŏ	pot
âr	care	ĭ	pit	ō	go
ä	father	ī	pie	ô	paw, for, ball

oi	oil	ŭ	cut	zh	vision
o͝o	book	ûr	fur	ə	ago, item,
o͞o	boot	*th*	the		pencil, atom,
yo͞o	abuse	th	thin		circus
ou	out	hw	which	ər	butter

a•bort (ə bôrt´) —*v.* **aborted.** To cancel before completing.

ab•so•lute (ăb´ sə lo͞ot´) —*adj.* Total; unconditional.

a•buse (ə byo͞oz´) —*v.* **abused.** To put to bad or wrong use.

a•bus•er (ə byo͞oz´ ər) —*n.* One who wrongly or improperly uses.

ac•ces•sory (ăk sĕs´ ə rē) —*n.* **accessories.** An extra item that goes with or improves a main item.

ac•cost (ə kôst´) —*v.* **accosted.** To approach in a hostile, aggressive manner.

ac•cu•rate (ăk´ yər ĭt) —*adj.* Conforming to fact; errorless.

ac•ti•vate (ăk´ tə vāt´) —*v.* **activated.** To set in operation or motion.

ad•van•tage (ăd văn´ tĭj) —*n.* A favorable position.
—*idiom* **take advantage of.** 1.To put to good use. 2. To profit selfishly by; to exploit.

ae•ro•sol (âr´ ə sôl´) —*n.* A mass of tiny drops of a liquid or pieces of solid material suspended in air or another gas.

af•front (ə frŭnt´) —*n.* An insult made on purpose.

a•gile (ăj´ əl) —*adj.* Capable of moving quickly and easily; nimble.

aim•less•ly (ām´ lĭs lē) —*adv.* In a manner without direction or purpose.

al•cove (ăl´ kōv´) —*n.* An inset or recessed part of a room.

a•li•en (ā´ lē ən) —*n.* An outsider; someone from a very different place and culture.

al•le•go•ry (ăl´ ĭ gôr´ ē) —*n.* A story in which characters and events are used to represent ideas.

alms (ämz) —*n.* Money or food given to the poor.

a•loof (ə lo͞of´) —*adj.* Cool and distant; not very friendly.

am•bi•tious (ăm bĭsh´ əs) —*adj.* Eager for success, fame, money, or power.

am•ble (ăm´ bəl) —*v.* **ambled.** To walk slowly and leisurely.

am•pu•tate (ăm´ pyo͞o tāt´) —*v.* **amputated.** To cut off all or part of an arm, leg, finger, or other part of the body.

a•muse (ə myo͞oz´) —*v.* **amused.** To cause enjoyment; to entertain.

a•nal•y•sis (ə năl´ ĭ sĭs) —*n.* Any careful study of a subject and its details.

an•cient (ān´ shənt) —*adj.* Very old.

a•nes•the•tize (ə nĕs´ thĭ tīz´) —*v.* To give someone or something a numbing drug.

angst (ängkst) —*n.* A vague feeling of fear and unhappiness.

an•i•mat•ed (ăn´ ə māt´ əd) —*adj.* Full of spirit; lively.

an•tics (ăn´ tĭks) —*n.* Funny acts or actions intended to draw attention.

a•pol•o•get•i•cal•ly (ə pŏl´ ə jĕt´ ĭ klē) —*adv.* In an excusing, humble manner.

ancient

ă	pat	ĕ	pet
ā	pay	ē	be
âr	care	ĭ	pit
ä	father	ī	pie
îr	fierce	oi	oil
ŏ	pot	o͝o	book
ō	go	o͞o	boot
ô	paw,	yo͞o	abuse
	for	ou	out
ŭ	cut	ə	ago,
ûr	fur		item,
th	the		pencil,
th	thin		atom,
hw	which		circus
zh	vision	ər	butter

ap•pren•tice (ə prĕn´ tĭs) —*n*. A person who learns a skill or trade by working for a skilled craftsman. Because an apprentice is learning and studying, he is paid a very small salary.

ap•proach (ə prōch´) —*v*. **approached, approaching.** To come near or nearer to.

ar•bor (är´ bər) —*n*. A shaded place or garden area closed in by trees, bushes, or vines growing on lattices.

ar•dent•ly (är´ dnt lē) —*adv*. In a passionate manner.

ar•ray (ə rā´) —*n*. An orderly arrangement; an impressive display or collection.

ar•ro•gant (ăr´ ə gənt) —*adj*. Proud; feeling that one is more important than everyone else.

as•sas•sin (ə săs´ ĭn) —*n*. A person who murders someone who is of political or public importance.

as•say (ăs ā´) —*v*. **assayed.** To try to do something.

as•sent (ə sĕnt´) —*v*. **assented.** To agree.

as•set (ăs´ ĕt´) —*n*. Something that is useful or valuable.

as•sume (ə so͞om´) —*v*. **assumed.** To believe something is true without thinking about it.

a•ston•ish (ə stŏn´ ĭsh) —*v*. To cause amazement or surpise.

a•stride (ə strīd´) —*adj*. With one leg on each side of a thing.

au•di•ence (ô´ dē əns) —*n*. 1. The people gathered to see and hear a public event. 2. A formal hearing or conference.

aug•ment (ôg mĕnt´) —*v*. **augmented.** To make greater in size or scope.

awe (ô) —*v*. **awed.** To fill with wonder or fear about something that is mighty or majestic.

awn•ing (ô´ nĭng) —*n*. A canvas or plastic screen that looks like a roof. An awning is put up over a window or door. Awnings protect the inside of houses from the sun and rain.

az•ure (ăzh´ ər) —*adj*. Light to medium blue.

arbor

B

bade (băd, bād) —*v*. A past tense of *bid*.

balk (bôk) —*v*. **balked.** To stop short and refuse to go on.

ball (bôl) —*n*. A spherical object such as a piece of metal shot from a gun or cannon.

balm•y (bä´ mē) —*adj*. Mild or pleasant.

ban•ish (băn´ ĭsh) —*v*. To force someone to leave a country.

ban•nock (băn´ ək) —*n*. A fried, flat bread that can be made of oatmeal, barley, or wheat flour.

bar (bär) —*n*. 1. The ruling association of lawyers. 2. A straight piece of wood or metal that is longer than it is wide. It is sometimes used to fasten doors, windows, or other openings.

barge (bärj) —*n*. A boat with a flat bottom used to carry freight.

awning

azure

bow net

brass

base¹ (bās) —*v.* **based.** To use as a foundation for; support.
—*n.* 1. A part on which something rests. 2. A starting or main place. 3. In baseball, one of the four corners of the infield.

base² (bās) —*adj.* Having low values or ethics.

bawl (bôl) —*v.* **bawling.** To cry out or call in a loud, strong voice.

bea•con (bē′ kən) —*n.* A fire, light, or radio signal used to guide or warn.

beat (bēt) —*v.* **beaten, beating.** 1. To hit or strike again and again. 2. To mix or whip rapidly. 3. To win against. 4. To flap, especially wings. 5. To pound heavily and fast; to throb. 6. To strike an opponent's blade with a single sharp blow of the fencing foil.
—*n.* A pulsation or throb.

beck•on (bĕk′ ən) —*v.* **beckoned.** To signal to someone with the hand or head.

be•siege (bĭ sēj′) —*v.* **besieged.** To crowd around and hem in.

be•sought (bĭ sôt′) —*v.* Past tense of *beseech:* to ask in a serious way; to beg.

be•stir (bĭ stûr′) —*v.* To rouse or encourage to action.

bet•ter (bĕt′ ər) —*n.* A superior in position, wealth, or intelligence.

be•wil•dered (bĭ wĭl′ dərd) —*adj.* Confused or puzzled.

bid (bĭd) —*v.* **bade.** 1. To tell someone to do something. 2. To say as a greeting or farewell.

bide (bīd) —*v.* To wait patiently

for the right moment.

bil•low (bĭl′ ō) —*v.* **billowed, billowing.** To rise or swell.
—*n.* A great rising of anything.
—**billowy** *adj.* Surging like waves.

blunt•ed (blŭnt′ əd) —*adj.* Having an edge that is not sharp.

boom (bo͞om) —*v.* **boomed.** To make a loud, resonant sound.

bor•age (bôr′ ĭj) —*n.* A European herb with blue or purplish star-shaped flowers.

bound (bound) —*v.* **bounding.** To leap forward; to jump at.

bow net (bō nĕt) —*n.* A special bowed net used for trapping wild birds.

brass (brăs) —*n.* A yellowish metal that contains copper and zinc.
—*adj.* Made from brass.

brave (brāv) —*v.* **braved.** To face courageously.

brawn•y (brô′ nē) —*adj.* Muscular; very strong.

bra•zen (brā′ zən) —*adj.* Brass-colored or made of brass.

breach (brēch) —*n.* A hole or blank space in something.

break (brāk) —*v.* 1. To burst into two or more pieces. 2. To separate. 3. To change direction suddenly. 4. To weaken or destroy. 5. To train a horse to respond to human commands. 6. To fill or be filled with sorrow.
—*n.* 1. An interruption; a pause or rest. 2. A broken place; an opening, crack, or gap. 3. A beginning. 4. An end.

ă	pat	ě	pet
ā	pay	ē	be
âr	care	ĭ	pit
ä	father	ī	pie
îr	fierce	oi	oil
ŏ	pot	o͞o	book
ō	go	o͞o	boot
ô	paw,	yo͞o	abuse
	for	ou	out
ŭ	cut	ə	ago,
ûr	fur		item,
th	the		pencil,
th	thin		atom,
hw	which		circus
zh	vision	ər	butter

break•er (brāk´ ər) —*n.* A wave that breaks into foam when it reaches shore.

breech•es (brĭch´ ĭz) —*n.* Short trousers that are fastened at or just below the knees.

brig•and (brĭg´ ənd) —*n.* One of a group of robbers.

bril•liance (brĭl´ yəns) —*adj.* Full of light; shining brightly.

bril•liant (brĭl´ yənt) —*n.* A gem cut with many facets to reflect light.

brine (brīn) —*n.* Water that contains much salt. It is used to prepare certain foods.

broach (brōch) —*v.* To bring up a subject in a roundabout way.

brood (brо̄о̄d) —*v.* To worry or think unhappily for a long period of time.

bronc (brŏngk) —*n.* Also *bronco.* A small, wild or partly tamed horse of western North America.

brute (brо̄о̄t) —*adj.* Physical or muscular.

bulk•head (bŭlk´ hĕd´) —*n.* One of the partitions that divide a ship or plane into compartments.

bulk•y (bŭl´ kē) —*adj.* Having great volume or size.

bur•ly (bûr´ lē) —*adj.* Muscular; strong; husky.

ca•dence (kād´ ns) —*n.* A steady, rhythmic sound.

ca•lam•i•ty (kə lăm´ ĭ tē) —*n.* A disaster; a terrible event.

cal•is•then•ics (kăl´ ĭs thĕn´ ĭks) —*n.* A series of exercises to build muscles and endurance.

can•is•ter (kăn´ ĭ stər) —*n.* An airtight container.

canister

can•yon (kăn´ yən) —*n.* A deep valley with steep cliffs on both sides and often a stream running through it.

ca•pac•i•ty (kə păs´ ĭ tē) —*n.* Position; role.

cap•tor (kăp´ tər) —*n.* One who keeps a person or thing as prisoner.

car•di•nal (kär´ dn əl) —*adj.* Of greatest or first importance; chief; foremost.

car•go (kär´ gō) —*n.* The freight carried by a ship, airplane, or other vehicle.

canyon

car•i•bou (kăr´ ə bо̄о̄´) —*n.* A large deer of northern North America. Both the males and the females have large, spreading antlers.

car•niv•o•rous (kär nĭv´ ər əs) —*adj.* Feeding on the flesh of animals.

case•ment (kās´ mənt) —*n.* The frame of a window that swings outward on hinges.

cast (kăst) —*v.* **casting.** To look toward.

cast•ing (kăs´ tĭng) —*n.* The indigestible part of a bird's food that the bird forms into a ball and spits out.

caribou

cat•call (kăt´ kôl) —*n.* A shrill call or whistle that shows disrespect or disapproval.

chandelier

cinch

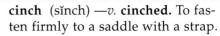

coffer

cat•e•chism (kăt´ ĭ kĭz´ əm) —*n.* Basic knowledge presented in a question-and-answer format.

ce•les•tial (sə lĕs´ chəl) —*adj.* Having to do with the sky or heaven.

chafe (chāf) —*v.* **chafed.** To be bothered or annoyed.

chan•de•lier (shăn´ də lîr´) —*n.* A hanging lamp holding many separate lights.

chan•nel (chăn´ əl) —*v.* **channeled.** To form a channel in or through something. —*n.* 1. The deepest part of a river or harbor through which ships can pass. 2. A body of water that connects two larger bodies.

char•ac•ter•is•tic (kăr´ ək tə rĭs´ tĭk) —*n.* A special feature of a person or thing.

chide (chīd) —*v.* **chided.** To reprimand or scold gently for the purpose of correction.

chink (chĭngk) —*n.* A narrow opening.

chit•ter (chĭt´ ər) —*v.* **chittering.** To chatter or twitter.

chock full (chŏk fōol) —*adj.* Having as much as possible.

cho•ral (kôr´ əl) —*adj.* Performed by a choir of voices.

chro•mi•um (krō´ mē əm) —*n.* A hard, steel-gray metal that resists tarnishing.

churn (chûrn) —*v.* **churned.** To move or swirl vigorously.

cinch (sĭnch) —*v.* **cinched.** To fasten firmly to a saddle with a strap.

ci•pher•ing (sī´ fər ĭng) —*n.* The figuring of basic math equations.

clam•ber (klăm´ bər) —*v.* **clambered.** To climb on all fours with some trouble.

cla•mor (klăm´ ər) —*v.* **clamored.** To make loud, confused noise.

clench (klĕnch) —*v.* **clenched.** To grasp or grip tightly.

cli•mate (klī´ mĭt) —*n.* The usual weather a place has during a year, including its temperatures, rainfall, and wind.

clus•ter (klŭs´ tər) —*v.* **clustered.** To gather or grow in clusters. —*n.* A group of similar things growing or grouped close together.

coax (kōks) —*v.* To try in a gentle or pleasant way to get a person or an animal to do something.

cob•ble•stone (kŏb´ əl stōn) —*n.* A small, round stone used for paving roads.

cock (kŏk) —*v.* **cocked.** To turn or tilt to one side.

co•coon (kə kōon´) —*v.* **cocooned.** To surround or cover as a cocoon.

cof•fer (kô´ fər) —*n.* A strongbox or treasury.

com•mence (kə mĕns´) —*v.* **commenced.** To begin; to start.

com•mo•tion (kə mō´ shən) —*n.* Violent motion; noisy activity; confusion.

com•pan•ion•ship (kəm păn′ yən ship) —*n.* The relationship of friends or comrades.

com•pare (kəm pâr′) —*v.* **compared.** 1. To say that something is similar. 2. To examine the differences and similarities of two or more things or people.

con•ceit•ed (kən sē′ tĭd) —*adj.* Having too high an opinion of oneself and one's abilities.

con•flict (kŏn′ flĭkt′) —*v.* (kən flĭkt′) **conflicting.** To clash; to be different. —*n.* A clash or struggle of ideas or interests.

con•grat•u•late (kən grăch′ ə lāt′) —*v.* To praise someone for something the person has done or for any good event.

con•se•quence (kŏn′ sĭ kwĕns′) —*n.* Something that happens as a result of another action.

con•sol•ing•ly (kən sōl′ ĭng lē) —*adv.* In a comforting manner.

con•su•late (kŏn′ sə lĭt) —*n.* The office of a government official when he represents a foreign country.

con•sult (kən sŭlt′) —*v.* **consulted, consults.** To go to for advice, an opinion, or information.

con•ten•der (kən tĕnd′ ər) —*n.* One who participates in competition.

con•trap•tion (kən trăp′ shən) —*n.* A gadget.

con•trast (kən trăst′) —*v.* **contrasted.** To compare in order to show differences.

con•vict (kən vĭkt′) —*v.* To persuade someone of his sinfulness.

co•or•di•nate (kō ôr′ dn āt′) —*v.* To work or cause to work together well or efficiently.

co•or•din•a•tion (kō ôr dn ā′ shən) —*n.* Harmonized functioning of the muscles.

cope (kōp) —*v.* To struggle with and overcome some problem.

cor•mo•rant (kôr′ mər ənt) —*n.* A large diving bird with webbed feet, a hooked bill, and a pouch.

cor•on•a•tion (kôr′ ə nā′ shən) —*n.* The ceremony of crowning a king or a queen.

corps-à-corps (kôr ə kôr) —*adv.* Literally, in a body-to-body position.

cor•ri•dor (kôr′ ĭ dər) —*n.* A narrow hallway or passage with doors opening into it.

cor•rup•tion (kə rŭp′ shən) —*n.* Decay, rot.

coun•ter•at•tack (koun′ tər ə tăk′) —*n.* A return attack.

cou•ri•er (ko͝or′ ē ər) —*n.* A messenger on official business.

crag (krăg) —*n.* A steep portion of rock that juts out of a cliff.

crag•gy (krăg′ ē) —*adj.* Resembling or similar to rugged cliffs.

crane (krān) —*v.* **craning.** To stretch or strain one's neck in order to see.

ă pat	ĕ pet
ā pay	ē be
âr care	ĭ pit
ä father	ī pie
îr fierce	oi oil
ŏ pot	o͝o book
ō go	o͞o boot
ô paw,	yo͞o abuse
for	ou out
ŭ cut	ə ago,
ûr fur	item,
th the	pencil,
th thin	atom,
hw which	circus
zh vision	ər butter

corps-à-corps

crayfish

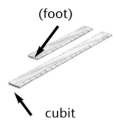

(foot)

cubit

cutter

cray•fish (krā´ fĭsh´) —*n.* A water animal that looks like a lobster but is much smaller.

cres•cen•do (krə shĕn´ dō) —*v.* **crescendoed.** To gradually increase in volume.

cre•vice (krĕv´ ĭs) —*n.* A narrow crack or opening.

crin•kle (krĭng´ kəl) —*v.* **crinkled.** To form wrinkles.

croon (krōōn) —*v.* To hum or sing softly.

crop (krŏp) —*n.* 1. A small pouch in a bird's digestive system that stores partly digested food. 2. Plants grown for their grain, fruit, or other parts that can be eaten.

crouch (krouch) —*v.* **crouched.** To stoop; to bend close to the ground.

crow•hop (krō´ hŏp) —*v.* **crowhopped.** To jump in a stiff-legged manner so that all four hooves are off the ground at the same time.

crys•tal•lize (krĭs´ tə līz´) —*v.* **crystallized, crystallizes.** 1. To form crystals. 2. To coat with crystals, such as sugars.

cu•bi•cle (kyōō´ bĭ kəl) —*n.* A small room or enclosed area.

cu•bit (kyōō´ bĭt) —*n.* A unit of measure about eighteen inches long.

cul•ti•vate (kŭl´ tə vāt) —*v.* **cultivated.** To develop by study or practice.

cur (kûr) —*n.* 1. A dog considered lowly. 2. A cowardly person.

cure (kyōor) —*v.* 1. To bring back to good health. 2. To prepare or preserve an animal skin for use.

cur•few (kûr´ fyōo) —*n.* A regulation forbidding people to be in the streets after a certain time.

cur•ry (kûr´ ē) —*n.* A blend of several very powerful spices.

curt•ly (kûrt´ lē) —*adv.* In a rude, abrupt manner.

cus•tom (kŭs´ təm) —*n.* 1. Something people do that is widely accepted or has become a tradition. 2. Something a person usually does; a habit. —*adj.* Made especially to fit a buyer or according to a buyer's instructions or desires.

cut•o•ver (kŭt´ ō´ vər) —*v.* To circle the blade over the opponent's foil.

cut•ter (kŭt´ ər) —*n.* A lightly guarded motorboat used by the coast guard.

D

dachs•hund (däks´ hōont) —*n.* A small dog with a long body, drooping ears, and very short legs.

dain•ty (dān´ tē) —*adj.* Delicate; discriminating.

darn (därn) —*v.* **darning.** To mend cloth by interweaving long stitches of thread or yarn across a hole.

dart (därt) —*v.* **darting.** To move quickly and suddenly.

day sail•er (dā sā´ lər) —*n.* A small sailboat for day trips.

ă	pat	ĕ	pet
ā	pay	ē	be
âr	care	ĭ	pit
ä	father	ī	pie
îr	fierce	oi	oil
ŏ	pot	ōō	book
ō	go	ōō	boot
ô	paw,	yōō	abuse
	for	ou	out
ŭ	cut	ə	ago,
ûr	fur		item,
th	the		pencil,
th	thin		atom,
hw	which		circus
zh	vision	ər	but

de•bris (də brē´) —*n*. The scattered pieces or remains of something that has been broken, destroyed, or thrown away; rubble.

de•ceive (dĭ sēv´) —*v*. To make a person believe something that is not true; to mislead.

de•con•tam•i•nate (dē´ kən tăm´ ə nāt´) —*v*. To destroy impurities or pollution.

deft (dĕft) —*adj*. Quick and skillful. —**deftly** *adv*. In a quick and skillful manner.

de•fy (dĭ fī´) —*v*. To resist or challenge.

de•lib•er•ate (dĭ lĭb´ ər ĭt) —*adj*. Done or said on purpose. —**deliberately** *adv*. In a purposeful manner.

del•i•cate (dĕl´ ĭ kĭt) —*adj*. 1. Requiring or needing great skill. 2. Easily spoiled or broken; fragile.

del•ta (dĕl´ tə) —*n*. A mass of sand, mud, and soil that settles at the mouth of a river.

de•mo•lish (dĭ mŏl´ ĭsh) —*v*. To get rid of completely.

de•pres•sur•ize (dē prĕsh´ ə rīz´) —*v*. **depressurized.** To release from pressure.

des•cend (dĭ sĕnd´) —*v*. **descended.** 1. To move from a higher to a lower place; to go or come down. 2. To come upon in a sudden manner.

des•ert[1] (dĕz´ ərt) —*n*. A very dry region covered with sand or pebbles.

de•sert[2] (dĭ zûrt´) —*v*. **deserted.** 1. To abandon or forsake. 2. To leave empty or alone.

de•ser•tion (dĭ zûr´ shən) —*n*. 1. Abandonment. 2. Leaving a responsibility without permission, especially a military post.

des•pair (dĭ spâr´) —*n*. Lack of all hope.

des•ti•na•tion (dĕs´ tə nā´ shən) —*n*. The end or goal of a journey.

des•ti•tute (dĕs´ tĭ tōōt´) —*adj*. Utterly lacking; poor.

de•tain (dĭ tān´) —*v*. **detained.** To slow down or delay.

de•tour (dē´ tōōr´) —*v*. To take a path other than the one planned.

de•vice (dĭ vīs´) —*n*. 1. Something that is made or used for a special purpose. 2. A plan, scheme, or trick.

di•ag•nose (dī´ əg nōs´) —*v*. **diagnosed.** To identify or distinguish clearly, especially a disease.

di•a•lect (dī´ ə lĕkt´) —*n*. A way of speaking a language in different places or parts of a country.

di•a•logue (dī´ ə lŏg´) —*n*. The words spoken by characters in a play or story.

dig•ni•ty (dĭg´ nĭ tē) —*n*. Worthiness or honorableness.

dire straits (dīr strāts) Urgent or desperate circumstances.

dis•card (dĭ skärd´) —*v*. **discarded.** To throw away.

dis•cern (dĭ sûrn´) —*v*. To recognize differences; to judge.

delta

descend

detour

drench

dugout

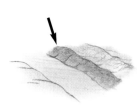

embankment

ephah

dis•charge (dĭs chärj´) —*v.* **discharged.** To release from work, service, or jail; to dismiss.

dis•dain (dĭs dān´) —*v.* **disdained.** To show or feel contempt or scorn.
—*n.* Contempt or scorn.
—**disdainfully** *adv.* Acting in a scornful or contemptuous manner.

dis•en•gage (dĭs´ ĕn gāj´) —*v.* 1. To circle one's blade under an opponent's foil. 2. To release from something that holds back.

dis•gust (dĭs gŭst´) —*v.* To cause a feeling of strong dislike or loathing; to sicken.

dis•mount (dĭs mount´) —*v.* **dismounted.** To get off or down.

dis•patch•er (dĭs păch´ ər) —*n.* One who sends out messages.

Dis•sent•er (dĭ sĕn´ tər) —*n.* One who refused to accept the doctrines of the Church of England.

dis•tinct•ly (dĭ stĭngkt´ lē) —*adv.* Clearly; definitely.

dis•tin•guish (dĭ stĭng´ gwĭsh) —*v.* **distinguished.** To set apart; to make different.

dis•tract (dĭ străkt´) —*v.* **distracted.** To draw away the mind or attention of; to divert.

do•jo (dō´ jō) —*n.* A school for learning martial arts.

dou•bly (dŭb´ lē) —*adv.* In a double manner; to a great extent.

draft (drăft) —*v.* **drafted.** To select for special service, especially for the military.
—*n.* 1. A current of air. 2. A rough sketch, plan, or outline.

drench (drĕnch) —*v.* **drenching.** To wet completely; to soak.

drov•er (drō´ vər) —*n.* One who drives cattle or sheep.

dug•out (dŭg´ out´) —*n.* A boat made by hollowing out a special type of log.

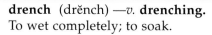

ear•nest[1] (ûr´ nĭst) —*adj.* Serious and sincere.

ear•nest[2] (ûr´ nĭst) —*n.* Money given in advance as part of a payment.

ec•sta•tic (ĕk stăt´ ĭk) —*adj.* Marked by a feeling of great happiness or joy.

e•lim•i•nate (ĭ lĭm´ ə nāt) —*v.* **eliminated.** To get rid of; to remove.

em•bank•ment (ĕm băngk´ mənt) —*n.* A mound of earth or stone built to hold back water or hold up a road.

e•merge (ĭ mûrj´) —*v.* **emerged.** To come into view; to appear.

em•is•sar•y (ĕm´ ĭ sĕr´ ē) —*n.* **emissaries.** An agent or messenger.

en•a•ble (ĕ nā´ bəl) —*v.* **enabled.** To make possible; to give ability to.

en•coun•ter (ĕn koun´ tər) —*v.* **encountered.** To come upon or meet.

en•vi•sion (ĕn vĭzh´ ən) —*v.* **envisioned.** To imagine; to form a picture in the mind.

e•phah (ē´ fə) —*n.* An ancient measurement nearly equal to a bushel.

ep•i•sode (ĕp´ ĭ sōd) —*n.* An event in one's life or experience.

er•mine (ûr´ mĭn) —*n.* 1. An animal whose fur in winter is white with a black tip. For the rest of the year, its fur is brown. The ermine is a kind of weasel. 2. The white fur of an ermine.

es•sen•tial (ĭ sĕn´ shəl) —*adj.* Of the greatest importance.

et•i•quette (ĕt´ ĭ kĕt) —*n.* A set of rules for behaving properly in different situations.

et•y•mol•o•gy (ĕt´ ə mŏl´ ə jē) —*n.* The history of a word, including where it came from and how it got its present form and meaning.

e•va•sion (ĭ vā´ zhən) —*n.* Avoiding or getting away from something or someone.

ev•er•glade (ĕv´ ər glād) —*n.* A large area of marshland covered with tall grasses.

ev•o•lu•tion (ĕv´ ə lōō´ shən) —*n.* The imagined processes by which living things supposedly formed by themselves without a Creator and then somehow kept improving themselves.
—**evolutionary** *adj.* Of the theory of evolution.

ev•o•lu•tion•ist (ĕv´ ə lōō´ shə nĭst) —*n.* A person who believes and promotes the theory of evolution.

ex•act (ĭg zăkt´) —*v.* **exacted.** To demand the payment of.
—*adj.* Correct or accurate in every detail.
—**exactly** *adv.* 1. Without any change or mistake; precisely; accurately. 2. In every respect; just.

ex•ile (ĕg´ zil´) —*n.* One who has been forced to leave his home or country.

ex•por•ta•tion (ĕk´ spôr tā´ shən) —*n.* Shipment to another country for sale.

ex•tend (ĭk stĕnd´) —*v.* To reach or stretch.

ex•tent (ĭk stĕnt´) —*n.* The point or degree to which something extends.

ex•tinc•tion (ĭg stĭngkt´ shən) —*n.* The state of being no longer in existence.

ex•tract (ĭk străkt´) —*v.* **extracted.** To pull out with force.

ermine

fac•tu•al (făk´ chōō əl) —*adj.* Based on or including facts.

fal•ter (fôl´ tər) —*v.* **faltering.** To move unsteadily; to stumble.
—**falteringly** *adv.* In an unstable manner.

fare (fâr) —*v.* To get along; to survive.
—*n.* The price of a ride on a bus, train, or other vehicle.

far•thing (fär´ thĭng) —*n.* A British coin worth less than a penny.

faux (fō) —*adj.* Fake; artificial.

feat (fēt) —*n.* An achievement; an act of courage.

fea•ture (fē´ chər) —*n.* A part or quality that stands out; something that can be noticed.

fee•bly (fē´ blē) —*adv.* In a manner without strength; weakly.

ă	pat	ĕ	pet
ā	pay	ē	be
âr	care	ĭ	pit
ä	father	ī	pie
îr	fierce	oi	oil
ŏ	pot	ŏŏ	book
ō	go	ōō	boot
ô	paw,	yōō	abuse
	for	ou	out
ŭ	cut	ə	ago,
ûr	fur		item,
th	the		pencil,
th	thin		atom,
hw	which		circus
zh	vision	ər	butter

ferry

feint (fānt) —*v.* **feinted.** To pretend to attack in order to draw an opponent's defense away.

fen•nel (fĕn´ əl) —*n.* A plant with clusters of small yellow flowers and seeds that are used in seasoning.

fer•ry (fĕr´ ē) —*n.* A boat used to carry people back and forth across a body of water.

fer•vent (fûr´ vənt) —*adj.* Showing warmth or enthusiasm.

fit•ful (fĭt´ fəl) —*adj.* Irregular or interrupted. —**fitfully** *adv.* In a fitful manner.

fix•ture (fĭks´ chər) —*n.* Something firmly fastened in place.

flail (flāl) —*v.* **flailing.** To swing wildly about.

flask (flăsk) —*n.* A small bottle with a narrow neck.

fuselage

fledg•ling (flĕj´ lĭng) —*n.* A young bird just learning to fly.

fleet•ing (flēt´ ĭng) —*adj.* Quickly passing.

flick (flĭk) —*v.* **flicked.** To give a light, quick blow. —*n.* A light, quick blow.

flinch (flĭnch) —*v.* To pull back quickly in pain or fear; to wince.

flint (flĭnt) —*n.* A type of quartz used to make a spark.

flit (flĭt) —*v.* **flitted.** To move in a quick and light way.

galabia

floun•der (floun´ der) —*v.* **floundered.** To move in a clumsy way or with difficulty; to struggle.

flour•ish (flûr´ ĭsh) —*v.* **flourishing.** To vigorously wave, gesture, or display.

foil (foil) —*n.* A long, light, thin sword used in fencing.

for•age (fôr´ ĭj) —*v.* To search for food.

franc (frăngk) —*n.* French currency.

fran•ti•cal•ly (frăn´ tĭ klē) —*adv.* In a frantic manner.

fren•zy (frĕn´ zē) —*n.* Wild, energetic excitement.

friv•o•lous (frĭv´ ə ləs) —*adj.* Not serious; unimportant.

frock coat (frŏk kōt) —*n.* A smock-like garment worn by men in olden times.

fur•row (fûr´ ō) —*n.* A deep wrinkle in the forehead.

fu•se•lage (fyōō´ sə läzh) —*n.* The main body of an airplane.

G

ga•la•bi•a (jə lä´ bē ə) —*n.* A long flowing garment worn mostly in Muslim countries.

gang•way (găng´ wā) —*n.* A passageway along the deck of a ship.

gape (gāp) —*v.* **gaped.** To stare at something with one's mouth open.

gar•ble (gär´ bəl) —*v.* **garbled.** To disorder; to scramble.

gaunt•let (gônt´ lĭt) —*n.* 1. A protective glove used by medieval knights. 2. A challenge.

gawk (gôk) —*v.* **gawking.** To stare rudely.

ga•zelle (gə zĕl´) —*n.* A very swift, deerlike animal of Asia and Africa.

ge•o•graph•i•cal (jē´ ə grăf´ ĭ kəl) —*adj.* Of or having to do with geography.

ges•ture (jĕs´ chər) —*v.* To move a body part to express emotion. —*n.* A movement of a body part, made to help express a feeling.

gi (gē) —*n.* A uniform used in the martial arts made up of loose cotton pants, a tunic, and a belt.

gib•lets (jĭb´ lĭts) —*n.* The heart, liver, or gizzard of a bird.

gid•dy (gĭd´ ē) —*adj.* Dizzy; feeling the head spin.

glazed (glāzd) —*adj.* Having a smooth, shiny coating.

glide (glīd) —*v.* In fencing, to exert pressure on an opponent's blade with the foil and slide it across to score on the opponent's jacket.

glint (glĭnt) —*v.* **glinted, glinting.** To gleam or flash briefly.

gnarled (närld) —*adj.* 1. Roughened as from age. 2. Knotted and twisted.

goi•ter (goi´ tər) —*n.* Swelling of the thyroid gland.

good•man (good´ mən) —*n.* A courteous old-time title for a man who was not a noble.

grade (grād) —*n.* 1. A class or year in school. 2. The amount of slope in a road or other surface.

grave (grāv) —*n.* A place of burial. —*adj.* Extremely serious; important. —**gravely** *adv.* In a serious solemn manner.

greaves (grēvz) —*n.* Leg armor worn below the knee.

grim (grĭm) —*adj.* Gloomy.

grip•ping (grĭp´ ĭng) —*adj.* Holding the interest of.

grope (grōp) —*v.* **groped.** To feel about; to search blindly or uncertainly.

grove (grōv) —*n.* A group of trees without underbrush among them.

gruffly (grŭf´ lē) —*adv.* In an unfriendly or harsh manner.

gur•gle (gûr´ gəl) —*v.* **gurgled.** To flow with a low bubbling sound.

gust (gŭst) —*n.* A sudden, strong breeze.

gauntlet

grove

ă	pat	ĕ	pet
ā	pay	ē	be
âr	care	ĭ	pit
ä	father	ī	pie
îr	fierce	oi	oil
ŏ	pot	ŏŏ	book
ō	go	ōō	boot
ô	paw,	yōō	abuse
	for	ou	out
ŭ	cut	ə	ago,
ûr	fur		item,
th	the		pencil,
th	thin		atom,
hw	which		circus
zh	vision	ər	butter

H

hack•a•more (hăk´ ə môr) —*n.* A rope halter used to break horses into wearing a bridle.

hale (hāl) —*adj.* Healthy, robust.

ham•mock (hăm´ ək) —*n.* A swinging bed made of rope or strong fabric and hung in the air between two supports.

hammock

harvesting

hedgehog

hand•guard (hănd´ gärd) —*n.* A rounded shield between the hand-grip and blade on a fencing foil or on a sword.

han•ker•ing (hăng´ kər ĭng) —*n.* A desire to have something or to do something.

ha'penny (hă´ pə nē) —*n.* A British coin worth half a penny.

har•den (här´ dn) —*v.* **hardened.** To make unfeeling.

har•dy (här´ dē) —*adj.* Strong and healthy; robust.

har•row (hăr´ ō) —*v.* **harrowing.** To break up and level off plowed ground.

har•vest (här´vĭst) —*v.* **harvesting.** To gather in a crop. —*n.* The crop that is gathered.

hasp (hăsp) —*n.* The metal loop to which a padlock is secured to lock a door.

haste (hāst) —*v.* **hasted.** To hurry or use speed in moving or getting something done.

hatch[1] (hăch) —*v.* **hatched, hatches.** 1. To break open and produce young. 2. To come out of the egg.

hatch[2] (hăch) —*n.* 1. A small door. 2. An opening in the deck of a ship that leads to a lower deck or to the hold.

hatch•el (hăch´ əl) —*v.* To separate fibers using a comb.

hay•wire (hā´ wīr) —*adj.* Not working properly; broken.

hearth (härth) —*n.* The brick or stone floor in front of a fireplace.

heave (hēv) —*v.* **heaved.** 1. To raise, lift, or throw with effort or force; to hoist. 2. To utter with a long, deep breath.

hedge•hog (hĕj´ hôg) —*n.* A small animal whose back is covered with short, stiff spines. It rolls itself into a spiny ball to protect itself.

herd (hûrd) —*v.* **herded, herding.** To gather, keep, or drive together.

her•e•tic (hĕr´ ĭ tĭk) —*n.* One who disagrees with established religion; literally, one whose religious beliefs condemn his soul.

her•i•tage (hĕr´ ĭ tĭj) —*n.* Something passed down from preceding generations.

her•ring (hĕr´ ĭng) —*n.* A salt-water fish well liked for its taste.

hes•i•tant (hĕz´ ĭ tənt) —*adj.* Stopping or waiting because one is not sure; doubtful. —**hesitantly** *adv.* In a doubtful manner.

hes•i•tate (hĕz´ ĭ tāt) —*v.* **hesitated.** To stop or wait because of doubt.

high•tail (hī´ tāl) —*v. slang.* To get away as fast as possible.

hilt (hĭlt) —*n.* The handle of a sword.

hitch (hĭch) —*v.* **hitched.** To tie or fasten with a rope, strap, loop, or ring.

hoard (hôrd) —*n.* A hidden supply of goods or valuables.

ă	pat	ĕ	pet
ā	pay	ē	be
âr	care	ĭ	pit
ä	father	ī	pie
îr	fierce	oi	oil
ŏ	pot	o͝o	book
ō	go	o͞o	boot
ô	paw,	yo͞o	abuse
	for	ou	out
ŭ	cut	ə	ago,
ûr	fur		item,
th	the		pencil,
th	thin		atom,
hw	which		circus
zh	vision	ər	butter

528

hob•ble (hŏb´ əl) —*v.* **hobbled.** To use a rope to restrict free movement of an animal.
—*n.* A rope or strap used to prevent free movement of an animal.

hob•by•horse (hŏb´ ē hôrs´) —*n.* A child's toy made of a stick with a toy horse's head on one end.

hogs•head (hôgz´ hĕd) —*n.* A large barrel or cask with a volume or capacity of sixty-three gallons.

hoist (hoist) —*v.* **hoisted.** To lift a heavy object, often with mechanical help.

hol•low (hŏl´ ō) —*v.* To make or become hollow.
—*n.* 1. An empty space; a gap or cavity. 2. A sunken area; depression. 3. A small valley.
—*adj.* A reverberating sound.

holt (hōlt) —*n.* An otter's den.

hom•i•ny (hŏm´ ə nē) —*n.* Kernels of corn hulled and boiled as a food.

horn•book (hôrn´ bŏŏk) —*n.* A one-page primer that was used in early America to teach children to read. The page was often mounted on a paddle-shaped piece of wood and covered with a transparent sheet of horn.

host (hōst) —*n.* 1. A large number; a multitude. 2. A person or group who invites guests and entertains them.

hov•er (hŭv´ ər) —*v.* **hovered, hovers, hovering.** 1. To stay in one place in the air; to float or fly without moving much. 2. To stay or wait nearby.

hub•bub (hŭb´ ŭb) —*n.* Confused noise.

hu•mid•i•fi•er (hyōō mĭd´ ə fī´ ər) —*n.* A device for adding moisture to the air.

hunch (hŭnch) —*v.* **hunched.** To make rounded by drawing up or in.

hur•dy-gur•dy (hûr´ dē gûr´ dē) —*n.* A instrument played by turning a crank.

huz•za (hə zä´) —*n.* A shout of joy; a cheer.

hwa•rang-do (hwä răng´ dō´) —*n.* A Korean martial art whose name literally means "the way of the flower of manhood." It was studied by the royal bodyguard of the emperor.

hy•ae•na or **hy•e•na** (hī ē´ nə) —*n.* An Asian or African animal that looks rather like a large dog.

hys•ter•ics (hĭ stĕr´ ĭks) —*n.* Excited or frightened behavior.

ig•nite (ĭg nīt´) —*v.* **ignited.** 1. To set fire to; to catch fire. 2. To inspire passion or interest.

il•lu•mi•nate (ĭ lōō´ mə nāt´) —*v.* **illuminated.** To light an area.

im•bue (ĭm byōō´) —*v.* **imbued.** To inspire.

im•mense•ly (ĭ mĕns´ lē) —*adv.* Greatly, hugely.

im•per•ti•nent (ĭm pûr´ tn ənt) —*adj.* Improper, rude, insolent.

hobbyhorse

hurdy-gurdy

hyaena

ignite

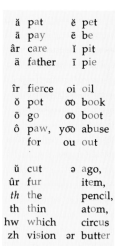

inlet

jade

ă	pat	ĕ	pet
ā	pay	ē	be
âr	care	ĭ	pit
ä	father	ī	pie
îr	fierce	oi	oil
ŏ	pot	ŏŏ	book
ō	go	ŏŏ	boot
ô	paw,	yŏŏ	abuse
	for	ou	out
ŭ	cut	ə	ago,
ûr	fur		item,
th	the		pencil,
th	thin		atom,
hw	which		circus
zh	vision	ər	butter

im•ple•ment (ĭm´ plə mənt) —*n.* A tool or piece of equipment used to do a particular job or task.

in•aud•i•ble (ĭn ô´ də bəl) —*adj.* Too quiet to be heard.

in•cor•po•rat•ed (ĭn kôr´ pə rā´ tĭd) —*adj.* Formed into or organized as a legal corporation.

in•den•ta•tion (ĭn´ dĕn tā´ shən) —*n.* A dent or hole in the surface of something.

in•den•ture (ĭn dĕn´ chər) —*n.* A contract binding service on one person to another for a specific time. —**indentured** *adj.* Bound to service to another by a contract for a specific amount of time.

in•dif•fer•ent (ĭn dĭf´ ər ənt) —*adj.* Without strong feelings; careless.

in•di•gest•i•ble (ĭn´ dĭ jĕs´ tə bəl) —*adj.* Inedible; unable to be used by the body.

in•dis•posed (ĭn´ dĭ spōzd´) —*adj.* Mildly ill.

in•ex•pli•ca•bly (ĭn ĕk´ splĭ kə blē) —*adv.* Without explanation or reason.

in•fa•mous (ĭn´ fə məs) —*adj.* Having a bad reputation.

in•fu•ri•ate (ĭn fyŏŏr´ ē āt´) —*v.* **infuriated.** To make extremely angry.

in•hab•it (ĭn hăb´ ĭt) —*v.* To live in; to make a home.

in•let (ĭn´ lĕt) —*n.* A bay or other recess along the coast.

in•ner•most (ĭn´ ər mōst) —*adj.* Most personal and private.

in•sist (ĭn sĭst´) —*v.* **insisted.** To be firm in making a demand. —**insistent** *adj.* Firm in making a demand.

in•stinc•tive (ĭn stĭngk´ tĭv) —*adj.* Coming from natural impulses.

in•tense•ly (ĭn tĕns´ lē) —*adv.* With strong emotion.

in•tent (ĭn tĕnt´) —*adj.* Focused; concentrated. —**intently** *adv.* With great concentration.

in•ten•tion (ĭn tĕn´ shən) —*n.* Purpose; plan.

in•ter•com (ĭn´ tər kŏm) —*n.* A device used for talking between different parts of a building, ship, or aircraft.

in•vest (ĭn vĕst´) —*v.* To spend in order to gain more.

in•vol•un•tar•y (ĭn vŏl´ ən tĕr´ ē) —*adj.* Not subject to the control of the will. —**involuntarily** *adv.* In a manner without the control of the will.

J

jack•al (jăk´ əl) —*n.* An African or Asian animal that looks like a dog. It often feeds on what is left of animals that lions or leopards have killed as prey.

jack•tar (jăk´ tär) —*n.* A sailor.

jade (jād) —*n.* A hard green or white stone often used in jewelry or ornaments.

jag•uar (jăg´ wär) —*n.* A large, spotted wild cat of Central and South America. The jaguar looks very much like a leopard.

jerk•in (jûr´ kĭn) —*n.* A short jacket worn by men during the fifteenth and sixteenth centuries. Jerkins were usually close fitting and sleeveless and were often made of leather.

jess (jĕs) —*n.* **jesses.** A short strap attached to the leg of a bird. A leash may be attached to the jess.

jet•ti•son (jĕt´ ĭ sən) —*v.* To eject into space.

jig•gle (jĭg´ əl) —*v.* To move back and forth with small, jerky motions. —**jiggly** *adj.* Having the motion of jiggling.

john•ny•cake (jŏn´ ē kāk) —*n.* A pancake made with cornmeal.

jos•tle (jŏs´ əl) —*v.* **jostling.** To push or bump.

joust (joust) —*n.* A combat between two knights on horses.

jut (jŭt) —*v.* **jutting.** To extend beyond the main part of something.

ka•ra•te (kə rä´ tē) —*n.* A style of self-defense in which the person uses hands and feet as weapons.

keel¹ (kēl) —*n.* A strong beam of wood or metal that runs down the center of the bottom of a ship or boat.

keel² (kēl) —*v.* **keeled.** To fall down.

keen (kēn) —*adj.* 1. Sharp; acute. 2. Intense; piercing. 3. Having a quick mind; intelligent. 4. Desiring greatly. —**keenly** *adv.* In an intense manner.

kin•dle (kĭn´ dl) —*v.* To stir up or arouse.

kin•dling box (kĭnd´ lĭng bŏks) —*n.* A box used for the storage of small firewood.

joust

la•goon (lə gōōn´) —*n.* A small body of water separated from the sea by sandbars or coral reefs.

la•ment (lə mĕnt´) —*v.* To regret deeply; to mourn.

lank•y (lăng´ kē) —*adj.* Tall and thin.

la•ser (lā´ zər) —*n.* A highly focused beam of light.

levy (lĕv´ ē) —*v.* **levied.** To impose or collect a tax, tariff, or other fee.

lib•er•ate (lĭb´ ə rāt) —*v.* To set free.

lieu•ten•ant (lōō tĕn´ ənt) —*n.* An officer in the military who ranks below a captain.

keel

limb (lĭm) —*n.* A jointed extension of the body, such as an arm or a leg.

lim•ber (lĭm´ bər) —*v.* **limbering.** To make supple or flexible.

live•li•hood (līv´ lē hŏŏd) —*n.* The way a person earns a living.

lodg•ing (lŏj´ ĭng) —*n.* A temporary place to sleep.

loin•cloth (loin´ klôth) —*n.* A piece of cloth worn around the waist.

loom (lōōm) —*n.* A machine or frame for weaving threads to make cloth.

laser

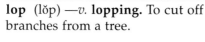

lop (lŏp) —*v.* **lopping.** To cut off branches from a tree.

lope (lōp) —*v.* To run or walk with a steady gait.

lull (lŭl) —*v.* **lulled.** To cause to sleep or rest.

lum•ber (lŭm´ bər) —*v.* **lumbered.** To move or walk in a clumsy manner.

lu•na•tic (lōō´ nə tĭk) —*n.* An insane or foolish person.

lunge (lŭnj) —*v.* **lunged, lunges.** To make a sudden, forceful attack. —*n.* A sudden attack.

lurch (lûrch) —*v.* **lurched.** To jerk violently.

lure (lŏŏr) —*v.* To attract in order to capture. —*n.* Something that attracts.

lust (lŭst) —*n.* A desire that is too strong and leads to sin.

lux•u•ry (lŭg´ zhə rē) —*n.* Something that is not considered necessary but that gives pleasure, enjoyment, or comfort.

M

mag•is•trate (măj´ ĭ strāt´) —*n.* A local government official.

main•land (mān´ lănd) —*n.* The main part of a country, territory, or continent, not including the islands off the coast.

main•stay (mān´ stā) —*n.* A chief support.

main•te•nance (mān´ tə nəns) —*n.* The act of caring for something.

make•shift (māk´ shĭft´) —*adj.* Something used as a temporary substitution.

mal•let (măl´ ĭt) —*n.* A sports tool with a wooden head and a long handle.

ma•neu•ver (mə nōō´ vər) —*v.* **maneuvering.** To move or guide in a clever, planned way.

man•grove (măn´ grōv) —*n.* A tropical tree or shrub that has many roots growing above the ground. Mangroves form dense thickets in marshes and along shores.

mar•i•on•ette (măr´ ē ə nĕt´) —*n.* A puppet operated by strings.

ma•roon (mə rōōn´) —*v.* To leave a person helpless and alone in a deserted place; to strand.

mar•row (măr´ ō) —*n.* The soft material inside bones.

mar•tial art (mär´ shəl ärt) —*n.* An oriental art of combat, usually studied as a sport or recreation.

mar•vel (mär´ vəl) —*v.* To be filled with wonder or admiration.

may•hap (mā´ hăp´) —*adv.* Perhaps.

mean (mēn) —*v.* 1. To have in mind. 2. To try to say. 3. To have sense of; to be defined as. 4. To bring about as a consequence. —*adj.* 1. Not kind or good. 2. Hard to handle; troublesome. 3. Low in value. —**means** *n.* 1. Something that is used to help reach a goal. 2. Money; wealth.

med•dle (mĕd´ l) —*v.* To interfere in other people's business.

mainland

mallet

marionette

me•di•eval (mē´ dē ē´ vəl) —*adj.* Of, from, or like the Middle Ages, or the period of European history from about A.D. 500 to about 1400.

mem•brane (mĕm´ brān) —*n.* A thin wall of tissue in living things.

men•ac•ing•ly (mĕn´ ĭs ĭng lē) —*adv.* In a threatening manner.

men•had•en (mĕn hăd´ n) —*n.* A species of fish of the American Atlantic and Gulf waters.

me•ni•al (mē´ nē əl) —*adj.* Relating to a task considered lowly.

mesh (mĕsh) —*n.* A material with many small open spaces.

met•a•phor (mĕt´ ə fôr´) —*n.* A figure of speech that compares one thing with another without using the words *like* or *as.*

mill (mĭl) —*v.* **milling.** To move around in a confused way. —*n.* 1. A machine that grinds or crushes something into very small pieces. 2. A building with machines for grinding corn, wheat, or other grains into flour.

mince (mĭns) —*n.* A mixture of finely chopped fruit, spices, suet, and sometimes meat; used as a pie filling; **mincemeat.**

mirth•ful (mûrth´ fəl) —*adj.* Full of gladness.

mis•hap (mĭs´ hăp) —*n.* An unfortunate accident.

mod•i•fy (mŏd´ ə fī) —*v.* To change; to alter.

mo•lest (mə lĕst´) —*v.* To bother or destroy.

moor•ing line (moͦor´ ĭng līn) —*n.* A line used to tie up or anchor a boat.

moral (môr´ əl) —*n.* The lesson taught by a fable, story, or event; the basic message. —*adj.* 1. Conforming to a standard of right conduct. 2. Teaching what is right conduct or behavior.

muck (mŭk) —*n.* A moist, sticky mixture, especially of mud and filth.

muff (mŭf) —*n.* A tube of fur or cloth into which hands can be put to keep them warm.

muff

mull (mŭl) —*v.* **mulled.** To ponder.

mul•let (mŭl´ ĭt) —*n.* A type of edible fish.

mur•ky (mûr´ kē) —*adj.* Stirred up; muddy.

mus•lin (mŭz´ lĭn) —*n.* A cotton cloth with a plain weave.

mus•ter (mŭs´ tər) —*v.* **mustered.** To gather; to assemble. —*n.* A gathering, especially of troops.

must•y (mŭs´ tē) —*adj.* Stale in odor or taste.

mu•ti•ny (myoͦot´ n ē) —*n.* Open rebellion against leaders, especially by sailors.

ă	pat	ě	pet
ā	pay	ē	be
âr	care	ĭ	pit
ä	father	ī	pie
îr	fierce	oi	oil
ŏ	pot	oͦo	book
ō	go	oͦo	boot
ô	paw,	yoͦo	abuse
	for	ou	out
ŭ	cut	ə	ago,
ûr	fur		item,
th	the		pencil,
th	thin		atom,
hw	which		circus
zh	vision	ər	butter

N

nav•i•gate (năv´ ĭ gāt) —*v.* To plan, guide, and control the course of a ship or aircraft.

notch

orangutan

peasant

ă	pat	ĕ	pet
ā	pay	ē	be
âr	care	ĭ	pit
ä	father	ī	pie
îr	fierce	oi	oil
ŏ	pot	ŏŏ	book
ō	go	ōō	boot
ô	paw,	yōō	abuse
	for	ou	out
ŭ	cut	ə	ago,
ûr	fur		item,
th	the		pencil,
th	thin		atom,
hw	which		circus
zh	vision	ər	butter

nee•dle (nēd´ l) —*v.* To tease, annoy, or provoke.

niche (nĭch) —*n.* A cranny or hole in a surface.

nick (nĭk) —*n.* A small cut or chip in a surface or edge.
—*idiom* **nick of time.** The moment before it is too late for something to happen.

notch (nŏch) —*n.* 1. A V-shaped cut. 2. A degree or level.

nub (nŭb) —*n.* The essence or core.

nudge (nŭj) —*v.* **nudged.** To push gently.

O

ob•so•lete (ŏb´ sə lēt´) —*adj.* No longer used; out of date.

ob•struc•tion (əb strŭk´ shən) —*n.* Something blocking the path of another thing.

off•ing (ô´ fĭng) —*n.* In the near future; soon.

off•side (ôf´ sīd´) —*adj.* Illegally ahead of the ball in soccer or football.

o•paque (ō pāk´) —*adj.* Not reflecting light; not shiny; dull.

op•po•nent (ə pō´ nənt) —*n.* A person who is against another person in a fight or contest.

o•rang•u•tan (ô răng´ ə tăn) —*n.* A large ape that lives on islands south of Asia.

or•di•nar•y (ôr´ dn ĕr´ ē) —*adj.* Usual; normal.

or•ner•y (ôr´ nə rē) —*adj.* Mean-spirited and disagreeable.

out•crop•ping (out´ krŏp ĭng) —*n.* Bedrock that rises above the ground.

out•ra•geous (out rā´ jəs) —*adj.* Far from what is right or proper; shocking; terrible.

P

pale (pāl) —*v.* **paling.** To cause to become whitish in color.

pal•let (păl´ ĭt) —*n.* A temporary bed arranged on the floor.

pan•ni•kin (păn´ nĭ kĭn) —*n.* A small saucepan or cup made of metal.

parched (pärcht) —*adj.* Dried or roasted.

par•lia•ment (pär´ lə mənt) —*n.* A governing body much like the American Congress.

par•ry (păr´ ē) —*v.* To ward off an attack.

pas•sion (păsh´ ən) —*n.* A powerful or very strong feeling.

pa•tent (păt´ nt) —*n.* A document given by the government to an inventor or a company. A patent gives a person or company the right to be the only one to make, use, or sell an invention for a certain number of years.

pa•thet•ic (pə thĕt´ ĭk) —*adj.* Causing one to feel pity or sorrow; sad; pitiful.

paw-paw (pô´ pô) —*n.* A tropical evergreen tree with a large yellow flower.

peas•ant (pĕz´ ənt) —*n.* A poor farm worker.

peeve (pēv) —*v.* **peeved.** To annoy; to make resentful.

pe•nal•ize (pē´ nə līz´, pĕn´ ə līz´) —*v.* **penalized.** To punish for breaking a rule.

peril (pĕr´ əl) —*n.* The chance of harm or loss; danger.

per•sist•ent (pər sĭs´ tənt) —*adj.* Refusing to give up.

per•suade (pər swād´) —*v.* **persuaded.** To cause someone to do or believe something by arguing, begging, or reasoning; to convince.

pes•ti•cide (pĕs´ tĭ sīd´)—*n.* A chemical used to kill harmful insects.

pe•ti•tion (pə tĭsh´ ən) —*n.* A special request to someone in charge.

pheas•ant (fĕz´ ənt) —*n.* A type of bird that is large and has a long tail.

phlox (flŏks) —*n.* A plant with clusters of reddish, purple, or white flowers.

pi•ous (pī´ əs) —*adj.* Very religious or holy.

pitch (pĭch) —*v.* **pitches, pitching, pitched.** To throw; to hurl; to toss.

pi•ty (pĭt´ ē) —*n.* A feeling of sorrow for another's suffering.

plank (plăngk) —*n.* A thick, wide board.

plank•ing (plăng´ kĭng) —*n.* Boards grouped together.

plea (plē) —*n.* An urgent request.

pledge (plĕj) —*v.* To promise. —*n.* 1. A delivery of goods in payment of a debt or obligation. 2. A solemn promise.

plumb (plŭm) —*adj.* Totally; completely.

plume (plo͞om) —*v.* **plumed.** To decorate or cover with feathers.

plump (plŭmp) —*v.* **plumped.** To make well-rounded.

poise (poiz) —*n.* Balance; muscular control. —**poised** *adj.* To be balanced.

pome•gran•ate (pŏm´ grăn´ ĭt) —*n.* A tree whose fruit has a tough, reddish rind and many small seeds.

pomp (pŏmp) —*n.* A spectacular display; splendor.

pon•der•ous (pŏn´ dər əs) —*adj.* Difficult to handle because of weight or size.

pon•toon (pŏn to͞on´) —*n.* A float that attaches to a structure.

por•ce•lain (pôr´ sə lĭn) —*n.* A brittle kind of fine china.

port (pôrt) —*n.* 1. The left side of a ship as it faces forward. 2. A place along a river, lake, ocean, or other body of water where ships may dock or anchor; a harbor. 3. A city or town with a harbor.

port•ly (pôrt´ lē) —*adj.* Fat or stout.

por•tray (pôr trā´) —*v.* **portrayed.** To represent in a visual manner.

post•haste (pōst´ hāst´) —*adv.* Speedily; rapidly.

po•ten•tial (pə tĕn´ shəl) —*adj.* Not real or definite, but possible in the future.

prat•tle (prăt´ l) —*v.* **prattled.** To talk or chatter idly or meaninglessly.

pheasant

pomegranate

porcelain

pre•cise (prĭ sīs´) —*adj.* Accurate; definite.

pred•a•tor (prĕd´ ə tər) —*n.* An animal that lives by catching and eating other animals.

pre•dic•a•ment (prĭ dĭk´ ə mənt) —*n.* A troublesome or embarrassing situation.

preen (prēn) —*v.* **preening.** To smooth or clean with the beak or bill.

prep (prĕp) —*v.* To prepare for a medical procedure.

pre•side (prĭ zīd´) —*v.* To act as the authority.

press (prĕs) —*v.* **pressed, pressing.** 1. In fencing, to exert pressure on an opponents' blade. It is usually followed by a quick release. 2. To put force or pressure against; to bear down.

pre•vail (prĭ vāl´) —*v.* **prevailed.** To be greater in strength or influence; to triumph.

prey (prā) —*n.* An animal hunted or caught by another for food.

prick•le (prĭk´ əl) —*n.* A sharp spine or thorn.

pro•ces•sion (prə sĕsh´ ən) —*n.* A group of persons walking or riding in an orderly line.

pro•jec•tion (prə jĕk´ shən) —*n.* A system of intersecting lines used to help represent a spherical shape as a plane surface.

prompt•ly (prŏmpt´ lē) —*adv.* In a quick manner.

pros•pect (prŏs´ pĕkt´) —*n.* Possibility.

pro•trud•ing (prō trood´ ĭng) —*adj.* Jutting out; projecting.

prov•ince (prŏv´ ĭns) —*n.* A political territory of a country.

pry (prī) —*v.* To raise or move with a lever or wedge.

pulp (pəlp) —*n.* A soft mass of material.

pum•mel (pŭm´ əl) —*v.* To pound or beat.

pup•pet•eer (pŭp´ ĭ tîr´) —*n.* One who operates puppets.

py•thon (pī´ thŏn´) —*n.* A very large, nonpoisonous snake of Africa, Asia, and Australia. Pythons coil around and squeeze to death the animals they eat.

Q

qualm (kwäm, kwôm) —*n.* A feeling of doubt.

quartz (kwôrts) —*n.* A milk-white mineral found commonly in rock around the world.

quay (kē, kā) —*n.* A stone wharf or strong bank where ships are loaded or unloaded.

que•ry (kwîr´ ē) —*n.* A question; an inquiry.

quest (kwĕst) —*n.* A search, especially for something valuable.

R

rack (răk) —*v.* To strain or try very hard.
—*n.* A pole with pegs or a frame with pegs or shelves.

python

procession

quartz

ram•rod (răm´ rŏd´) —*n.* A straight metal rod used to push the ammunition into the barrel of a gun.

ranks (răngks) —*n.* All soldiers who are not officers.

realm (rĕlm) —*n.* A kingdom.

rec•on•cile (rĕk´ ən sīl´) —*v.* **reconciled.** To reestablish friendship between; to forgive.

re•count (rĭ kount´) —*v.* **recounted.** To tell or tell again.

re•cov•er•y (rĭ kŭv´ ə rē) —*n.* A return to a normal condition.

re•duce (rĭ dōōs´) —*v.* **reduced.** 1. To make smaller. 2. To pulverize.

ref•er•ence (rĕf´ ər əns) —*n.* 1. A note in a book that directs the reader to another page for additional information. 2. A passage or source referred to. 3. A work often used as a source of information.

ref•u•gee (rĕf´ yōō jē´) —*n.* A person who flees from his own home or country to find safety.

ref•use[1] (rĕf´ yōōs) —*n.* Something useless or worthless; trash.

re•fuse[2] (rĭ fyōōz´) —*v.* **refused.** 1. To be unwilling to do something. 2. To decline to accept; to turn down; to reject.

re•gain (rē gān´) —*v.* **regained.** To get again.

re•gale (rĭ gāl´) —*v.* **regaled.** To entertain.

reg•i•ment (rĕj´ ə mənt) —*n.* A unit of soldiers made up of two or more battalions.

reg•u•la•tion (rĕg´ yə lā´ shən) —*n.* A law or set of rules by which something is ruled.

re•gur•gi•tate (rē gûr´ jĭ tāt) —*v.* To bring back up after chewing and swallowing.

re•lay (rē´ lā) —*v.* To pass or send along.
—*n.* A crew, group, or team that relieves another; a shift.

re•lent (rĭ lĕnt´) —*v.* **relented.** To become softer and gentler in nature.

rel•ic (rĕl´ ĭk) —*n.* Something that survives from the distant past.

re•lin•quish (rĭ lĭng´ kwĭsh) —*v.* To give up or abandon.

re•luc•tant (rĭ lŭk´ tənt) —*adj.* Hesitant; unwilling.

re•morse (rĭ môrs´) —*n.* Sorrow or regret.

ren•e•gade (rĕn´ ĭ gād´) —*n.* An outlaw.

re•press (rĭ prĕs´) —*v.* **repressed.** To hold back by an act of the will.

re•proach (rĭ prōch´) —*n.* A shame; a dishonor.

rep•u•ta•tion (rĕp´ yə tā´ shən) —*n.* The general worth of someone judged by others.

re•sent (rĭ zĕnt´) —*v.* **resented.** To feel angry.
—**resentment** *n.* A bitter, angry feeling.

res•er•voir (rĕz´ ər vwär´) —*n.* 1. A container for storing liquids. 2. An extra supply; a reserve.

ă	pat	ĕ	pet
ā	pay	ē	be
âr	care	ĭ	pit
ä	father	ī	pie
îr	fierce	oi	oil
ŏ	pot	ŏŏ	book
ō	go	ōō	boot
ô	paw,	yōō	abuse
	for	ou	out
ŭ	cut	ə	ago,
ûr	fur		item,
th	the		pencil,
th	thin		atom,
hw	which		circus
zh	vision	ər	butter

rigging

rhubarb

rodent

salute

res•ig•na•tion (rĕz´ ĭg nā´ shən) —*n.* The act of giving up or quitting a position or job.

res•o•lute (rĕz´ ə loot´) —*adj.* With strong will and determination. —**resolutely** *adv.* In a determined manner.

res•o•lu•tion (rĕz´ ə loo´ shən) —*n.* An explanation; a solution.

re•solve (rĭ zŏlv´) —*v.* To decide with determination.

re•source (rē´ sôrs´) —*n.* Supplies for a task.

re•spect (rĭ spĕkt´) —*v.* **respected.** To regard or esteem. —*n.* A favorable opinion; admiration. —**respectful** *adj.* Showing proper esteem.

re•sponse (rĭ spŏns´) —*n.* An answer or reply.

re•strain (rĭ strān´) —*v.* **restrained, restraining.** To hold back by physical force.

re•straint (rĭ strānt´) —*n.* Control.

re•sume (rĭ zoom´) —*v.* **resumed.** To begin again.

re•ver•ber•ate (rĭ vûr´ bə rāt´) —*v.* To resound; to echo.

re•vive (rĭ vīv´) —*v.* **revived.** To bring back or return to life.

rhu•barb (roo´ bärb´) —*n.* A plant having large, poisonous leaves and long, fleshy stalks. The stalks are reddish or green.

rift (rĭft) —*n.* A break in rock.

rig•ging (rĭg´ ĭng) —*n.* Masts, sails, lines, and other equipment on a boat.

ri•ot (rī´ ət) —*v.* **rioting.** To take part in a wild, violent disturbance.

ri•poste (rĭ pōst´) —*n.* In fencing, a thrusting attack made after deflecting an opponent's blow.

risque (rĭsk) —*n. obsolete spelling of* **risk.** Possibility of loss or harm.

ri•val (rī´ vəl) —*n.* A competitor.

ro•bust (rō bŭst´) —*adj.* Full of health and strength.

ro•dent (rōd´ nt) —*n.* A small, nibbling animal such as a mouse, rat, squirrel, or beaver.

rogue (rōg) —*n.* 1. A dishonest person; a cheat. 2. A playfully mischievous person.

ros•ter (rŏs´ tər) —*n.* A list of names.

rouse (rouz) —*v.* **roused.** To awaken.

rud•dy (rŭd´ ē) —*adj.* Having a healthy pink or reddish color.

rue•ful•ly (roo´ fəl ē) —*adv.* Sorrowfully; regretfully.

Rug•by (rŭg´ bē) —*n.* A British game similar to football.

rum•mage (rŭm´ ĭj) —*v.* **rummaging.** To search thoroughly by moving things around.

S

sag (săg) —*v.* To sink or hang down.

sa•lute (sə loot´) —*v.* **saluted.** To greet with polite or friendly words or gestures.

sar•cas•tic (sär kăs´ tĭk) —*adj.* Using cutting, bitter remarks to make fun of someone or something. —**sarcastically** *adv.* In a cutting, bitter manner.

sat•ur•ate (săch´ ə rāt´) —*v.* **saturated.** To soak or become soaked; to fill completely.

sa•vor (sā´ vər) —*v.* **savoring.** To relish or enjoy something.

scaf•fold•ing (skăf´ əl dĭng) —*n.* A system of raised wooded frames or platforms.

scal•a•wag (skăl´ ə wăg´) —*n.* A reprobate; a rascal.

scale¹ (skāl) —*v.* **scaled.** To climb up to the top of or climb over. —*n.* 1. The size of a model, drawing, or map compared with the actual size of what it represents. 2. A series of marks placed at equally spaced distances along a line. It is used on different devices.

scale² (skāl) —*n.* An instrument or machine for weighing.

scale³ (skāl) —*n.* **scales.** One of the platelike structures that cover fish, reptiles, and certain mammals.

scav•en•ger (skăv´ ən jər) —*n.* An animal that feeds on decaying matter.

sche•ma•tic (skē măt´ ĭk) —*adj.* Having to do with a simplified diagram.

schol•ar (skŏl´ ər) —*n.* A person who has a great deal of knowledge.

scis•sor (sĭz´ ər) —*v.* **scissored.** To move in a manner resembling scissors cutting.

scoff (skŏf) —*v.* **scoffing.** To mock or treat in an unkind manner.

score (skôr) —*v.* **scored.** To make points in a game, contest, or test. —*n.* 1. A record of the points made in a game. 2. A group of twenty items. 3. A large number.

scourge (skûrj) —*v.* **scourged.** To punish by beating.

scowl (skoul) —*v.* **scowled.** To show disapproval with a frowning facial expression.

scrip (skrĭp) —*n.* A small bag or satchel used for carrying money.

script (skrĭpt) —*n.* 1. Letters or symbols written by hand; handwriting. 2. The written text of a play, motion picture, or television or radio show; a manuscript.

scuff (skŭf) —*v.* **scuffing.** To shuffle; to scrape a foot along the ground.

scur•ry (skûr´ ē) —*v.* **scurried.** To run or move quickly.

scut•tle (skŭt´ l) —*v.* **scuttled.** To move in a short, hurried manner.

scythe (sīth) —*n.* A tool with a long, curved blade attached to a long, bent handle. It is used for mowing and reaping.

seize (sēz) —*v.* **seized.** 1. To take hold of suddenly; to grab. 2. To take possession of by force; to capture. 3. To have a sudden, overwhelming desire.

scaffolding

schematic

scythe

ă	pat	ĕ	pet
ā	pay	ē	be
âr	care	ĭ	pit
ä	father	ī	pie
îr	fierce	oi	oil
ŏ	pot	o͞o	book
ō	go	o͞o	boot
ô	paw,	yo͞o	abuse
	for	ou	out
ŭ	cut	ə	ago,
ûr	fur		item,
th	the		pencil,
th	thin		atom,
hw	which		circus
zh	vision	ər	butter

shinny

shuttlecock

ă pat	ĕ pet
ā pay	ē be
âr care	ĭ pit
ä father	ī pie
îr fierce	oi oil
ŏ pot	ŏŏ book
ō go	ŏŏ boot
ô paw,	yŏŏ abuse
for	ou out
ŭ cut	ə ago,
ûr fur	item,
th the	pencil,
th thin	atom,
hw which	circus
zh vision	ər butter

sen•tence (sĕn´ təns) —*v.* To give a penalty to.
—*n.* 1. A penalty passed by a court. 2. A group of words, or sometimes one word, that tells or expresses a complete thought.

sen•ti•men•tal (sĕn´ tə mĕn´ tl) —*adj.* Easily moved by feeling or emotion.

sen•ti•nel (sĕn´ tə nəl) —*n.* A guard; a sentry.

se•vere (sə vîr´) —*adj.* Hard or harsh; stern.

shake (shāk) —*n.* A wide, flat board used as a shingle.

share•crop•per (shăr´ krŏp´ ər) —*n.* A farmer living on and farming another person's land. He gives part of his crop as rent.

sheaf (shēf) —*n.* A collection of papers.

shek•el (shĕk´ əl) —*n.* A Hebrew coin weighing about half an ounce.

shil•ling (shĭl´ ĭng) —*n.* A coin in the old British currency. It was worth about fifty cents if compared to today's dollar.

shin•ny (shĭn´ ē) —*v.* To climb by gripping and pulling with the hands and legs.

shoal (shōl) —*n.* A shallow place in a body of water.

shov•el (shŭv´ əl) —*v.* **shoveled.** To throw in a quick, rough way.

shuf•fle (shŭf´ əl) —*v.* **shuffling.** To move from place to place.

shut•tle•cock (shŭt´ l kŏk) —*n.* A piece of cork with feathers in it, used to play badminton.

sil•ver (sĭl´ vər) —*v.* **silvered.** To give a silver color to.

skim (skĭm) —*v.* **skimming.** To glide or move quickly across the top of something.

skit•ter (skĭt´ ər) —*v.* **skittered.** To skip, glide, or move rapidly along a surface.

skulk (skŭlk) —*v.* To wait in hiding; to lurk.

sky•rock•et (skī´ rŏk´ ĭt) —*v.* **sky-rocketed.** To rise quickly and suddenly.

slay (slā) —*v.* To kill violently.

sleight (slīt) —*n.* Cleverness; skillfulness.

slink (slĭngk) —*v.* **slinking.** To sneak around.

sluice•way (slŏŏs´ wā) —*n.* A man-made channel for water with a gate or valve to control the flow.

smirk (smûrk) —*v.* **smirked.** To smile in a knowing, superior manner.

smol•der (smōl´ dər) —*v.* **smoldering.** To burn with little smoke and no flame.

smote (smōt) —*v.* Past tense of *smite:* to hit or strike.

sneer (snîr) —*v.* **sneered, sneering.** To show contempt or say something with scorn.

sod•den (sŏd´ n) —*adj.* Completely soaked; full of water.

sol•i•tar•y (sŏl´ ĭ tĕr´ ē) —*adj.* Existing or living alone.

sol•i•tude (sŏl´ ĭ tōōd´) —*n.* A lonely or secluded place.

sop (sŏp) —*v.* **sopped.** To dip or soak in a liquid.

span (spăn) —*n.* Formerly, a unit of measure equal to about nine inches.

spar (spär) —*v.* To practice fighting techniques.

sphere (sfîr) —*n.* A round object like a ball or globe.

spin•ster (spĭn´ stər) —*n.* An unmarried woman past the normal age for marrying.

spir•it (spĭr´ ĭt) —*v.* **spirited.** To carry off secretly.

spruce (sprōōs) —*n.* An evergreen tree with short needles and soft wood.

squelch (skwĕlch) —*v.* To produce a squishing, sucking sound.

stag•nant (stăg´ nənt) —*adj.* Foul or stale from standing still.

stalk (stôk) —*v.* **stalked.** To move in a proud, scornful manner.

stance (stăns) —*n.* A position of readiness assumed by a fencer.

sta•ple (stā´ pəl) —*n.* A major product grown or produced in a region.

star•board (stär´ bərd) —*n.* The right-hand side of a ship as it faces forward.

state•ly (stāt´ lē) —*adj.* Elegant, dignified, or grand in appearance; majestic.

states•man (stāts´ mən) —*n.* A person who has experience, wisdom, and skill in dealing with government affairs or important public issues.

staunch (stônch) —*adj.* Firm and steadfast; true.

stave (stāv) —*n.* A staff or club.

stealth•y (stĕl´ thē) —*adj.* Marked by caution and secrecy; intending to avoid notice.

steel (stēl) —*v.* **steeling.** To make hard; to strengthen.
—*n.* Any very hard, strong metal made by combining iron and carbon.
—*adj.* Something made of steel.

stern[1] (stûrn) —*adj.* Grave and severe.
—**sternly** *adv.* In a grave and severe manner.

stern[2] (stûrn) —*n.* The rear part of a ship or boat.

stick•ball (stĭk´ bôl) —*n.* A type of baseball played with a rubber ball and a stick or broom handle for a bat.

stile (stīl) —*n.* A ladder over a fence.

stir•rup (stûr´ əp) —*n.* A loop or ring with a flat bottom, hung by a strap from either side of a horse's saddle. It is used to support the rider's foot.

stock (stŏk) —*v.* To keep for future use.
—**stocks** *n.* A timber frame with holes used to confine the ankles or wrists. A form of punishment in earlier times.

spruce

stave

stile

stocks

submerge

stout (stout) —*adj.* 1. Not giving in easily; bold; brave. 2. Bulky in size; heavyset.
—**stoutly** *adv.* In a brave, bold manner.

stow (stō) —*v.* To put or place; store.

strat•e•gy (străt′ ə jē) —*n.* A plan of action.

stride (strīd) —*n.* A long step.

stu•por (stoo′ pər) —*n.* Mental confusion; a daze.

sub•due (səb doo′) —*v.* **subdued.** To quiet; to bring under control.

sub•merge (səb mûrj′) —*v.* **submerged.** To place or go beneath the surface of the water.

sub•tle (sŭt′ l) —*adj.* **subtler.** So slight as to be difficult to detect or recognize.

sub•urb (sŭb′ ûrb′) —*n.* A residential area lying outside a city.

suf•fice (sə fīs′) —*v.* To fulfill current needs.

suit•or (soo′ tər) —*n.* A man who is courting a woman.

sulk (sŭlk) —*v.* To be withdrawn or aloof because of anger or selfishness.

sum•mon (sŭm′ ən) —*v.* **summoned.** To call together; to gather.

sump (sŭmp) —*n.* A hole at the lowest point of a mine shaft into which water is drained in order to be pumped out.

talon

target

su•per•sti•tious (soo′ pər stĭsh′ əs) —*adj.* Likely to have an irrational belief that one event will cause another event not related to it.

su•per•vi•sion (soo′ pər vĭzh′ ən) —*n.* The act of watching over or inspecting an action, work, or performance.

sup•ple (sŭp′ əl) —*adj.* Moving with ease; limber.

surge (sûrj) —*n.* A sudden increase.

sus•pend (sə spĕnd′) —*v.* **suspended.** To forbid attendance for a period of time.

sus•pense•ful (sə spĕns′ fəl) —*adj.* Filled with uncertainty or doubt about what might happen.

swash•buck•ler (swŏsh′ bŭk′ lər) —*n.* A showy sword fighter.

T

tal•on (tăl′ ən) —*n.* The claw of a bird that seizes other animals as prey.

Tao•ism (tou′ ĭz′ əm) —*n.* A Chinese religion founded in the sixth century before Christ.

tap•es•try (tăp′ ĭ strē) —*n.* **tapestries.** A heavy cloth woven with designs or pictures in many colors. It is hung on walls as decoration or used to cover furniture.

tar•get (tär′ gĭt) —*n.* 1. A small, round shield. 2. An object aimed at to test accuracy.

tarp (tärp) —*n.* A waterproof sheet of canvas used to protect from moisture.

taunt (tônt) —*v.* To tease or mock.

taut (tôt) —*adj.* Pulled or drawn tight.

tech•ni•cian (tĕk nĭsh´ ən) —*n.* A person trained in a specific type of technical work.

tech•nique (tĕk nēk´) —*n.* A method or way of doing something difficult or complicated.

teem (tēm) —*v.* **teeming.** To be full of; to abound or swarm.

tee•ter (tē´ tər) —*v.* **teetered.** To walk in an unsteady manner; to totter.

ten•don (tĕn´ dən) —*n.* The tough fiber that connects muscle to bone.

teth•er (tĕ*th*´ ər) —*n.* **tethered.** A restraining rope that allows an animal some limited movement.

tex•ture (tĕks´ chər) —*n.* The look or feel of a fabric. The texture results from the way the threads are woven or arranged.

thatch (thăch) —*n.* **thatched.** Straw, reeds, or palm fronds used to cover a roof.

the•ol•og•y (thē ŏl´ ə jē) —*n.* The study of the nature of God and religious truths.

thong (thông) —*n.* A thin strip of leather used to fasten something.

thrash (thrăsh) —*v.* **thrashing.** To move wildly or violently.

thrift•y (thrĭf´ tē) —*adj.* Careful in the use of money or other resources.

thun•der (thŭn´ dər) —*v.* **thundered.** To produce loud sounds like thunder.

thy•roid (thī´ roid´) —*n.* A body organ that produces necessary chemicals.

tick•er tape (tĭk´ ər tāp´) —*n.* A thin strip of paper that reported the latest stock market information by telegraph before the invention of the computer.

tide (tīd) —*v.* To carry through a difficult time.

tid•ing (tī´ dĭng) —*n.* A piece of information; news.

till•age (tĭl´ ĭj) —*n.* Cultivated land.

til•ler (tĭl´ ər) —*n.* A lever or handle used to turn a rudder and steer a boat.

tin•ker (tĭng´ kər) —*v.* **tinkering.** To make unskilled efforts at doing something; to fiddle around. —*n.* A traveling salesman of various household supplies.

tit•ter (tĭt´ ər) —*v.* **tittered.** To giggle.

tol•er•ate (tŏl´ ə rāt´) —*v.* To put up with; endure.

toll[1] (tōl) —*v.* To sound a bell slowly and regularly.

toll[2] (tōl) —*n.* A tax for a privilege.

top•i•cal (tŏp´ ĭ kəl) —*adj.* Concerning a particular topic or subject.

tote (tōt) —*v.* **toting.** To carry.

trans•ac•tion (trăn săk´ shən) —*n.* A piece of business conducted between two parties.

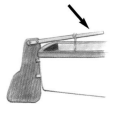

tiller

toll[1]

ă	pat	ĕ	pet
ā	pay	ē	be
âr	care	ĭ	pit
ä	father	ī	pie
îr	fierce	oi	oil
ŏ	pot	o͝o	book
ō	go	o͞o	boot
ô	paw,	y o͞o	abuse
	for	ou	out
ŭ	cut	ə	ago,
ûr	fur		item,
th	the		pencil,
th	thin		atom,
hw	which		circus
zh	vision	ər	butter

trap (trăp) —*v.* **trapped.** To catch in a trap.
—*n.* 1. A light, two-wheeled carriage. 2. A device for catching animals.

trap

trawl•er (trô´ lər) —*n.* A boat used for a special kind of fishing.

treach•er•ous (trĕch´ ər əs) —*adj.* Deceptively dangerous.

trea•son (trē´ zən) —*n.* A crime against one's country.

trench (trĕnch) —*n.* A long, narrow ditch.

tres•pass (trĕs´ pəs) —*v.* **trespassed.** To invade someone's property without permission.

tres•tle (trĕs´ əl) —*n.* A framework consisting of diagonal supports and a horizontal beam or flat surface.

tripe (trīp) —*n.* The stomach lining of a cow, sometimes served as food. It is considered a delicacy.

trudge (trŭj) —*v.* **trudged.** To walk in a heavy manner.

trun•dle (trŭn´ dl) —*n.* A bed on small wheels that is rolled under another for storage.

tu•mult (tōō´ mŭlt´) —*n.* An agitation of the mind or emotions.

tunic

tu•nic (tōō´ nĭk) —*n.* A loosely fitting garment that hangs below the knees.

tur•bid (tûr´ bĭd) —*adj.* Muddy; heavy; dense.

tur•bo•charged (tûr´ bō chärjd´) —*adj. slang* Very fast.

turn•pike (tûrn´ pīk´) —*n.* A toll highway.

tu•tor (tōō´ tər) —*n.* A private teacher.

twitch (twĭch) —*v.* **twitched.** To pull or draw.

twit•ter (twĭt´ ər) —*v.* **twittering.** To make light, chirping sounds.

ty•rant (tī´ rənt) —*n.* A ruler who is unjust and cruel.

U

ul•ti•mate (ŭl´ tə mĭt) —*adj.* Final or last.
—**ultimately** *adv.* Finally.

unc•tu•ous (ŭngk´ chōō əs) —*adj.* Having a calming effect.

un•der•stud•y (ŭn´ dər stŭd´ ē) —*n.* A person who learns a part in a performance so that he can replace the regular performer if called on to do so.

un•fal•ter•ing (ŭn fôl´ tər ĭng) —*adj.* Steady; unwavering.

un•wiel•dy (ŭn wēl´ dē) —*adj.* Not easily managed.

up•land (ŭp´ lənd, ŭp´ lănd´) —*n.* **uplands.** The higher parts of an area, usually inland.

ut•most (ŭt´ mōst´) —*adj.* Of the highest or greatest degree.

V

va•cant (vā´ kənt) —*adj.* Having no expression on the face; blank.
—**vacantly** *adv.* Acting without expression on the face.

vac•ci•na•tion (văk´ sə nā´ shən) —*n.* The giving of a vaccine to protect against disease.

vague (vāg) —*adj.* Not clear or distinct.

vain (vān) —*adj.* 1. Of no real worth. 2. Thinking too much of oneself or one's appearance.

van•i•ty (văn´ ĭ tē) —*n.* Emptiness; foolishness; worthlessness.

var•mint (vär´ mĭnt) —*n.* A troublesome or obnoxious animal.

veer (vîr) —*v.* **veered.** To swerve suddenly to avoid something.

ven•ti•late (věn´ tl āt´) —*v.* **ventilated.** To circulate fresh air. —**ventilation** *n.* The act or process of causing fresh air to enter or move about.

ven•ture (věn´ chər) —*v.* **ventured.** To take a risk; to expose to possible loss or danger. —*n.* A task or action that involves risks and possible danger.

ver•dict (vûr´ dĭkt) —*n.* The decision made by a jury at the end of a trial.

ver•min (vûr´ mĭn) —*n.* Small animals that are annoying or harmful.

ver•sion (vûr´ zhən) —*n.* A description or an account from one particular point of view.

vice (vīs) —*n.* A bad character trait or sin.

view•point (vyo͞o´ point´) —*n.* A way of thinking about something.

vig•or (vĭg´ ər) —*n.* Strength, energy, or enthusiasm for a task.

vil•lain•y (vĭl´ ə nē) —*n.* Evil mind or character.

vir•tue (vûr´ cho͞o) —*n.* Goodness; purity.

vi•tal signs (vīt´ l sīnz) —*n.* The heart rate, breathing, and temperature of a person.

vo•cif•er•ous (vō sĭf´ ər əs) —*adj.* Marked by a strong outcry.

vermin

W

wal•lop (wŏl´ əp) —*v.* A hard or severe blow.

ward (wôrd) —*v.* **warding.** To stop from striking; to avoid being hit. —*n.* Someone placed under the care and protection of a guardian.

war•y (wâr´ ē) —*adj.* Watchful; careful.

wa•ver (wā´ vər) —*v.* To be uncertain; to tremble or flicker.

wench (wěnch) —*n.* A young woman or peasant girl.

whack (hwăk) —*v.* **whacking.** To slap with a sharp sound.

wharf (hwôrf) —*n.* A landing place or pier at which ships may tie up and load or unload.

whee•dle (hwēd´ l) —*v.* **wheedling.** To persuade by flattery or deceit.

whence (hwěns) —*adv.* From where.

whim (hwĭm) —*n.* A sudden wish, desire, or idea.

wharf

ă	pat	ě	pet
ā	pay	ē	be
âr	care	ĭ	pit
ä	father	ī	pie
îr	fierce	oi	oil
ŏ	pot	o͝o	book
ō	go	o͞o	boot
ô	paw,	yo͞o	abuse
	for	ou	out
ŭ	cut	ə	ago,
ûr	fur		item,
th	the		pencil,
th	thin		atom,
hw	which		circus
zh	vision	ər	butter

whirr (hwûr) —*v.* To move in a way that produces a buzzing sound.

whit•tle (hwĭt´ l) —*v.* 1. To cut small bits or pieces of wood with a knife. 2. To make something by whittling.
—**whittler** *n.* One who whittles.

whittle

will (wĭl) —*v.* To desire something deeply and strongly.
—*n.* 1. The power of the mind in a person to choose or decide what to do. 2. A wish or decision. 3. Strong purpose; determination.

wince (wĭns) —*v.* **winced.** To pull back quickly in pain; to flinch.

wist•ful•ly (wĭst´ fəl lē) —*adv.* In a sadly longing manner.

wrap (răp) —*v.* **wrapped** or **wrapt.** To cover or enclose by folding or winding something around.

wrath•ful•ly (răth´ fəl ē) —*adv.* In an angry manner.

wrench (rĕnch) —*v.* A sudden, hard twist or turn.

wretch•ed (rĕch´ ĭd) —*adj.* Very unhappy or unfortunate.

zinc

wroth (rôth) —*adj.* Angry.

yam•mer (yăm´ ər) —*v.* **yam-mered.** To complain or whine.

yearn (yûrn) —*v.* **yearning.** To desire something desperately.

yearn•ing (yûr´ nĭng) —*n.* A desperate desire.

yield (yēld) —*v.* **yielded.** To give forth; to produce; to provide.
—*n.* That which is brought forth as a crop.

Zen (zĕn) —*n.* A form of Buddhism, a major religion in China and Japan.

zinc (zĭngk) —*n.* A shiny, bluish-white metal that is not affected by air and moisture.

zyz•zy•va (zĭz´ ə və) —*n.* A tropical American weevil that is destructive to plants.

ă	pat	ě	pet
ā	pay	ē	be
âr	care	ĭ	pit
ä	father	ī	pie
îr	fierce	oi	oil
ŏ	pot	ŏŏ	book
ō	go	ōō	boot
ô	paw,	yōō	abuse
	for	ou	out
ŭ	cut	ə	ago,
ûr	fur		item,
th	the		pencil,
th	thin		atom,
hw	which		circus
zh	vision	ər	butter